Also by William C. Davis

LOOK AWAY!
A History of the Confederate States of America

THREE ROADS TO THE ALAMO
*The Lives and Fortunes of David Crockett, James Bowie,
and William Barret Travis*

LINCOLN'S MEN
*How President Lincoln Became Father to an Army
and a Nation*

WILLIAM C. DAVIS

LONE STAR RISING

The Revolutionary Birth of the Texas Republic

FREE PRESS

NEW YORK   LONDON   TORONTO   SYDNEY

*f*P

FREE PRESS

A Division of Simon & Schuster, Inc.
1230 Avenue of the Americas
New York, NY 10020

Copyright ©2004 by William C. Davis

FREE PRESS and colophon are
trademarks of Simon & Schuster, Inc.

Manufactured in the United States of America

1   3   5   7   9   10   8   6   4   2

Library of Congress Cataloging-in-Publication Data
Davis, William C., 1946–
lone star rising : the revolutionary birth of the Texas Republic / William C. Davis
p.   cm.
Includes bibliographical references (p.) and index.
ISBN: 0-684-86510-6
1. Texas—History—Revolution, 1835–1836. I. Title.

F390.D2757 2004
976.4'03—dc22
2003065051

For information regarding special discounts for bulk purchases
please contact Simon & Schuster Special Sales at 1-800-456-6798
or business@simonandschuster.com.

For Bird

CONTENTS

CHRONOLOGY

1835

2 OCTOBER Outbreak of war. When Mexican soldiers demand that the Texians of Gonzales hand over their one little cannon, the hastily assembled volunteers tell them to "Come and Take It," attack and repulse the Mexicans, and Revolution is inaugurated.

10 OCTOBER The fall of Goliad. An "army" of one hundred volunteers march on the Mexican garrison at Goliad, demand their surrender, then storm their defenses and force their surrender.

11 OCTOBER Soldiers in the newly forming army elect Stephen F. Austin as their general to command them in the march to take Béxar.

12–20 OCTOBER The Texian army of four hundred fifty marches from Gonzales to the outskirts of San Antonio de Béxar bent on evicting the six hundred fifty men in the Mexican garrison commanded by General Cós.

28 OCTOBER James Bowie and James Fannin engage Mexican cavalry and artillery at Concepción, the first genuine battle of the Revolution.

28 OCTOBER–9 DECEMBER The siege of Béxar. As Austin's army grows, shrinks, then grows again, General Cós and his garrison hold out during intermittent shelling and skirmishing, hoping for relief from Mexico.

3–4 NOVEMBER Texians force the surrender of Fort Lipantitlán and repulse a Mexican attack on the banks of the Nueces River.

24 NOVEMBER Austin turns over command of the army at Béxar to the newly elected commander Edward Burleson.

26 NOVEMBER James Bowie leads a reconnaissance that turns into an attack on a Mexican pack train, inaugurating the semicomic "Grass Fight."

5–9 DECEMBER The attack on Béxar. Led by Ben Milam and Frank Johnson, the Texians fight house by house through the town until Cós and his men are forced into their last defense at the Alamo and surrender.

1836

18 JANUARY James Bowie arrives to take command of the dwindling volunteer garrison in San Antonio and decides that it needs to be held.

3 FEBRUARY William Barret Travis arrives in Béxar, followed a few days later by his small company of cavalry.

12 FEBRUARY James Neill leaves Béxar, turning command of regulars over to Travis, who shortly agrees to share joint command with Bowie.

16 FEBRUARY The main van of Santa Anna's Army of Operations crosses the Rio Grande, heading toward Béxar.

20 FEBRUARY The Mexican cavalry led by General Ramírez y Sesma reaches the Medina River, just five miles from Béxar.

23 FEBRUARY Mexican cavalry rides into Béxar as Travis and Bowie pull their garrison into the fortified Alamo. The Texians refuse a demand for surrender.

23 FEBRUARY–6 MARCH The siege of the Alamo.

26 FEBRUARY Fannin makes a halfhearted attempt to march to the relief of the Alamo but turns back.

2 MARCH The convention at Washington-on-the-Brazos votes to declare independence from Mexico and adopts a constitution.

6 MARCH The fall of the Alamo. Some two hundred or more defenders are killed; not a combatant survives.

11 MARCH The "Runaway Scrape" begins as volunteers and citizens alike flee eastward out of the path of Santa Anna's forces.

18–20 MARCH Fannin and his garrison attempt to retreat from Goliad but are forced to surrender on the road.

27 March Under orders from Santa Anna, Fannin and his men are marched out of Goliad and executed. Only twenty-eight manage to escape the massacre.

March–April Houston retreats east of the Colorado, then beyond the Brazos River, while trying to hold his army together as Santa Anna pursues.

4 April Santa Anna crosses the Colorado River, his army increasingly strung out and separated behind him.

16 April Houston's army refuses to retreat any farther and of its own accord turns to march on Santa Anna's isolated advance element.

20–21 April The Battle of San Jacinto. The Texians almost spontaneously attack and overwhelm surprised Mexicans in their front, inflicting dreadful casualties and virtually ending the war.

22 April Santa Anna himself is captured posing as a peasant and is forced to order his remaining forces in Texas to return to Mexico.

14 May The Treaty of Velasco is signed, ending the Revolution and inaugurating the independent Republic of Texas.

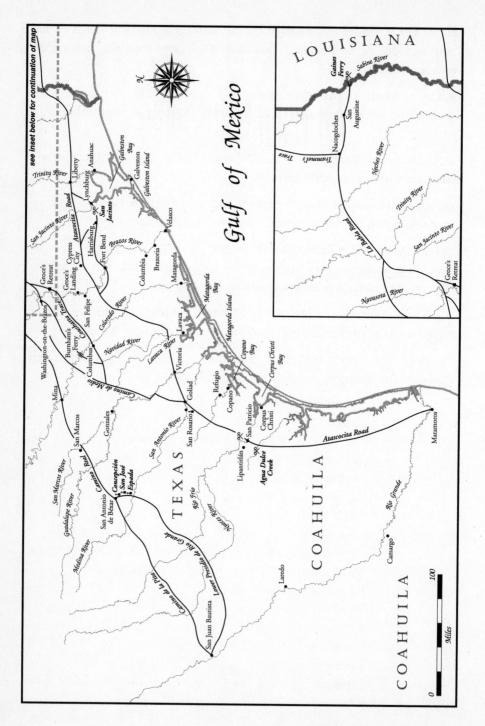

see inset below for continuation of map

LOUISIANA

Sabine River

Gaines Ferry

Nacogdoches

San Augustine

Trammel's Trace

Neches River

La Bahía Road

Trinity River

San Jacinto River

Navasota River

Groce's Retreat

Gulf of Mexico

N

Trinity River

Liberty

Anahuac

Lynchburg

San Jacinto

Galveston Bay

Galveston

Galveston Island

San Jacinto River

San Jacinto Road

Atascocita Road

Harrisburg

Cypress City

Fort Bend

Velasco

Brazos River

Columbia

Brazoria

Matagorda

Matagorda Bay

Matagorda Island

Groce's Retreat

Groce's Landing

San Felipe

Colorado River

Navidad River

Lavaca River

Lavaca

Victoria

Copano Bay

Corpus Christi Bay

Washington-on-the-Brazos

Burnham's Trace

Burnham's Ferry

Columbus

Camino de la Medio

Refugio

Copano

Mina

San Marcos

Gonzales

San Antonio River

Goliad

San Rosario

San Patricio

Corpus Christi

Atascocita Road

San Marcos River

Camino Real

Concepción

San José

Espada

San Antonio de Béxar

Río Frío

Lipantitlán

Agua Dulce Creek

Guadalupe River

Medina River

Nueces River

Lower Presidio

Camino de la Pita

Matamoros

Río Grande

Río Grande

Camargo

Laredo

San Juan Bautista

TEXAS

COAHUILA

COAHUILA

100

Miles

0

INTRODUCTION

An Immigrant Land

᏶ᏮᏮᎥ

EVERYTHING IN TEXAS came from somewhere else, beginning with the land itself. In ancient eons unseen by human eyes the Texas that later men fought over lay beneath a vast inland sea, or estuary, created even earlier by a gigantic rift in the continent. During the Late Cretaceous period it extended hundreds of miles northward from the latter-day Gulf of Mexico, its mouth on the Gulf more hundreds of miles in width. Then ensuing millions of years began to fill it in. The formation of the Rocky Mountains created rivers flowing southeastward like the Colorado and Rio Grande, while the Mississippi, then among the shortest rather than the longest of North American rivers, began its inexorable work of building the middle of the continent.

Suddenly—in geological time—parts of Canada began the downriver trip as sediment to become Illinois and Missouri. Pennsylvania and Ohio commenced a journey down the Ohio River to meet the Mississippi and continue the construction. In time, soil from as far west as Montana and Wyoming met with bits of New York and even Virginia, as they traveled the Mississippi current and washed up on the advancing banks. Gradually the estuary filled as the Mississippi and its tributaries made then followed the serpentine courses rivers create on alluvial beds. In time all of them—the Mississippi, the Colorado and Rio Grande and others—steadily filled in more and more of the estuary until all that was left was the rivers and the Gulf.

Meanwhile, regional uplifting in the Miocene epoch began to raise what later became central Texas above that sedimentary plain where once lapped the waters of the extended Gulf. The action created fault

I

lines and raised plateaus, so that by the beginning of human memory there were two Texases. One was that very immigrant Texas Coastal Plain created by the rivers, and the other was the Hill Country, an elevated and rocky plateau beginning along the Balcones Escarpment some one hundred sixty miles inland from the coast. They were as different from each other as any two neighboring territories on the continent. The Coastal Plain was virtually identical to inland Louisiana, Arkansas, and even Mississippi and Alabama, all of them siblings of the fecund Mississippi River. They boasted rich soil, gentle rolling hills, broad plains, and numerous gentle streams in no hurry to reach the Gulf. But at the Balcones Escarpment a dramatic change took place, and from its bluffs everything west in Texas became arid, rocky, unsuited for agriculture, and more like the farther Southwest. It was a difference destined to dominate the settlement and history of the human community to come.

By the advent of historic times, the Texas that men would explore, settle, and ultimately fight over was not the Texas of later days, but essentially that Coastal Plain east of the Balcones Escarpment. The Nueces River—not the Rio Grande—constituted its accepted southern boundary. It meandered some two hundred miles or more in a roughly southeasterly direction from its origins in the lower Hill Country, flowing into the Gulf at Corpus Christi Bay. The territory between the Nueces and the Rio Grande would be largely uninhabited, a mixture of salt domes, mountains, and deserts, with too little available water to encourage settlement. By the dawn of the nineteenth century only scattered *ranchos* and an occasional settlement clung to the sporadically flowing creeks, or along the rivers themselves.

Above the Nueces, and east of the Balcones Escarpment, the arable and fertile Texas known to the world of the time was a strip one hundred twenty to one hundred forty miles wide running along the Gulf coast for more than two hundred miles. Periodically more rivers poured out of the Hill Country to run southeasterly across the land. The San Marcos and the Guadalupe came together at Gonzales to continue together as the Guadalupe and emerge at San Antonio Bay sixty miles northeast of Corpus Christi. Thirty miles above that, the Lavaca passed into Matagorda Bay, and immediately above it flowed the Navidad River. Then came the Colorado, which flowed all across central Texas for hundreds of miles before it emptied into Matagorda Bay as well. Between twenty and sixty miles northeast of the Colorado ran the Brazos, which ended at the Gulf at Velasco, and forty miles above Velasco sat the great bay of Texas, Galveston. Into it emptied the San Jacinto River and above it some miles the Trinity. Roughly along the San Jacinto began the Great East Texas Forest, a frequently dense range of oaks and other trees that extended northward for hundreds of miles, and eastward another hundred miles or more to the Sabine River that divided old Texas from Louisiana.

The rivers, especially the Colorado, Brazos, Guadalupe, and Nueces, were only crossable at a few fords when in full flow, and sometimes not even then, making ferries vital for bridges as yet could span only the minor tributaries. The communities that appeared by 1800 grew up beside the rivers: San Antonio de Béxar, capital of the early province under Spain, and known colloquially both as San Antonio and simply as Béxar, sat on the upper reaches of the San Antonio River, one hundred forty miles from the coast. Downstream, and just fifty miles from the Gulf, the river passed La Bahía, which men would later rename Goliad. Gonzales grew up seventy miles due east of Béxar, and fifty miles north of Gonzales sat Mina on the edge of the Hill Country. The major future settlement would land between the Lavaca and the Trinity, but as of 1800 that stretch of territory sat virtually uninhabited except by a few tribes of Coushatta, Karankawa, and other native peoples. Above the Trinity almost no settlement appeared except at Nacogdoches some fifty miles from the Sabine. Meanwhile, all of that vast empire north and west of the settled area was the home ground of the feared Comanche.

Primal forces of the earth itself created this Texas, ripped it apart in the separation of the continent, then drove it back together in a geological metaphor for the human history to come. Indeed, even as the first European men ventured north of the Nueces to find that rich land of gentle breezes and tall waving grass, the strains in the earth's crust continued their epochal battle to shape the land. But then came men with their own ideas about shaping a world above all that terrestrial turmoil, men with younger traditions than those of tectonic stresses, but just as deeply ingrained in them as were the shifting of the plates beneath their feet. They, too, carried in their blood a compulsion for change, for destruction, revolution, and rebuilding, only theirs was not the patience of the eons. The primal forces that drove them wanted metamorphosis within the scale of a lifetime rather than over uncounted millennia.

They came because the earth itself made this Texas a lure. They stayed because of what they saw they might do with it. And inevitably, they warred among themselves in the conflict of their dreams.

Chance and geography placed Texas at one of history's crossroads. At the dawn of a new century in a New World, that intersection was about to become very busy indeed.

CHAPTER ONE

"Cast in a Contentious Crowd"

T HERE SEEMED TO BE SOMETHING inevitable about Texas and revolution. It lay near the center of a hemisphere called the New World, bracketed by revolutions above and below. It experienced the last in a series of revolutions, and the most sudden and yet briefest of all, as if the men and women involved sought to accelerate the process in order to catch up to history. Texas became almost a compulsion, not just for isolated men, but in the personality of a whole generation. Hiram Taylor, a thirty-five-year-old New Yorker, confessed himself caught in the irresistible gravity of the idea of Texas when he complained of "the inexorable will of providence" that had "impelled me onward to the verge of poverty, ruin and contempt." Abandoning even wife and children, his mind chafed "nearly to a PHRENZY," he gave in to magnetic forces beyond his control. "In a moment of enthusiasm I agreed to join the expedition to *Texas*," he shamefully confessed to the wife he left behind. "I have now cast myself in a contentious crowd; I have to struggle for the palm with thousands, to obtain the wayward and far spreading renown which rends the air with the loud huzza of praise."[1]

That compulsion, those contentious crowds, threw the New World into a revolutionary soup just coming to the boil when a new century dawned in 1800. The uprising in Britain's colonies that became a revolution, then spawned a new and independent nation, shook the American hemisphere and the Western World both to their foundations. Almost inevitably Spain's American colonies soon followed the path of revolt against their European overlords, for colonialism had brought with it, in human nature, the seeds of its own disruption. First, it guaranteed that its chief victims, the native peoples of the new continents, finding themselves exploited and dispossessed of their homes and the worlds they had known, even of their religion, must naturally harbor bitter resentments that only force and fear contained. Whole peoples were eliminated in the process, the once mighty Inca and Aztecs and their own empires brought down and reduced to penury, if not slavery. For centuries in the Spanish colonies they lived at the bottom order of a new social scale imposed from afar, one in which the *peninsulares*, men from Spain, came and ruled over all, while beneath them served the *creoles*, men of Spanish blood born in the New World who could rise and succeed but never achieve the top rungs of a ladder controlled by Madrid and its New World capital at Havana. Below them were the *mestizos*, the half-breed products of Spanish interbreeding with the native peoples, and finally at the bottom of the pile were those natives themselves, some of whom descended from the once-exalted ruling class of the Aztec, Inca, and Maya.

It was a system destined to generate multiple and overlapping levels of resentment and unrest. Some of the *peninsulares* in time resented being ordered about by masters in Havana and Madrid. Some of the *creoles* resented being denied access to the social and political strata reserved for the *peninsulares*, and the inability to determine for themselves their own affairs in a world that they themselves helped to carve from the wilderness. The *mestizos* felt some common cause with the *creoles* as they managed to grasp some position and prosperity in their world, limited though it was by their blood, while the Indians, of course, were well entitled to resent everyone. Several things kept the system in place and restive forces in check, starting with the habits of centuries. Spain, England, France, and the rest had been relatively well-ordered feudal then aristocratic cultures for half a millennium by the time they began colonizing the New World. People were born into a social caste and knew to keep their place and be satisfied with it unquestioningly, making peasant revolts almost unheard of. Every colonial empire exported that social system to its New World colonies, but in doing so reckoned without the effect of the wilderness experience on Old World establishments.

In North America, for example, virtually everyone worked in the new colonies. Later mythology about Cavalier aristocrats settling in the Southern colonies and Puritan shopkeepers inhabiting the North to the contrary, from Massachusetts Bay Colony to Georgia there were no aristocrats sitting idly like lords. Only men and women willing to work hard came to the colonies, and only those who worked hard survived. Naturally, some prospered more than others, acquiring more land and more wealth, but their enhanced property only required them to work harder themselves and to employ—or buy—more labor. Even the master of a large plantation who owned many slaves still had to work long hours himself over his account books and with the merchants, or riding the circuit of his domain to oversee the fields. The very few genuine aristocrats who came here, most as royally appointed governors and officials, returned home at the end of their tenures. Everyone else who stayed felt a personal investment in the land and the place, and in time in the *idea* of where they lived. The shoots of revolution began snaking their way upward through the topsoil toward daylight, and the idea, once born, could not be stopped. Once even limited local government gave them the taste for ruling themselves, the generation of increasing protests and confrontations began.

That Britain's North American colonies were the first to revolt against their mother empire was hardly surprising. Unlike Spain, Britain saw a vastly larger number of its people emigrate to a New World that absorbed much of the overflow of a middle-class explosion at home that required more scope for enterprise than the small island nation could offer. Only America offered new land for the farmer and the socially relaxed atmosphere that could allow the professional class to prosper and, in time, thoroughly infiltrate—even dominate—the upper social and political elites. Moreover, the North American colonies had the hidden benefit of not being surfeited with fabulous mineral riches, at first a disappointment to colonists and mother country alike. The result was that people came there to plant roots of crops and families, to stay and become a part of the New World, and often in some degree of peaceful coexistence with the natives, for all the conflict that ensued. Consequently, Britain's colonies were never armed camps, nor did they have to be maintained or governed by military authority. Until the opening of continental warfare with the French in 1756, the American colonists were largely allowed to maintain their own peace, and thus formed yet another habit of independence.

To this growing tradition of limited self-rule, self-reliance, and self-defense, the mother country added the catalysts that had begun New

World adventuring in the first place: ambition and aspiration. Both exploded on the scene in the sixteenth century in the greatest and most dramatic change in the Western personality since the consolidation of Christianity as the one and only European religion. After millennia of acceptance of birth and station, suddenly the class system relaxed dramatically. Royalty and nobility remained the exclusive province of the highborn, but trade, the need for expansion in the professions, and the New World all allowed men—and only men—at almost every lower level to begin for the first time to dream of something better. At the same time, the relatively sudden integration of European nations into a larger trading community, thanks to mastery of the sea, provided the dynamo to power prosperity. Classes bred to lack ambition suddenly found some attainable purpose in aspiring for more education, a better home, more property, a place and means to expand.

Expansion, of course, meant the New World, and the word became almost a motto for those who forged their futures across the Atlantic. Never before had Europeans encountered a limitless horizon. Suddenly people whose families may have spent five hundred years tilling the same patch of land could see just beyond the sunset whole new worlds awaiting plow and axe and community. Accustomed to making decisions for themselves in the freer atmosphere of their American colonies, the colonists saw no reason why they could not—should not—decide to expand their fortunes westward, or that constantly arriving new emigrants should not be able to go immediately to the edge of settlement and drive it a little farther west as they, too, carved themselves new homes. Accustomed to defending themselves, they naturally felt that what they defended was their own, subject to their dictates and not to those of a foreign potentate. Accustomed to acting in concert with their community and with neighboring communities, their sense of themselves and their interests and rights naturally expanded beyond their individual hearths.

By the middle of the eighteenth century they identified themselves as Virginians and New Yorkers and Carolinians, with a collective sense of what was naturally their due. They had worked and sweated and bled to make a civilization out of this wilderness, and it seemed only natural that it was their right to continue to do so, regardless of opposition from London or the protestations of less numerous and apparently less civilized native peoples who did not use the land to its fullest anyhow. At the eve of 1775, when settlement of the British colonies of North America was still primarily confined east of the Appalachian Mountains, there were already men defying regulations against going farther west, filtering into the Ohio River Valley, planning settlements in the so-called dark and bloody ground of Ken-tuck-ee, and venturing even into the Spanish provinces on the lower Mississippi, to Natchez and New Orleans, and as far west as Natchitoches in the vast and as-yet scarcely comprehended territory of Louisiana. Indeed, the attempt to restrict westward expansion became one of the multiple irritants that led to shots heard around the world, shots that began the century-long death knell of European empire in the Americas. In less than a single life span, the echo of those shots began to be heard in a faraway corner of the Louisiana Territory that the Spaniards called *Tejas*, and which the Anglo-Americans thought of somehow in the plural at first as "the Texas."

Those Texas belonged to someone else, of course, but by the time the British colonies won their independence, Spanish America itself stood close to the same threshold over which its northern neighbor had crossed. At first Spain allied itself with the colonies in their bid for independence, as did France, though it was a move calculated more to halt the growing dominance of Britain on the world stage than from sympathy with the ideals of British colonists. Indeed, European empires felt uneasy about supporting the American Revolution for fear of the example and precedent it might set within their own colonial holdings. After the loss of Canada in the war of 1756–1763, however, France largely gave up on the New World except for a few islands in the Caribbean.

Spain was another matter. Its empire in the New World predated Britain's by more than a century, and was vastly larger and richer. It stretched from La Plata and the southern tip of South America, northward across the entire western half of the continent, and as far north as a territory not yet called Oregon, from the Pacific shores eastward to the Mississippi, and onward along the Gulf Coast to the Florida peninsula. It embraced fully one third of the later United States. The Spaniards had divided it into four massive viceroyalties, each with its subordinate captaincy-generalships and local *audiencias*, while Portugal maintained one huge viceroyalty over Brazil. La Plata embraced modern-day Argentina, Paraguay, Uruguay, and Bolivia. New Granada contained most of latter-day Ecuador, Colombia, and Venezuela, while the viceroyalty of Peru oversaw Peru and Chile. Of them all New Spain was the largest, encompassing Mexico all the way to Oregon, the Caribbean islands that made up the *audiencia* of Santo Domingo, and the captaincy-general-ships of Guatemala and Cuba. [2]

The very size of the colonial hold posed a problem for Spain from the first, one compounded by the mother country's unabashed policy of rabid exploitation. The native population was simply swept aside, eradicated or enslaved, mollified with a new religion and controlled by intimidation. Three hundred years of enforced subservience, on top of many more centuries of subjugation under their earlier native empires, went as far as possible in driving aspiration and assertiveness out of the whole native culture, yet still some sparks of resentment smoldered on. Unwittingly, in the Catholic Christianity that Spain imposed on its new serfs, it gave them an ideology that acknowledged oppressors in the Romans, lauded attempts to rebel and cast off chains in a holy cause in the exodus from Egypt and the revolt of the Hebrews against the Herods, and held out the prospect of something better for those who suffered. The more the Spaniards had to impose rule by force to maintain order and keep the mines working and the treasure galleons returning to Spain, the more the crown sounded like pharaoh and the greater grew the store of resentment against it.

The land itself also worked against a pacific population in Spanish America. So much of it was simply uninhabitable. The Andes Mountains cut north to south through the center of the South American continent. Huge deserts covered much of Mexico and all of the west coast of the lower continent as well as portions of its interior. Much of the rest lay hidden beneath an impenetrable canopy of jungle, with the result that out of all of this immense land mass, only a very small part of it could be broken by the plow and made habitable. That, and the fixation of Spain on exploiting mineral wealth, exerted a natural pressure to confine expansion and settlement. As late as 1800, most communities hugged the shoreline of the Atlantic and Pacific or the Gulf of Mexico. What agriculture and livestock herding there was remained confined to the near environs of the coastal plains and the fertile higher plateaus of South America, or central Mexico, and a great deal of that lay in the hands of *grandees* controlling vast acreage tended by *peons*.

The result was a population easier to control than that of North America, partially out of long habit, but also because it had not dispersed very far from the centers of power and authority. Whereas distance from the mother country and rather benign local authority allowed the revolutionary spirit to flourish in the British colonies once ignited, in New Spain it took much longer for such ideas to spread. The disproportionate distribution of wealth and education also kept the masses either from being exposed to republican ideas, or having the wherewithal and organization to mount resistance. Revolutionary dissatisfaction was thus confined to a substantially smaller part of the population than in North America, chiefly the middle and upper classes among the *creoles*, thanks to their being the only ones with access to education and the dissemination of information. Still they could command, either by force, habit, or inspiration, the loyalty of some of the lower classes, and would find as well some support among the *peninsulares*, though most of that class remained loyal to Spain to the end.

One influence in New Spain that positively promoted revolutionary spirit in a way not known in North America was the absolutely abominable nature of the colonial administration both by Spain itself and the viceroys on the scene. The mission of the colonies was to send wealth home and to be a market for goods from the mother country, all of it geared to the prosperity of Spain and not the colonies, which found themselves exploited on all sides. Rule was arbitrary and authoritarian, the *peninsulares* dominating over a *creole* aristocracy, both of them looking down on the cadre of entrepreneurs from Spain who came as merchants and managers, and at the same time trying to keep down the growing class of professionals, the lawyers and physicians, who comprised the intelligentsia such as it was. So absolute and unbending was colonial rule by the viceroys that in New Spain, unlike the Old World, the infamous Inquisition was looked upon largely as a protector rather than as a threat. The resentment and dissatisfaction was always there as an undercurrent, but so long as the harsh authority of the viceroys remained in place, it had neither the organization nor the courage to emerge from hiding.[3]

And then the world began to teeter on its ancient axis, and even remote parts of New Spain felt dizzy. Iberia and France became intellectually and culturally linked with each other early in the eighteenth century, and in step with Great Britain began gradually retreating from the absolute monarchy of preceding centuries. Reforms at home allowed rights to trickle down from the nobility into the professional classes, the burdens on the land-tied poor were lightened, art and education were encouraged and expanded, and the Enlightenment was well under way. Once men began talking freely about human rights and the nature of the state, it was an invitation to ask for redress. All three great nations, Britain, France, and Spain, steadily reduced the power of the throne and the aristocracy during the first half of the eighteenth century, commensurately granting more and more political influence to the professional, middle, and upper classes. Unwittingly, they were opening the gates to the flood.

Wise heads in Spain might suspect that such relaxations were only asking for trouble either at home or in the colonies, but the ruling class believed that it was, if anything, diffusing unrest in the Americas by allowing greater local rule and thereby encouraging more prosperity for the middle and *creole* classes. But when in 1759, Charles III ascended the throne, the pendulum swung toward greater exploitation. Taxes and export duties all but killed Mexican industries other than mining, and even the autonomous church was brought under viceroyal rule for a time. The later shift to a more lenient regime under a new viceroy came too late, for even as the *creoles* and the professions enjoyed more freedom, they did not forget how easily and quickly it could be taken from them. Reform, efficient administration, free trade, the encouragement of industry and agriculture, all became their talking points, and not surprisingly each, if pursued, led toward local prosperity and solidarity. When they also began demanding more of a political role in their own government, the revolution was born in their hearts. After centuries of being exploited by the mother country and arbitrarily ruled by appointed *peninsulares* who knew nothing of their interests and concerns, educated men throughout Spain's New World empire were tired and frustrated. It needed only example, encouragement, and opportunity for the status quo to collapse.

All three came a step closer in the wake of the 1756–1763 war between Britain and France, when Spain sided with the latter. The ultimate British victory lost Spain some of its Cuban holdings and a part of the Honduran mainland, and required a trade of Florida to regain Havana. To reward Spain for its ill-fated alliance, France ceded to it the Louisiana Territory in 1762, and thus the balance of power in the New World shifted, leaving Spain and Britain the only competitors for hemispheric hegemony. They remained bitter enemies. When the revolutionary inundation washed over the British Empire in 1775 with the

American Revolution, Spain was happy to join with France once more to try to weaken Britain. This time it worked. An independent set of thirteen colonies, weak and isolated to the Atlantic seaboard, seemingly posed far less threat of competition to Spanish interests. But still there was that worrying precedent. For the first time in modern history a group of colonies had revolted with sufficient strength, organization, and commitment to succeed in wresting away its independence. To be sure, it was only French military aid in the New World, and the distraction of French and Spanish armies confronting Britain in Europe, that sufficiently weakened Britain for it finally to let the colonies go in 1783. Still there was a lesson, that a distant and isolated colony could be hard to hold on to by a mother country distracted by internal upheaval. At least one man in Spain, Conde de Aranda, a minister in the court of Charles III, warned that dissident elements in New Spain might look enviously at what their northern neighbors had done and one day seek to emulate them. The king, however, was too pleased by the recovery of Florida and Honduras to see troubles ahead.[4]

Next into the revolutionary cauldron in 1789 fell France, an example that still stuns and confounds for its unchecked violence and radicalism. The rebels of 1776 created a stable, democratic state. The rebels of 1789 launched themselves on a self-consuming orgy of bloodshed that led first to the dictatorship of Napoleon and later to a restored monarchy as Frenchmen sought nondemocratic solutions for their own folly. Which example would Spain's colonies follow? When Charles III died in 1788, he was succeeded by his son, a man simply unfit for rule even at home, let alone over a set of colonies thousands of miles distant and populated by increasingly dissatisfied elements. Indeed, the first weak fumbles at revolution had taken place already, though quickly quelled. In the very year that the Americans effectively ended the military part of their revolution in 1781, a descendant of the Inca rulers of old in Peru named José Gabriel Condorcanqui managed to incite thousands of the native peoples of Peru in an uprising against Spanish rule. They besieged Cuzco, captured the Spanish governor, and killed him. The Spaniards retaliated with massive force, putting down Condorcanqui's followers and taking him and his family prisoner. His family they butchered before his eyes and then his captors cut out his tongue, tied his arms and legs to saddle horses, and ripped him to pieces. However disorganized and ill prepared, however bloody and unsuccessful, it had been the first real revolutionary uprising in Spanish America after over two hundred years.[5]

The Peru revolt may have been nothing more than an outburst of frustration, with no thought-out long-range plan, yet even the temporary success of Condorcanqui's revolt sent shivers throughout Spanish America, and the quaking continued when the excesses of the French Revolution found echoes in the New World. The same kind of pent-up frustration and anger that put Condorcanqui's followers on the road to Cuzco excited half a million slaves on the island of Hispaniola to rise up against their French overlords. Vincent Ogé, an educated free mulatto of comparative affluence, went to Paris at the outbreak of the French Revolution to beg for extension of civil rights to free mulattoes and for the emancipation of slaves on Hispaniola. Rebuffed, he returned to the island in 1790, and when the French governor refused to remove restrictions on slaves and free blacks, Ogé incited and led an insurrection. Defeated and captured, he was tried, convicted of treason, and broken on the wheel, but within months erupted the bloody coup led by Toussaint L'Ouverture, a former slave serving as an officer in the French colonial garrison. It saw thousands murdered and most of the balance forced to flee, many of them to French Louisiana.

The unrest on Hispaniola, and the exodus of refugees, continued for a decade off and on, until 1803 when, after retaking Louisiana from Spain, Napoleon then sold it to the United States and simply abandoned French attempts to hold on to Hispaniola. Thus, for the first time, a colony within the very environs of New Spain had given sway to revolution, an ethnic one at that, and had apparently achieved its de facto independence. By 1803 Spain was just as weak in the New World as France had been, and just as distracted and overextended militarily and financially in Europe. If a rabble of slaves could achieve independence on Hispaniola, what could discontented *creoles* and a rabble of *mestizos* and even Indians bring about, especially if outside agitators incited them to take advantage of Spanish weakness?

The ideal place for a separatist movement or revolt would be at an isolated outpost of the Spanish empire, far from the seat of power in Mexico City. Poor communications meant perhaps weeks in passing information, and the long distances over rough ground would cause delay and hardship to any military forces sent to keep order. Not surprisingly, eyes looked to "the Texas." A few, in fact, had looked in that direction for some time. In 1791 a twenty-year-old Irish-born clerk named Philip Nolan, working in New Orleans for General James Wilkinson, obtained a passport from the Spanish governor of Texas to trade with the inhabitants. His work for Wilkinson made him alive to the untapped trade opportunities presented by the communities in Texas, which had raw resources that Louisianians could use, and whose closer proximity to New Orleans than to Mexico City promised a market hungry for consumer goods. His being a member of the Wilkinson household also no doubt influenced his interest, for the general was a perennial plotter after Spanish empire west of the Mississippi.

The mercantile enterprise failed, but Nolan spent much of the next three years living with the natives and trading in wild horses. Watchful Spanish officials did not miss the attention Nolan paid to local terrain, his mapping of rivers, and his friendliness with the United States officials then trying to establish the western boundary of the United States along the Mississippi River. In 1797 Nolan went into Texas once more on a horse-trading trip, this time going as far as San Antonio de Béxar, the provincial capital, but by now officials believed they had evidence that the horse-trading expeditions were a blind and that Nolan's real purpose was to incite the native population into a revolt against Spain. Still Nolan was allowed to stay in Texas more than a year, in violation of Spanish trade regulations, and when he returned to Natchez, Mississippi, in 1799 he brought with him twelve hundred horses and a great deal of information. It is hardly coincidental that his employer and mentor Wilkinson, one of American history's greatest schemers, already had well-developed personal interests and ambitions that involved the southwest. A few years earlier he went secretly on the payroll of the Spanish to advise them of American designs on their territory, and now was commanding general of the United States Army and still taking Spanish bribes. Yet Wilkinson always worked essentially for himself, and what Nolan was able to tell him of the temper of the native population in Texas, of its roads and river crossings, and of the state of Spanish colonial outposts, all helped to inform his grand designs for some kind of empire of his own. Nolan was widely believed to have made the first map of eastern Texas, the portion chiefly inhabited by the Spaniards, and if so a document that would be of inestimable value to any expedition setting out to take the province. Certainly the Spaniards suspected this, for the word soon went out to the Indians that Nolan was, as he himself put it, "a Bad man," with a warning that he should not be allowed to enter their villages.[6]

Thus, if not at Wilkinson's instruction but certainly with his blessing, Nolan went once more to Texas in 1800, this time at the head of a party of twenty-seven armed men, though still under the pretense of being on a trading mission. By October he was building a fort near Nacogdoches, then corrals for captured horses, but Spanish authorities had seen enough. Spanish *soldados* from Nacogdoches appeared with orders to arrest him and his men on March 21, 1801. They resisted, and a small battle broke out in which Nolan was killed and his men all taken. Ever afterward there remained uncertainty as to just what his purpose had been, and how much involved were Wilkinson and other would-be empire builders at the expense of New Spain. Certainly Wilkinson remained interested in Texas for years to come, and within two years one of Nolan's associates, Robert Ashley, was believed to be planning an expedition of his own into Texas, coincident with the Louisiana Purchase in 1803 that gave the United States its first shadowy claim on the province.[7]

PHILIP NOLAN—WHOSE STORY later writer Edward Everett Hale considerably fictionalized in turning him into his *Man Without a Country*—was probably not the first of the future so-called filibusters, a term likely of uncertain Dutch origin in the word *vrijbuiter* for pirate. But he was one of those shadowy figures who appeared so drawn to Texas, men of mixed and shifting motives, bent on quick personal gain and yet somehow impressed with the larger opportunity represented in the untamed and largely unclaimed land. Most likely he was chiefly—perhaps only—interested in the lucrative horse trade, yet the fact remained that he was willing to risk his life and break American and Spanish law by interloping into Texas to seek fortune. That at least made him the spiritual precursor of the armies of Americans who would follow, and in much greater numbers, while the fears that he implanted in Spanish minds about the intentions of their neighbors to the east awakened the rulers of Texas to its vulnerability to outside intervention and the potential for internal revolt.[8]

Meanwhile, Spain's hold on its Caribbean empire was crumbling. It gave up to the French its claim on Saint Domingue, which shared the island of Hispaniola. Then the British began brazen occupations of Puerto Rico and Trinidad, and by the turn of the century the *creoles* and even the *peninsulares* saw their mother country being insulted and buffeted with impunity by Britain and France alike. That led to a disdain of Spain and their royal rulers that only fed already deep-seated resentments over centuries of local exploitation and incompetent and corrupt viceroyal rule by favorites appointed in Madrid. When Napoleon sent an army to Hispaniola in 1802 to put down Toussaint L'Ouverture's uprising on Hispaniola and restore slavery, inhabitants of Spain's colonies were horrified, wondering when it would come their turn to fall under French rule. The expulsion of the French from Hispaniola in 1804 by another black uprising, and the declaration of independence of the newly named nation of Haiti, gave hope to restive elements in New Spain. Haiti was the first colony in the Spanish colonial sphere to declare and maintain its independence. The lesson was clear. If even France, under the legendary Napoleon, could be evicted from the New World, surely Spain could, too. Disorganized, weakened, and distracted colonial powers could be pushed out of the New World and self-rule established. When Spain unwisely allied itself with France in Napoleon's continuing war with Britain, the Spanish fleet was all but erased from the seas at Trafalgar, and in a stroke the mother country simply lost the means of enforcing its authority from afar in the New World.

Even in remote Texas and its capital at Béxar, such fears and ideas took root. The Nolan expeditions left Spanish authorities there anxious about what might come next from the *americanos,* especially after Napoleon sold Louisiana to the United States, and now the Americans and Texas became wary neighbors. Texas had been an unarmed border between two Spanish provinces and later between two friendly powers, Spain and France. Now events in Europe and Washington shifted the situation dramatically, especially after refugees from Catholic Louisiana began pressing to move away from feared Protestant domination under the Americans, and live instead in a neighboring Catholic province. To meet all of these feared and anticipated pressures, authorities in Mexico City began the steady militarization of Texas. In 1801, the year Nolan's last expedition had sparked the first serious concern, royalist *soldados* in Texas numbered fewer than 200. By 1806 their number had soared to 1,368, most of them centered at Béxar.

Interestingly, more than one tenth of those were local men, either native *béxareños* or men who had been on duty there for some time, meaning that the local garrison was not entirely free from the domestic discontents troubling other elements in the province.[9] Then came more blows, first the confiscation of charity funds raised by the church to bolster a bankrupt Madrid treasury, and next Napoleon's astonishing occupation of Spain itself, and his installation of a puppet king, his brother, on the throne. In Mexico City, whose rule extended to Texas, the authorities had no intention of remaining loyal to a French usurper. The *peninsulares* and *creoles* seemed in the main disposed toward creating a provisional government in their colony, remaining loyal to their deposed king until he should be restored to his crown. Yet they did not dare risk expanding either civil or political power lest they threaten their own hold on the colony. The example of the French Revolution that led to Napoleon's tyranny over them was worrisome, because they saw it as a triumph of the rabble. If that idea spread to Mexico, then the *mestizo* and native Indian population, so successfully kept at bay for centuries, might erupt. Numbering four of every five inhabitants, they would be unstoppable if aroused.

Mexico and its Texan province drifted on the verge of insurrection for the next few years. Not so the rest of Spanish America, however. Almost everywhere at once it seemed to explode in a revolutionary frenzy. In Venezuela republicans overthrew its *peninsulare* ruler and the following year declared for independence under the leadership of Simón Bolívar. Chile had already done the same with a declaration of its own, and Buenos Aires soon followed suit. The idea of revolution and republicanism spread rapidly, rumbling like one of South America's frequent earthquakes all along the Andes and right up the backbone of Central America into Mexico. There the *peninsulares* split with the *creoles*, the former arguing to remain obedient to the sitting viceroy, while the latter, sniffing the opportunity for more autonomy, argued for an interim provisional government.

When the viceroy came out in favor of the *creole* plan, the *peninsulares* rose against him and sent him back to Spain under arrest, then chose their own safely royalist viceroy in his place. That kept Mexico City quiet until September 16, 1810. In Guanajuato, just one hundred fifty miles north of the capital, a cabal of *creoles*, a local priest, and others aroused the smoldering unrest of the Indians and *mestizos* and broke out in rebellion. The *mestizos* looted Guanajuato, killing full-blooded

Spaniards regardless of caste and showing that once unleashed, their anger could be vented indiscriminately. The *peninsulares* and the *creoles* were forced to unite for their own survival. They immediately shifted their allegiance to the viceroy, who sent in forces to attempt to put down the rebellion and scatter its leaders.[10]

None of this escaped notice in Texas. Indeed, a few of the refugees from the quashing of the rebellion found their way across the Rio Grande, while the Mexico they left behind still teetered on the edge of a *mestizo* revolution. Mexican officials in Texas braced themselves in fear both of a similar outbreak in their own bailiwick and the spread of the existing rebellion northward. Almost monthly they saw more disruption to the south. In Nueva Santander loyalist forces ousted a governor, and then in Coahuila, just across the Rio Grande from Texas itself, the entire military force of the royalist governor changed sides to join the rebels as they advanced.

By January 1811 it appeared to men in Béxar as if the old Spanish regime was about to be ousted completely. The governor of Texas, Manuel de Salcedo, received credible information that revolutionary agents were acting in his own province, plotting to funnel arms and munitions from sources in the United States through Texas to the rebels. Salcedo remained loyal to Spain and arrested the agents, and then began to ready an expedition with his small force to assist in defending against the rebel advance. Yet on January 22 *béxareños* rose up and arrested Salcedo and all of the *peninsulares* in the area. This was no movement for local Texan independence, to be sure. The Béxar rebels were simply siding with the larger *creole* revolution against rule by the *peninsulares*—now called *gachupines*—and soon carried out a purge of their foes from all offices, confiscating their property. Their leader, Juan Bautista de las Casas, sent troops to Nacogdoches, arrested *gachupines* there, too, and then established a provisional government for the province in this new capital. It marked a milestone. For the first time, Texans themselves, both Spanish-blooded *creoles* and *mestizos*, acted as a regional people rather than as castes. It was the beginning of the "Texas spirit," the first time that Texas was seen as something more than an appendage to a larger entity, and the first time that Texas was its own political melting pot. The first true Texians, in this sense, were called *tejanos*, people of Spanish and Indian ancestry living in Texas. And now they had risen in rebellion.[11]

Just as interesting, Casas sought to shift the center of power in Texas northeastward some two hundred fifty miles from San Antonio to Nacogdoches. In part, no doubt, he did so to place his provisional government that much farther away from any attempt by royalist forces to reimpose their power. But it cannot be denied that the move also put his capital a scant sixty-five miles from the Sabine River, and thus within easy reach of the United States. His motive is unclear, but that he was positioning it to be able to receive that same military aid from the Americans that had initially upset Salcedo seems inescapable, especially when representatives from the main body of revolutionaries in the interior passed through Béxar on their way to Nacogdoches and the United States to try to buy arms.

How much more he may have envisioned he never had time to reveal, for his revolution proved short-lived. Elements within Casas's own organization changed sides to the royalists still at large, and under the leadership of Juan Manuel Zambrano they soon waged a counterrevolution. In March, Casas was overthrown and sent south of the Rio Grande to Monclova, the capital of Coahuila, where he was tried and executed for treason. Now completely in charge, Zambrano created his own new ruling junta and declared for the royalist cause, placing Salcedo back in power. The revolution farther south in Mexico also disintegrated, and though the remnants of the revolutionaries planned to retreat into Texas toward the Sabine and safety in Louisiana, they were dispersed or captured by the end of March.

One of the few who escaped was José Bernardo Maximiliano Gutiérrez de Lara. He had been sent to Washington to try to excite support for the revolutionary cause, and thus was absent when the Casas regime collapsed. But he did not abandon his cause, nor would he. Surviving a Spanish plot to assassinate him on his journey, Gutiérrez met a warm reception on his trip to Washington. Along the way influential men wined and dined him, governors suggested that thousands of men could be forthcoming for his plans, and President James Madison and Secretary of State James Monroe listened as he outlined plans for a republican government in Texas and set his goal at enlisting enough adherents to invade Texas and reclaim it from the royalists. If that was all he could do, then Texas would be a free and independent republic, but his dream extended beyond that to using Texas as a springboard for sending liberating forces south into Mexico to drive out the royalists for good. He asked for men and money, and most of all arms, and the president initially promised him ten thousand muskets and extensive credit, but the deal fell apart when Gutiérrez insisted that he must himself command any insurgency. Gutiérrez did not suspect that Madison cared little for Texas dreams in their own right, but had his own agendum, for with war with Britain looming, and Spain now allied with Britain, any distraction in Texas worked to Washington's advantage. For Gutiérrez an independent Texas was only a means, not the end in itself, but still for the next decade he would strive to keep alive the ambitions of one cadre of Hispanic people to release the colony from the grip of another. The drive to involve support, money, and manpower from the United States only widened the door opened by Nolan a decade before. Hereafter, no one looking toward a change of regime in Texas could do so without American influence and ambition being a part of the equation. After 1811, the center of revolutionary gravity for Texas shifted dramatically to the north and east, across the Sabine, to Louisiana, Mississippi, and even as far as the Potomac.

No place on the North American continent was destined to be the scene of so much revolutionary and insurrectionary activity as Texas. The background of revolt in Mexico and among its own *tejanos* merely set the stage for a generation of expeditions and invasions. Before 1811, with the exception of Philip Nolan's efforts, pressure had come only from the south, and within. Increasingly, Americans from the north now swarmed into Texas and catalyzed an already unstable solution. No sooner did Anglo-Americans east of the Mississippi feel secure in their own independence than they rapidly spread westward to the great river itself. In 1803, with the purchase of the vast Louisiana Territory from Napoleon, the grasp of the new United States in a single leap spanned the continent to the northwest Pacific coast, north to British Canada, and across the southwest along an ill-defined border with Spanish possessions. Of special importance to the story of Texas, however, was the fact that the border between that Spanish province and the Louisiana Territory was ambiguous at best.

The treaty of San Ildefonso, confirmed in October 1800, and by which Spain transferred Louisiana to the French, did not actually define the western boundary of the territory. It merely declared the line to be the same as it had been when France previously owned the area. Napoleon soon declared that the southern boundary was the Gulf of Mexico, and the western one was the Rio Grande. When President Thomas Jefferson bought the territory in 1803, his negotiators tried to get a more precise definition, but the French insisted on retaining the vague wording used when they acquired it from Spain three years before. As a result, Jefferson himself was not at first certain that his acquisition extended any farther west than the north side of the Red River, which excluded almost all of modern Texas. Soon, however, he changed his mind. "We have some pretensions to extend the western territory of Louisiana to the Rio Norte [Grande], or Bravo," he confided in August 1803. However, having already gotten a remarkable bargain from Napoleon, Jefferson was reluctant to press for more. He would have to negotiate with Spain, which claimed that Texas had never been a part of Louisiana, but Spain was still a larger power in the hemisphere than the United States. Jefferson anticipated that Spain soon would be at war with France and hoped to press his advantage to make yet another bargain New World buy.[12]

The Spaniards felt nothing but chagrin at seeing Napoleon sell their onetime empire to the infant United States, for at a stroke it made the Americans a far more equal competitor for hegemony in the region. Furthermore, it now gave them a common border—wherever it might be— with the Yankees. Spain had already seen enough of the expansionist temper of the Americans to expect that such a border would really be little more impassable than a fence, for Spain already felt American expansionist pressure in Florida and Oregon. They wanted a buffer zone. Moreover, the Spaniards objected to Napoleon selling what they considered to be a part of their own territory. Negotiations commenced and continued during which they argued that the Red River was the true border of the Louisiana Purchase. Jefferson and his Congress held to their own construction, and thus there was no settlement, though always Jefferson expected at some time to press his claim to the Rio Grande, even if he had to back it with more money to a war-strapped Spain.[13]

The difference went unsettled for years. In 1806 the United States and Spain conducted negotiations to agree on a so-called Neutral Ground, in order to avert unnecessary border friction. At one point Jefferson almost expected war with Spain to erupt over the boundary dispute. It did not, but they never finally agreed, as each side kept trying to press the buffer zone east or west according to its interests.[14] Not until 1819 and the Adams–Onís Treaty would the line finally—yet still tentatively—be set, and by that time Texas was already thoroughly embroiled in the kind of expansionist agitation the Spaniards feared from the first. The buffer had enclosed a strip roughly forty miles wide, running north and south between the Sabine on the west and the Calcasieu River on the east. The intent was that neither side was to occupy or settle the Neutral Ground, pending any subsequent definite settlement of the boundary, but there was no binding proscription on either side when it came to settlement. Into that sort of vacuum thousands of budding entrepreneurs, expansionists, and simple adventurers stood poised to leap.[15]

Regardless of the treaty, the result was an open invitation to those seeking the most liberal—and westerly—interpretation of the Louisiana boundary. Spain was no longer the power that once it was, and the revolutions of South America were sure to continue after Napoleon invaded Spain itself in 1807. Anglo adventurers from the United States, knowing Spain's weakness and the claim the United States had to ownership of a substantial portion of the province by the Purchase, could hope—dream even—that if they simply marched into Texas and took it, the Spaniards would be too weak, distracted, and irresolute to stop them. Their own fellow Americans would be happy to take advantage of the position thus gained to lend them support and security. In short, whether legally purchased or not, Texas was there for the taking. Logic, the Purchase, geography even, all seemed to dictate that even if Texas was not part of the United States, it should be, and if not that, then still it ought to be free and independent of its Iberian masters. The term "Manifest Destiny" would not be coined for another generation to define American attitudes toward westward expansion, but the words were already reflected in the glimmer in the eyes of ambitious men who turned their gaze toward Texas.

The first American attempt to grab Texas may have lain within the still shadowy dreams of a onetime vice president of the United States, Aaron Burr of New York. In 1806 he organized a substantial party of men and set off down the Ohio toward the Mississippi, ostensibly aiming to seize Spanish West Florida, the region west of Pensacola that would later form portions of the states of Alabama, Mississippi, and the Louisiana parishes east of the Mississippi. He may have intended to create his own empire, or perhaps to take West Florida with a view to annexation by the United States. Anglos living there had already been agitating to do the same thing for two years by this time. Some of them, especially the three Kemper brothers, were beginning there what would become virtual careers as revolutionaries.[16] Reuben, Samuel, and Nathan Kemper were Virginians who moved to Spanish West Florida in 1801 and made turbulence a way of life thereafter, perpetually at odds with Spanish authorities as they divided their time between farming and tavern keeping, and fomenting one rebellion after another. Or Burr may have had grander dreams, for even as his expedition moved down the Ohio, rumors spread in Mexico that his aim was Texas. Whether true or not, it cannot be denied that a marked number of Burr's followers later became agitators in the drive to wrest Texas from Spain, and later Mexico.[17]

The Burr episode ended comically, with Burr and his men captured and the expedition broken up before it even reached the Mississippi River. Future, unequivocal, blows at Texas liberation would not be so easily disrupted, or so bloodlessly. By 1810, when Gutiérrez made his journey to Washington to seek official aid in a Mexican revolution against Spain, there were already hundreds of adventurers gravitating to west Louisiana and New Orleans in the hope of somehow joining an expedition into Texas for adventure, plunder, and perhaps to create a new state or nation. Though ultimately unsuccessful in his effort to gain Madison's aid in his scheme, Gutiérrez found a partner for his enterprise in Augustus W. Magee, who launched his own invasion of Texas in August 1812. Magee, a West Point graduate from Massachusetts, finished third in his class just four years before and seemed to be one of the most promising young officers in the army. But then in an episode of thwarted ambition of the kind that sent so many men to Texas, he was denied a promotion despite the earnest recommendation of his immediate superior, who just happened to be the ubiquitous General Wilkinson. Magee's frustration may account for his actions early in 1812, when he was stationed near the Neutral Ground to protect Spanish traders from marauding bandits. On one occasion when he captured two of the robbers, he tied them to trees, whipped them, then held hot coals to their backs in a needless act of torture before handing them over to civil authorities. Not content with that, he also burned their homes to the ground.

Unable to contain his anger at being refused promotion, the twenty-four-year-old resigned his commission in June and went to the Neutral Ground to help organize the adventurers there gathered. Scores had come, among them Louisianians like Rezin Bowie and Warren D. C. Hall, and Magee whipped nearly one hundred fifty of them into a semblance of an "army," if such a word could be affixed to so small a force.[18] Gutiérrez had hoped to command the force himself, but his vanity and pomposity discouraged any confidence in his ability, and thus he wound up only as second-in-command.

Magee enjoyed initial success in skirmishing with Spanish defenders once he crossed the Sabine. Soon he was in Nacogdoches, the Spaniards continuing to retreat before him or even deserting to the adventurers' banner. It looked as if the political center at San Antonio might be taken before long, and that within two months or more all of Texas would be in Magee's hands, though the once boastful Gutiérrez had now lost his nerve and seemed reluctant even to be with the command. Not so the adventurers who flocked to Magee in even greater numbers after his initial success. By mid-September more than seven hundred followed him when he set off for San Antonio. Fortune continued to favor the bold as Magee took La Bahía in November, but then he met determined Spanish resistance, his men began to desert, and suddenly he became pessimistic of his future chances. After he fell ill, his men lost their confidence in him and were ready to turn over the command to Samuel Kemper. Gutiérrez did nothing but stand on the periphery and watch. Magee died on February 6, 1813, of unknown causes, some said from fever, while others hinted at suicide, even assassination by poison.[19]

With Magee's death the expedition took renewed determination and a few days later drove the Spaniards in their front from the field. Suddenly all of Texas as far as San Antonio de Béxar lay open to them. When the capital at San Antonio itself fell to the invaders, it seemed nothing could halt the march toward an independent Texas. In a city now under the green flag of Texian independence, a few days saw the appearance— for the first time, but not the last—of a declaration of independence and a constitution for Texas. Yet it would also witness that swift and brutal violence that itself so often accompanied events in the province. When the Spaniards capitulated, fourteen of their officers remained, unable to get away with their commands, among them the Spanish governor of Texas, Manuel de Salcedo, and another Simón de Herrera, the governor of the neighboring province of Nueva Leon. On April 3 they were taken out on the road from San Antonio, told they were being taken to the coast to be sent to the United States. They got only a mile and a half on the journey before the commander of their escort suddenly stopped the column, ordered the men to undress, robbed them, and then gave chilling orders. The escort drew swords and beheaded them one by one, not even allowing them to pray before their deaths. The executioners cut out Salcedo's tongue before they killed him.[20]

The atrocity cast a pall over the remainder of the expedition. Some of the better men deserted, among them Warren D. C. Hall, of Natchitoches, who would be heard from again in Texas. Still, on April 6 they framed a declaration proclaiming themselves "free and independent" of Spain and asserting that henceforward they had no allegiance or duty to any foreign power. Not surprisingly, though no one knows who drafted the declaration, it showed some remarkable similarities to one issued in Philadelphia in 1776. Gutiérrez was asked to appoint a commission to frame a government and select a governor. Not surprisingly, Gutiérrez appointed himself governor, and he immediately published a proclamation opening Texas to settlement, especially encouraging Americans to come and make it their home. Unfortunately, he outlined the new government in a constitution that showed that he viewed himself more as a Spanish governor than a democratically responsible American one. In the newly created office of president-protector, he was in all but name an autocrat, all legislative acts subject to his approval. His constitution also revealed that Gutiérrez, at least, wanted Texas to be an independent nation, and not just a latterly claimed part of Louisiana. The first article of his constitution asserted that Texas was a part of the Republic of Mexico, even then struggling to wrest independence from Spain. Beyond this there were to be no gestures toward religious freedom. Texas, like Mexico, was a Catholic province.

There would be little opportunity for Gutiérrez to exercise his authority, however. That summer a Spanish command returned to attempt the retaking of San Antonio. Samuel Kemper had already left on furlough in disgust with Gutiérrez, and his successor in command of the army, Major Rueben Ross, resigned in June, to be succeeded by Major Henry Perry, who marched his nine hundred men out of San Antonio and drove back the would-be besiegers. That done, Perry joined with other American leaders, including advisers and wire pullers in the Madison administration, to maneuver the ouster of Gutiérrez and his replacement. On August 3 Gutiérrez had no choice but to turn over his office and agree to be banished to the United States. The next day José Alvarez de Toledo took over, just in time to preside over the death of the first Texas revolution.

Knowing of the approach of a new Spanish army toward San Antonio, Toledo marched his own out to meet the foe. By August 18 Toledo had his army of about fourteen hundred men just east of the Medina River, a few miles outside Béxar. He did not expect Spanish forces to appear just yet, but when Perry saw an enemy officer appear on the horizon, he told Toledo the foe must be closer than they thought. Reasoning that the Spaniards would still be spread out along their line of march and somewhat disorganized, Perry argued that this was the moment to strike before the foe could form battle lines. Toledo agreed, and the little army set out, only to find itself on a hot, dusty march of two miles or more without sighting the Spaniards. They stopped for water when they came to the Medina, then saw another Spanish party, which quickly fled before them. Toledo and Perry did not realize that it was a feint designed to lure them into following the hastily retreating party back onto the Spaniards' main line. What started as a seemingly victorious pursuit turned into a hot, disorganizing march. Men fell out with thirst, the sand made walking exhausting, their cannon fell behind, and some men became unruly to the point of demoralizing others. Then they suddenly bumped into almost two thousand Spanish *soldados* well positioned in ambush. While most of the Americans in the little army still stood their ground after the initial surprise, even rushing forward to attack the enemy line, some Mexican companies with them refused to answer orders and after several hours simply left on their own. Seeing that, the Americans, too, joined in the retreat. The victors pursued, executing most of those whom they captured—primarily *tejanos* who had joined the revolutionaries, 327 in San Antonio alone—while the remainder of the Americans did not stop running, in most cases, until they reached Louisiana, bringing their families with them.[21]

In just three years Texas had suffered three revolts: one against royalist rule, one against the republicans, and now the repulse of the first insurrection fomented and supported by outside filibusters from the United States. From now on all of its internal upheavals would come at the hands of outsiders. Revolution and invasion would soon be hard to tell apart.

CHAPTER TWO

Bad Causes and Bad Men

ᎧᏗᏅᎧ

DISASTER RARELY DAMPENS the dreams of ambitious men. Even as Toledo and Perry met disaster on the Medina, another dreamer was on his way. Some people thought General Jean Robert Marie Humbert was at least a little crazy, and perhaps rightly so. After all, he made a former commander's widow his mistress, drank too much, and had a nose that looked like an overripe strawberry. He was approaching sixty as he made his way toward Texas in 1813, and left behind him a full and adventurous life. He rose to prominence as a young officer in the French Revolution, survived it with his head, then distinguished himself in Napoleon's subsequent campaigns including an expedition to Ireland that Humbert led in person, only to be forced to surrender. In the wake of the eruption on Santo Domingo, the emperor sent him there in 1802 to put down the insurrection; he was unsuccessful. And now he appeared in Philadelphia, apparently on a mission from Napoleon to engage American aid in starting revolutionary backfires in Mexico to distract Spain from aiding its British ally. Humbert threw about wild promises that he could raise an Irish army to come seize Canada for America, but Washington wisely ignored him. When he suggested that he would be happy to start a military academy to teach the lessons of the emperor to Americans, that, too, generated no enthusiasm. Instead, authorities suggested that he lend his aid to Gutiérrez in Texas or even revolutionaries in Colombia. So Humbert went to New Orleans, and for the next decade the mercurial Frenchman stood either at the center or on the periphery of every plot to take Texas away from Spain.

Within months he bragged that he had found fifteen hundred French

Louisianians awaiting his command to take Texas. After their disenchantment with Gutiérrez and Magee the Kempers refused to join his enterprise, but there were rumors that the band of smugglers and privateers that haunted the region of Barataria south of New Orleans, loosely commanded by the brothers Pierre and Jean Laffite, agreed to use their ships to transport an expedition against the Texan coast while Humbert's burgeoning army marched overland.[1] Meanwhile, Toledo actually managed to rally some of his veterans at Natchitoches, Louisiana, and secure their support for another expedition. In fact, the several incipient bands of revolutionaries became rivals, each hoping to beat the others to the prize. Such a lack of coordination and spirit of self-interest would bedevil attempts to take Texas from Spain—and later Mexico—for two decades.

Humbert got as far as Natchitoches and then somewhat prematurely formed a provisional government for the "Internal Provinces of Mexico" in which he had not yet set foot. Some of his followers crossed the Sabine, just barely entering Texas by a matter of a few hundred yards to give their act legitimacy, and there "elected" Juan Picornell president. Toledo condemned their actions as premature. Meanwhile John Robinson, who had been a gadfly on the fringes of the Gutiérrez-Magee operation, now took the filibustering fever and brought arms and ammunition to Natchez, in December 1813, bent on leading an expedition of his own. Toledo condemned this effort as well.[2]

In time it assumed an almost comic aspect, Toledo trying to steal "soldiers" away from Robinson, each trying to delay the departure of the other for Texas, and Humbert and Picornell strutting about New Orleans with ridiculous titles and pretensions. "As is usual, the prejudices & passions of the People have been awakened 'by the voice of Reason & Liberty,' while the Leaders are stimulated by avarice and ambition," complained a man in Natchitoches who watched it all in March 1814. "Royal Honors, Dukedoms, Principilities [sic] &c are forever rising before them. The gilded tombs of Mexico are not too remote for their mercenary vision."[3] Robinson finally crossed into Texas that same month, but he had barely fifty men with him, hardly an army of invasion. When Toledo sent word for him to stand aside, as Texas was a concern properly left to Mexican revolutionaries like himself, Robinson told him to mind his own business, as Robinson's was an entirely American concern with its own agendum. Soon afterward Toledo unceremoniously had to leave

Natchez when he learned that he was the subject of an arrest warrant for violating laws against fitting out filibustering expeditions on United States soil. Toledo escaped to Natchitoches and then crossed the Sabine into Texas on May 2, to find that one of his subordinates had arrested Robinson. As if that were not comical enough in itself—an American officer arresting an American civilian on orders of a Mexican revolutionary in a Spanish province where none of them had authority to interfere with each other—Toledo then went one better. He issued a declaration ordering all Mexican citizens then in western Louisiana—in which a Mexican revolutionary in a Spanish province hardly had jurisdiction—to join him immediately. Soon Toledo released Robinson after extracting from him a commitment to support the Mexican revolution rather than his own designs on Texas—which Robinson promptly ignored—and then Toledo tried to induce United States military authorities in Louisiana to arrest Robinson's command by falsely accusing it of committing acts of plunder on Mexican citizens west of the Sabine. Thereafter Toledo and his one hundred twenty men simply glared at Robinson and his fifty or fewer at a distance of a few miles, both so lost in their own pretensions and mutual jealousy that neither could advance his own cause or his command another foot into Texas. Neither would ever find his dream. Robinson gave up, went back to Mississippi, and died of yellow fever five years later, and well before then Toledo had switched allegiances and become a good Spaniard once more.[4]

It must be remembered that all of these sometimes harebrained schemes did not operate in a vacuum. They counted on—and were a part of—two separate upheavals. The revolution in Mexico had resurfaced once more to occupy Spanish attention, thus making Texas the more vulnerable. In May 1812 a new leader, José Maria Morelos y Pavón, declared Mexico independent from Spain, convened a congress, and oversaw drafting a constitution with some significant reforms that showed its debt to the United States Constitution that so many emerging republics used as a model. It was a short-lived triumph, for royalist forces soon forced the revolutionaries under Morelos y Pavón on to the defensive and inflicted heavy losses on them. Within a few months Morelos y Pavón himself would be captured and later executed in 1814, and the Spanish hold on Mexico seemed once more secure.

For the next two years the revolution in Mexico went largely underground, but still the ideal was kept alive, aided by the constant distraction to royalist forces elsewhere in Central and South America. Bolívar was waging a costly campaign in Venezuela, alternating between success and disaster, while Chile expelled the Spaniards for a time and then José Francisco de San Martín began making advances against the royalists in Argentina. With such a weakened mother country behind them, and so much rebellion in their front, Spanish authorities simply could not devote much attention to Texas. Thus it is not surprising that even tiny bands of a few hundred Americans might think they could take and hold the province.

And of course the new war between Great Britain and the United States worked in their favor, too. Madison and Monroe considered supporting more than one of these expeditions because of the potential of creating a buffer state on their border, and also because anything that distracted Spain could help distract Spain's British allies. Moreover, the dreams of men like Humbert and Toledo went far beyond just an independent Texas, for they sought independence of all of Mexico, and to some degree sought to coordinate their efforts with those of the main body of revolutionaries south of the Rio Grande.

It was Humbert's worldliness, perhaps, and certainly his French background, that finally established him with a more promising avenue into Texas than either Robinson or Toledo. Humbert, at least, understood the international ramifications of the Texas quest and the Mexican Revolution in ways that Robinson certainly did not, and probably not Toledo either. Moreover, operating in New Orleans, Humbert found himself able to gain the acquaintance of other worldly men, men who had spent two years showing they knew how to take advantage of the war with Britain for their own advantage, and men who also commanded ships, resources, armaments even. Perhaps best of all, they were less than welcome in their current venue and might see much to gain from a change of base.

Jean Laffite certainly had a taste for flair mixed with his opportunistic nature. When the governor of Louisiana offered a reward for his apprehension and that of his brother Pierre, Laffite promptly published a notice of his own offering a larger reward for the arrest of the governor. The brothers Laffite were probably natives of France who grew to young manhood on St. Domingue until about 1803, when revolts there made the island inhospitable for whites and thousands came to Louisiana. Pierre, at least, arrived in New Orleans in 1803, his brother Jean then or later, and for the next ten years they were frequently in the city. Pierre may have been a seafarer already, and there is evidence that he spent some time in the then Spanish outpost at Pensacola. Both were merchants to an extent, and though they never actually owned domiciles in New Orleans, they did apparently rent a warehouse. Like many other Creole men, they took mulatto mistresses whom they maintained in houses in the city, drank in the coffeehouses, gambled in the inns, and in most other respects assumed the mode of respectable businessmen. After the abolition of the African slave trade in 1808, however, they like others quickly realized that there was considerable profit to be made in smuggling slaves into a labor-hungry Louisiana. Somehow in the process they became increasingly associated with a growing and unorganized band of privateers who lived beyond the arm of the law at Grand Terre on the Louisiana coast and in and around Barataria Bay, preying primarily on Spanish shipping. While Pierre may have taken out a privateering commission from Cartagena, Colombia, in 1813, the real occupation of the two was as middlemen for the merchandise brought in by the privateers, bypassing customs and therefore evading tax duties, and selling it to a hungry market in New Orleans.

Through it all they established some very useful connections in the best of Louisiana society and government and, moreover, enjoyed the widespread approval of the populace for the service they provided. The blockade imposed by the British during the war made consumer goods scarce, but the Laffites were able to bring all manner of staple and luxury goods to New Orleans's markets, and if they were taken from English or Spanish ships so much the better. Thus privateering was easily distinguished from piracy in the public mind, and the Laffites—or more properly, the men whose goods they marketed—were regarded as patriots in a way, for they robbed the ships of the common enemy. It was easy to look away from the money the Laffites' smuggling denied to the treasury and thus to the war effort, but the governor and Washington were hardly willing to remain blind. Periodically they were arrested, released on bond, arrested again, but easily disappeared into the fastness of Barataria when necessary. The rest of the time they walked the streets and haunted the coffeehouses of New Orleans with impunity, and Pierre often lived openly with his mulatto mistress in a house he helped her buy on Bourbon Street.

The Laffites and those like Humbert with Texas dreams were ready for each other. Sooner or later their smuggling operations were likely to come to an enforced end, especially once the War of 1812 ended. Regardless of who won, neither British nor American rulers would welcome illicit trade once the guns fell silent. For all their powerful friends, the Laffites had also made powerful enemies. Indeed, even now they were in secret communication with Spanish authorities in Cuba, providing information on rumors of threats against Texas. Masters of playing both sides at once, they could hope for commercial preferments in Texas if Spain held on to it, and at the same time expect similar advantages if Humbert or any other filibuster succeeded in wrenching the province from the mother country. Meanwhile, they could keep in the good graces of both sides by pretending loyalty and providing information about the other. And whoever won in Texas, the Laffites could hope to gain a secure land base on the Texas coast far away from the pesky jurisdiction and legal pettifogging of the United States. Serious allegiances apparently had nothing to do with the matter. The Laffites, like so many others on this frontier, sought first and foremost their own advancement and took advantage of any circumstance that served their purpose.

Soon Humbert had an ally in his planning with the Laffites—of all people, the discredited Gutiérrez. By the summer of 1814 they hatched a plan to make a landing somewhere on the Texan coastline. Gutiérrez fumbled his part of the agreement by failing to raise sufficient money to arm and equip their expedition, meanwhile letting news of their plans become common knowledge. The plotters reduced their goals to a simple raid on Texas by sea, but even that failed to materialize, despite Humbert fetching Peter Ellis Bean, a veteran of Philip Nolan's ill-fated adventure of more than a decade before, to help with the planning. Then the Laffite enterprise itself hit foul weather as first Pierre was arrested and jailed, and a United States Navy attack on Barataria that fall all but cleaned out their operation. The naval attack was motivated only in part to arrest the smuggling. It also reflected the desire of Commodore Daniel Patterson, who planned and led the attack, to profit personally from the enormous haul of ships and goods taken that he was then able to sell for his own profit as legitimate seizures. Finally, there had been rumors for months that if or when the British made an effort to come up the Mississippi to attack New Orleans, they would try to form an alliance with the Baratarians, who knew the water approaches through the swamps and bayous better than anyone else. Thus the erasure of the

Baratarian operation seemingly removed a threat to the security of Louisiana itself. Yet Patterson reckoned without the Laffites' instinct for allying themselves with a winner. All along they had scrupulously refused to sanction taking American vessels, knowing that to do so would destroy their support in New Orleans. Moreover, they knew there was no profit for them in a British victory, for the British, too, had abolished the slave trade in its colonies and enforced it—and smuggling laws in general—far more effectively than did Washington. A British victory would likely see the Laffites put out of business, whereas the United States, if successful, could be hoped to continue pursuing its essentially lax policy toward them. Thus, the Laffites—Pierre having escaped from jail—rebuffed the British approach for assistance, and all the blandishments that came with it, and instead threw their support to General Andrew Jackson and his small army when the climactic battle came in January 1815. The participation of the Laffites and their privateers and smugglers has been greatly inflated in its importance, but it was enough to gain the "pirate-patriots" a presidential pardon for their past transgressions.

Meanwhile, many of the Baratarians, driven out of their lair, flocked to New Orleans, and hard on that none other than Toledo arrived. Suddenly New Orleans was a ferment with Humbert, Gutiérrez, Toledo, and Bean, all in the same place, with hundreds of unemployed privateers looking for employment, and the Laffites so recently evicted from their base of operations.[5] Even after the Patterson raid, the Laffites still had two ships, which was enough upon which to base some kind of enterprise, and all of the rival filibusters seemed briefly willing to work in accord. What they needed was a plan.

Into this situation stepped the New Orleans Association, a group of businessmen, lawyers, planters, even Patterson, all interested in the profit to be made from taking advantage of Britain's withdrawal from the war and Spain's crippled condition thanks to Napoleon's conquest and occupation of the Iberian Peninsula prior to his own defeat. The associates talked with Gutiérrez about supporting his Texas dreams, and then Humbert and Toledo resurrected their own prior plots for invasion. Toledo boasted that he had four hundred men ready, and Humbert actually proclaimed his plans in a published broadside that gave everything away to Spanish agents in New Orleans. Toledo got involved with Vincent Gambi, perhaps the Laffites' most rebellious and unruly corsair, and soon Gambi was taking Spanish vessels on the Gulf despite the fact that the United States and Spain were now at peace. Patterson arrested Gambi and charged him with piracy, and then arrested Toledo as an accomplice. Both escaped the noose, but no one was any the closer to Texas.[6]

Finally in the summer of 1815, Henry Perry came back on the scene, like so many with the Texas dream, unwilling to stay long away. He and Gutiérrez agreed to cooperate on a joint land-sea invasion, to converge on La Bahía and San Antonio, while some of the Laffites' associates were to attack Tampico on the Mexican coast. By March 1816 Perry had perhaps 350 men gathered on the Louisiana coast, among them Warren Hall and others from the Gutiérrez–Magee fiasco, but then, like Humbert before him, he gave it all away with a boastful announcement calling on volunteers and promising them "an easy road to distinction" and "glorious reward for merit," meaning plunder.[7] Meanwhile, going it alone again, Toledo began trying to organize his own fleet for a landing at Vera Cruz, his goal this time Mexico itself.

The efforts of these men, and their foolishness in being so public about their enterprises, brought on an inevitable reaction, not only from the governor of Louisiana, but even from faraway Washington. President Madison promulgated a proclamation condemning all such filibustering expeditions against a nation with whom the United States was at peace and promising the swift action of military and naval forces in stopping them and bringing their leaders to justice.[8] Of course, many in New Orleans took Madison's proclamation at less than face value, for it seemed common knowledge that while Washington was required to maintain a public posture of opposition to unlawful expeditions, privately leaders in the capital still had not abandoned the belief that Louisiana had included Texas all along, and if private adventurers could take it for them—perhaps with a little covert aid from the United States government—then perhaps America could extend to its lawful borders without risking an international incident.

That fall the Laffites met with Toledo, and now Patterson was working with them on a plan to send materiel to desperate revolutionaries on the Mexican coastline. With Napoleon's defeat, his puppet ruler lost the Spanish throne, and the crown had been restored to Ferdinand VII, who quickly attempted to institute absolute rule over the New World colonies once more. Armies sailed from Spain to retake what had been lost to the revolutionaries, and for a time men such as Bolívar were on the run. But by late 1816 San Martín and the new Chilean leader Bernardo O'Higgins were taking ground again, and Bolívar returned to Venezuela. Again there was simply too much for Spain to try to do to control all of the fires in its colonial house. In Mexico the revolt was confined to the southern provinces and seemed ill fated, hence Toledo's plan to inject some new life into the cause with his expedition. Meanwhile, Humbert left with what men he had raised to rendezvous with Perry and his command just offshore from the mouth of the Sabine. Toledo intended soon to join them. These men would march their little army overland across Texas to San Antonio, there to be joined by more men landed on the coast below La Bahía. Several privateer vessels would take a port on the Mexican coastline somewhere below the mouth of the Rio Grande, use it as a base of privateering operations to capture supplies and valuables to convert into guns and ammunition, and then another fleet would attack Tampico itself.

Perry actually made the first move in November, landing some of his men at Point Bolivar—named for Simón Bolívar, even then waging war for Colombian independence, and granting commissions in his navy to Baratarian privateers including the Laffites. A second group including Hall soon followed, only to be shipwrecked and mostly drowned on Culebra Island, also known then to the Spaniards as Galvez-town, or Galveston. The remainder of Perry's men never left, tired of waiting for information and transportation, and eventually dissolved. After a year of plotting and planning, only Perry and a handful of men had actually set foot on Texas soil. It would be some time before any more joined him, and thus another flicker of flame fell back into ember.

Anxious men watched the flames and embers closely, all the same. Almost all that happened was being reported regularly to Spanish officials by the accommodating Laffites, who went to work for them at least as early as November 1815 and perhaps earlier. Not long thereafter Toledo changed sides and sought a pardon from Spain, and then he, too, began revealing what he knew about the plans of Humbert, Perry, and the rest. The whole Texan enterprise was seriously compromised. Not forgetting his old enmities, Toledo suggested to the Spaniards that of all the filibusters, only Gutiérrez did not deserve pardon.

No sooner did Toledo leave the scene, destined for the obscurity that he richly deserved, than a replacement arrived to take up the cause, a man no less dedicated foremost to his own adventure and profit, yet one with far more ability and stamina: Louis Michel Aury. Only this century could have produced his like. He was yet another dreamer, a wealthy twenty-eight-year-old Parisian whose personal reality had been formed by romance novels. He daydreamed of buccaneering, heroic conquests, glory in battle, and of making himself a lord, even a king, much of it to impress parents and a sister to whom he was devoted, and a young woman he dreamed of making his wife. He had served with distinction in the French navy, and then commanded privateers in the war against Britain before he bought his own fleet and set sail for Cartagena, where he received letters of marque from New Granada to prey on Spanish shipping in the Gulf. He fell out with Bolívar in 1816, however, and Cartagena had to be evacuated, and thus Aury sailed for Louisiana. The combination of Louisiana and corsairing had fascinated Aury for some years before, and now he was about to combine the two.[9] Indeed, he had brought prizes into New Orleans before, and that is no doubt how he came into contact with the Association, which now engaged him to carry out the naval part of its Texas scheme.[10] Their eyes were most immediately set on taking Florida, which they expected then to be able to sell to the United States for some $2 million that could finance more ambitious schemes in Texas and Mexico. However, American neutrality laws precluded them from basing their operations on United States soil. Aury would need a port, and the nearest that lay outside American waters was Galveston. Consequently, in July and August 1816 Aury and a fleet of ships rendezvoused with men and supplies engaged for the enterprise and set sail from the mouth of the Mississippi, soon making landing on Galveston Island and beginning the construction of a village of huts that would be, in its way, the first community of non-Spanish nationals on Texas soil. Here they could outfit and equip the expeditions by sea to Florida, and by land and sea to take Texas. It was a modest beginning, to be sure, but a beginning all the same.[11]

Of course Pierre Laffite informed the Spanish consul in New Orleans of all that occurred with the association and Aury. Other events added to the tension of the moment. The revolutionary congress in Mexico had dissolved, returning the country to internal confusion without a constituted authority, and then rumors appeared of a massive naval expedition, well funded and equipped, bent on taking Vera Cruz or some other major port on the Mexican coast. The chaotic events of the past decade seemed to show no sign of letup. Unexpectedly, Aury's own men on Galveston mutinied against him in reaction to his dictatorial regime. They entered his tent and shot him through both hands and in the chest. It was thought for a time that he would not recover. Then they took most of the goods brought with them from Louisiana and taken on prizes along the way, loaded three ships, and left.[12]

Aury was left behind with about two hundred men, mostly blacks recruited in the Caribbean, and one partially burned ship. Though discouraged, while he healed he planned to return to New Orleans. Before he could do so, more ships arrived from the Associates bringing supplies, Humbert, one hundred sixty more men, and José Manuel de Herrera, an ambassador to Washington from the recently defunct Mexican congress. Learning of Aury's plight, Herrera and the Association decided to shift their sights to the new opportunity presented by the collapse of the revolutionary government in Mexico. They were still interested in Florida, but now Texas and Mexico were up for grabs once more. They agreed to cooperate with Herrera—representative of a defunct government with no power at all—in using Galveston as a base for declaring yet another new revolutionary regime for Mexico. If successful, they stood to profit much more by backing Herrera than they did from their Florida scheme. It would require a real invasion, however. In addition to sending the veteran plotter Humbert to work with Aury in planning naval operations, they decided to call once more on Gutiérrez to cooperate with Henry Perry in leading an army across Texas to Galveston by land. It was to be almost a reunion of past plotters on a newer, better funded and equipped scale.[13]

Revolutionaries from Washington to Robespierre to Lenin suffer from ambition. Some, like Washington, temper it and maintain the interests of their cause and people above their own. Most, however, including the early Texas filibusters, all too quickly mistake patriotism with their own ends, betraying their revolutions and themselves. The associates wanted Herrera to take charge in Galveston, with Aury demoted to his subordinate in fact if not in name. Herrera set up a "government" on behalf of the Mexican Republic, made Aury and his men swear allegiance to the republic, but then gave in to Aury's petulant demands that he be put in command of the Galveston base. As soon as Herrera left for Mexico to try to secure ratification of his actions, however, Aury declared himself general and supreme commander, alienated many of the men who had come from New Orleans with Herrera, and began feuding with Perry.

The international communist party of the twentieth century would have only a few more schemers. In November, Francisco Xavier Mina brought a force of more than one thousand men from the United States, bent on pressing the revolution in Mexico, but by the time he reached Galveston desertion and sickness thinned his ranks to only about one hundred forty, the ever-present Warren Hall among them. Aury did not like the idea of a competing commander with his own men, and for a week refused even to allow Mina and his men to land. Perry, meanwhile, welcomed Mina's arrival, and finally Mina was allowed to come ashore and set up a camp at some remove from the soldiers ashore commanded by Perry. Now Mina's and Aury's ambitions collided. The former wanted the ships to land the entire force below La Bahía, then march to take San Antonio and proceed from there across the Rio Grande into northern Mexico. Aury—now calling himself governor of Texas—still wanted only to make a raid on Tampico with a greater prospect of prizes and far less exertion and risk, and then continue the plan to take Florida. Unable to agree between themselves on anything, they simply argued until Mina left for New Orleans in February 1817 to get a definitive decision from the associates.[14]

When Mina returned with two ships of his own, his relations with the associates were all but shattered, as they continued to favor the Florida scheme, and he was on his own to continue his Mexican endeavor. But he arrived to find that in his absence Aury had fomented yet another near mutiny at Galveston. Aury announced that the entire command was to shift to Matagorda Bay, one hundred miles farther south, but Perry refused to go along unless everyone including Mina's men made the move. Aury arrested Perry and threatened to open fire on his men if they did not agree, but Perry's men called the bluff and asked Mina's command to join them in resisting Aury. Actual violence was averted only when Aury released Perry, and then the two of them and the interim commander of Mina's band met in a council and agreed that henceforth Aury would command only the naval forces, his ships, and the two hundred men aboard them, while Mina would be commander of the land forces when he returned. But then when Mina's small squadron was about to enter the port, Aury made one last treacherous attempt to have his own way by posting one of his ships outside the harbor and ordering it to fire on Mina to prevent his coming ashore. No real battle ensued, and outnumbered as he was ashore by Perry's and Mina's men, Aury backed down and Mina landed. Any further talk of a move to Matagorda was pointless.[15]

Mina decided to land his small army on the Mexican coastline at the mouth of the Rio Santander, north of Tampico. Perry and his men would go with him, making their total force only about three hundred fifty. Aury's command remained with him and Aury's only role in the expedition would be to convoy the men to their destination. That done, Aury would return to a Galveston now exclusively his own. On April 7, 1817, the fleet sailed off, leaving Galveston all but abandoned, and two weeks later Mina led his men ashore, never to be seen in Texas again. Within a few weeks Perry and Mina fell out over strategy, and Perry and about fifty of his men set off on their own to march north back toward Texas. They reached La Bahía and were on their way to Nacogdoches when Spanish soldiers from San Antonio caught up with and surrounded them on June 19, killing or capturing all. Perry, wounded and seeing the situation hopeless, shot himself in the head. He was the first and only American filibustering leader to lose his life on Texan soil during the generation of attempts to take it from Spain.[16] As for Mina, he lost half his men when he split his force and one part surrendered, and he and the pitiful remnant simply abandoned any independent hopes they had and joined forces with local revolutionaries. He tried unsuccessfully to organize scattered patriots and was himself captured in a skirmish in October. On November 11, 1817, in Mexico City, he stood with his back to a wall to meet his end.

That left only Aury, or so it seemed. But when he returned he discovered to his surprise that he no longer ruled Galveston. Jean Laffite had arrived shortly before the fleet left for the Santander, and the day after Aury departed he declared a new government and placed himself in charge, with no resistance from the men Aury had left behind. Allegiance was cloudy at best. Laffite was an agent of the Spanish, but he had close ties to the New Orleans Association. He had authority from neither to take over Galveston, but merely took bold initiative on his own and got away with it. While Herrera reluctantly chose to recognize Laffite's government as a de facto satellite of the Mexican revolution, Laffite himself reassured the Spaniards to whom he reported that his move only put him in a better position to monitor filibustering efforts like Mina's. Meanwhile, his own agendum seems to have been to continue selling merchandise taken from Spanish ships by his corsairs sailing under Colombian colors. Arguably no one in the whole convoluted arena of Texan-Mexican-Spanish affairs in the Gulf wove a web more tangled than Jean Laffite's.[17]

Aury found himself a commander without a base, and almost without a command as some of his men defected to Laffite and returned with the new commander to New Orleans for more supplies. In May, Aury simply left with the tiny remnant of loyal followers willing to go with him and sailed for Matagorda, unaware that in New Orleans the Laffites were plotting with their Spanish employers to take Galveston by strength, capture and destroy all of Aury's vessels, and imprison him, an act that not only removed Aury as a competitor, but which would also leave Mina isolated without a supply line or a line of retreat. At a stroke, the Laffites would remove all competition for this new base on the Texas coast, not to use it as a base for the conquest of Texas, but as a safe headquarters for their privateering and smuggling empire. Aury meanwhile lost most of his ships anyhow due to the treacherous sandbars in Matagorda Bay, and was forced to return to Galveston in June with his two remaining vessels. By now he acknowledged that his future in Texas, even in the Gulf, was over, and soon he sailed away to continue his schemes and dreams on the Atlantic coast of Florida. Four years later he would die in obscurity on an island off the coast of Colombia, having failed in everything he had attempted.[18]

A GENERATION OF ASPIRATION for Texas, from the unfortunate Nolan to the equally ill-fated Aury, had thus far come to nothing, all ending in disruption, disgrace, or death. Yet undeniably something had been born in those years, something that refused to expire in the succeeding episodes of fiasco and misadventure. Partly it was the pure opportunism inspired by such a vast and unexploited territory. Beyond that, however, Texas had become an idea, a place in the imagination as well as on the map. Now and for decades to come, Texas represented intangibles like aspiration, rebirth, and self-renewal, potentials as limitless as the land itself. As Nolan and Perry and so many more discovered, it was easy to kill men. The rulers of Texas were just beginning to discover, however, how much more difficult it was to kill men's dreams, and Texas had become a dream whose allure spread eastward to the Atlantic and across the sea even to the Old World.

The little American foothold on Texas, backed covertly by the Spaniards, and with ostensible ties to the Mexican revolutionaries, now belonged to the Laffites, who speedily built it into a major haven and port of entry for the privateers sailing under Mexican and Colombian flags who preyed on Spanish shipping. Soon the Laffites and their subordinates fed information of new plans by Humbert and Gutiérrez to the Spaniards. The New Orleans Association soon abandoned its hopes for Florida and Texas altogether, and virtually all filibustering activity ground to a halt in the summer and fall of 1817. No sooner did that happen, however, than Spain perceived another, perhaps more insidious threat from a new quarter.

In the wake of the failure of Napoleon's brief resurgence at the Battle of Waterloo, thousands of his followers fled the country, some of them exporting the emperor's dreams of empire to the New World with them. Among them was General Charles Lallemand, who conceived a number of schemes to free Napoleon from his exile at Sainte Helena, but who also became involved in the effort to make a home for fellow refugees in the New World, at first with land grants in what was then the Mississippi Territory. However, after only halfhearted efforts to settle there, Lallemand and many of his followers sold the grants to finance a more ambitious scheme to build a settlement in the Neutral Ground beyond United States authority, and presumably beyond the power of Spain. No one knew with certainty what he intended next, whether just to start a new life or to use the settlement as a base for carving out a new French state that could itself be used as the base for a move to liberate more of Spanish America, and perhaps then place Napoleon's brother Joseph on a new throne. Maybe he even hoped to free the emperor himself and bring him to the New World. It was a time when men dreamed large, expansive, even silly dreams, which to them seemed anything but frivolous.[19]

Lallemand reached New Orleans early in 1817, probably contacting his fellow French exile Humbert. Almost immediately rumors began to circulate of Lallemand being in touch with revolutionaries in Mexico, who supposedly promised him large armies of soldiers. Much was exaggeration, but Lallemand did buy substantial armaments in the north, and in December 1817 embarked with about one hundred fifty men for Texas, trying to mollify Spanish authorities by saying that he would be happy to place himself and his settlers under Spanish rule and that he would himself take a commission in the army of Spain if desired. The Spaniards were not fooled and believed with a certainty that any foothold in the Neutral Ground taken by Lallemand would be used not as a permanent new home, but as a launching place for an invasion of Texas or Mexico itself.[20]

Lallemand's first ship anchored at Galveston in January 1818. As Lallemand's men outnumbered the privateers under Jean Laffite at the moment and were well armed, Laffite could do nothing but accept their coming, meanwhile watchfully reporting all movements to his Spanish employers. Lallemand himself reached New Orleans the next month, and there Pierre Laffite gained his confidence and heard from his own lips his true intention of building a new Bonapartist France in Texas and then expanding to take all of Mexico. Pierre arranged a trap intended to lead to the capture at sea of most of Lallemand's officers, Humbert among them, but it went awry, and then without warning the Spanish abruptly cut off all further funds for the Laffites' espionage activities. Nevertheless, the Laffites continued to serve several masters, while all the time acting chiefly in their own interest.[21]

They need have feared little from Lallemand and his followers, for they proved almost hopelessly incapable of sustaining themselves, let alone posing a threat to Texas or Mexico. In March the French exiles rowed across the harbor from Galveston Island and up the Trinity River about twenty miles, where they went ashore and began to build the community they would call Champ d'Asile. These soldiers and aristo-crats knew little about eking out a living in the wild. They were mili-tary men, not farmers. Their own inexperience and internal discord, added to climatic hazards beyond their control, soon saw them all but starving, even as the governments of the United States and Spain wor-ried unnecessarily about Lallemand's intentions. When they heard rumors that the Spaniards were about to send an expedition to eject them from their settlement, it so put the fright into them that they abandoned their unfinished community and withdrew to the mouth of the Trinity opposite Galveston, appealing to Laffite for aid. He happily obliged, protesting his sympathy and support for their welfare, while keeping Spanish officials informed of Lallemand's condition. The French refugees perched precariously on the banks of the Trinity until Septem-ber, watched and reported on constantly by Laffite, when a hurricane destroyed their camps and they gave up entirely. Laffite gladly provided transportation for the hundred or so who remained, and by November they were almost all back in New Orleans.[22]

Once more the Laffites parlayed ingenuity and treachery into a means to preserve their unchallenged hold on the Texas coast. Their lair on Galveston Island soon housed as many as two hundred men and women of all nationalities, Jean Laffite acting as overall commandant and brother Pierre handling their business in New Orleans and the United States. They built a community of rude wooden huts and houses, with streets, saloons, billiard parlors, even reportedly a newspaper. The Laffites themselves lived in the only masonry structure, called "Red House," Jean keeping a young mulatto mistress and living a life of some luxury, thanks to what the privateers took from Spanish vessels and what it bought in New Orleans. He created an admiralty court in order to handle prizes in Galveston rather than risking the scrutiny of United States admiralty courts, and ruled the island with a firm grip, in the process managing the most extensive smuggling enterprise on the continent.

Not surprisingly, the United States paid increasing attention to Galveston, including a visit in 1818 from an American inspector, suggesting that the Laffites might not be able to hold on indefinitely without active diplomatic support from Spain. But Spain had cut off further payments to them. Moreover, the insurgency in Mexico was at a low ebb, fragmented into a number of ineffective local uprisings, and the long-term threat to Spain's hegemony seemed much reduced. The same hurricane that so damaged the Champ d'Asile refugees' camp on the Trinity had also ravaged the Laffites' community, wrecking many of their ships. In such a state of affairs, Spain had little to gain from continuing to support the Laffite operation in Galveston, especially if it was drawing Washington's eyes westward. Any move by the United States to clear out the privateers could well be used as a pretext for permanent occupation of the Texas coast, and with a force and organization far beyond that of any of the filibusters thus far. Thus the Laffites were rapidly on their way to becoming an embarrassment to Spain, which had always viewed them as a necessary evil at best. Indeed, had they but known it, for several months in late 1818 and early 1819 the subject of their tenure or eviction from the island was hotly debated in Spanish dispatches. By April 1819 officials were actually planning their own attack on Galveston and the destruction of the Laffites' lair.[23]

But then came what was destined to be the last of the filibustering efforts directed at Texas, and it gave the Laffites one more opportunity to divert attention from themselves by being useful to Spain. Dr. James Long was a twenty-five-year-old Virginian practicing medicine in Natchez at the dawn of 1819. He already had at least a distant connection to the filibustering story by virtue of his having married the daughter of General Wilkinson, and must have achieved some standing in his community among those who believed that Texas ought to belong to Americans and not the Spaniards, regardless of the Adams–Onís Treaty. That treaty, signed in February 1819, finally settled the issue of the southwestern boundary of the Louisiana Territory, placing it along the Sabine River.[24]

Expansionists like Long felt outraged, believing that legitimate interests of potential entrepreneurs like themselves had been abandoned by Washington relinquishing its claim to the vast territory of Texas west of the Sabine. Long became the spokesman for the disgruntled in Natchez, and in seemingly no time at all it was decided to raise an army and invade to take by force what craven politicians in the east had surrendered. Not surprisingly, one among those voices in Natchez was Gutiérrez, though he no longer had the credibility to lead. They nominated Long to be their general, though his only military experience was as a surgeon in the late war with Britain. Somehow expansionists, looking back on the sorry and often silly history of filibustering in Texas over the past two decades, may have felt this was a last chance, and so Long managed to attract great enthusiasm, including pledges of close to half a million dollars in financing.

The adventurers flocked to Long's banner. "Never was a more propitious moment for effecting their purpose," a Natchez editor wrote while the men gathered in and around his town. "Should New-Mexico and Texas unite in the great cause, the consummation of the independence of all America will be soon and certain."[25] By late June there were seventy-five immediately at hand under Long, with others on the way, their ranks including the veteran filibuster Warren Hall; Rezin Bowie's dynamic younger brother James Bowie; James Gaines, who operated the principal ferry across the Sabine into Texas, and a Kentuckian named Ben Milam.[26] Meanwhile, an advance party of one hundred twenty led by Eli Harris went ahead and crossed the Sabine on June 8. Long and the balance rendezvoused with Harris two weeks later at Nacogdoches.

Once Long had his force consolidated, he followed the usual practice of filibusters by declaring a new government for Texas, naming officials, issuing decrees, and the rest of the usual futile blustering of a would-be Napoleon trying to take hold of an empire with two hundred men. On June 22 he and his men selected a "provisional government" composed of a twenty-one-man Supreme Council, which in turn elected him president and commander in chief. The next day the Council issued a declaration of independence for Texas. The declaration showed its debt to the 1776 document by stating a list of grievances, not failing to make repeated reference to "Spanish rapacity," "odious tyranny," and "most atrocious despotism." They promised that their new and independent Texas would protect religious freedom, an unfettered press, and free trade, the last a clear lure to American interests already rankling over the enactment in 1816 of the first protective tariff, driving up the cost of imported goods. No one needed to spell out the hint that a free-trade Texas, separated from the United States only by the Sabine, could in effect be a free port of entry for all manner of merchandise that could then be smuggled across the river to a market eager for bargains, just as the Laffites were then smuggling slaves into Louisiana from Galveston in spite of the abolition of the foreign slave trade.[27]

Indeed, Long's new operation quite consciously defied both Spanish and American authority. Americans had a right to Texas, he believed, and it was lawfully theirs, bought and paid for, and if their own government and politicians chose to abandon their legal claim, then they would simply take it themselves. "Our citizens have a right to migrate whithersoever they choose," wrote a publicist for Long back in Natchez, "and it is beyond the power of government to prevent them."[28] As evidence that this was the real impetus for this and most filibustering projects, the Supreme Council then passed an ordinance giving ten sections of Texas land to each man in the expedition and authorizing the further sale of even more at minimal prices as a means to raise cash for a treasury that at the moment held nothing more than the contents of Long's saddlebag.[29] To farmers from east of the Mississippi, accustomed to eking out a living from a few acres, the prospect of receiving ten square miles of land for free was almost beyond dreaming. In an era of expanding empires and wars for them, here in Texas every man who took big risks could hope for a miniature empire of his own.

Long's small army grew to more than three hundred by late July, but foolish as he may have been, he was not so much a fool as not to know that he needed a great deal of help to effect his dream. Laffite and his reduced privateer enclave were still on Galveston Island with ships, some men, arms, and ammunition. Moreover, in an echo of the old plans of the New Orleans Association, Gutiérrez, and others, Long's campaign had a naval component in a small flotilla under José Félix Trespalacios transporting volunteers led by Milam, bound for a landing at Vera Cruz. The Laffites, were they willing, would be in a position to lend aid and support to either Long or Milam. Thus, Long sent emissaries to Laffite at the beginning of July, carrying a personal letter entreating his cooperation and dangling lures of another kind before the privateer lords of Galveston. Long's letter suggested that the new government of Texas would establish an admiralty court at Galveston, meaning that prize ships and goods could be cleared and sold there to buyers from all nations, rather than having to clear them through other less convenient ports. Moreover, Long tendered to Jean Laffite himself a commission as governor at Galveston.[30]

For his part, Laffite played Long brilliantly, giving nothing in reply but excuses, putting him off by saying he needed to consult with his absent brother Pierre, and at the same time disingenuously promising much while asking Long for detail on his own strength and intentions, information that he could immediately communicate to the Spanish.[31] Indeed, the Spaniards were already well aware of Long and his intentions. "I am fully persuaded that the present is the most serious expedition that has threatened the Kingdom," the Spanish Consul in New Orleans warned the viceroy in Mexico City on July 16, "for its directors lack for neither pecuniary means to effect it, nor for better organised heads, than all that have conducted the previous ones."[32] They would learn even more from the Laffites in time.

Meanwhile, Long tried to consolidate his new government in Nacogdoches. He sent parties out to establish strong points on the Red River and the Trinity, and established trading houses near Anahuac on the Trinity and the Brazos Rivers. In Nacogdoches he helped start the first English-language newspaper in the province, the *Texas Republican*, which first appeared in August, destined for a life span of just one month.[33] In its first issues the *Republican* spoke of a future beyond Texan independence, meaning possible annexation by the United States, and in an editorial declared that inhabitants of the province north of the

Rio Grande "have long hoped that they would one day be governed by its [the United States'] laws."[34] By what authority the editor spoke for the *tejano* inhabitants he did not say, perhaps not realizing that he was really giving voice to the aspirations of Americans who wanted Texas for their own. Had not men in Louisiana and elsewhere long expected that Texians—whether the Hispanic natives or a rump junta of fili-busters—would rise up and achieve their independence with the proba-ble aid of the nation on their eastern border, and then apply for statehood? That done, would-be patriots must soon start immigrating to Texas with their guns and their dreams to make such predictions a real-ity. The abandonment of American claims to the province reflected in the Adams–Onís Treaty had "unkindly" scotched those dreams and vir-tually forced Texian settlers to take action in order one day to become Americans in title as well as heritage.[35] "At no remote period it may become a question of expediency with them to propose to be admitted into the union, unkindly as we have deserted them," complained a Ken-tucky editor.[36]

Such ideas were enthusiastically seconded in New Orleans and else-where, where the press emphasized that Long and his adventurers were not just plunderers bent on grabbing free land, but principled men mak-ing a stand for free democratic government. How invading a province to which their own nation had abandoned any claim, and whose own native population had not invited them to come as liberators, qualified Long's expedition as a blow for democracy, none bothered to explain. It was America on the march, and that was all that mattered to most. Only men of the highest character served in Long's ranks, argued one editor, and all "friends of liberty" felt encouraged to see "so many fine-looking young men" in the service of Long, Texas, and liberty.[37]

That was not the face of things as seen by people closer to the scene, however. In Natchitoches, Louisiana, the closest overland point of con-tact in the United States with Nacogdoches, disturbing reports came in from the west. "As to the Spanish expedition [sic] it has Past its zenath [sic] and many of the officers Deserting the cause which I Beleeve [sic] was at Best a Bad one and conducted By Bad men," a man in Natchi-toches complained that September. Moreover, "reports say some things of the officers at the Head of affairs that is not prudent to put on Paper as there is things of a femanine [sic] nature involved in it."[38] Just what he meant by that last item he did not say, but it suggests that whatever discipline Long had managed to instill in his men was breaking down rapidly. Meanwhile, disenchanted members of the expedition began casually to "muster" themselves out as they saw nothing but ruin on the horizon. Bowie left and went home to Louisiana, though with a taste for Texas still in his mouth. Gaines disassociated himself from the enterprise and returned to operating his ferry, and others simply melted eastward from time to time.[39]

Laffite's equivocal reply, and worse his failure immediately to send provisions, meant that Long had to disperse his men to forage. Meanwhile, Long tried again with Laffite, sending another embassy to Galveston in August. This one, too, gained only platitudes and promises from the privateer establishment, but then at the end of September Jean Laffite finally received his brother Pierre's advice from New Orleans, or so he said, and he sent two emissaries of his own—New Orleans lawyers, interestingly enough—to draft an agreement between Long and the Laffites for the government of Galveston.[40] On October 9 the negotiations concluded, and the Supreme Council decreed Galveston to be a port of entry for the new republic of Texas and commissioned Jean Laffite its governor. Long could not know that just two days earlier Pierre sent a report on Galveston affairs to the Spanish governor in Cuba, even as a Spanish expedition with five hundred men—possibly generated by information from Jean Laffite—was on its way to drive Long out of Texas.[41]

He learned soon enough. Leaving with a party of thirteen men to go to Galveston himself to confer with Laffite and oversee establishment of his authority, Long got only a short distance on his way before he learned of the approach of Spanish forces, who had already captured ten men in one of his outposts on the Brazos. Long returned to Nacogdoches at once. Then on October 26, learning that the Spanish command was not more than two days away from Nacogdoches itself, Long abandoned the post and withdrew his remaining men to the Sabine. The Spaniards managed to catch about thirty of the filibusters, but Long and the rest eluded them, and the general and president himself fled to Natchitoches. Ironically, even as the flotsam of the expedition was washing up on the streets of New Orleans, a delayed letter from Galveston appeared in the press praising the new Long regime. "The inhabitants have all submitted to the constituted authorities of the republic and taken the oath of allegiance," it said. Law was imposed over the privateers, tariff duties established and imposed, and the admiralty court functioning efficiently.[42]

Some of Long's men, cut off from the retreat, made their way to Galveston. Pierre Laffite, then in New Orleans, apparently was informed of their arrival by his brother and wasted little time in reporting their presence to the Spaniards. "It would be well to dispose of these gentlemen in one way or another," he advised. Erroneously, he believed Long himself to be among them, and suspected that far from being hapless refugees, they came to Galveston with the intent of taking it from his brother's now much weakened commune. What damage the 1818 hurricane had not done, discontent and desertion had, and the Laffites were now down to only two or three ships and perhaps no more than one hundred men. Moroever, repeated visits from United States naval ships made it clear that Washington wanted them out of Galveston. Thus, feeling doubly threatened from within and without, Pierre did not scruple at exaggerating the threat posed by Long's men. "I foresee the most woeful consequences if they take possession," he said, "since it is evident that they are the instruments of a Government [the United States] that seeks means of territorial expansion and that is setting them at work as pioneers." He recommended sending one hundred men on a vessel he would provide out of New Orleans, and which he would get by stealth into Galveston Bay, there to subdue Long's men and raise the flag of Spain.[43]

There would be no such expedition, nor any real need of it, the Spanish authorities perhaps seeing through the Laffites' attempt to finesse them into providing an occupying force and a legitimate flag for Galveston to discourage American attempts to force out the privateers. In fact, the Laffite Galveston enterprise was in its last days, and with it their involvements in Texan scheming. They traded a little with Long's refugees, who settled on Bolivar Point at the tip of a spit of land just across the entrance to the bay from Galveston Island, but the fact that the Laffites exchanged ammunition for deer and other game suggests that they were running low on food themselves. When Long arrived on April 6, 1820, in company with Hall, Trespalacios, Milam, Gutiérrez, and more of the old filibustering fraternity, the privateer empire was completely collapsed. Under threat of naval action from Washington to drive him out, Jean Laffite had burned his community's buildings, including his own house, and was living aboard a brig anchored in the bay, his empire reduced to just two ships and their crews. He had torn down his fortifications and was only awaiting a favorable sea to set out for some new horizon to seek his fortune, while some of his followers left for New Orleans, others took off on their own, and a few remained as coasters and scavengers on the island. Long could expect no help from the onetime "governor" of Galveston. Ahead of the Laffites lay dissolution and mutiny in their own command, and vague ends shrouded in myth and rumor, including for Pierre a likely death from fever in Yucatán, and for Jean a probable death in action as a Colombian privateer in 1823.[44]

With some difficulty Long raised the money to equip another expedition and enlist more men, but when some fifty recruits tried to leave Louisiana to join him, United States authorities arrested them. Meanwhile, forced to wait until his command grew large enough to set out on the road to conquest, Long installed another man in his former office of president, though the new incumbent would never leave New Orleans to claim his position, and once more declared Galveston a port of entry for his renewed, and reduced, Republic of Texas. Indeed, it seemed apparent to many now that this effort was destined to be even less effectual than the one the year before. Long discovered that a nephew of Trespalacios sought to foment a rebellion within the expedition, and had him tried and shot, which naturally led to a falling-out with Trespalacios, who nevertheless remained a part of the overall plan.[45] The men became disgruntled when they had to wait for supplies and found that they were being given their pay in worthless scrip rather than hard coin. One by one they began to desert until by December 1820 Long had scarcely more than fifty men with him on Bolivar Point, not much of an army with which to take on Spain even in its crippled condition in the New World. By July 1821 the garrison had but two weeks' supplies, and Long was in New Orleans frantically trying to resupply it with men and food.

By September, Long could count on only fifty-two men, but with his dreams they were enough. While Milam and Trespalacios sailed for Vera Cruz to try to make contact with the revolutionaries, Long set sail to make a landing in Matagorda Bay, then moved up the Guadalupe River and disembarked to march on La Bahía, hoping to ally himself with the local revolutionaries and thus perhaps gain legitimacy for his Texas republic from any new government. In fact, Long's party all but walked into the small community unopposed, shouting a battle cry "Republicanos!" only to find that no one was on guard. Four days later a force appeared in his front and launched an attack. The fighting continued in a desultory fashion until a parley revealed that the attackers—flying the

Spanish flag—were themselves revolutionaries who mistook Long's men for royalists loyal to Spain. They flew royalist colors, they explained, in case they encountered other Spanish commands believed to be in the area. Odds are, they felt uncertain just which side of the political quicksand offered better footing in the current chaotic state of affairs, and thus were prepared to jump either way. Once the confusion was explained, Long welcomed the attackers into town and laid down his arms, only to discover that he had been duped as they now proclaimed themselves to be, in fact, a royalist party sent out from San Antonio to take him.[46]

Much had happened in recent months, but communications between Mexico and Bolivar Point were imperfect. Chile, Argentina, Venezuela, and the new Colombia were all independent or virtually so, and though there would still be Spanish victories in the ensuing years, Spain was within a decade of being forced out of South America and Central America altogether. With Spanish control broken down and revolutionaries in control of most of Mexico by that summer, the local Spanish governor had no choice but to sign a treaty on August 24 granting at last the independence of Mexico. But to whom? Revolution in Mexico had always been as much one between classes as ideologies, and the *creoles* who were now to take power from the old *peninsulares* were no more interested in republican forms of government, a situation guaranteeing continuing unrest even in their own house.

There were still numerous royalist military enclaves scattered about the vast country, and it would be some months before all of them either shifted sides or surrendered, and not until May 1822 would a new regime take an unsteady—and brief—seat of power in Mexico City. Thus, in a fitting climax to the seriocomic story of the past fifteen years of filibustering attempts to take Texas, Long had burst into La Bahía and succeeded in taking only a small piece of Texas from men he mistook to be his own allies, only to be duped by men who did not themselves know where their allegiance lay. He and his men were sent under guard to San Antonio, then to Laredo, where they were treated with unexpected consideration before being sent on to Monterey. Long and the commander of his captors actually became rather friendly, the Spaniard quipping that Long was a natural-born revolutionary, and that "if he went to heaven and found no republicans there, he would revolutionize it."[47]

Eventually the balance of Long's followers were allowed to return to the United States, while Long himself, still under arrest, reached Mexico City just as the new republican government was being organized. He was soon imprisoned with Milam, Trespalacios, and others from the Vera Cruz venture. Most, among them Milam, would eventually return to the United States after they convinced the new regime that their intentions had been friendly to the republican cause. Trespalacios actually secured appointment as governor of Texas in a few months under the new regime. Long himself remained in prison for six months, and had just been released when a soldier shot him fatally, perhaps by accident, though Milam and others believed it was done at the connivance of Trespalacios in revenge for Long's execution of his nephew, as well as to remove one whom he still considered a rival for rule in Texas. Milam and others plotted the death of Trespalacios but failed, and finally the intercession of the United States secured their release and return.[48]

WITHIN DAYS OF Long's death there arrived in Mexico City the man who would accomplish by persuasion and diplomacy almost all that the filibusters had failed to achieve in their designs for an independent Texas. A failed young businessman fresh from living in bachelor quarters provided by his New Orleans employer, he was no conqueror and an unlikely father of anything, let alone a new state or nation. Yet the story of Texas was about to enter a dramatic, and decisive, new phase that he more than any other would dominate. Without the cautious, sometimes reluctant, yet ultimately incisive guidance of Stephen F. Austin, an independent Texas might have remained only a dream.[49]

CHAPTER THREE

"The Labyrinth of Trouble and Vexation"

⟋⟋⟋⟋⟋⟋

AFATHER-AND-SON pair living in the Louisiana Territory had been watching the steady challenge to Spanish authority in Texas for some years before Mexico finally achieved its independence. At least as far back as 1818 Stephen F. Austin, an attorney practicing without much success in the Missouri territory, looked with keen interest on Mexican affairs as the revolution dragged toward its climax. "The same spirit that unsheathed the sword of Washington and sacrificed servitude and slavery in the flames of the Revolution, will also flash across the Gulph of Mexico and over the western wilderness that separates America from the enslaved colonies of Spain," he declared on July 4. "Despotism totters, liberty expands her pinions, and in a few years more will rescue Spanish America from the dominion of tyranny."[1]

Less than a year later, however, his father, Moses Austin, a typical frontier entrepreneur, looked at the successful conclusion of the Adams–Onís Treaty and its virtual abandonment of any American claim to Texas, and in it he saw an opportunity that he must have had on his mind for some time before. The filibustering expeditions had all failed, in part from their own internal weakness, but also because of their belligerent nature. Of course, Spain would oppose anyone marching into the province and simply trying to take it. But would the Spaniards be more amenable to the establishment of a commercial and agricultural colony? The benefits were many. It would develop a land thus far mostly left wild. The colony would provide a market for Spanish goods and produce some tax revenue, and thus far indigenous Mexicans had shown little inclination to develop the economic potential of the place. It could serve as an overland conduit for trade between Mexico and the United States, and by its nature it would be a buffer between the two powers. If Texas were settled under permission by American colonists loyal to Spain, then future filibusters from the United States would have to think twice before invading a land now populated and settled by their brethren. At the same time some American colonies would act as a defensive barrier against the depredations of the Comanche and other tribes, protecting the Mexican interior.

The problem, however, had been the uncertain status of Texas. Was it Spain's or America's? If an entrepreneur like Moses Austin got permission from Spanish authorities to move in and begin a colony, but then the boundary line of the Louisiana Purchase were settled to the south, giving Texas to the United States, his colonists' title to their lands could be moot. But when the 1819 treaty unequivocally yielded the claim of the United States to the province, that reservation almost evaporated. In 1819 Moses Austin first suggested to his son Stephen the idea of applying for a grant of land and permission to bring a body of colonists into eastern Texas. For some days they discussed the idea and were in accord, thus planting the dream of an Anglo Texas.[2]

Rather than take immediate action, father and son let the idea mature in their minds. Among other concerns, the Adams–Onís agreement had yet to be ratified. They pursued other interests, in particular Moses Austin's existing land development at Herculaneum, Missouri. It may have been his successful land dealings there that helped suggest to him the potential in Texas, while son Stephen worked on a land speculation of his own farther south along the Caddo and Ouachita Rivers in the Arkansas territory where he hoped to begin several towns.[3] Neither looked on these activities as necessarily a preparation for a future Texas venture, but it cannot be denied that their experience at land dealings naturally disposed them to consider similar opportunities where land might be even cheaper to acquire and develop. As throughout the story of the United States thus far, cheaper land meant land farther west and southwest, and from Missouri and Arkansas that meant Texas.[4]

Meanwhile, they looked on at the Champ d'Asile and Long expeditions, and in September 1819, thinking that Long was making great progress and had taken San Antonio, Moses Austin decided that he would himself pay a visit to Béxar. If Long or another filibuster successfully took Texas away from Spain, then the Austins would need to deal with the new ruling authority should they wish to investigate a land speculation in Texas. The next year, Moses went to the Arkansas territory, visited with his son, and then rode off for Texas in November. By December he had reached San Antonio and learned much of interest, especially that Long's first expedition had failed and the Adams–Onís Treaty had been ratified. He appeared before Governor Antonio Martínez and stated that he came to apply for permission to settle himself and his family and plant cotton and sugar. Having lived in the Louisiana Territory when it was under Spanish rule before being ceded to France then sold to the United States, he like other inhabitants of the time had to swear fealty to Spain, and he still had his Spanish passport showing that he was a loyal subject of the king.[5]

The governor was not convinced, especially since he knew what Austin perhaps did not, that Long had come back with another invading party. The fewer of these troublesome Anglos there were in Texas the better, and so he ordered Austin out of the colony. But three days later he relented when others vouched for Austin, and on December 26 Martínez recommended approval of the entrepreneur's application for a permit to bring three hundred American families—all Catholics, of course—to settle a colony near the mouth of the Colorado River at Matagorda Bay.[6] Austin had great dreams, as befit a chronic entrepreneur. "One year would make a Change in the State and condition of Saint Antonio beyond any thing, you can now believe," he told a friend in January 1821. "I have a full confidence that a Town at the Mouth of Colorado in three years would become of the utmost Consequence." Moreover, men with shares in the enterprise would make thousands of dollars, while the people who came to settle the new colony would be "of the first class," and the property that they brought with them as settlers would be their security of "fidelity to the King and Constitution of Spain."[7]

Unfortunately, Austin lost the next several months in settling chaotic financial affairs in Missouri, but good news came with the notification that his colonization application was approved. Then he persuaded his son Stephen to join him in the venture. The younger Austin was reluctant, as indeed he would demonstrate a conservative and cautious disposition for the rest of his life with Texas. His own Arkansas venture had collapsed in debt and ruin, and he had moved to New Orleans to practice law. He resented his father's habit of involving him in schemes that frequently came to naught. Indeed, for some months Stephen had no idea of what his father had been doing in Texas or how his efforts succeeded. "I know nothing as to my father's objects or prospects," he told his mother in January 1821.[8]

But Moses could be persuasive. By March he boasted that he already had commitments from the full three hundred families allowed under his contract, each one to pay him about $60 for its share of the land to be granted to him by Spain.[9] He would not take them all to Texas at once, but only a few to start, as he needed to perform a survey on the land grant in order to lay out the tracts for each colonist family in advance. When Stephen proved stubbornly opposed to taking part, his father exercised every device he could. "Discharge your Doubts, as to the Enterprise," the father urged. "Times are changing a new chance presents itself [and] nothing is now wanted but Concert and firmness."[10] It was the last communication young Austin ever got from his father. That summer Moses became seriously ill, probably from pneumonia. Perhaps knowing that he was dying, he imposed one last deathbed obligation on his son that Stephen could hardly ignore. Through his wife he sent a message imploring his son to take his place and "go on with his enerprise in the province texes." So many felt enthusiastic and anxious to be a part of it, but only Stephen Austin could make it a reality now. A week later Moses Austin died, leaving his son a legacy that was the last thing on earth he wanted.[11]

In fact, it would have cheered the dying man to know that by this time his arguments had already worn down his son's resistance, for before he learned of his father's condition and dying wish, Stephen had already left New Orleans with a few companions and gone to Natchitoches to meet with Erasmo Seguín of San Antonio, who would take him to inspect the grant on the Colorado on behalf of his father. Before he left Louisiana, however, Austin sent a circular letter to newspapers announcing the new colony and soliciting applicants. To counter longstanding prejudice against the bloodthirsty Spaniards, he also added that Spain had returned to its 1812 constitution with more generous personal, civil, and economic freedoms, "and recent accounts state that the beneficial effects of it are already perceptible." In short, no Americans need feel apprehensive about their freedom of life, liberty, and pursuit of wealth under the Dons.[12] In return Spain required all colonists to observe the Catholic faith, take an oath of allegiance to king and constitution, and be *"honest, industrious* farmers and mechanics," not filibusters with dreams of empire.[13]

Austin set out from Natchitoches in July, stopping first in Nacogdoches, Texas, where he discovered that many of its few remaining American families wanted to join his new colony close to the sea and its trading opportunities. Finally, in early August he reached the Colorado, and then on August 12 arrived in San Antonio, being greeted by the surprising news that Mexico had just achieved its independence from Spain. Governor Martínez himself quickly made the transition from royal to republican loyalty and met Austin warmly. Now the young *empresario,* as he and those who came after him would be called, made plans for distribution of land to the three hundred. Each family should have three hundred twenty acres of riverfront land and double that amount of grazing land in the interior. Additionally, there would be more acreage allotted for each head of family, his wife, and for each child, as well as fifty acres per slave. That done, Austin rode southeast to La Bahía on the San Antonio River, soon to be renamed Goliad. Finally, in September he reached the Colorado again and began the exploration of the land grant, spending several days at it before making his way back to Nacogdoches, and thence to Natchitoches early in October. Behind him he had laid out the boundaries of his new colony, a vast tract stretching from the Lavaca River at a point some miles above where it emptied into Matagorda Bay, thence some one hundred miles northeast to a point inland from the southern tip of Galveston Island, then northwest between the Brazos and San Jacinto Rivers another one hundred thirty miles to the El Camino Real connecting San Antonio with Nacogdoches. From there the line ran southwest along the highway one hundred twenty miles to the Colorado, and then southeast again to the Lavaca.[14]

It was enormous, more than fifteen thousand square miles, some twenty-four hundred square leagues in the old Spanish measure, and yet it was only a small part of the vastness of Texas. Significantly, settlement along the Gulf Coast itself was prohibited, though he could hope for that to change. Austin found a line of people waiting to settle in this new empire. Fifty families were in Natchitoches ready to go, and the advertisements in the press spurred interest among hundreds of others. Austin started issuing contracts to settlers as early as October 6, not forgetting that he was personally to receive $12.50 for every hundred acres to cover his expenses in surveying.[15] His enthusiasm seemed boundless. "I am convinced that I could take on fifteen hundred families as easily as three hundred if permitted to do so," he boasted to Governor Martínez. Indeed, seeing the response, he suggested that he superintend emigration from the United States beyond the boundaries of his grant, throughout the arable part of Texas, from the forests between the Trinity and San Jacinto Rivers on the northeast, to the San Marcos and Guadalupe Rivers on the southeast, almost on the doorstep of Béxar. Pleading the efficiency of such a plan, and arguing that his own familiarity with the country, his previous experience at land development, as well as surveying and the law, made Austin an ideal candidate, he asked that his grant be so extended. Martínez agreed to expand it on the northeast, but left the southwest border on the Lavaca, which already put the Anglos close enough to the provincial capital.[16]

In the fall of 1821, as Austin was settling his first colonists in Texas, Dr. John Sibley at Natchitoches agreed with the *empresario*'s optimistic predictions when he looked on and suggested that the settlement tide could hardly be stopped at three hundred families. Sibley foretold that within eighteen months there could be as many as fifty thousand Americans migrating west of the Sabine if the Mexican government allowed. "The Country is Larger than all France & finer Climate & the soil as rich as any & can support a great population," he declared. "The Climate will grow Sugar, oranges, Pine-apples, coffee figs & grapes & the existing Spanish govt. [is] very desirous of getting as many Americans as possible settled there." Sibley may have overestimated Spanish intentions, but he clearly saw at this early date that American intentions were for a much greater settlement than Austin's incipient colony. Even as Sibley wrote, he saw wagons from Missouri and other places passing through Natchitoches on their way to Texas with or without Spanish permission.[17]

By the summer of 1824 at least 272 of the allotted 300 titles were issued. The colonists settled along the bottom lands of the Brazos, San Jacinto, Colorado, and San Bernard Rivers, while Austin located the administrative center of the colony in the new village of San Felipe de Austin, about ninety miles inland on the Brazos. The names of the colonists told the story of their origins—Bell, Borden, Harrison, McCormick, McNair, McNeel, Muligan, Nelson, Phillips, Williams. With a few exceptions they came almost entirely of Anglo-Celtic backgrounds, had been born in the United States, and found their way to Texas via the well-established migration route through the Appalachians in the Virginia gaps, and then onward across Tennessee, Alabama, Mississippi, and Louisiana.

They were largely the grandchildren of men who fought in the American Revolution and came steeped in that tradition. The intervening generations imbued in them a strong doctrine of self-help, and had taught them self-reliance and resentment of arbitrary authority. Their own previous frontier experience instilled in them a hunger for land, a disdain for brown-skinned native peoples, a contempt for Spanish culture (thanks to the excesses of Spain in the New World), and a willingness to act quickly in their own interest without due regard for statute and protocol. Austin would find such men difficult to control in the years ahead, in spite of precautions he took that he thought would have obviated such problems. He chose colonists from among a large pool of applicants, and only those who met his standard for industry—the "better classes" he called them—were given grants. As a result, the "Old Three Hundred," as these first settlers would be called, were perhaps unique in frontier annals. They were far better off financially than most settlers anywhere else, bringing some substance with them from the east. Nearly one fourth of them owned slaves, one man, Jared Groce, holding ninety by himself. All but four of the colonist men could read and write, an unheard-of literacy on the frontier.[18]

While these first settlers would become, by prior arrival, a sort of aristocracy among future Texians, they were not unrepresentative of those who followed. Property and personal liberty were virtually inseparable twin ideals to them, and any threat to either was to be met and resisted forcefully. They resented absentee rulers trying to direct their affairs, and thanks to their literacy, they absorbed and spread the knowledge and news always essential to uniting people to a common purpose. Being overwhelmingly Protestant, they felt especially uneasy about being ruled by Catholic overlords and required to observe the faith of Rome, though they still acquiesced in that stipulation or else simply ignored it, while Mexico never seriously tried to enforce the religious requirement. Coming as they did from an assertively republican culture in the United States that even then made almost a religion out of the cult of the "common man," these immigrants were hardly likely to tug their forelocks meekly in a province ruled chiefly by military authority. Contrary to Austin's hopes, influences such as these would not be conducive to producing a passive or harmonious colonial body politic.

Moreover, the Texas they were about to inhabit was itself far from stable. The past decade of unrest, and especially the minor bloodbath in the wake of the Gutiérrez-Magee expedition and the Battle of Medina, had severely disrupted the province. In 1800 there had been nearly four thousand inhabitants excluding the Indians. When Austin started his colony the only towns were San Antonio and Goliad. Nacogdoches was all but abandoned, and overall the white and mixed-blood population had sunk to about twenty-five hundred, many of them *tejanos* resentful of the treatment meted out by the Spanish authorities to several hundred of their compatriots who had joined the revolution, and equally unhappy that Spanish authorities did not protect their outlying *ranchos* from Indian depredations. That decline in population, the scarcity of settlement outside the towns, and the need for a buffer against the Indians were among the most compelling reasons for allowing the Anglos to come there to settle. The success of Austin's enterprise could ensure the revitalization of a ravaged and stagnated Texas. Ironically, however, it could also pose the greatest danger yet to Mexico's hold on the province.[19]

For the first two years Austin's colony grew steadily and showed every sign of prosperity. It also remained quiet and orderly, not surprisingly given the constant distraction of building homes, planting crops, fencing pasture, and the like. Mexico itself, however, was anything but quiet. The treaty granting independence was followed by a plan agreed upon among the revolutionaries to install a new constitutional monarch, and the throne went to revolutionary leader Agustín de Iturbide, proclaimed Agustín I in May 1822. Unfortunately he proved to be as autocratic and insensitive to the *creoles* and other orders of society as his Iberian predecessors, and within months a new revolt rose against his regime. Part of his problem was that in proclaiming a new independent Mexican empire, he encouraged the idea of a degree of autonomy in the far-flung provinces, but he proved unable to extend enough central government control to them to reinforce that they were still a part of a larger entity, Texas least of all. That forced the local authorities in such provinces to act largely on their own, and it sent to the inhabitants, both Anglo and *tejano*, the message that they must look out for themselves. In Texas, as elsewhere, local authorities—the *ayuntamientos*, or town councils—that ran the few communities, and the mayors, or *alcaldes*, were forced to fill the civil vacuum. Indeed, what brought down Iturbide's brief empire was the very idea of provincial autonomy that had been one of the sparks of the revolt against central absolutism in the first place.[20] When Iturbide dissolved the Constituent Congress in October 1822, it signaled his abandonment of the idea of genuine representation, of the provinces having a voice in their own affairs and those of the nation. That Texas had only one delegate out of the 242 in the Congress revealed that even in a system intending some degree of representation, the remote and less populated provinces would be, indeed, voices crying from the wilderness.

When the revolt against Iturbide forced him to abdicate in March 1823, it was led by, among others, a dynamic young officer whose commitment to the idea of a genuine federation of autonomous provinces no one had any reason to question—Antonio López de Santa Anna. What followed was a period of chaos in which the several provinces, Texas included, really did rule themselves for some months in the absence of a central government with the mandate to govern. The Constituent Congress reconvened itself, but then delegates from some provinces demanded selection of a new congress. The provinces began organizing their own governments and rescinding their recognition of the existing congress. Calls went out for the creation of a federal republic. One province declared its own councils to be the supreme law within its borders and ceased any allegiance to Mexico City, and others declared that they would become sovereign states in their own right. Santa Anna declared for a federation and began to position himself as the only real military power. Finally, the all but impotent Congress voted in June 1823 for a federal republic.[21]

Texas and its neighboring province Coahuila across the Rio Grande were authorized to select provisional delegates to a new constitutional congress in September, and Texas elected the *tejano* Erasmo Seguín as its delegate. He went burdened with instructions to protect the autonomy of Texas as best he could, seeking for it statehood on a par with the other provinces to become states in the new federation. But he soon found that Texas was too poor, too unpopulated, and too outpoliticked in Mexico City. In the end, when a new constitution was being drafted in 1824 and the nation redefined, the best he could get was for Texas to be joined with Coahuila, with the promise that Texas could separate on its own when it achieved sufficient population. On May 7, 1824, the new state of Coahuila y Texas emerged, to little joy when the news reached north of the Rio Grande. Now Texas would have no governor of its own, as it had when a province, but would be required to answer to one seated in a capital at Saltillo, in Coahuila. Indeed, Texas was only to have one delegate in the state legislature in Saltillo, guaranteeing virtual nonrepresentation.

One of the first acts of that legislature was to dissolve the supposedly permanent Texan deputation to Mexico City and then demand the transfer of all archives to Coahuila, action that outraged the *tejanos*. Only months of conciliation and soothing finally quieted the outcry. The *tejanos* strongly resented the loss of their autonomy, and though their grievance was more with Coahuila than with Mexico City, still the dissatisfaction and sense of alienation ran deep, meaning that more than ever these descendants of the *creoles* and *mestizos* could provide good soil for a future revolt against their own Mexican brethren. It helped that before long, Texas did at least secure an agreement to be allowed to have a subordinate or lieutenant governor seated in Béxar, and they gained an extra two seats in the legislature in time, but they never forgot the lesson that only they were going to look out for their interests. Officials, even revolutionary leaders, in Mexico City or Saltillo were simply too far away, and within a few years the Béxar *ayuntamiento* would complain of them as "men who are ignorant of the political state of the Department of Tejas . . . who know neither her topographical situation nor her class of inhabitants." It was only a short step from that dissatisfaction to concluding that in either capital "the government cannot be convinced that the Department of Tejas is not just a new-born population which lacks the strength to govern itself."[22] There was an old *tejano* saying about their relations with Spanish kings and now Mexico City that took on added meaning: *"obedezco pero no cumplo"*—"I obey but do not comply."[23]

For the next several years the *tejanos* strove to gain some degree of local autonomy, and with the introduction of Austin's colonists they saw a mutual opportunity. Indeed, the two peoples, for all their outward differences, had at least some similarities. Texas had never seen the degree of *peninsulare* and *creole* population of the more central provinces. Its early inhabitants were mostly *creoles*, Spanish soldiers, half-breed *mestizos* or *castas*, and Tlascalan Indians, and over succeeding generations the latter three groups intermarried widely. As a result, the old caste definitions became less meaningful, and in their place arose a simpler, more elemental differentiation in local society that was very familiar to the *americanos* now coming into the province. *Tejanos* were either *ricos* or *pobres*, rich or poor. Certainly that was nothing new to Austin's immigrants, either those of property or those coming now because they failed to prosper in the East. The *ricos* held more of the old Spanish blood, while far the greater of the population of the mixed-breed peoples were among the *pobres*. The propertied men mainly raised cattle, while the poor did day labor or worked smallholdings of their own.

Tejano society revolved around the church, the community, and the home, just as it did for the Anglos. Nominally Catholic, the *tejanos* had been all but abandoned by the mother church in Mexico years before. As a result, they observed all the religious holidays and seemed obsessed with prayers, but looked on both as ritual obligations requiring little deeper faith or feeling. It was again a case of *obedezco pero no cumplo*, which mirrored almost exactly the attitude of the Anglos now arriving. Though they all took the oath promising to observe only the Catholic faith, almost from the first, Mexican authorities complained that no masses were being held. While a few Americans were already Catholic, or felt no compunction about conversion, most adopted a posture of passive disobedience, not openly flouting their Baptist or Methodist beliefs, but not outwardly observing the rites of Rome either. Before long, when itinerant Protestant ministers did come into Texas to preach to the colonists, Mexican authorities objected but did not exert themselves to enforce the law.[24] When it came to work, especially with livestock, the Americans quickly acquired a high regard for the skill on horseback of the *vaqueros* and sought to learn from them.

This did not mean, however, that the Anglos were going to look on the *tejanos*, whether *ricos* or *pobres*, as their equals. Americans came to Texas in the 1820s with almost exactly two centuries of experience with darker-skinned peoples behind them, and the predominantly Southern emigrants arrived with an even more particularly refined attitude. The native Indians had been an obstacle to settlement and expansion, a constant hazard on the early frontier, the authors of massacres and kidnappings innumerable. Experience taught that they were to be pushed aside when necessary, not to be trusted, and would inevitably become a nuisance to white society. Within a few years the United States would actually commence a policy of Indian removal to lands west of the Mississippi, a clear indication that peaceful coexistence and competition for the bounty of the land were not ideals with which whites felt comfortable. Even darker than the natives were the Negro slaves introduced early in the 1600s and by now a fixture of Southern society and economy. The Americans regarded them as being even lower on the social scale than Indians. Given such a background, it was inevitable that racial attitudes were going to get in the way of relations between Americans and *tejanos*. "There are few among them who should be called white," a Quaker abolitionist wrote after visiting Texas. Others thought them almost on a par with their blacks, "a mongrel breed of negroes, Indians, and Spaniards of the baser sort."[25] It was an attitude that might keep them from assimilating entirely with their new *tejano* neighbors, but much more significantly, it also gave hints of just how these whites from the East were going to feel about being ruled over the long term by Mexico, or by anyone not as white as themselves.

Meanwhile, the *tejanos* and the Anglos had some common interests, especially economically. The best and most accessible market for their cattle lay to the east in Louisiana, not to the south in Mexico, and that required good relations with the Anglos, some of whom would become themselves intermediaries and wholesalers. Until now their crops had been mainly subsistence, but as the Americans began to introduce cotton into the fertile bottom lands along the rivers, the *tejanos*, too, saw prosperity in growing a cash crop. Above all, regardless of the commodity, there was so much opportunity in trading with the United States, and so little in dealing with the rest of Mexico, that *tejanos* were naturally obliged to see their future more profitably tied with the former than the latter. If policies coming out of Mexico City, like trade restrictions or export duties, threatened to retard that prosperity, then again the attitude was going to be *obedezco pero no cumplo*, and another seed of revolution planted.

Thus, the *tejanos* actively pursued local provincial control over the massive unsettled public lands outside their own holdings and the Austin grant. The new Constitution of 1824 delegated that control to the states, but it was not enough for Texas's public lands to be under the thumb of politicians in Coahuila. Instead, the *tejanos* pushed for, and largely got, local control of public lands in 1825. They would also in time succeed in taking colonization decisions out of Mexico City and moving them northward to Saltillo, allowing them to do even more to encourage American immigration. To lure Anglo cotton planters from east of the Mississippi, they pushed through their legislature statutes affording protection from outside creditors, thus making colonists' lands secure from seizure to settle old debts. They managed to pass a ten-year exemption on payment of land taxes in order to encourage more settlers, and even instituted a form of squatters' rights in allowing the occupation of land not yet surveyed or divided into tracts.

Working with Austin and his followers, the *tejano* officials in the *ayuntamientos* would wisely give appointments as land agents to Americans rather than keeping such offices for their own, knowing that the Anglos would have much more success in persuading more of their people to cross the Sabine. In perhaps the easiest of all their concessions, *tejano* leaders let it be known that they had no intent or desire to enforce the rule on Catholicism. In an extra effort to accommodate their new neighbors, the *tejano* faction even managed to get a temporary exclusion for Texas from an 1829 presidential decree from Mexico City that abolished slavery. Then, going that one better, their faction in the Saltillo legislature succeeded in rewording existing statutes covering colonists by cleverly redefining slavery as indentured servitude or lifetime "contract" employment, implying that somehow the slaves were actually paid laborers.[26] There could hardly have been more the *tejanos* could have done both to encourage expanding American settlement, or to indicate that whatever their ethnic differences, their fortunes were inextricably intertwined.

During the period of upheaval following independence, Austin had had to make a trip to Mexico City to affirm his right to the grant and his authority to settle colonists. It had been a frustrating time, as Iturbide repeatedly dissolved congress or arrested some of its members, all of it delaying the bills that would secure the Texas enterprise. Even when the legislation finally was working its way through to passage, Austin still encountered difficulty over the slavery issue. The Mexicans wanted it abolished and all existing slaves freed within ten years, while Austin argued to retain lifetime slavery and allow emancipation only for children of slaves once they reached majority. His conclusion after months of working with the Mexican leadership was the rather condescending assertion that "these people will not do for a Republic."²⁷ The "contract employee" might have begged to differ. Still, in spite of revolution and counterrevolution, the rise of Santa Anna and the fall of Iturbide, when Austin left to return to Texas in April 1823 he had confirmation of his grant.

The first years of the colony did much to foster the sense of self-reliance that colonists brought with them and which their *tejano* neighbors encouraged. The Comanche and Karankawa, Tawakonis, Wacos, Tonkawas, and others all posed a hazard, not so much to the survival of the colony as a whole but to the more isolated settlers' homes and livestock. Since Mexican *soldados* were few and confined mainly to the *presidios* at Béxar and Goliad, Austin organized his colonists into a militia for self-protection, thus transplanting a frontier tradition from the United States and at the same time inaugurating a new ethic in Anglo Texas. Very quickly colonists became accustomed to expecting little aid from Mexico City or Saltillo, and to looking out for themselves instead. The same approach applied to government within the colony. Mexico City would expect its own forms and institutions to be observed, but at the same time the colonists came with their own traditions. Once more the practical solution was *obedezco pero no cumplo*. The colonists would acknowledge the authority of the *alcaldes* and *ayuntamientos*, and Austin would introduce them into the new districts created within his grant, but then he wrote his own civil and legal code for the ruling bodies to follow. Whereas Mexican law did not provide for trial by jury in civil suits, Austin did. While an *alcalde* still presided over criminal trials in the courtroom, as in the rest of Mexico, here the equivalent of grand juries were to do the investigation prior to indictment. And Austin added a section to his code uniquely American in its motivation and interest, one covering slaves and their punishment, borrowing provisions wholesale from the slave codes in place in the slave states of the United States.²⁸

Oddly enough, though perhaps not unsurprisingly, Austin found that his own settlers would be the source of almost constant confrontation and discontent. Despite Austin's caveats that they would have to act as loyal subjects of Mexico, most of the colonists could not leave behind them the independent nature fostered in the land of their birth. Austin himself exercised decidedly undemocratic authority. In June 1824 unrest came to the fore over the fees to be paid to Austin. His original grant anticipated that each colonist family would be able to claim up to two square miles of land. However, when the confirmation and colonization legislation finally passed the Congress in 1823, maximum grants were expanded to a square league, more than three times as much acreage, meaning that the 12.5-cents-per-acre surveying fee that was part of Austin's contract with every colonist now escalated cost to the settler from $160 to $554.[29]

Even though the expansion of the grant size was not of Austin's doing, to some settlers—forgetting the incredible bargain they were paying to buy estates unheard of east of the Mississippi—it looked as if he was trying to become wealthy at their expense. Some accused Austin of "deceving and swinling the people," and some of his ardent supporters felt nothing but outrage. "Befor I would be imposed on by the ungratefull inhabitants of the Coloney I would at once Dam the Hole," complained one friend in June 1824. "I would not permit the Interisted and ambicious Blood Suckers [to] live from the benifits of my exertions and labor."[30] The outcry became sufficiently vocal that José Antonio Saucedo, the Mexican political chief in Texas, had to support Austin by calling on the colonists to cease their agitation and obey their *empresario*. But having given with the one hand, Saucedo then took away with the other, silencing the cry himself by arbitrarily throwing out Austin's 12.5-cents-per-acre charge and reducing the surveying charge for a league to $192, of which not a cent was to go to Austin himself. No wonder the *empresario* complained to the colonists soon afterward that he found himself "in the Labyrinth of trouble and Vexation" thanks to them.[31]

The wedge driven between Austin and the colonists grew wider when some perceived that he gave larger tracts to friends and cronies if they imported more slaves or agreed to set up machinery such as mills and cotton gins to encourage commerce as a whole. Single men complained that married men got more land, thanks to the entitlement for their wives and children. Poorer men felt cheated that slave owners got extra acreage for their chattels. Discontented settlers could find anything to complain about, and the fault all lay with Austin or his Mexican masters. A friend warned him late in 1824 to give it all up and leave. "You certainly Can by this Time form an Opinion of a Majority of your people now," advised James Gaines. All he could expect from them were "Curses and Abuses, this you may Rely on, as they accuse you of Every thing bad and threaten Continually Revenge."[32]

Eventually one malcontent went too far. Aylett C. Buckner issued a call for a secret public meeting of colonists to investigate Austin's authority and then "shake off the Yoke and disperse that dark cloud that has so long kept the settlers in darkness." So far as Austin was concerned, such language could have but one meaning, that being to shake off the "yoke of Government." Austin arrested Buckner and charged him with sedition, then scolded his colonists publicly for the "spirit of discontent and contention [that] has manifested itself in a few individuals of this colony since its first commencement." Were they ready for revolution? he asked. "Are you prepared to join any man in an open rebellion against the government under which you have voluntarily sought a settlement?" What message would it send to Mexico City if, upon the threshold of their career in Texas, they were "to impress upon the Government the idea, that, the Americans are disposed at the very moment of their entrance into the country . . . to *array themselves* in opposition to the authorities placed over them?"[33]

Always a conservative man reluctant to take action, Austin had vividly thrust before him the fact that many of these new Texians were determined to be turbulent and were unwilling to accept any government but their own, regardless of any expedient pledges they may have made to get their grants. In September 1825 Austin aptly characterized the nature of his difficult subjects. "It is innate in an American to suspect and abuse a public officer whether he deserves it or not," he said, anticipating by more than a decade the same observation made by Alexis de Tocqueville. "I have had a mixed multitude to deal with collected from all quarters strangers to each other, to me, and to the laws and language of the country," he complained. They came ignorant of the laws and customs of Mexico, but expecting to find something much like what they left behind, and when they did not they became resentful and unruly. "Very many of them have all the licentiousness and wild turbulence of frontiersmen," he continued. "Among the ignorant part of the Americans indipendence means resistance and obstinacy right or wrong—this is particularly the case with frontiersmen—a violent course with such dispositions might have kindled a flame that would have destroyed them and the settlement entirely." Indeed, he had constantly to attempt to persuade Mexican officials that Americans were not by nature "a turbulent people, difficult to govern and predisposed to resist," especially when his own experience with his colonists suggested that he did not believe it himself.[34]

The proof of that lay in what happened next. His own crisis abated, thanks to Austin's conciliatory management, and he was soon able to obtain additional grants from the government to expand his colony, which grew to 1,357 white and 443 slave inhabitants by 1825. Indeed, anxious to spur further growth, and in spite of the objections of Austin, the government in Coahuila now started granting colonial franchises to other *empresarios* as it tried to speed settlement. Among the successful applicants was Haden Edwards, a Mississippian who came with his brother Benjamin and a plan to locate eight hundred families in the area of Nacogdoches. The terms of his grant, like all others, provided that he must recognize and honor all preexisting grants made under Mexican or Spanish administrations. There were many of these in the area around Nacogdoches encompassed by the Edwards grant, though quite a few families had moved away during the revolutionary disquiet of previous years. Edwards announced that all with claims would have to present documentation of proof to him now, however, or he would consider their claims null and their land his to sell. Some of course no longer had their documents, and a vigorous opposition to Edwards's high-handedness ensued, though the actual number of threatened claims was few.

When an election was held in December 1825 to select an *alcalde*, those angered by Edwards's imperious stance put forward Samuel Norris in opposition to Edwards's chosen nominee, his own son-in-law. Once the ballots were counted, the son-in-law legitimately had the majority, but when Edwards certified him the victor, the older settlers opposed to Edwards's authority appealed the decision to the political chief José Antonio Saucedo, charging that many of the victor's votes came from outside the colony and were therefore invalid. Saucedo found in favor of the protesters and threw out the election, declaring Norris the victor. For months thereafter the situation festered, as Edwards refused to acknowledge the decision. Finally in the summer of 1826, authorities in Mexico City wearied of his petulance, revoked his grant, and ordered his expulsion from the state. Even then he refused to leave, and finally in December, Saucedo sent *soldados* out of San Antonio to march to Nacogdoches to enforce the expulsion.

By then, however, open rebellion had broken out, and Saucedo intended to put it down. On November 22 some thirty-nine men rode into Nacogdoches, arrested Norris and some other officers, and then stepped even further over the line by arresting the commander of the tiny Mexican garrison. Under the leadership of Martin Parmer, a former Missouri politician regarded as sufficiently impetuous to earn the sobriquet "Ringtailed Panther," they convened a rump court and tried the arrested men on charges of corruption and found them guilty. All were sentenced to the loss of their offices, and Parmer appointed a new *alcalde* on his own, all of this probably with the connivance of the Edwards brothers themselves. Saucedo's *soldados* took the road in response, and even before they reached Nacogdoches, Austin wrote to Hayden Edwards in bald amazement. "It appears as tho. the people in your quarter have run mad or worse," he declared. "They are distroying themselves." If he wanted to save his life, Austin warned, he must immediately surrender himself and his companions "and acknowledge at once and without any reserve or stiff and foolish republican obstinacy that wrong steps were taken."[35]

But the Edwardses, Parmer, and their compatriots were not for contrition. On December 16 they returned to Nacogdoches and five days later drafted and signed a declaration of independence for a new republic they called Fredonia. Somehow they expected that all would flock to their banner. Emissaries went to the Cherokee Indians to the north to conclude an alliance, and another was sent to San Felipe to ally Austin's colony with them. Austin responded in anger. "You are deluding yourselves and this delusion will ruin you," he told them on December 24, making it abundantly clear that there was no hope that "this colony will unite in such mad schemes." Scheming men might suggest that, in the crisis, American blood and old loyalties would unite all the colonists, but he promised that the men of his colony "are unanimous in disapproving all such violent proceedings and they will all be faithful to the Govt. of their adoption and if necessary take up arms in its defense." Indeed, he predicted that the government could march two thousand soldiers to Nacogdoches in a couple of months, and that most of his own colonists would gladly join them in putting down the Fredonian rebellion. The alliance with the Cherokee was equally absurd. "Great God, can it be possible that Americans, high minded free born and honorable Americans will so far forget the country of their birth, so far forget themselves, as to league with barbarians and join a band of savages?" Again he implored them to disband and submit to lawful authority, or else leave the country and save their lives.[36]

Austin's final word on the Fredonians was to his own colonists on

January 1, 1827, when he issued an address announcing that "infatuated madmen at Nacogdoches have declared Independence." His predictions of where his settlers would stand proved correct, as overwhelmingly they supported his call to volunteer to assist the *soldados* in putting down the rebellion. It was, he said, a sign of respect to their Mexican authorities, and a mark of their own loyalty as subjects.[37] He sent ahead Peter Ellis Bean, a survivor of the last fight of Philip Nolan, to scout Nacogdoches, and began arrangements for volunteers, some of them *tejanos*, to march on their own against the rebels.[38] Meanwhile, the rebels were falling out among themselves, for there was no unanimity in the Edwards colony for this rash course. Armed groups of loyalists began to threaten the Edwards–Parmer party, and on January 4 unsuccessfully attacked them in a fortified stone building in Nacogdoches over which flew their Fredonian flag proclaiming "Independence, Liberty, Justice."

In the end, flight was their only option. With no support from Austin and no aid from their Cherokee allies, they sent to Louisiana hoping to enlist United States military aid, but American authorities were not about to foment an international incident over the petty squabble of a disgruntled entrepreneur. By the time Mexican soldiers reached Nacogdoches on January 31, 1827, both Edwardses, Parmer, and most of the others had already disbanded and fled for the Sabine and the safety of Louisiana. "There never was a more silly, wild, Quicksotic scheme than that of Nacogdoches," John Sibley wrote Austin from Natchitoches. There seemed to be universal gratification at its speedy and bloodless overthrow.[39]

Austin's handling of the episode, especially his anxiety to have his own colonists involved in putting down the uprising, revealed his keen perception of the diplomatic task that he faced in making Anglo settlers and Mexican rulers meld. He showed it again a few months later when an unruly colonist was arrested and tried by his peers without involving Mexican authorities. Not only did it demonstrate the good faith of the colonists that they would put down upstarts, but it also prevented such "firebrands," as he called them, from being transformed into martyrs. "Let the firebrands alone, and the good sense of the sound and reflecting part of the colony, will put them down much sooner and more effectually than opposition or irons, by the authorities," he advised, looking back on the incident. Let Mexican authorities take charge of trial and punishment, however, and the challenge to the Anglo spirit of independence and ethnic prejudice changed the equation completely, and a simple miscreant "would have become popular, altho he was a most perfect jack ass and a scoundrel."[40] It was an important insight, one that would be demonstrated all too vividly within a few years.

Mercifully for Austin, the Fredonian fiasco did not have the effect of stunting immigration to the colony as he had feared. Mexican authorities did not overreact, and people in the United States still felt keen interest. Indeed, throughout the period of the Fredonian imbroglio the press in Louisiana and farther eastward carried constant public letters and narratives advertised as "direct from Austin's settlement," and most were glowing, not failing to mention the abundant cheap land.[41] Indeed, Texas began to take on a special allure to those mired in debt, thanks to its denial of rights of seizure or collection by foreign creditors. "Whenever an individual becomes somewhat embarrassed he crosses the Sabine with all his property," complained one creditor in Louisiana, "& then remains in perfect security."[42] Before long there would be stories that account books in stores and court ledgers alike were entering beside the names of the bankrupt the simple phrase "gone to Texas."[43]

"A person may travel all day; and day after day, and find Americans only," Amos Parker would write of early Texas. "He can hardly make himself believe he is not still in the United States."[44] The colony also possessed a lure for men who had come to Texas years before as failed conquerors, among them men like Rezin Bowie, veteran of the Gutiérrez–Magee expedition, and his brother James, who left the first Long enterprise in 1819 in time not to be caught. Both would visit Texas again, James coming on an exploratory trip in the summer of 1827 in the wake of the Fredonian collapse. He visited San Felipe, which a disappointed later visitor from more effete Virginia thought to be "a wretched, decaying looking place," with "no appearance of industry, of thrift or improvement of any kind," and then went on to San Antonio.[45] There, like many another man coming to Texas, Bowie unwittingly commenced spinning yet another thread that would strongly—if not unbreakably—bind the new colonists to the Mexican and *tejano* inhabitants. He met the daughter of Juan Veramendi, destined to be lieutenant governor of Coahuila y Texas in future years. She was one of the *ricos*, of course, but so were some of the *tejanos* like Seguín. Intermarriage with a Mexican citizen brought a land bonus to the grants of immigrant men, not to mention a tie to an established family, though in setting his sights on Veramendi's daughter Ursula, Bowie aimed higher than any other potential colonist.[46]

Austin, too, was establishing important cross-ethnic relationships, and by late 1827 he and his supporters had succeeded in bringing together his American colonial interests with those of the *tejano* leadership like Seguín and Veramendi and other leaders in Béxar. Finding common cause now in the economic development and political autonomy of Texas would help to bind them in times of crisis ahead, when the stakes were even greater. Their successful alliance got through Saltillo a colonization law that liberalized entry for new settlers and at least forestalled the incipient movement to abolish slavery altogether. Saucedo was close to them, and his successor at the end of the year, Ramón Músquiz, felt the same.[47]

These political allies would need each more than ever before when 1828 saw Mexico explode in insurrection yet again. Independence had not brought stability, and now the struggle was between the "centralists," who wanted a strong government centered in Mexico City, and the "federalists," who favored a more Jeffersonian approach allowing much greater power to the states. One short-lived centralist revolt had been put down in 1827, but in the presidential election held in September 1828 the centralist candidate won, only to spark a rebellion by federalists led by, among others, Santa Anna, now the governor of Yucatán. This revolt succeeded, and the federalists installed Vicente Guerrero in the presidency. A federalist regime boded well for Texas, but the fact that it had been put in place by military force, and by overturning a lawful election, set an ominous precedent. In a time of economic collapse and political uncertainty, the army had been growing steadily larger, reaching some fifty thousand by 1828. The will of the people, having yielded to the bayonet this time, could do so again, and ambitious men like Santa Anna saw the balance of power shifting from the ballot box to the bullet.[48]

One offshoot of this disruption was the arrival in Texas in April 1828 of General Manuel de Mier y Terán, sent by those worried about unruly Texians—American Texans—to inspect the colony and suggest ways to prevent its eventually becoming overrun and destabilized by the *americanos.* He came to generally favorable conclusions about the industry of the Texians, observing that they were really better suited to capitalize on the land than the native *tejanos,* many of whom did not have agricultural skills. But Mier y Terán was emphatic in offering a warning about the temperament of the Anglos. Speaking generally, but using the Fredonian revolt as background, he reported that "the uproar is incessant and a week never passes without the disturbing news that Nacogdoches is besieged, and that from such and such point there has entered an army of troublemakers." In San Antonio he found many among the *tejano* community who expected the Anglos to erupt in revolution any day. If Mexico were not prudent and preemptive, it could lose Texas to the Americans, which would put them at the Rio Grande, ready to invade Coahuila and threaten the interior.[49]

Mier y Terán suggested sending more *soldados* to Texas. More important, he recommended an immediate cessation to further introduction of colonists. Though the existing colonies—and now there were others besides Austin's—should be allowed to continue, he argued that it was vital that Mexico address the substantial imbalance now existing. While there were only about four thousand *tejanos* in Texas, the number of Anglos was now approaching thirty thousand.[50] To counter this he suggested that the region immediately east of Austin's colony, the territory between the Trinity and the Sabine Rivers, should be colonized with at least six thousand Mexican farmers from Yucatán.[51] Mier y Terán's report may never have gotten back to Mexico City, but he sent numerous letters south while he spent some time in Texas surveying and sparring with Austin in a cordial manner over how best to manage the region in the years ahead. Austin even made for the first time a case for separating Texas from Coahuila and making it a state in its own right, now that the population was swelling. To that, Mier y Terán showed no enthusiasm at all.

And then, as if to punctuate the danger Mexico faced from outsiders, an ill-fated Spanish invasion based out of Cuba landed at Tampico in July 1829. Spain had not given up its claim to rule over Mexico. Mier y Terán himself was back in Mexico to take command of part of the forces resisting the invasion, while Santa Anna commanded another army that helped surround them in a siege that saw the Spaniards surrender in September.[52] The victory was in a sense Pyrrhic, however, for the invasion weakened the already shaky hold of Guerrero on power, and in December an army commanded by the centralist Anastasio Bustamente marched on Mexico City and installed Bustamente in office as president. Almost at once Bustamente began to concentrate political power in Mexico City, and just at a time when Texas was getting some significant concessions from its state legislature in Saltillo. For Texas, the change boded ill. Mier y Terán, already disposed to halt immigration, now stood high in the new administration, while Bustamente himself had been commandant general over the region including Texas when the Edwardses rebelled. In the months ahead Bustamente would reveal himself to be under the sway of those dedicated to withdrawing individual rights and state autonomy, especially where Texas was concerned.

In their view it was the only way to stop the rot before American settlers simply took away one of their most promising provinces and opened the way for expansionists to imperil Mexico itself. In Mier y Terán's own words, "if the colonization contracts in Texas by North Americans are not suspended, and if the conditions of the establishments are not watched, it is necessary to say that the province is already definitely delivered to the foreigners."[53] A French visitor to America just then viewed the situation in precisely the same light, though he watched from the other side of the Sabine. "Daily, little by little, the inhabitants of the United States are infiltrating into Texas, acquiring land there, and, though submitting to the country's laws, establishing there the empire of their language and mores," wrote Alexis de Tocqueville. "The province of Texas is still under Mexican rule, but soon there will, so to say, be no more Mexicans there."[54]

The result came the next spring when the new congress passed the Law of April 6, 1830. It was based chiefly on recommendations from Mier y Terán. Non-American colonization must be encouraged, not only by Mexicans but also by non-English-speaking Europeans. Trade must be encouraged between Texas and Mexico in order to break the commercial bonds linking the province with the United States. More *soldados* must be stationed in Béxar and other posts to ensure tranquility, and settlement of the coastline with its vital ports must remain under Mexican control. Though Mier y Terán left it out of his latest recommendations, Congress went beyond them and included a closure of Texas to further immigration from the United States and a stop to issuing any more *empresario* contracts, nor were any more slaves to be allowed into the province.[55]

Austin was stunned. "The law of the 6 of April will have a fatal tendency," he warned, and he complained directly to Bustamente that it seemed calculated to destroy his colony.[56] Within just weeks it would also lead to what it was intended to prevent, armed outbreaks of protest.

CHAPTER FOUR

"What Will Become of Texas?"

ᏎᎭᎭ

T HE OUTBURST WAS ALMOST immediate, and unlike the Fredonian episode or anything else that came before, it cut across
both geographical and ethnic lines, a reaction that was neither *tejano* nor
americano, but genuinely Texian, though taking different manifesta-
tions. The province's two current representatives in the Saltillo legislature were both *tejanos*, and they spoke out against the Bustamente
policy, only to find themselves attacked and reviled, and one of them
would soon be expelled from the legislature altogether. The *ayuntamientos* in Béxar, Goliad, and Austin's San Felipe all came out in support of
their representatives, though that is as far as *tejano* protest went for the
moment. The Americans were much more kinetic in their response. An
excited Austin, walking a fine line between conciliation and outrage, for
the first time came out publicly in favor of separation of Texas from
Coahuila. If Coahuila was so much in the hands of centralists as to eject
lawful delegates from Texas, then "it has become a matter of serious
doubt whether Texas will ever rise or prosper, so long as it is united with
Coahuila," he said to his colonists in a public letter in September 1830.[1]
Privately to friends he declared that "Texas does not suit to be united
with Coahuila."[2] In the immediate instance, he began trying to get an
exemption for his colony from the law's onerous provisions.

When Mexico City ordered the establishment of a new military post
at Anahuac on the northern end of Galveston Bay, immediately outside
the limits of Austin's colony, the outrage only escalated. This post was,
among other things, to ensure observation of the customs laws. Texas
colonists had been granted a seven-year freeze on paying import duties

in 1823, but now that would expire, and already it was evident that the Anglos would go to great lengths to ignore the law, just as they ignored the rules on immigration itself, for thousands were coming into the colonies without proper permission or papers. When further particulars of the Law of April 6, 1830, became more widely known, especially the prohibition of further importation of slaves, and a ban on commercial trade by non-Mexicans, both blows to the vitals of Texian commerce and prosperity, the volume of colonial outrage only grew louder.[3]

Now more than ever Austin tried to keep a lid on American tempers. He got his exemption from the immigration ban, but it was hard to sell that or the exemption of Texas from an 1829 abolition of slavery to his colonists as signs of Mexican good faith. "Things are quite at sixes and sevens," he observed in October, noting the unrest in Béxar among the *tejanos* as well as the anger of his colonists.[4] In spite of that, he ordered a militia muster and census for early November, and directed that an incomplete company finish its organization. State law required it in any case, but in the current circumstances Austin ran some risk by assembling armed colonists who were disgruntled, though the muster came off without incident.[5]

By that time, in a sign that for all the divisions there were between *tejanos* and the Americans they saw mutual goals as well, Austin was informed that he had been elected to fill the seat of the ousted Texas representative in the Saltillo legislature. That meant he had to leave the colony in December at a particularly critical time, and full in the knowledge that most crises in the past had come when he was absent. This time was to be no exception. Mexico remained on the edge of civil war, with Santa Anna already secretly planning to lead a revolt against Busta-mente in the name of federalism, and behind him Austin had to leave colonists—and to a lesser extent *tejanos*—festering in anger over the Law of April 6, 1830. Before he could return to San Felipe, shots would be fired.

It began over the customs regulations. In December 1831 a small flotilla of merchant vessels defied the Mexican officials posted at the mouth of the Brazos River to collect exportation duties and tried to sail out into the Gulf without stopping. The officer in charge attempted to stop the vessels, and someone on the ships replied, wounding a Mexican soldier. The result was predictable. Austin himself happened to be in Brazoria at the time. Everyone in the town was in a "fever heat," he found. "All the violent passions of the *body politic*" had been aroused and the crisis loosed from him thoughts he had not previously released.[6] "Our situation is extremely delicate," he wrote on December 29. "To remain as we are is impossible." He still wanted peace. "One word from me *now* would anihilate every Mexican soldier in Texas," he declared, "but I am opposed to all violence—all bloodshed—so long as there is even a plausible hope of avoiding such extremes." And he still opposed separation from Mexico, but if all efforts at continuing conciliation should fail, he warned, then *"the last resort will be adopted."* Leaving little room for misunderstanding, privately he told friends that for him this last resort meant that "we shall go for *Independence,* and put our trust in our selves, our riffles, and—our God."[7]

A day later he wrote to the commandant of the one-hundred-seventy-man garrison at Anahuac, a Kentuckian-turned-Mexican named Juan Davis Bradburn, a man who had, by coincidence, served in the War of 1812 in the same regiment with Warren Hall and the Bowie brothers, and later served under Henry Perry and then with the Laffites at Galveston. The situation in Texas was critical, Austin told him, and he implored Bradburn to keep a tight rein on his men, for an overreaction by the *soldados* now could ignite an explosion.[8] "We are still entirely in an unsettled state," one correspondent wrote from Matagorda in February.[9]

The news that Santa Anna had openly rebelled and was leading his army to overthrow Bustamente did not quiet the unrest, even if the general was regarded as being on the federalist platform. It was just one more evidence of the instability of Mexico and of the Mexicans' inability to rule themselves, let alone Texas. Austin just prayed that he could keep the peace in Texas and not see it embroiled in the revolution.[10] By March, now in Béxar, Austin found there a political turmoil over the revolution and the future of Texas. "Personal feelings are more violent here now, than ever," he lamented, and they were becoming *ad hominem* as much as political. Furthermore, somehow two small cannon had been introduced into Brazoria without his knowledge, but the Mexicans had found out about them and were not pleased. In a conciliatory mood, Bradburn had offered to purchase them for his garrison, the unspoken message being that he would not allow them to remain in the colonists' hands. Austin heartily agreed. The guns would "do more harm than good in their present situation," and he confessed his own fear that "there should be some imprudent act committed at Brazoria, which will put the colonists in the wrong, and afford a pretext to harrass them." It looked as if Santa Anna was going to win, and one move now could put the colonists on his wrong side in spite of his professed liberal sentiments.[11]

As happens so often, into just such a situation ripe for explosion stepped just the right man to set the match. Just the year before, in May 1831, one of those many newcomers leaving failure behind arrived in San Felipe. William Barret Travis, born in South Carolina, had grown to manhood in Alabama, where he showed himself to be both a prodigy and prodigiously immature. By 1830, when just twenty-one, he was a lawyer, newspaper publisher, teacher, civic leader, and husband and father, and a failure at all. Perpetually broke, he went deeply into debt with creditors until none would extend him more. "Never have I seen a more impressive instance of depression from debts," a fellow attorney recalled of Travis. "He was unquestionably an honest man, but debt will weigh down the loftiest soul, and humble the brightest intelligence." Certainly it humbled Travis's. In a humiliating incident, creditors took Travis to court, and he was prosecuted by the very man under whom he had himself read law. His only defense was to take refuge from his debts by pointing out his age and the fact that virtually all of his debts had been incurred when he was a minor, and therefore presumably not liable to be held responsible. It was an unfortunate decision, however, for in Alabama law the grounds for such an argument rested literally upon use of the word "infancy" as a defense. Travis made his case, but then his old mentor brought Travis to the jury box, observed that the defendant was five feet nine or ten inches tall, fully bearded, and weighed about 175 pounds, and with devastating effect remarked upon the wondrous size of such an "infant." Not surprisingly, the jury first thundered in laughter and then found against him.[12]

That humiliation was bad enough, but Travis's marriage—rather forced upon him by an unexpected pregnancy in the first place—was going badly as well, and there was another child on the way. Humiliated in his community and unhappy at home, with far more pride than prudence and not yet enough maturity to match his social and career ambitions, he now faced the prospect of debtor's prison. His only alternative was to leave and start over somewhere else. In April 1831, before any formal papers could be served on him for collection or prison, he stole out of Alabama without farewells to any except his wife and infant son, whom he told he would send for when he could, or else return to get when he had made his fortune and could repay his debts. Some years later, as he grew up, he would start to repay those debts, but he all but abandoned his wife, who would eventually secure a divorce.[13]

Two months later he had settled in Anahuac, a small community on the northeastern shore of Trinity Bay, which opened into Galveston Bay. There were little more than two dozen log houses and shops atop the bank leading down to the water. With the exemption on customs duties having just recently expired, Mexican authorities chose Anahuac as the point of entry for taxing goods passing into or out of Galveston. That meant there would be work for lawyers here, and almost from the first Travis's practice flourished in a modest way. For reasons long lost to history, Travis—who seems never to have suffered the diminutive "Bill"—carried the nickname "Buck."[14] It suited his temperament, for he was still intemperate in speech and behavior, with a seeming instinct to "buck" authority. Within less than a year got himself on the wrong side of the Mexican commander Bradburn, who had indeed alienated himself from most of the community by high-handed interpretation of his duties.

Travis and Bradburn locked horns repeatedly over customs and land issues. Unlike his superiors in San Antonio and elsewhere, Bradburn was not willing to ignore the prohibition on slavery, nor would he recognize the thinly disguised subterfuge of the "lifetime indentures" or the ninety-nine-year "labor contracts." After all, Anahuac was just outside the Austin colony, and so the exemption granted to Austin did not apply here. Moreover, many runaway slaves from Louisiana crossed the Sabine and wound up in Bradburn's jurisdiction, and not a few of Travis's new cases were suits from the owners for the return of their property. Bradburn refused to yield them to writs, declaring that only through diplomatic channels in Washington and Mexico City could he be ordered to return slaves to Louisiana. As a committed believer in the sanctity of slavery and individual property rights—as interpreted in the United States Constitution, of course, and not in the Mexican—Travis felt outraged by Bradburn's position, which also, of course, interfered with his business. Bradburn also prohibited new arrivals in Anahuac from getting surveys of their new land grants even when they predated the April 6 halt, thus preventing them from getting formal titles, and some of these litigants, too, became Travis's clients.

Then in April 1832 one of the Anahuac *soldados* allegedly raped an Anglo woman. It was witnessed by a Texian man who chose not to interfere, and citizens of Anahuac felt so outraged that they tarred and feathered the bad Samaritan on April 26. Bradburn sent some of his men to stop the business, words and then shouts were traded back and forth, then blows, and finally random shots in a small riot. The Texians left the field to the Mexicans, ending the disturbance, but Bradburn was incensed at the resistance to his authority, and rightly or wrongly concluded that Travis and fellow attorney Patrick Jack had been the instigators.[15] Perhaps they were, for just five days later the Anahuac Texian men met publicly, and in violation of a prohibition on creating new militia companies, they organized themselves into one, ostensibly for protection from Indian attack. The excuse was transparent, since the closest raiding Indians were more than two hundred miles distant. In a clear threat to local authority the Texians intended to have some means of resistance if there were another confrontation with Bradburn's *soldados,* and they chose Jack as their captain. A centralist himself, Bradburn might have been a martinet, but he was not a fool. With Santa Anna's federalist revolt occupying central Mexico itself, there would be little assistance to Bradburn if he were to face an armed uprising of colonists in support of Santa Anna. He responded by immediately arresting Jack.

During the next two weeks Travis and others made repeated protests for Jack's release, and finally Bradburn relented. But then the commandant heard a rumor of a band of well-armed Louisianians about to cross the Sabine and raid Anahuac to reclaim runaway slaves by force. The rumor proved false, as did another one deliberately leaked to the Mexicans, but both forced Bradburn to put his small garrison on full alert. Having been made a fool of by the hoaxes, he concluded that Travis lay behind them and on May 17 he arrested the lawyer, and immediately afterward arrested Jack, too, confining them in a guardhouse in his stone barracks.[16]

To some Travis and Jack became heroes overnight, confirming Austin's prediction that the wrong reaction by the authorities to even a minor Texian indiscretion could make the accused a popular hero and rallying point for the disgruntled and turbulent "altho he was a most perfect jack ass and a scoundrel." That their own foolish prank—if indeed Travis and Jack were the authors of the rumors—had gotten them into trouble did not matter. Now they sat—and would sit for fifty days—in a Mexican cell, victims of the arbitrary authority of a Mexican commander—if not himself a Mexican—who defied the personal and property rights common to all Americans, and therefore presumably, by their logic, to Texians as well. Quite aware of their symbolic position, and though they were well treated by Bradburn, Travis and Jack tried to capitalize on the moment by encouraging confrontation. Early in their confinement they tried to smuggle out a plea to David G. Burnet, a fellow malcontent, calling on Texians at large to *"come and rescue them from the claws of [blood]thirsty, ra[s]cally and convict soldiers."*[17] It was not quite a call for an armed uprising, but Travis was not such a fool as not to realize that it could lead to that.

Bradburn intercepted the message first, yet continued to allow his prisoners some privileges. Travis and Jack determined to break out rather than submit themselves to a Mexican trial in Matamoras, where Bradburn intended to send them, especially since Bradburn would likely be charging them with attempted insurrection leading to Texian independence not just from Coahuila, but from Mexico itself.[18] A conviction for that kind of treason historically had only one outcome on conviction. Worse, they learned that Bradburn was taking testimony to support his case without allowing Travis and Jack themselves to question the deponents, and the accused further believed that Bradburn was forcing perjured testimony from some. When Bradburn learned of their escape plan, he transferred his prisoners without warning to a newly completed brick kiln that was more easily guarded and positioned his artillery pieces directly in front of it.

Despite Bradburn's fears and the attempts of the incarcerated to get their pleas out to their friends, fewer than half a dozen men actually felt aroused, and even they had no interest in actually taking action. Meanwhile General Mier y Terán, Bradburn's superior officer, began plans to prevent Jack and Travis—whom he described as a "plague of locusts"—from practicing law in the event of their release or acquittal by requiring that they have licenses issued in Saltillo, which everyone knew neither possessed.[19] But then Jack's brother William began to campaign on their behalf throughout the Austin colony, joined by Robert M. Williamson, Frank Johnson, the ever-present Warren Hall and others, and soon more than one hundred were gathered on the San Jacinto River a few miles west of Anahuac. Under the leadership of Johnson and Hall they readied themselves for a raid on the kiln to release the prisoners. Bradburn heard of their gathering and immediately assumed that their aim was more far-reaching, to start a rebellion. In his imagination he exaggerated their strength to six hundred or more and pleaded for reinforcements from his superiors, even as his immediate superior Colonel Domingo Ugartechea sent a plea for Bradburn to defuse the situation by showing some discretion and releasing the men before violence broke out.

By the morning of June 10 it was too late. Johnson and Hall and their little army rode into the environs of Anahuac. Bradburn reacted by taking Travis and Jack out of their kiln, tying them to the ground, and having several *soldados* train their muskets on them. At the first sign of an attack, he would order them to be shot, he warned Johnson. Travis defiantly shouted to Johnson's negotiators to go ahead and attack, promising that he could die manfully if he must. Instead, the volunteers retired a few hundred yards to debate what to do next, an early indication of the sometimes counterproductive democratic spirit that would animate these men even when enlisted for a specific purpose. Not only would they insist upon electing their own officers, but then they still expected their voices to be heard—even by ballot—in deciding what those officers were to lead them in doing. Bradburn's *soldados* and Johnson's Texians exchanged a few occasional shots at a distance during the rest of the day and into the next, no one really making a serious effort to bring on a battle, though the Texians took some Mexican prisoners. Then on June 12 Bradburn and Johnson came to terms on an exchange of captives if the Texians would retreat some six miles to Turtle Bayou. Bradburn was being disingenuous. He had no idea of giving up Travis and Jack, but by getting Johnson's men away to a safe distance, he could proceed unseen with further fortification of his own position and also buy time to call in all his outposts to strengthen his garrison to one hundred sixty or more, easily enough to defend against anything the Anglos could send at him. Adding further insult to what Texians would naturally see as his duplicity, he then had his *soldados* ransack the Texian houses in Anahuac for anything that they could put to their own purposes. That done, he then sent word to Johnson on June 13 to come and get Travis and Jack if he thought he could take them.

Yet when the men back at Turtle Bayou got word of a significant victory of Santa Anna's in his fight to overthrow Bustamente and the centralists, they opportunistically decided that if they were going to fire on Bradburn and his garrison, they could legitimize themselves by declaring support of the federalist cause, which seemed on the verge of victory. They drafted the Turtle Bayou Resolutions, condemning Bustamente's violations of the Mexican constitution of 1824 and calling on all Texians to support Santa Anna, made several copies, and sent them to other Anglo communities. If doing so freed them of the fear of being branded outright revolutionaries, still they were now openly declared to be in revolt against Bustamente and the military authorities in Texas, but they had cunningly placed themselves on the winning side. That done, they marched back toward Anahuac and continued some desultory but inconclusive skirmishing.[20]

All of this took time, while Travis and Jack languished in their cell. The scene of confrontation shifted elsewhere. John Austin, the *alcalde* of Brazoria, a member of the 1819 Long expedition, and a good friend—though no relation—of Stephen Austin, had been at Anahuac with Johnson trying to effect the prisoners' release, then participated in the Turtle Bayou discussions. He then helped to spread the call for volunteers, and returned to Brazoria to get a small cannon to use against Bradburn. On June 26 he and Henry Smith, a farmer and schoolteacher, got the cannon aboard a boat and with as many as one hundred fifty men sailed down the Brazos some fifteen miles to its mouth on the Gulf. To get into the Gulf, they had to pass the Mexican fort at Velasco commanded by Ugartechea himself. When he attempted to halt their passage the Texians went ashore and attacked the fort, and in the ensuing skirmishing some forty-two men became casualties, including fifteen killed or mortally wounded, a third of them Mexicans. Ugartechea, probably outnumbered, in the end had no option but to surrender. Three days later his garrison were put on a ship and sent home to Mexico.

That done, Austin and his men returned to Anahuac, only to discover on arrival that Colonel José de la Piedras and part of his garrison from Nacogdoches had come to reinforce Bradburn. Piedras, himself a centralist but much more sympathetic to the Texians, stopped outside town and immediately entered negotiations with Johnson and agreed to release Travis and Jack. On June 29, the same day of the Velasco surrender, Piedras agreed to release the prisoners to be tried by their own civil authorities if any cause for indictment could be found—which would never happen—and to relieve Bradburn of his command upon the promise of the assembled Texians to disperse and go home. On July 2 Travis and Jack walked free once more, and a humiliated Bradburn sulked in Anahuac for a few days, now in fear for his life. When Piedras left to return to face problems of his own in Nacogdoches on July 8, he left Anahuac in command of a mere lieutenant, and three days later Travis took advantage of the power vacuum to bring a barrel of whiskey into town and have a party for the whole male community, Texians and *soldados* alike. By the end of the evening he and friends persuaded the garrison to mutiny and declare for Santa Anna. Two days later, now in fear of his own former men as well as of the Texians, Bradburn and a few followers escaped east to Louisiana, chased by vengeful Texians including probably Travis himself.[21] Behind him Bradburn left a legacy by his arbitrary policy that achieved exactly what Austin had warned against. He had overreacted and made heroes of two local malcontents whose actions their own people otherwise had not been much inclined to sanction.

The confrontations of this summer were not done yet, for when Piedras returned to Nacogdoches he found another crisis at hand. All over Texas communities were following the lead of the Turtle Bayou Resolutions and coming out in support for Santa Anna. In San Felipe members of the *ayuntamiento* called for a declaration for Santa Anna and Austin's own deputy Samuel May Williams proclaimed on July 1 that "this once happy and prosperous country is now a perfect charnal house of anarchy and confusion."[22] The men of Nacogdoches and surrounding communities were in the act of forming themselves into militia companies and raising arms when Piedras returned. Having seen the desultory outbreak in Anahuac, and well aware of what had happened at Velasco, he tried to preempt a similar confrontation at home by issuing a proclamation demanding that the Texians surrender their arms and disperse. If he could prevent the defection of his community to the federalists, then perhaps he could stop the *santanista* tide here before it swept all of Texas.

It was not to be. Piedras issued his order to the *ayuntamiento*, which refused to act and instead began organizing its own militia and sent pleas to communities as far away as San Felipe begging for men to come to their aid. They came from all over, some traveling as far as fifty miles, and by July 31 more than three hundred Texians were gathered just a few miles east of Nacogdoches, where they elected James W. Bullock their leader. The next day they sent into Piedras their ultimatum to withdraw his order and transfer his allegiance to the federalist cause. Piedras refused, and so on August 2 the militia marched into Nacogdoches. As they approached the square, the *soldados* opened fire and then Piedras's cavalry made a charge to try to clear the street. While many of the Texians dispersed, one hundred or more took refuge in houses and then began a daylong skirmishing as they advanced house-by-house to drive the Mexicans out of their own fortified buildings. All told, some thirty-three Mexicans were killed and another seventeen or more wounded, while Texian losses were light, just four dead or mortally wounded, and six more injured.[23] By nightfall Piedras found that he was in danger of being surrounded and decided to evacuate under cover of darkness. Before leaving, he ordered his men to throw all the arms they could not carry with them into wells. The next morning, expecting a renewal of the battle, the Texians were stunned to discover that their quarry had escaped.

It was the moment for another potential leader to emerge as a symbolic hero of resistance. Travis had no previous martial experience to commend him. His newfound reputation came to him by accident. Neither were John Austin nor Henry Smith naturally men to whom others looked for leadership. But late the night before, even while Piedras was getting ready to slip out of town, James Bowie rode into Nacogdoches. He brought with him a reputation for combativeness well known, if much exaggerated, thanks to his participation in the September 1827 brawl outside Natchez known as the Sandbar Fight. It was a local affair that grew out of political and personal rivalries. Two men determined to fight a duel met on the sandbar, exchanged fire without doing harm, and declared themselves satisfied. But then their numerous seconds decided the moment was ripe to settle other old scores, a gun was drawn, and suddenly more than a dozen men were exchanging fire. Bowie went down with two bullets and at least seven stab wounds, his lung twice punctured, but still he killed an opponent with whom he had a long-standing feud, using a long-bladed butcher knife given him by his brother Rezin. No wonder he came with the smell of violence about him, of illegal slave trade dealings with Laffite, and a wide reputation for forged Spanish land grant frauds by which he had tried—unsuccessfully—to gain possession of hundreds of square miles of Louisiana and Arkansas. His game was played out in Louisiana, but after that first visit to Texas in 1828 he had not forgotten the seeming opportunity for his kind of enterprise west of the Sabine. In January 1830 he returned in company with Martin Parmer of Fredonian ill fame to seek land, citizenship, and the opportunity to rebuild his own dreams anew. His marriage to the daughter of Veramendi made the highest possible alliance. He tried unsuccessfully to get a textile mill going, attempted a little trade as a dry-goods merchant, and began searching for lost silver mines in the interior, always looking in vain for the big financial killing. For all his penchant for opportunism and a lenient attitude toward the law, he was also a man of unshakable bravery, one who inspired calm and confidence in dangerous moments, a man with a strong sense of fair play, a sense of humor, a fondness even for Methodist hymns. Most of all, he carried with him an aura that attracted men to him, and that infused them with confidence that in a crisis, Bowie's side was the one that would win.

Bowie stayed out of the political ferment of 1831–1832, though he, like others, recognized that until the revolution in Mexico settled where rule would lie, the colonists ran great risks if they took sides. He was off on another treasure-hunting trip when a message from Stephen Austin himself asked Bowie to rush to San Felipe. There Austin asked Bowie to go to Nacogdoches to try to keep a lid on Texian rumblings there. The two men were not exactly friends. Indeed, there had been some misunderstandings between them, and Austin's own rigidly upright character could never admire a chancer like Bowie.[24]

What Bowie found on reaching Nacogdoches was disarray. When Bullock's men discovered that Piedras had escaped their grasp, they seemingly lost heart and Bullock himself apparently lost control of his men. It was a moment meant for Bowie. With no authority—for Austin could give him none outside his own colony—Bowie simply took over. Ignoring Bullock, he asked for twenty mounted volunteers, and undeterred by odds of ten-to-one, immediately set out to chase Piedras and his two hundred *soldados*. Easily riding around the marching soldiers, Bowie placed his company ahead of them on the road where they would have to cross the Angelina River, and then took refuge in ambush. When the advance of Piedras's column started across, a Texian volley killed one and the rest fled. For the balance of the day, Bowie dogged the Mexicans' march, staying in sight but concealing his own weakness. The next morning, August 4, believing that enough time and uncertainty had passed to unnerve the Mexicans, Bowie sent a demand for surrender into Piedras's camp, threatening that if they did not, then all would be put to the sword, an ultimatum that would be heard again in Texas in the days ahead.

Piedras, not knowing of his own overwhelming superiority in numbers, was still game to fight, but one of his own officers mutinied, took command from him, and agreed to Bowie's terms. Before the Mexicans could realize their error, Bowie had them disarmed and on the march back to Nacogdoches. A few days later he marched them to San Felipe, and along the way wrote ahead to Austin that the Mexican command had been, as he dryly put it, "induced by certain American arguments" to declare in favor of the federalist cause.[25] When he reached San Felipe he was the hero of the hour. Not only had he cleared eastern Texas of Mexican soldiers, thus buying time free from threat for the political activities soon to follow, but by his persuasion of the Mexican column to conversion he had implicitly allied himself with the *santanista* cause. He also joined Travis, whom as yet he knew only slightly, as one of the acknowledged leaders of the men of action, though both were still in concert with Stephen Austin on the need for Texas to remain a part of Mexico. They had revolted in favor of local autonomy and self-determination, but not for independence.

In any other context the outbreaks at Anahuac, Velasco, and Nacogdoches might well have led to revolution, especially since the participants were overwhelmingly Anglos, and there is no telling what might have been the response from south of the Rio Grande. But by aligning themselves with their declarations in favor of Santa Anna, the colonists managed to strike blows for their own freedoms and clear their midst of several Mexican garrisons, without arraying themselves against Mexico itself, revealing no small degree of political sophistication and a good deal more willingness to take risks than poor Austin, struggling always to cling to the status quo for fear of what might come in its place. So long as Santa Anna and the federalists prevailed in the continuing contest in Mexico itself, that risk could be rewarded.

But still they needed to take care, for in the wake of the first shots being fired, new voices arose calling for more, for absolute Texian independence. While Travis was yet in his kiln cell, James Bailey, one of Austin's original three hundred and a man known for extreme views, declared: "The first blow has already been struck. Now or never is the time to sever all ties."[26] Once Travis was released he wasted no time in taking advantage of his recent situation. He wrote an unsigned editorial in which he spun rather a different tale. His arrest was not for pranks, but because of his political views as a man standing up for Texian liberties. *"Americans know their rights and will assert and protect them,"*

he blustered. Moreover, he boasted that "the Americans"—he did not
call them Texians—had gained everything they wanted by their bold
stand.[27] The message seemed clear. Mexicans, especially in their current
distracted and divided state, could not or would not stand up to a determined and united front of Americans. The subliminal message was that
now was the time to assert a demand for separation from Coahuila and
the regional rule of Mexicans. Unlike Bailey, Travis did not openly call
for independence, but after talking with Bradburn and both of his former
captives, Ugartechea at least concluded that Travis and Jack "and other
accomplices" were planning by some means to separate Texas not only
from Coahuila, but from Mexico itself.[28]

While Travis moved to San Felipe and continued his agitation there,
Bowie did the same in San Antonio, as did others such as William Wharton, the Jacks, and Hall, among others. From San Antonio there came a
call from the Anglo—but not the *tejano*—citizens for a convention of
representatives from all of the several colonies to decide on common
action to capitalize on an advantage they all knew could be fleeting.
Through it all, Austin had been follower rather than leader. He did not
entirely trust the sincerity of Santa Anna's federalist protestations. By
now the history in other former Spanish colonies had shown that when
a military man used the army to establish a government, he usually did
so in the name of liberty and reform, then too often reverted to authoritarian rule. Austin called Santa Anna accurately a "sort of Mad Cap difficult to class."[29] Knowledgeable Mexican leaders with whom Austin
met in Saltillo confided that they regarded the general as essentially a
centralist at heart, and even Austin's friend Mier y Terán did not trust
the general. Indeed, Mier y Terán despaired for Mexico itself. On July 2,
the very day that Travis was released, Mier y Terán decided that he had
had enough of the miseries of Mexican politics. "We are lost," he told a
friend. "Texas is lost." Indeed, almost his very last known words were of
that faraway province. "What will become of Texas?" he asked in what
was surely a rhetorical question, since he never expected to hear an
answer. The next day he committed suicide by thrusting his own sword
through his chest.[30]

Seeing that Texians had taken control of affairs from him, Austin had
no alternative but to endorse their actions and then try once more to
place himself at their head where at least he could try to contain their
impetuosity. When he returned from Saltillo to find the results of

Anahuac, Velasco, and Nacogdoches, Austin went to San Felipe, where he found that its *ayuntamiento* had joined the call for a convention. Unable to stop it, he simply went along, and was there on October 1, 1832, when some fifty-five delegates representing sixteen colonies and communities gathered in San Felipe. It was the first time that Texians from all across the settled colonies tried to meet in a representative assembly to discuss their common aims. Though the number of colonies represented here differed from that other colonial assemblage of 1774 that met in Philadelphia to discuss common problems and try to assert their rights as Englishmen, still the Continental Congress was a part of their common heritage and political identity. Few could have been unmindful that they might be starting on the same road taken half a century before by their grandfathers.

There were aspects of this convention that reflected the immediate events of the past summer. The *tejano* community had not taken part in the outbreaks of June and July, largely regarding them as unwarranted actions brought on by the *americanos'* own folly. Invitations to send delegates to this convention now went to the *tejano* leaders, but not a one came, and the *ayuntamientos* of San Antonio de Béxar and Victoria, dominated by *tejanos,* sent no delegations at all. The political chief in San Antonio, Músquiz, frankly responded to the invitation that loyal *tejanos* could not participate in a convention that was clearly an unlawful assembly under Mexican law. The *ayuntamiento* was the proper and legally constituted medium for forwarding protests to higher authorities. The fact that the Anglos also knew a convention to be unlawful but went right ahead and did as they wished, and were apparently ready to presume to try to make policy for Texas without reference to *tejano* concerns and sensibilities, did not bode well for their future relations. Indeed, while there had never been entire harmony of interests between Anglo and *tejano,* still their coexistence until this time had been mostly cordial and supportive, but a small gap was widening. "Let us be honest with ourselves, Sir," a member of the Goliad *ayuntamiento* would write to the legislature in Coahuila a few months later, "the foreign empresarios are nothing more than money-changing speculators caring only for their own well-being and hesitating not in their unbecoming methods."[31]

Unbecoming or not, and representative or not, the convention of 1832 went ahead. The names of Austin and Wharton were both put in nomination for president, and Austin won, showing that he certainly still had substantial moral authority in the community. Fortunately, few of the men now identified as hotheads, like Travis or Bowie, were sent as delegates (Bowie could not have been since San Antonio sent none). Patrick Jack was there representing the district of Liberty, just north of Anahuac, and William Wharton came from Victoria, and both were certainly on the more aggressive side of the questions before them, as was Rafael Manchola, the only delegate from Goliad, and the only *tejano* sent to the convention, though he only arrived after it adjourned. Still, the bulk of the delegates gave the meeting a more thoughtful, though hardly conservative, complexion.

For six days they talked both in their meeting hall and in the taverns of San Felipe in the evenings. In a series of resolutions they made their concerns—they stopped short of allowing hubris over recent successes to make them demands—plain in a memorial to be sent to the state capital in Saltillo and in Mexico City itself. They wanted the exemption from customs duty to be extended until 1835 in order to stimulate more settlement by merchants and encourage their economy, and they wanted a means of controlling the sometimes corrupt customs officers sent to date. They asked for a repeal of the portions of the Law of April 6, 1830, that prohibited immigration from the United States. Revealing their constant preoccupation with land, they asked for a refinement of the system of issuing land titles to make it faster and more efficient, and they also requested a gift of public domain lands to be sold to raise and support bilingual schools for the education of both Anglo and *tejano* children. To protect themselves from the threat of hostile Indians—or so they said—they petitioned for permission to raise their own militia. Certainly they had seen how weak and easily beaten the Mexican garrisons had been that were sent to Texas, so naturally they trusted far more to their own ability to defend themselves. Still, it could not be argued that they were also asking for lawful sanction to maintain an armed militia that could always be used to revolt against Mexican authority. In their most provocative resolution of all, they asked for separation from Coahuila and the creation of Texas as a separate state within the federation.

Beyond these resolutions, the delegates also agreed to create a seventeen-man central committee authorized to convene such meetings again in the future when circumstances warranted, as well as committees of correspondence in each of the municipalities, yet another echo of 1774.

Should there be another time of crisis like that precipitated at Anahuac, they would be prepared by being kept steadily informed of each other's affairs. On October 6 the convention adjourned, its last act being to appoint Wharton and the just-arrived Manchola to present their resolutions to the legislature in Coahuila and to Congress in Mexico City.[32] Disingenuously, Austin would declare on October 10 that "we have just had a convention of all Texas, native Mexicans and foreign settlers—all united as one man." If that was manifestly not true, he shaved a little closer to the truth when he averred that "we have done our duty faithfully as Mexican citizens." Civil insurrection against the *current* lawfully constituted regime hardly seemed good faith to either the shredding Bustamente administration or even the Texians' *tejano* neighbors. Certainly Austin spoke accurately when he admitted "what will be the fate of our application I know not." However, he revealed after the convention that the incipient sentiment of resistance, fed by recent easy successes, could no longer be explained away or hidden.

> Whatever may be the view which the Mexican government may take of the past, we can with honest truth say, that our consciences are clear. Should the future drive us into an attitude of hostility in defense of what we have so dearly earned, the public opinion of good men, I think, will acquit us of all wrong—we shall *then* expect that the sympathies which cheered the struggling Greeks and Poles—that sanctioned the independence of Spanish America—that applauded the liberals of France, and the reformists of Great Britain, will also cheer the humble watch fires of our undisciplined militia, and if necessary soon swell their ranks to a respectable army. . . . This country, as a state of Mexico, would prosper—it would be of great service to the nation, and add much to the national strength and resources—it is not our interest to separate if such a thing can be avoided, *unless indeed we should float into the Northern Republic with the consent of all parties, ourselves included.*[33]

When all was done, Austin tried, as usual, to straddle the fence by downplaying the significance to Músquiz. "With regard to the meeting," he told him, "it did not originate with me, but I believe some good will result from its action." More important, though, he tried to soothe any apprehensions on Músquiz's part by adding that "the public is quiet," suggesting that by having their convention the discontented were now satisfied and no harm done, with the result that "we have enjoyed more quiet than heretofore." When political chief Músquiz finally handed down a stern ruling on November 7 that the convention had been extralegal and thus annulled its resolutions, there was no point in Wharton and Manchola taking their embassy south. Austin confessed his relief. "In times like the present, any measure is bad, that tends to irritate, and produce excitement," he said a few weeks later.

Yet at the same time, he despaired of anything good for Texas coming out of the upheaval in Mexico, declaring that "Texas is lost if she takes no measure of her own for her welfare." He may have been pleased that Músquiz killed the resolutions, but he was uncomfortable with the grounds. "I cannot approve the principle, that the people have not the right to assembly peaceably and honorably to represent their wants," he told the political chief, "but we may fear to see it still worse."[34] Mindful of that, Austin went to San Antonio at the beginning of December hoping to bring the *tejano* and American community back together and "secure union and harmony throughout Texas."[35] He had to keep Béxar in tune with the rest of the Anglo-dominated communities. He met with Erasmo Seguín and other *tejanos* and gave them what he thought was "an exact description of the evils that are retarding the progress of Texas." Plainly put, he said they must separate from Coahuila, and they agreed. Their complaint with the convention had been its means, not the end. The proper route to seek redress was a petition from the *ayuntamiento*, they argued, and Austin readily assented. It would state grievances and means of remedy and submit them to the government, but then, showing that despite their sense of alienation from the Texians they still shared common goals, the *tejanos* went on to agree with Austin on giving an ultimatum that if their protests were not addressed and remedied by the following spring, then Texians should unite in organizing their own state government as if Coahuila did not exist. "Texas can *then* say to Coahuila and to the world—we were insulted and oppressed—we asked redress—it was refused, and we have redressed."[36] It would be secession from Coahuila, not Mexico, but would still be a challenge to Mexican law.

The San Antonio *ayuntamiento* was as good as its leaders' word, and the petition was drafted on December 19, then endorsed by the *ayun-*

tamientos of Goliad, San Felipe, and Nacogdoches. All the laws and forms had been observed, and thus Músquiz had no choice but to send it on to Saltillo and Mexico City. But by this time events elsewhere had dramatically changed the context of their efforts. In September the governor of Coahuila y Texas died, and Bowie's father-in-law, the federalist Veramendi, went to Saltillo to assume the governorship. He immediately dissolved the centralist legislature and called for the election of a new one in its place, at the same time proclaiming his allegiance to the 1824 constitution that was the bedrock of federalist hopes. Aided and encouraged by his son-in-law Bowie, he also began making plans for an attempt to move the capital to Monclova on the Rio Grande, just forty miles from the Texas provincial border on the Nueces. Then Bustamente finally gave up all resistance and resigned his presidency, followed by the arrival of Santa Anna and his army in Mexico City on January 3, 1833. Two months later, in a foregone conclusion, the Mad Cap was elected president of the federation.

His madness, if it be so, was founded on a wonderful instinct for advancement and self-preservation. Stories of Santa Anna's risks and indiscretions abounded, most of them true. As a young officer he paid debts by forging his commander's signature on a bank draft. Everyone remembered how he suddenly became a federalist in 1821, beginning the day a captain in the Spanish army, then changing sides and rising immediately to colonel in the insurgent forces. When Iturbide was the power of the moment, Santa Anna gained a general's star by courting Iturbide's sister despite her being more than twice his age, then turned against Iturbide shortly after pledging lifetime loyalty to him. Santa Anna liked cockfights, himself raising prize cocks for the ring, and tried to assume the mantle of the country gentleman, forever protesting that all he really wanted to do was stay on his plantation near Vera Cruz. "My whole ambition is restricted to beating my sword into a plowshare," he declared, but somehow it never happened.[37]

Santa Anna or no, Austin or no, events in Texas were moving. The central committee appointed by the October convention, unhappy at the stalling of their resolutions, did not wait to learn the result of Austin's attempt to get the Béxar *ayuntamiento* moving. Instead, just before Christmas it issued a call for March elections for delegates to another convention to meet in San Felipe on April 1. From the tone of the call it was evident that the committee had no intention of being circumvented this time in making Texians' case known.[38] Many still felt uneasy over such an action by what one colonist called "the Junto of San Felipe," but they were now quickly to be left behind, especially when the complexion of the future convention became evident after the elections. It was thoroughly in the hands of men committed to action.[39]

This time the less conservative Wharton was elected to preside over the fifty and more delegates, a public declaration that while Austin was still respected, his moderate course would no longer be followed. This time, too, San Antonio participated, and Bowie was elected among its delegates. San Felipe elected Pat Jack once more, while Nacogdoches sent a distinguished new arrival, Sam Houston of Tennessee. He was on the rebound from several years of failure and dissipation after suddenly resigning as governor of Tennessee in the wake of a marital collapse. He had moved west of the Mississippi to live among the displaced Chero-kee, where he became a notorious drunk in the dusty streets of Fort Gib-son, telling bawdy stories to soldiers in return for money to buy drink. His friendship with President Andrew Jackson saved him, as Old Hick-ory employed Houston as a go-between for Indian affairs relating to the Cherokee, and by 1832 Houston was on an inspection tour of the west-ern tribes for the president. He may also have been using his mission as a pretext for a close look at Texas for an expansionist administration that had no love for Spanish-speaking peoples. Indeed, in February 1833 he wrote to Jackson reporting that the colonists seemed determined on separation from Coahuila and that if they did not get that, then he thought 95 percent favored independence followed by annexation by the United States. "She can defend herself against the whole power of Mex-ico," he said, "for Mexico is powerless and penniless."

Houston anticipated that at the coming convention the delegates would frame a constitution for Texas as a state apart from Coahuila, and in the process lay claim to all territory down to the Rio Grande as prop-erly lying within its boundaries. Still, the fact that Houston's first act on reaching San Felipe in December was to apply for a grant of land sug-gests that he came as well on his own interest to establish a new home and start life anew. "I may make Texas my abiding place!" he told Jack-son, but then added that—like so many other Anglos there now chafing at the uncomfortable fit of Mexican citizenship—"in adopting this course, I will *never forget* the country of my birth."[40]

It remained for the convention itself to determine how right Houston would be. It opened with the predictable speeches on the wrongs they had suffered and justifications of their actions of the past season. At Anahuac the men who attacked Bradburn were not resisting the power of Mexico, but only that of an arbitrary local official. The Texians expelled garrisons from Texas because they had been oppressors. Houston himself said that the Turtle Bayou Resolutions and similar declarations of support for the federalists had been a subterfuge. "Santa Anna was only a name used as an excuse for resistance to oppression," he argued. On the broader issue, Houston like others averred that Mexico simply was not competent in its current state to legislate over Texas. The mother state was in chaos without either constitution or civil law in authority, and then in an echo of the "taxation without representation" outcry of the American Revolutionary generation, Houston and others asserted that Texas could not be bound by laws made in Mexico City by a congress in which Texas had no representation, ignoring the fact that, like it or not, Texas was represented as part of the state of Coahuila y Texas by the delegates sent from Coahuila. The solution to that, of course, was separation from Coahuila and a constitution of their own as a new state in the federation.[41]

Austin laid before the group a lengthy review of the past year's events in Mexico and Texas that the central committee had asked him to prepare. In it he rehearsed their grievances, the inefficiency of their current system of political and judicial administration within the province, and he made anew the case in favor of separation from Coahuila so that they could attend to their own concerns. He then pointed out the provision in the 1824 constitution for Texan statehood when it should inform the congress that it was ready to meet such responsibilities.[42] "We are now able to sustain A State Govt. and no country ever required one more than this," he told a friend on the second day of the convention, predicting that it would vote to apply for admission to statehood, and that the Congress would grant the request.[43]

In anticipation of that, Austin then presented an outline for a new state constitution to a committee headed by Houston, who immediately by his presence assumed a prominence in the convention at least equal to Austin's by virtue of his close connection to Jackson, his experience in the United States Army and as a major general of the Tennessee militia, his two terms in the U.S. Congress, and his two years as governor of Tennessee. As a model, Houston, Austin, and others used the Massachusetts constitution of 1780, which someone happened to have available. Their state government should have a house and senate, and their chief magistrate would be a governor serving a two-year term of office. Their judiciary would be headed by a supreme court, with district and lesser courts as the legislature should require. All males over twenty-one would be eligible to vote, and a lengthy twenty-seven-article bill of rights well defined what they believed to be the liberties any Texians should enjoy. They provided the guarantee of trial by jury, unlike the Mexican system of trial by *alcalde.* There should be no impediment to freedoms of speech and assembly, though they decided to leave out religious freedom rather than risk seeking too much relaxation of their Catholic rulers' insistence on the state religion. They wanted to establish free public schools for their children, and to establish a monetary system within the state based on hard specie and banning unsecured paper currency. Burnet was appointed to chair a committee to draft a statement to Congress outlining the merits of this new constitution and its organization of their state government on a model quite obviously owing much more to American than to Mexican precedents.[44]

While debating the constitution, the convention renewed its call for annulment of the Law of April 6, 1830, then passed new resolutions requesting better defense against the Indians, more efficient transportation of the mails, and the extension of their exemption from tariff duties. Then they went on to other issues that might more properly have belonged to a real sitting legislature than a supplicant convention. They passed resolutions banning the African slave trade—the importation of new slaves from Africa, already banned by Great Britain and the United States—and expressing their concurrence in "the general indignation which has been manifested throughout the civilized world against that inhuman and unprincipled traffic." The resolution came in response to the recent importation of a cargo of Africans from Cuba, but it also presented an opportunity to try to arrest fears in Mexico about the Texians' attachment to slavery. That almost all favored the institution and felt they needed slaves to work their plantations was not open to question. Their efforts for years to get around the national abolition law proved that. But this resolution could demonstrate to Mexican officials that they had no desire to make Texas a slave empire as was feared.

As evidence of the fact that Mexicans, not Texians, were the real target of the resolution, the resolution provided for its publication throughout the newspaper press of Mexico.[45]

Finally, they passed anew the petition for separation from Coahuila and the granting of separate statehood. That, above all, was the key to their session. Their constitution and other resolutions were pointless unless they got statehood. Indeed, some proposed that they not wait to hear from Congress, but that they proceed on their own to hold elections for governor and legislature and put a new state government in operation, either in the hope that Mexico City would take the line of least resistance and ratify a fait accompli, or else that they could defend themselves against any attempts to disperse them. Austin strenuously opposed such a move, since there was no sanction for it in the 1824 constitution, but mollified the radical delegates by proposing that if their application for statehood should be rejected or ignored, then they ought to go ahead. Whatever his reservations about the wisdom of the long list of requests and demands that came out of the convention hall, Austin at least felt secure that they were doing the right thing on statehood. He had sometime since come to accept that it was the only hope for the province's future. "Texas must have a state Government," he told a kinsman a few days after the convention adjourned on April 13. "Nothing else will quiet this country or give any security to persons or property."[46] And saddened though he was at how Texas had gotten away from him in the past year, he could not, under the present circumstances in Mexico, see how it could have been avoided. "No one can be blamed in any manner for what has happened since June 1832, in Texas," he soon told an acquaintance. "It was inevitable."[47]

The last act of the convention before its adjournment was the selection of Austin, Seguín, and Dr. James B. Miller, as a commission to take their resolutions and petition for statehood to Mexico City. Austin had no choice but to go, and yet felt optimism that the new regime in power would look favorably upon statehood.[48] He also probably felt it augured well that Seguín was one of the commissioners, since it would indicate *tejano* support. However, Seguín had not been a delegate to the convention, though this time San Antonio had sent a delegation. Austin's first stop on the road south was Béxar, where he called on Seguín to notify him of his appointment and show him the petition and resolutions they were to present. Meanwhile citizens held public meetings to discuss the documents brought by Austin, and they revealed a varying agendum from that of the convention.

Thanks to the influence of Veramendi, and aided in person no little by Bowie before the frontiersman left to serve in the convention, the interim governor had managed to persuade the legislature to approve moving the capital from Saltillo to Monclova.[49] Bowie's primary interest in the move was to put those with power to grant large tracts of land for speculation in a more congenial political climate for speculators like himself, and Monclova certainly offered that. Indeed, Austin was already wary of "such men [as] Bowie etc." and even now warned friends not to get too closely involved with him.[50] But having seen the one move, the *tejanos* in Béxar now decided that the capital could be moved again, and should be relocated to their own community. If that were done, then they could safely remain linked with Coahuila, since the axis of power would have shifted into their orbit. If it were not done, then they would favor separation, but still they protested that this recent convention, like the last one, had been unlawful, and under the 1824 constitution only a legislature—not a rump convention—could petition congress. Seguín was the only one who spoke out in support of the convention's petition for separate statehood now.

But then the citizens bogged down on the technicalities of just how and by whom any petition could be sent to Congress, and in the end they did nothing, which may have been their subconscious intent all along. The best Austin could conclude was that if Béxar would not step forward in support of the convention's petitions, then at least the *tejanos* would not actively oppose it either. "The people here agree in *substance* with the rest of Texas," he concluded, "but differ as to the manner, and will express no opinion for, nor against."[51] The *tejano* statesman Seguín then told Austin that his "private affairs" made it impossible for him to accompany him to Mexico City, and at least so far as the public was concerned, Austin chose to accept the excuse at face value. But he did not disguise the realization that the eruptions of the previous summer, when headstrong Texians had threatened to embroil the whole province in insurrection regardless of the sentiments of the *béxareños,* had cost the Anglos support. "It has neutralized many who before that were openly warm friends," he wrote after the close of the public meetings, "and it has made some decided enemies to the colonists."[52]

Dr. Miller also would not be going. A dangerous cholera epidemic had broken out in Texas and in Coahuila as well, and already people were dying. He decided that it was his duty to remain behind to treat the sick. In any case, the hope of the commission always rested on Austin himself and the degree of prestige and good will that he enjoyed among leading officials in Mexico City. Thus, he had no choice but to go on by himself. When he reached Matamoras on the Rio Grande, he found that rumors of the actions of the convention had become so exaggerated that it was believed locally that Texas had declared its independence from Mexico and was raising an army of revolution. Even as he tried to dispel such talk, he must have realized that the rumors would have spread farther south. Indeed, he also learned that Santa Anna himself was believed to be outraged at the colonial uprisings at Anahuac and elsewhere, thinking that they had forfeited whatever sympathy they were entitled to by being "so headlong and passionate" to obtain redress that they only made their situation worse by alienating sympathy in Mexico. "They put weapons in the hands of their enemies, and injured and mortified their friends," Austin was told. Now to hear talk that there were "American Generals in Texas"—perhaps meaning Houston—trying to incite unrest against Mexico "and that the common talk is about independence, fighting, and abuse of the Mexicans" was worrying in the extreme, or should have been. People even told Austin that he could not expect to be cordially welcomed by Santa Anna, though he refused to believe that he would be "roughly received" by the new president.[53]

On June 1, 1833, Austin set sail for Vera Cruz on the next leg of his journey to Mexico City. Within six months he would be under arrest.

CHAPTER FIVE

"Confusion Doubly Confounded"

⟨∾∾∾⟩

OF ONE THING ALMOST all the Texian colonists were certain, and that was that in 1833 Mexico was a mess, and given what its people had endured for the past several years, it was no wonder. Independence from Spain had not brought the relief that so many in that wonderful but ill-starred land expected, but rather just a brief respite before the years of unrest and revolt continued, sometimes even following the same names and faces. From the time Iturbide successfully drove the Spaniards out in 1821, Mexican leaders faced a set of challenges that many simply had not anticipated. Now that they were independent, what should they be—republic or monarchy? Should they establish a confederation like their neighbor to the north, granting significant sovereignty to the constituent states and reserving power to the central government only for issues too broad to be left to states to handle individually, such as national defense, trade, and commerce? Or should Mexico face up to the fact that it had too little tradition of local government and autonomy, and too large a population accustomed only to authoritarian rule, and decide in favor of a centralization of power to decide things for people unused to deciding for themselves? How were they to form the *ricos* and the *pobres*, the *creoles* and the *mestizos* and Indians, into a single body politic, or should they? Mexico lay shattered after constant internal revolt since 1810, and the only real source of power at the moment centered in the armies, each chiefly loyal to its still-royalist officers. No one even knew the exact boundaries of the nation—if it could be so called. At the north there was still disagreement over the extent of Texas in spite of the Adams–Onís Treaty, a debate that would continue until 1841. At the other end, for two years Central America had considered itself a part of Mexico, but then in 1823 left on its own again.

Given its history, geographical extent and ambiguity, lack of social homogenization, and now near destitution, any hope of Mexico stabilizing was tragically slim. At first the line of least resistance seemed to be a local monarchy under Iturbide, but that lasted less than a year and only made the internal divisions wider. The rebellion of Santa Anna and others in the name of granting more autonomy to the wide-flung provinces was only a recognition of what the peoples in the provinces themselves were saying when they resisted the laws and levies coming from Mexico City. That same year four of the provinces went into open rebellion with sovereign declarations, expressing willingness, if necessary, to defy even the armies. No wonder, then, that when delegates went to Mexico City to try to frame a new constitution, it was a foregone conclusion from the start that it would have to recognize and grant greater autonomy to the provinces in the form of statehood, with their own governors and legislatures. What emerged was a constitution, like that of the United States of America, with sovereignty shared so as to allow the states to handle their own domestic affairs but leaving the new president and congress in Mexico City with enough authority to provide for defense.

The histories of the United States and Central and South America frequently seem to have run in parallel, both beginning their recorded historical lives as colonial conquests, then passing from colonial to revolutionary stage, and onward into independent national phases with varying degrees of constitutional democratic aspirations, and success. Yet Mexico, Brazil, Argentina, and most of the rest walked a very fine line between revolutionary success and administrative chaos. Even the relatively enlightened 1824 Mexican constitution was doomed to a rocky career, and one that made it a talisman for the disaffected elements in Texas and elsewhere after 1830. Meanwhile, the ever-present threat from Spain, which refused to recognize Mexican independence and posed a constant threat of invasion, meant that far too much of the new government's time and all-too-scarce revenue had to be occupied in fielding and maintaining a large military, at the same time virtually guaranteeing that the army and its commanders would remain the same sort of semi-independent power base that they had been in the old regime. It was just such a threat that kept Santa Anna at the forefront, especially after he helped defeat the ill-fated 1829 Spanish landing at Tampico. A popular hero, perceived as a champion of the people, at the head of an army in a poor and unstable emerging nation, will always be a threat to the longevity of republicanism.

More than a decade of war had exacerbated social divisions, encouraged a tradition of resistance to authority in the more distant provinces-cum-states, given rise to a culture of partisan warfare in the more remote areas, and thoroughly entrenched the army as the dominant influence in society. Even on the streets of Mexico City itself there was little law and order, with banditry so commonplace that most men did not go unarmed. The lack of money and the magnetism of the army that siphoned so much of what there was away from domestic needs meant that even as late as 1833 the damage from the 1810–1821 revolution had not been repaired. Burned villages were still in ruins, roads unrepaired, and the bones of men and animals often still lay where they fell years before. Abandoned houses littered the cities and villages, and many fields had gone untilled for years. Instead of the tranquility that any such state needed to get over the shock of revolution and begin to establish new traditions of domestic harmony and the beginnings of stable social and civic institutions, Mexico only got more unrest to exaggerate its problems under the successive regimes of Guadalupe Victoria, Guerrero, and Bustamente. All of it made the eventual military strong-man rule of a Santa Anna the more likely, even welcome.[1]

Too often caricatured and even more often underestimated, Santa Anna was a remarkable man, noteworthy alike for his great attributes and his equally imposing shortcomings. By 1833 he was just approaching the pinnacle of his career, and for all that this and future generations of Mexicans would love and fear him, the fact that he would hold the presidency no fewer than eleven times in his lifetime reveals just how essential he would become to the identity of the new Mexico in the middle of the nineteenth century. Born Antonio López de Santa Anna Pérez de Lebrón in 1794, he was a native of Jalapa, Vera Cruz, and came from a respectable *creole* family. At the age of sixteen he became a cadet in the local infantry regiment, and almost immediately grew to his majority involved in the intermittent skirmishing of the revolution throughout the massive northern part of Mexico extending as far as California, and including Texas, where he participated in the operations that put down the Gutiérrez-Magee insurgency at the Battle of Medina. As a result, he also witnessed the wide-scale executions of the captured filibusters, and then returned to northern Mexico again to take part in the defeat of Mina in 1817. By 1821 he was a brevet, or honorary lieutenant colonel, aged only twenty-seven, and still, like most Spanish-blooded officers, loyal to the royalist cause.

Then in 1821 Santa Anna suddenly changed allegiance. For him, as for so many others, it was Iturbide's February 24 Plan of Iguala that turned his loyalty. Iturbide had himself switched sides and joined with the insurgents he was supposed to put down, to declare at Iguala that Mexico should be independent, with religious freedom, and national unification under a constitutional monarchy. The Plan spoke to all constituencies except the *mestizos* and Indians, and above all it promised stability with a minimum of governmental change, goals ever popular with military men in times of upheaval. Santa Anna was only one of scores of influential young officers who crossed the line, among them Bustamente and Vicente Filisola. The Plan protected the interests of their class while promising benefits that a weakened Spain no longer could, and thus the change of allegiance was very much a cold-blooded decision out of self-interest. That Iturbide was opposed to the Spanish royalists did not mean that his followers were necessarily republicans, as evidenced by the constitutional monarchy that followed, though Santa Anna's leading role in the overthrow of Iturbide in 1822–1823 helped his republican image. In December 1822 Santa Anna issued his own Plan of Casa Mata, declaring that centralism had failed and implying that power needed to be returned to the provinces via a republican federation. He had become one of the *caudillos*, powerful men, backed by military force, who entertained political ambitions for themselves and their country.

His youth, his demonstrated bravery—he would be wounded in action several times in his life—and his dignified and attractive personal demeanor made Santa Anna, now a general, a natural magnet for loyalty. He was no democrat. In 1828, when a centralist won the presidency, Santa Anna and others rose in rebellion once more, and after some months of civic rioting and skirmishing between rival military factions, the lawful government in Mexico City gave up and allowed the installation of Guerrero as president, setting the precedent of the military overturning a lawful election. When Santa Anna, not Guerrero, played a leading role in the defeat of the Spanish invasion at Tampico, the general only became even more a hero to Mexicans, having presumably saved their republic. The president, meanwhile, forced to ever-greater tax measures to combat the nation's debt, even to the confiscation of church property, grew ever more unpopular until he was overthrown by his own vice president, the centralist Bustamente. And then commenced the policy that led to the Law of April 6, 1830.

Santa Anna did not participate in the Bustamente revolt, remaining at least nominally loyal to Guerrero. Few but his closest associates ever really understood the general's underlying bedrock principles. Seen chiefly as an opportunist who at one time or another would be liberal, conservative, autocrat, and democrat, he undoubtedly served whatever cause best promised to protect his own interests—chiefly his social class and the military. That made him a *caudillo,* but it also brought with it an obligation to defend the people of his region—Vera Cruz for Santa Anna—from threats to their prosperity, peace, and domestic tranquility, and to encourage their agriculture and industry. The Bustamente regime, more than any since Iturbide, posed a danger to all of those things, and Santa Anna and others like him saw the best hope of reform in local autonomy and a weak president and federal republic.[2]

Nevertheless, he also followed in the tradition of many who came before him, from Caesar to Napoleon, military men who emerged in a context of chaos and disintegration and saw no hope for their nation except in the imposition of order and stability as essential first steps toward internal harmony and prosperity as a nation. His goals were his own rise and fortune to be sure, but he was also unquestionably motivated by the dream of a stable, unified, strong, and independent Mexico. Unlike Bolívar and San Martín and O'Higgins and Washington, he had to try to achieve that dream on a geo-ethnic-political field of a scale greater than that confronted by anyone before him in Western culture since the days of Alexander the Great.[3]

Thus, and not surprisingly, when Bustamente's increasingly repressive policies aroused first protest, and then outright resistance in several states, including Zacatecas, Jalisco, and Tamaulipas, as well as Texas, the stability of the country again stood under threat. Santa Anna rose in resistance once more in 1832, organized his troops at Vera Cruz for a campaign, and then conducted a largely guerrilla campaign to wear down the government troops sent against him. When similar uprisings took place elsewhere throughout the country, Bustamente had no choice but to give up and hand over the government in December. The next month, Santa Anna entered Mexico City with Manuel Gómez Pedraza, who would serve out the weeks remaining in Bustamente's presidential term, though Santa Anna himself was now surely the power behind the office. With a new presidential election scheduled for March 1, 1833, the outcome was in little doubt. The legislatures of the several states did the voting, and Santa Anna emerged as the victor, along with vice president Valentín Gómez Farías, who felt a considerably greater ideological commitment to federalism than his more opportunistic companion in victory.

This last proved to be of decisive importance, for no sooner did Santa Anna take office than he left Mexico City and returned to Vera Cruz complaining of ill health and the need for recuperation. He did this repeatedly during his life, suddenly abandoning important duties at often critical times to go home, so often that his genuinely mercurial health cannot have been the sole reason. He was a man who rose to his best in crisis. Whether in building an army, planning a campaign, or leaping into a political fray, he showed dynamic leadership and resourcefulness in organization, sometimes achieving wonders. But once a campaign was under way, or a political objective achieved, he became detached, inattentive, lethargic even, as if his interest wandered once the initial crisis had been overcome. Then too, he was a pragmatic politician, and knew that in this ambiguous mass of shifting allegiances that was Mexico, the wise statesman tended his home fences regularly, and so he spent much time in Vera Cruz stabilizing and strengthening his home base. He also knew that there was need for reform in the army, some of it that would be very unpopular among the officer corps, and by going home he would be leaving Farías to run the government, and therefore to take the brunt of army resentment. Santa Anna was nothing if not a man who knew how to stay on the right side of his essential constituencies.[4]

Not surprisingly, Farías's administration soon became a lightning rod for complaint, not the least of it from Santa Anna himself. The government ejected centralists from hundreds of official positions at the national and state levels, replacing them with federalists. In an attack on the remaining vestiges of royalist power, they nationalized some of the large estates of the old *peninsulares* and actually debated a bill to banish all Spanish-born citizens. In an assault on one of the two main pillars of the old order, Farías and the congress introduced reforms to make the formerly untouchable clergy liable for prosecution in civil courts. They took control of schools away from the church and turned it over to civil authorities, and then substantially weakened the unilateral authority of the church even in clerical matters. Farías also sought to compromise the independence of army commanders in their districts by making their actions subject to approval by the state authorities. He also tried to reduce the actual size of the standing army, recognizing that fifty thousand men under arms always posed a threat to regime stability.[5]

All of this aroused indignation and soon forced men of the cloth and the sword into a partnership of expedience in opposition to a government they believed had spun out of control, finally forcing the president to return to Mexico City. He had allowed Farías to experiment to see how far he could go in army reform before alienating the officers, and having seen the limits of the acceptable, Santa Anna could now emerge as the army's savior by himself intervening to stop them. That done, he went back to his *rancho* and once again let Farías continue on the reform path, this time with an explosive proposition to give the government the power to grant priesthoods, thus interposing civil authority between the Catholic church in Mexico and papal authority in Rome. But soon, in response to pleas from a coalition of church, army, and landed aristocrats, he would again come back to the capital and again stop Farias's plans.

Santa Anna had had an epiphany. Or perhaps he was just acting out the last phase of a very carefully calculated and predetermined plan. In October, when he had finished putting down the outbreaks of resistance in some of the states that refused to acquiesce, he entered Mexico City. In one stroke he had cemented his base with church, army, and elite, and now he ruled alone, almost begged to install a centralist regime by all of the major players in Mexican politics. Santa Anna still believed in the wisdom of a federal system. No fool, he recognized that a territory as vast, undeveloped, unpopulated in places, and of such diverse ethnic and economic makeup simply could not prosper under a heavy central hand. But at this time the absence of such a hand risked handing the states over to anarchy. Before long he would banish several radicals from the country, and in time would lock congress out of its chambers, dissolve it and declare its enactments null, dissolve most of the state legislatures, and all but abrogate the Constitution of 1824. He issued a call for elections for a new congress and announced the need for major revision of the constitution.[6]

In the middle of all this, Stephen Austin had arrived in Mexico City on July 18. He could not have come at a worse moment. At a time when several states forcibly resisted the new regime, Austin came as the emissary of a distant province that had spent the previous summer defying the national authority and generating rumors—however untrue—of a design for revolution. At a time when the military in Mexico reasserted itself after a period of serious threat to its power and prestige, Austin came as the ambassador of a province that had challenged, fired upon, captured, and expelled lawfully assigned garrisons in the act of carrying out their orders. With the church bouncing back from the blows to its spiritual hegemony in Mexico, Austin represented colonists who had never honored their Catholic obligations. In an atmosphere in which the prevailing cry was for centralism, the Texian brought resolutions from a province that agitated for ever greater relaxation of central authority in favor of local determination. And while several of the existing state legislatures even then sent local militia into skirmishes with national troops in resistance to the forces of order, here came Texas, with a year of recalcitrance behind it, demanding independent statehood after not one but two illegal conventions.

Austin arrived in the last months of Farías's latest incumbency. At first he met a cordial reception, and felt encouraged for reform of the Law of April 6 and favorable action on the petition for statehood. But within days it all began to go wrong. He fell prey to a cholera epidemic then sweeping Mexico, one in which the whole Veramendi family, including Bowie's wife, would die. Austin recovered, but the epidemic forced Congress to adjourn, and by early October still no action had been taken on his petitions. He was fed up with the Mexican government and its constant state of revolution. "I have had much more respect for them than they deserve," he complained on October 2.[7] Word reached him—and therefore must have reached Mexican ears, too—that back in Texas some of the Anglos were determined not to wait longer, but to hold yet a third illegal convention and go ahead and declare themselves to be a new state. It would cause untold trouble, he knew, and to circumvent that, he tried to enlist the *tejanos* in lighting a backfire.[8] That same October 2 he wrote to the San Antonio *ayuntamiento* suggesting that, as he expected no satisfaction in Mexico City, the time had come for them to correspond with the other *ayuntamientos* about organizing a state government on their own. His expectation was that such a movement would cut the ground from beneath the feet of the radicals. Ignoring the obligatory closing sentiment of "God and Liberty," he ended his letter instead with *"Dios y Tejas"*—God and Texas.[9]

Though he would later try to talk his way around it, there is no disguising the fact that Austin's letter could be construed as inciting violation of the constitution and defiance of the powers of president and congress. It was not a call for revolution or for independence from Mexico, but no one then functioning in the halls of power in the capital could fail to fear the possible result. With bona fide states actually in insurrection already and undergoing pacification, the prospect of an upstart new state creating itself extralegally, especially one populated by non-Mexicans who had shown themselves repeatedly to be resentful, querulous, and headstrong, raised dire fears. Too many times a revolt started in one state or province had spread itself to others, and those northern states had in the past shown themselves to be susceptible to disorder and difficult to control. Even after congress finally repealed the ban on immigration from the United States a few days later, the increasingly belligerent tone he took in his meetings with Farías did not help. Sometime in the third week of October he told the vice president that if the government did not make Texas a state, then she would do it on her own, and Farías reacted with outrage. The hint was implicit. If Mexico would not make Texas a state, the United States of America would, and Austin himself now acknowledged that such was his thinking.[10]

Santa Anna arrived in the capital a few days later, and Austin had two interviews with him and various gathered generals, congressmen, and cabinet officials, one meeting lasting for three hours. He came intending to make one last appeal for statehood.[11] For a change, he found the meetings encouraging as Santa Anna listened politely. "He speaks very friendly about Texas," Austin said of the president. He told the president of his firm objection to a rumored plan to reduce Texas's status from semistatehood in tandem with Coahuila to mere territorial status as with the territories in the United States, a status that would hand virtually all power over Texas affairs—including its public lands—to the central government. Santa Anna apparently favored such an idea, but Austin persuaded himself that he had convinced the president otherwise, and that "Texas matters are all right." If Texians would just stay calm and quiet they would soon be granted what they asked.[12] Others at the long meeting, however, believed that Austin lost every point.[13] Thus concluding that he could do no more, but that the attitude of the president and the actions of the Congress thus far indicated a favorable outcome in time, Austin left Mexico City on December 10, bound for home. He got as far as Saltillo when, on January 3, 1834, the military officer in command there arrested him.[14]

Austin's October 2 letter was the immediate cause. Not only did the *ayuntamiento* of Béxar find his suggestion inflammatory and unlawful, but in rejecting it the *tejano* leaders also sent it to officials in Coahuila, where street rumors soon said that Austin had preached treason and would be apprehended. Worse, word also filtered up to Monclova of Austin's implied threat to Farías, and soon the impression was abroad that the *empresario* hoped to capitalize on Mexico's distracted and chaotic situation to make Texas a state. The idea that their government was so weak that it could be bluffed into submission by Texas was insulting. The suggestion of doing so was treason. Word of Austin's actions reached Mexico City only after he left, but Santa Anna lost no time in ordering his arrest as soon as he could be apprehended.[15]

He had finally had enough of Texas. Like many another of his class, Santa Anna had a decent Western education and, like everyone else among the *ricos*, he knew that when the Roman Empire fell, the rot began not at its center, but in a far-flung outpost almost exactly the same distance from Rome as Texas was from Mexico City. Whether Austin was genuinely trying to foment insurrection or not hardly mattered. Any threat to the central authority in Texas could be a threat to the stability of the nation, and it had to be met and quashed quickly and definitively. Santa Anna had gone back home by the time Austin was arrested, and Farías was once more in charge. Before long Austin would be placed in a cell once used by the Inquisition, and at first kept in close confinement, though he would be neither tortured nor mistreated.[16] It was to be his home for virtually all of 1834.

Austin feared the reaction in Texas to his arrest. Indeed, almost as soon as he could, he began to send back from his incarceration letters urging calm and restraint. "The people must keep quiet, obey the state authorities and law, harmonise fully with Bexar and Goliad and with the Mexican population," he counseled, and "discountenance all violent men or measures and speak to the govt. through the legal channels, that is the ayuntamientos."[17] His meaning was clear. Hold no more illegal conventions that could only further arouse Mexican ire against them. Try to build unity by cooperation with the *tejano*-run councils in Béxar and Goliad. Stop agitating. Now was not the time to press an already irritated and volatile regime.

The reaction in Texas was something different. Though Texians had just received the news of the repeal of the anti-immigration law on January 13, 1834, which Travis called "joyous intelligence!", the news of Austin's arrest hit hard.[18] Williamson expressed the disappointment and outrage of many, as well as their determination not to be cowed. "We still continue our unnatural connexion with Coahuila," he declared on April 28. They must go ahead and follow the course informally agreed upon at the last convention in the event that Mexico City refused to act on the petition for statehood. "Desertion by *us* then, of this *Our own cause, would be worse than political apostacy*," he chided the *ayuntamiento* of San Felipe. He suggested that San Felipe and the other municipalities draft memorials on statehood, and also petitioned the Congress for Austin's release, promising in return that Texians would remain loyal to the Constitution of 1824 and to the laws of the nation, pledging "their lives, their fortunes and their sacred honor" on their word. Even if its felicitous expression was hard to improve upon or equal, still he might have been wise to quote some document other than the Declaration of Independence.[19]

In fact, as the spring and summer of 1834 wore on, several of the *ayuntamientos* would do just as Williamson proposed, their memorials respectful, but still keeping alive the independent statehood issue. Meanwhile, and contrary to all of Austin's hopes, events were not quiet in Texas. In May the new federalist legislature in Monclova, urged along by subtle persuasion and bribery by Bowie and others who were on the scene, passed a law opening all public land in Coahuila y Texas for sale at auction. It was a triumph for the speculators. From the point of view of Mexico City, of course, that land did not belong to the state. Moreover, such a bargain sale, when linked with the recent repeal of the immigration ban, meant that tens of thousands of Anglos might soon flood the area.

Actions such as this led part of the military that same month to formally denounce the national and state governments alike, and this and the outcry among those threatened by the reforms was so great that it gave Santa Anna a virtual mandate to do as he wished, even to take the full power of government in his own hands to stave off civil war. Certainly he could point to the uproar created by the Farías reforms as evidence that Mexico was not yet ready for true republicanism and devolution of power to the states, which left no alternative but for him to assume full control. He could still pose as a dedicated republican—and perhaps he still was, to the extent that he ever committed himself fully to any ideology—who now had to redress the excesses of radicals. He once more returned to Mexico City to take charge as president, and even though he relaxed the severity of Austin's confinement, he ignored all matters of statehood and instead quickly began the concentration of power.[20]

There followed the very sort of chaotic chain of events that Austin and Santa Anna both feared. The federalist Monclova legislature passed measures condemning Santa Anna's action and issued a call for a special session to consult over what should be done. No one was yet saying revolution, at least not out loud, but there were several who called on the newly resurgent army to restore order by force. The men who formerly constituted the centralist legislature in Saltillo seized the opportunity to reconvene in a rump session, choose their own governor, and proclaim themselves the loyal government of the state, backed by the local military. In August, when the special session was to convene, the fear of assault by local military loyal to Santa Anna kept many members from taking their seats, and at that point centralist officers supported a coup. Commandant General Pedro Lemus, announcing that "the disturbances against the authorities in some of this state's towns have brought me to this city" to avoid civil war, proceeded to put the centralist governor from Saltillo in office and then referred the conflict between the two capitals and the two legislatures to the president.[21] Santa Anna actually found in favor of Monclova, suggesting that he still felt some republican sympathy, but at the same time he now decreed there would be an election for a new Congress in December 1834, and that the special session of the Monclova legislature should be put off until March 1835. The clear tide of centralism left little doubt about the complexion of the new congress to be elected or the likely fate of federalist state legislatures.

In Texas the *ayuntamiento* of San Felipe heard from Monclova dire warnings of a military overthrow of the state government and of the two

rival legislatures, with advice to recognize neither. Rather, they suggested that now was the time to go ahead and organize a separate state
government at Béxar. "Is not Texas as much entitled to a government?"
as Coahuila was to not one but two, they asked.[22] Faced with the chaos,
the new political chief in Béxar, Juan Seguín, son of Erasmo Seguín,
showed himself to be more radical as a republican than his father by
issuing a call in October for a new convention.[23] The *tejano* leadership
in Béxar had been changing in the past eighteen months, fed up at last
with the turmoil in Mexico. In December 1832 they had met to protest
the impediment to immigration, not so much because they wanted
more Anglos in Texas, as that they recognized that the Americans
brought money and enterprise that could benefit all. The ban on foreign
trade also kept them and their American neighbors from capitalizing on
the lucrative fur trade carried on by Anglo trappers at Taos and Santa Fé,
New Mexico, for Texas offered the easiest and most direct route to the
fur markets of New England and Europe.[24] These and other affronts,
especially the ejection of the Texas delegate from the legislature in
Saltillo in 1832, gave *tejanos* a "most justifiable cause to secede" from
Coahuila. The *tejano* leaders in Nacogdoches and Goliad framed similar
complaints early in 1833. "We have had enough," said Goliad in its
remonstrance.[25] Now came Santa Anna's apparent abandonment of the
federalist agenda. At last the *tejano* community was ready to unite—
even if uncomfortably—with the Anglos as they saw a mutual threat
from the march of centralism.

Through all this turmoil Texians became increasingly concerned
over Austin's long imprisonment. Between June and early September
they heard nothing directly from Austin, and indirectly only varying
rumors that he was in ill health or doing fine, soon to be released, or
even that he had escaped. "It is pretty certain that Austin has been
released," Travis wrote to his friend Burnet on September 12. It was
good news, though premature. Meanwhile, even in his absence Austin
was elected San Felipe's deputy to the state congress in Coahuila.[26]
Finally a letter from Austin reached Brazoria in mid-September. In it he
revealed himself to be still a prisoner though in good health and now
well treated, largely thanks to Santa Anna, of whom he continued to
express favorable sentiments. Indeed, he believed Santa Anna called for
a new congress in order to reform and reshape the 1824 Constitution,
which had been so badly battered in intervening years. "The President

Santana is friendly to Texas and to me," Austin asserted. "Of this I have no doubt." To his friends in Texas he counseled, as before: "Only proclaim with one unanimous voice *Fidelity to Mexico, opposition to violent men or measures,* and all will be peace, harmony and prosperity in Texas." But then he said something more, and showed a more realistic appraisal of the current political mood. "I hope the State question is totally *dead* and will so remain." Either he was writing for the eyes of jailors who surely read his mail, or else he was giving up on the original cause for his mission to Mexico City.[27]

Either way, it was not the tune Texian ears wanted to hear, especially as matters escalated north of the Nueces. Then in October came a rumor that Mexican *soldados* in Béxar might take action against Seguín for what the Mexican general in command in the state, Martín Perfecto de Cós, called the "scandalous" action of "an officer who would be better occupied in putting out the flames of revolution rather than fanning them."[28] In fact, that officer represented elements of all the parties in the Texian imbroglio. His blood was Spanish, his citizenship Mexican, his loyalties *tejano,* and his aspirations Texian. Few others in this uprising so fully reflected all of the conflicting issues of political, family, even racial ties.

Juan Nepomuceno Seguín was born into a family long resident in Texas, one soldier ancestor helping to found San Antonio more than a century before the uprising. No wonder that by 1834 the twenty-eight-year-old Seguín identified his first loyalty with the land that was his by birth and blood for generations. The civic rolls of Béxar showed his forefathers as aldermen and councilmen. By the time of his birth they were also prosperous farmers with substantial *ranchos* in the nearby countryside. His father, Erasmo Seguín, became known and respected throughout the province and even as far south as Mexico City as an influential civic leader. Beginning as postmaster of San Antonio, he first opposed revolutionaries who rose up for Mexican independence from Spain in 1810, but then later became involved with one of the filibustering expeditions that failed, survived charges of treason, and rose to become *alcalde* of San Antonio after independence was achieved in 1821, and in 1823 a member of the congress that met in Mexico City to frame a new constitution. It was he whom the governor sent in 1821 to communicate approval of Moses Austin's application for permission to bring American colonists to Texas.

Erasmo's son Juan thus grew up in a tradition of public service and independent thinking, and in a climate in which revolution was a fact of life. Moreover, it was natural that, just as American Southerners in the secession crisis of 1860–1861 would identify more personally with the states where they lived than with the idea of government from far-off Washington, so would Juan Seguín see his interests and loyalties most closely attached to his native Texas, and not to a Mexican congress or president a thousand miles away. As his father gradually lost confidence in the new government in Mexico City, so the son became more closely identified with dissident elements in Texas. When the first serious protests erupted in 1832, the twenty-five-year-old Juan Seguín was to be found among the ranks of those sympathetic with Travis and the other leaders. He had already become close to Veramendi, and through him with Bowie, which may have helped lead him into the land speculation that Bowie and others practiced even before they got into politics. It was almost exclusively an Anglo enterprise, and thus Seguín combined business interests with political sensibilities, cementing his sympathies with the colonists even more. In 1829 he won his first political office, *regidore*, or justice of the peace, when he was just twenty-three, and thereafter would be acting *alcalde* more than once. Four years later he became *alcalde* in his own right, and immediately thereafter became the temporary political chief of the entire administrative department of Béxar. Now that Santa Anna had finally come out apparently as a centralist, Seguín was forced to choose sides, and came over to those in favor of separation from Coahuila. The adherence of such an influential *tejano* to the statehood enterprise promised much for any future movement in that direction, or beyond.

Other radicals showed solidarity with Seguín. Henry Smith was now *alcalde* of San Felipe but seemed to spend most of his time elsewhere hoping to avoid confrontations. In his place, Travis, as secretary of the local *ayuntamiento*, held local affairs together. In the wake of the rumor of Cós possibly using troops to quell the convention movement, he declared frankly that "we are at a loss" and that "Texas is forever ruined unless the citizens make a manly, energetic effort to save themselves from anarchy and confusion." They now had virtually no legal government in Coahuila y Texas or in Mexico itself, he argued. "We are subject legally and constitutionally to no power on earth, save our *sovereign* selves. We are actually in a situation of revolution and discord, when it becomes the duty of every individual to protect himself." If they did not so act now, he warned Smith, law and order were dead in Texas. "Something *must* be done to save us from our inevitable fate," he warned, "and the sooner the better." Smith was the only Anglo in Texas holding the position of *alcalde*, Travis noted, and as such he must set the tone for other Americans to follow. "Let all party animosities drop," said Travis. "Let us march like a band of brothers to the same saving and vitally important point." They must have a convention, they must send a delegation that had *"absolute powers"* to "dispose of the destinies of the country," and whatever it decided, they must support its conclusions.[29]

It seemed to Smith, Travis, and others a wonderful chance for coalition with the *tejanos.* "Let us meet their advances," Travis told Smith on October 25. "It is all important to our success now and in future to have them with us. Now is the time to secure them & their influence in our favor." Unfortunately, there was still serious opposition to a convention, this time not from the *tejanos* but from some of the Anglo elements on the still-operating central committee of 1832, including Frank Johnson and William Jack, whose radicalism should have meant their support. They were suddenly cautious, however. Santa Anna had allowed some reforms the previous spring. Land was made more easily obtained and on good terms, and immigrants were coming from the United States again. Moreover, the Texas delegation in the legislature was expanded to three representatives, and two of the posts went to Americans, one being Austin himself. Authorities relaxed the prohibition on aliens engaging in foreign trade, instituted trial by jury, and even made Texas a bilingual entity by recognizing English as an official language, meaning that all legal and official papers were no longer obliged to be translated into Spanish. The number of *ayuntamientos* grew by four as new communities were chartered, thus encouraging a stronger number of authorized civic voices in state affairs, and with it the potential for a more powerful justification for local rule.[30]

Austin himself learned of these reforms that May and rejoiced. "Every evil complained of has been remedied," he told Oliver Jones in a letter on May 30. "This fully compensates me for all I have suffered." It was one more reason why the explosive statehood question could be dropped.[31] Anglos on the central committee agreed and felt it imprudent to risk going too far, especially with the threat of military force from Cós. Some thought that the committee should simply be ignored. "It has never done any good," complained Travis. The people should act through the *ayuntamientos* to call for the convention, he said, noting now that those bodies were, after all, the lawful authorities for civic action. But the opportunity to bind the *tejanos* to their cause should not be missed. Seguín and his people had "thrown themselves into our arms & upon our protection," Travis argued. It was a "golden opportunity."[32]

In fact, some communities elected delegates for a convention scheduled to meet November 15 in Béxar, but that is as far as the movement got. "Public opinion runs so high against any change that I doubt whether anything can be done towards an organization of Texas at this time," a disgusted Travis declared on November 1. "As long as people are prosperous they do not desire a change," he added, and he was right.[33] The central committee met and ruled against a convention, and so the delegates never gathered, and that was that. Instead, the committee published a declaration discountenancing the war of the legislatures in Coahuila and putting itself on record as accepting that the current state of affairs did not justify a violation of the 1824 constitution by an extralegal convention.[34]

EVER SINCE THE SUMMER of 1832 and the disturbances at Anahuac and Nacogdoches, a gap widened among those Texians pushing for statehood and action and those who were more conservative. Radicals like Travis, the Jack brothers, the Wharton brothers, John and William, Bowie, Johnson, Smith, and Williamson, had consistently aligned themselves in favor of an aggressive stance with Mexico and were largely bound as well by their desire for a more open land policy, not surprising since many of them were speculators like Bowie. By this time virtually all favored separation from Coahuila, and unilaterally if Mexico City did not allow it. A few privately talked about going further and striking for complete independence, but there was little open discussion of that as yet. They were young, largely bachelors, and ardently pro-slavery. Travis commented to Burnet on the number of new immigrants arriving on the Gulf coast of Texas, including a number of slaves, a topic of discord not only between Texians and Mexico, but even between men like Travis and Burnet, the former heartily in favor of expanding slavery within the province.[35] Often these recently arrived immigrants from the South came imbued with all the resentments against central authority that had so

recently swept across South Carolina and other slave states in the Nulli-
fication crisis of 1833. President Jackson threatened to use military force
to compel South Carolina to comply with anathemathetic tariff legislation, though the crisis calmed short of violence. These men did not leave
one system they regarded as tyrannical just to live under another. Frank
Johnson recalled that these men formed "a small party in Texas ready to
make the most of any occasion for friction with Mexico."[36]

A larger faction arrayed itself against them, composed of older men,
many of them from the Old Three Hundred, with families and deeper
roots in Texas, and a better understanding of—and respect for—their fellow Mexicans. Headed by Austin *in absentia,* and including Burnet,
Miller, and others whose names were not as well known (since they did
not stir unrest), their numbers were considerably greater. In all instances
they sought to quell open conflict with Mexico, especially outbreaks
like Anahuac, and now they openly opposed and condemned the agita-
tions of the more reckless. Some called them "tories" for their continuing loyalty to Mexico, and though much reviled, still they had been
strong enough to contain unrest at all but the most extreme provocations, just as now they succeeded in killing the convention movement.[37]

It was a great disappointment to the more aggressive Texian element,
though Austin would have been pleased at the sudden restraint being
shown. Ironically, now it was the *tejano* leaders who were ready to act,
not their Anglo counterparts. Recognizing that, disappointed radicals
accepted what they could not change and instead counseled quiet for the
time being. "Unless we are all united Texas can never sustain herself
alone," Travis told Smith, though he remained committed to separate
statehood if they could get it short of insurrection. "I am, however, for
Texas, right or wrong, and will never oppose anything for her benefit," he
declared, but the want of Anglo support now "would only be to make
confusion doubly confounded to attempt to do anything."[38] Smith did
not listen, not for the first time showing a temperament slow to come to
a decision and then inflexible in the face of changing circumstances. He
called a referendum on participating in the planned Béxar convention,
and of the few who bothered to vote, the majority rejected the idea.
William Jack wrote to the imprisoned Austin immediately afterward that
the rejection would kill Smith politically and end the statehood talk for
the time being.[39] Travis, meanwhile, counseled that "we must wait
patiently for the moving of the waters." In the end all would be well.

"The course of events will inevitably tend to the right point, and the people will understand their rights; yea, and assert them, too."[40] That immature young man who ran away from Alabama was growing up.

The sudden quietus on the statehood issue worked to Austin's benefit, for it helped to calm somewhat the fears about Texians in Mexico City. Santa Anna had returned to Vera Cruz again, leaving Farías once more in charge, and back in February he sent an agent, Colonel Juan Nepomuceno Almonte, on what was publicly announced as an inspection tour of Texas to survey the condition of the province and its people. His real orders, however, called for him to learn as much as he could about public sentiment and the plans of the Texian leadership, survey their potential military strength if they should revolt, advise the government on how best they could be defeated, and if possible to stymie their efforts while he was among them. Fortunately, what Almonte found on his arrival was the very same calm that so frustrated Travis and Smith. At the same time, however, he could not overlook the deep concern over Austin's imprisonment, or the explosive impact that any harm to Austin might have at home. Almonte recommended striking a balance. Releasing Austin too soon might be a show of irresolution or weakness, but his release in time would be a gesture of good faith, though perhaps it should not be done until after additional troops had been sent to strengthen the Texas garrisons. That way Mexico would be ready in case Austin's return should spark a renewal of colonists' intransigence. By July, however, as he completed his inspection tour, Almonte concluded that the *americanos* were sufficiently pacified now that there need be no obstacle to Austin's release.[41]

The quiet in Texas did the job, and on Christmas day the door to Austin's cell opened and he walked out on a bail bond, though still required to remain in the city until either trial or dismissal of the charges against him. By early February word of his release reached San Felipe. Indeed, Austin had written to Travis himself to say that he expected to be able to leave Mexico shortly, though unfortunately it would be well after the forthcoming election for the state governor and lieutenant governor, and for representatives to go to Mexico City for the new congress decreed by Santa Anna. Ironically, it would be the Texians' final effort at democratic participation within the decidedly undemocratic centralist regime of Santa Anna, and Austin would not be there to cast his own meaningless vote.[42]

It was just as well. Affairs could change quickly in Mexico. In January 1835 the new Congress convened, largely in the hands of centralists, and thoroughly infiltrated with friends of Santa Anna's from both the clergy and the military. Almost at once it attacked the Farías reforms. It started to raise a massive national army to be entrusted with taking over most of the role of the state militias in defense—and not incidentally to shift the loyalty of the bulk of men in uniform from their state capitals to Mexico City. The militias would be scaled down dramatically as unnecessary and as potential pockets of support for resistance to authority. The outcry from the states was immediate and predictable. Oaxaca, Zacatecas, and other states openly declared resistance to this repeal of their rights under the 1824 constitution. Guerrillas began to arm, and in Zacatecas the governor assembled the militia and began to fortify against attack. Santa Anna immediately took the field at the head of military forces that easily defeated the militia in May, and then he allowed his *soldados* to loot indiscriminately to teach the rebels a lesson. Then he visited several other cities just to demonstrate his power before he returned to Mexico City, intent this time on a major change.

Henceforward, he would rule on his own, and among his first actions was the repeal of many of the reforms that he and Farías between them had enacted. Federalism had failed. More and more Mexicans of prominence rejected it, and now Santa Anna himself gave up on it. It was plain to him that only a strong central government could maintain control and prevent the provincial unrest that seemed continually to be upsetting economic growth and political stability. Only central authority could preserve his own domination of the national course. He banished Farías, thus cleverly blaming the lieutenant governor for all the controversial reforms for which Santa Anna would gladly have taken the credit had they been popular, and then began the dismantling of Congress. That done, he commenced a program of evicting federalists from their positions throughout government, soon convened a new centralist congress, ordered the state legislatures to adjourn and disperse, and began preparations for a new constitution that within eighteen months simply declared the states no longer extant. There would be only departments under the central government, ruled directly by appointees from Mexico City. In a stroke it was the end of federalism and the dawn of dictatorship.[43]

This was all happening when Governor Augustín Viesca was

installed in Monclova as governor of Coahuila y Texas on April 14, 1835. A federalist who himself had much to do with the maneuver to move the capital from Saltillo, Viesca would mount a troubled chair. The centralists in Saltillo were on the point of insurrection over loss of control and the capital, and their pleas to Mexico City for support had become more and more strident even as Farías continued to ignore them. Viesca's first important act was to muster militia to send to Saltillo to put down any uprising, but the centralist Cós decided to interfere to the extent of quashing the militia order. Then Farías appeared in Monclova with the news of Santa Anna's takeover and his own banishment. When Zacatecas erupted in armed resistance, and as Santa Anna moved to put it down forcefully as an example to others, Cós planned to march on Monclova himself to enforce law and order in the growing confusion, not least because rumors warned him that Viesca and Farías might use their militia force to stage a counterrevolution. Rather than dissolving, the Monclova legislature simply voted on April 21 to remove to a new location soon, and Viesca ordered that it reconvene in Béxar the following month.

When Cós and his *soldados* arrived in front of Monclova, the militia confronted them outside the city, and among those present was Bowie, who had been back in the capital engineering land speculation advantages. He exerted himself to try to bring on a fight, and not surprisingly. As one of the more hawkish Texians, he was one of the leading heroes of the 1832 resistance, so naturally he would do the same now. More subtly, he could easily see that with the sudden and dramatic change in the political landscape, his land concessions from the legislature would henceforward be meaningless with Santa Anna's revocation of the legislature and its acts. The only hope for his personal fortunes now lay in an outright break with Mexico, either for Coahuila and Texas together, or Texas on its own. Viesca himself was determined to try to raise an insurrection in Texas in support of resistance to centralism, and if Bowie could get a fight started here first, it would go a long way toward lighting the match to ignite both provinces.[44]

Cós failed to take the bait and instead held his fire. Santa Anna had quickly put down the rebellion in Zacatecas, and there was no need for another "example" here. Instead, Cós withdrew his command, though he returned late in May to break up "designing and naturally turbulent foreigners" whom he heard were trying to rekindle the fires of resistance and revolution. On May 25, Cós confronted the town anew, but the fearful legislature had already adjourned and Viesca was even then camped outside town, to be joined by Bowie and others in the attempt to ride to Béxar to reconvene the government. Two weeks later, on June 8, they were all captured and Viesca sent to prison, though Bowie would escape to ride two hundred forty miles in ten days to reach the Lavaca to begin spreading the news of what had happened.

He had seen the *centralistas* seizing vessels at Matamoros and combining that with rumors that three thousand *soldados* were to be sent to garrison Texas, it was easy to conclude that the vessels were for their transport and supply. Clearly, Texas was going to be reoccupied by the army and ruled by a heavy hand from Mexico City.[45] Just a few weeks before, on his return to the capital, Santa Anna had visited Austin and reassured him of his good will toward Texas. Indeed, on April 14 he actually told Austin that he would like to visit Texas and take Austin with him after the current unrest was quelled. "He is very friendly to Texas," Austin wrote to Samuel Williams, "and it would be an advantage to that country if he would pay it a visit."[46]

Visit he would.

CHAPTER SIX

"We Shall Give Them Hell If They Come Here"

NACOGDOCHES WAS ALREADY in a ferment on July 20, 1835, when James Bowie spoke with a passing mail rider who told him something confidential. The courier had been carrying a package of sealed dispatches addressed to the Mexican consul at New Orleans, and left them at a house in San Augustine for another courier to take it on to its destination. The rider did not know the contents of the letters, apparently, but he could tell from their size and number that they must be important. San Augustine was just thirty miles east of Nacogdoches. A swift rider could be there in a few hours to intercept the package before it continued its journey. Bowie proposed the plan to a few townsmen and they agreed, whereupon he sent a friend galloping eastward to have friends there secure the packet and send it back to him. As soon as he had it in his hands, Bowie called a public meeting in the town square, and there he dramatically opened the package and read the letters. They contained accusations of treason against Texians, definitive word of an arrest order for Travis, and confidential information of a prospective military force coming to occupy Texas. Bowie made certain that the information soon circulated throughout the colonies. In the current mood, an attempted army occupation was all it would take to start a shooting war, and by now he and many others were ready to fight.[1]

It was not quite the sort of visit Austin expected when Santa Anna talked of coming north with him. In the event, Austin would not visit Texas with Santa Anna, but by July he was finally free to leave Mexico and begin what would be a long journey home via New Orleans. Ahead of him lay a province more confused than ever. If Bowie expected that his alarm would turn out the militias to come to the defense of the Monclova government in exile, he miscalculated. It produced some agitation, and a few *ayuntamientos* mobilized their militias, but Viesca's legislature had become so tainted in the eyes of many Texians by its relationship with Bowie and the other speculators that far too many now thought they were being asked not to defend a lawful government, but only the chance for Bowie and others to make fortunes in land speculations. "Wolf, wolf, condemnation, destruction, war, to arms, to arms!" one colonist accused them of crying, but he thought Bowie's real purpose was "to deceive many persons and make them believe that *an army is coming to destroy their property and annihilate their rights in Texas.*"[2]

Yet others waited to act even before Bowie's alarm, Travis one of the foremost. Ironically, the catalyst for him, as three years before, was Anahuac. With the repeal of the reforms, customs officials at the port of entry seized merchandise being imported by Texian merchants once again. "I am vexed," complained one victim, Robert Wilson. "We are determined not to stand it." He and others agreed to resist future confiscations at the risk of violence if necessary. "A few we can kill and that with a fine good will," he declared.[3] Wilson's plight aroused Travis as it did many others. He called the seizures "piracies and robbings," and "the oppressions of a govt. that seems determined to destroy, to smash & to ruin us." All around him in San Felipe he heard the same sentiments and vows to resist. Moreover, they saw in the Mexican newspapers that there were rumors of a plan by Santa Anna and his new congress to restrict or abolish citizenship for Texians, rumors that were partially true. "These are alarming circumstances," he told his friend Burnet. "We stand or fall now by ourselves."

What should they do? Was there any point in trying for another convention, when Santa Anna could dissolve congresses? "I have as much to lose by a revolution as most men in the country," pondered Travis. "Yet, I wish to know, for whom do I labor—whether for myself or a *plundering* robbing, autocratical, aristocratical jumbled up govt. which is in fact no govt. at all—one day a republic—one day a fanatical hep-

tarchy, the next a military despotism—then a mixture of the evil quali-
ties of all."[4] By early June the provocations from Anahuac proved simply
too much. On June 4, twenty men, including Travis, gathered at Harrisburg forty miles east of Anahuac, to decide what action to take. They
agreed to meet again in two days and march on the town and evict the
Mexican commandant Captain Antonio Tenorio, his men, and the customs officers.

Unexpectedly, in the following days they learned of Austin's final
discharge and of the arrest of Viesca and others fleeing Monclova. That
seemed to defuse the situation momentarily, and suddenly Travis
advised the others to be cautious. "Let us wait with patience, the issue
of things," he counseled on June 9. "The time will come when we shall
be called upon to act."[5] They did not have to wait long. The next day
there was an incident at Anahuac when a *soldado* shot a citizen and
Tenorio arrested two of Travis's plotters. Less than two weeks later the
Texians intercepted dispatches to Tenorio advising him to expect a substantial reinforcement from Mexico shortly. The next day the San Felipe
ayuntamiento met to debate what to do but adjourned in indecision.
Angrily, Travis and men of like mind met on their own that evening and
decided to form a militia and march on Anahuac.[6]

As the men made their way to their rendezvous at Lynch's Ferry,
about thirty miles opposite Anahuac on Galveston Bay, they got news of
Bowie's warning of Cós's breakup of the Monclova government, which
added urgency to their mission. They put a cannon tube on a makeshift
carriage, and on June 28 twenty or more men boarded a sloop with their
artillery and chose Travis as their commander. The next day they sailed
across the bay and as they approached fired a shot to get Tenorio's attention before they went ashore nearby. Unloading men and cannon that
afternoon, they immediately got a note from Tenorio asking their purpose, and Travis sent back a surrender demand. Tenorio, perhaps thinking that his reinforcements might be near, asked for a day to consider,
but Travis gave him one hour and then ordered an attack before even
that had expired. He led a dusk assault himself, guided by torchlights,
only to find when they reached the garrison barracks—where once
Travis himself had been a prisoner—that the Mexicans had abandoned
them and gone into the woods. The Texians followed and opened fire
with their cannon, but the Mexicans did not respond. Instead Tenorio
sent a note asking for terms.

The two men met at the water's edge, where Tenorio again asked for a delay, and Travis once more refused and then proceeded to dictate not only terms for this local incident, but to lay out a program for Texas itself. He told Tenorio that the Texians intended to release Viesca from imprisonment and seat him as governor with the Monclova legislature reconvened in San Felipe or some other secure location. That was a lot to assume for a man at the head of twenty men and a cannon on cart wheels. As for Tenorio, Travis gave him fifteen minutes to surrender, with the threat that if he did not the Texians would "put every man to the sword."

It was the second time in Texas troubles that the colonists had made such a threat, the first being Bowie back in 1832. Of course it was all rhetoric. The political, social, and cultural traditions of two centuries of American experience showed that wholesale butchery of the vanquished in battle lay far outside their ethics. Even in clashes with the Indians, the Americans may have inflicted awful carnage—on a very limited scale— but still men were usually allowed to throw down their arms and give up without fear of being murdered. In a fight with uniformed soldiers of another nation, Americans had never come even close to such a thing, and forced to the issue now, Travis would not have done it any more than Bowie would have three years before. But the threat in itself was a dangerous precedent to set, especially if Travis was aware of different traditions among the onetime Spaniard overlords of New Spain. They could and sometimes did perform such acts on rebels. Travis almost certainly never heard of José Gabriel Condorcanqui or of the fate met by his family and supporters, but if he had it would have been instructive. Mexican leaders were no longer Spaniards, perhaps, but from Santa Anna on down the ladder to Tenorio, they still shared the same colonial tradition and attitudes of their Iberian ancestors.

Fortunately, Tenorio did not test Travis's intentions, and quickly agreed to surrender. He handed over all weapons and public property and promised to take his garrison out of Texas. Travis actually took the Mexicans back to Harrisburg on his vessel to get them on their way; then proclaiming to one and all that he was for "*Victory or death,*" he awaited the public acclaim.[7] "This act has been done with the most patriotic motives," Travis told Smith as soon as he got home to San Felipe, "and I hope you and my fellow citizens will approve it, or excuse it."[8] It was the first hint that Travis realized that he could have gone too far for his fellow Texians, and if there were any question, the outcry that followed removed all doubt. Of support and praise there was precious little; of condemnation far too much. Travis and his little band had acted unilaterally, without consulting the other *ayuntamientos* or civic leaders, even among his own more militant compeers like John Wharton, and at a moment when Santa Anna's plans for Texas were as yet only rumored but not fully revealed. Now he found himself accused of trying to precipitate a revolution. "Travis is in a peck of troubles," observed one of the conservative men still hoping for accommodation. Calling attention to Travis's own domestic status, and to the fact that most of the other radicals like Bowie had similar backgrounds, another opponent warned Texians, "listen not to men who have no home, who have no family, who have nothing to lose in case of civil war."[9]

If anything, it was this Anahuac episode that finally brought the polarizations among Anglo Texians into the open. For some time now the growing undercurrent of disagreement within the Texian community over their proper course was becoming formalized in the appearance of "parties," not membership bodies with slates of candidates, but groups with defined views who increasingly brought their disagreements out in the open. Indeed, it was in speaking of Travis and Anahuac that James H. C. Miller, a Gonzales resident anxious to remain loyal to Mexico, declared on July 25 that with the public reaction to Travis's action, "all here is in a train for peace, [and] the war and speculating parties are entirely put down." Travis and others of his ilk ought to be arrested and dealt with by Texian authorities as a sign to Mexico of good faith. "Till they are dealt with," said Miller, "Texas will never be at quiet."[10]

Miller had finally given a name to them, if it was not already in common usage, and hereafter Travis, Bowie, Johnson, Houston, the Whartons and more would be known to their opponents as the "War Party," or "War Dogs" to some.[11] They never called themselves that; it was the epithet used by their political adversaries. As Miller's comment suggested, they were all tainted by the number of speculators like Bowie in their midst, men whose motives in supporting the Monclova government and opposing Mexican authority were at least suspect. There were perhaps all told no more than two dozen of them, and the speed and effectiveness with which their political foes quickly produced an overwhelming condemnation of Travis's actions showed that though their voices were strong, the War Party's influence was still weak.

Ironically, it was Travis himself who first publicly identified a name with his opponents, and it was perfectly logical coming from a War Dog. Commenting to his fellow War Party member Bowie at the end of the month on the outcry raised against them both, he noted that "the *peace-party*, as they style themselves, I believe are the strongest, and make much the most noise."[12] They were certainly more numerous than their War Party opponents, and at the moment at least carried more convincing credentials with the bulk of Texians and *tejanos* because they were not involved in the speculations and had in the main deeper roots in the colonies. The outcry about war frightened many like Anson Jones, a successful doctor in Brazoria making as much as $5,000 a year, who felt the anxiety that the propertied class always feels at change and disruption. Granting that a separation of Texas from Mexico seemed now almost inevitable, still he counseled his friends and others who would listen against war itself. Turning a deaf ear to the War Dogs, he refused all invitations to get involved in politics, but that did not keep him from being, as he put it, "an anxious observer of the political horizon." Like many another man who had taken his chance in coming to Texas and already found prosperity, he found revolution to be a word to stir more anxiety than incipient patriotism.[13]

In a near replay of 1832, Anahuac was followed almost immediately by a clash in Nacogdoches, and as in 1832 coincidence put Bowie at the head of events just after Travis. He reached Nacogdoches in mid-July following his escape from Matamoros, to find local militia forming in fear that the Mexican garrison would react to Anahuac by tightening its rein on the community. On July 13 about one hundred men mustered in the center of the village and elected Bowie their leader. They might logically have turned to their neighbor Houston, but he kept almost completely silent during the past year, absent much of the time, and pointedly stayed out of Texian politics without publicly jumping into either party. That left Bowie the logical choice for men of action.

Bowie immediately marched them to the Mexican armory where they broke in and armed themselves in spite of protests from local commander Peter Ellis Bean, who wound up fighting first for the royalists and later the republicans during the Mexican revolution. Bowie took his garrison by surprise, or else Bean felt himself too weak to resist Bowie's mob, but he did immediately notify his superiors that he suspected Bowie intended to incite a general rebellion. Nevertheless, Nacogdoches in the main reacted as San Felipe did to Anahuac; the people failed to rise to the bait.[14] Then a week later Bowie intercepted the Mexican dispatches threatening a military occupation. That changed things dramatically, and at once some of the Peace Party people in Nacogdoches began to make the difficult decision as to where lay their ultimate allegiances, with a distant foreign dictator or with their own kind on their own ground. One citizen wrote immediately thereafter that Bowie's revelation to the people of Nacogdoches "moved their deep wrath and indignation."[15] Almost overnight Nacogdoches began to turn a corner, but authorities still counseled caution. Nevertheless, to make sure of a peaceful northern border in case a fight with Mexicans should erupt on the south, the *alcalde* conceived a mission to make peace with the Comanche. Houston had returned home by this time, but despite his experience at dealing with Indians in Texas, the *alcalde* sent Bowie instead, perhaps to get him out of the way where he could not do anything more provocative.

Back in San Felipe the outcry so thrust Travis on the defensive that he published an open letter to Texians asking them to reserve their judgment until he put his narrative of the whole story before them. It was a vain hope, and at the end of the month he admitted to Bowie that San Felipe was badly divided and the Peace Party holding sway. "Unless we could be united, had we better not settle down and be quiet for a while," he asked. "God knows what we are to do! I am determined, for one, to go with my countrymen; 'right or wrong, sink or swim, live or die, survive of perish,' I am with them."[16] He still anticipated that his time would come. He had seen enough of Mexican politics and Santa Anna's shifts and changes not to expect that before long there would be another provocation like the Law of April 6, 1830, that could galvanize Texians into action. "Let us be firm and united in defending Texas to the last extremity," he advised Henry Smith. "In offensive war we can do nothing, in defensive everything."[17] He fully expected that in time the Mexicans would bring a war to Texas.

Even while he worked on his account of Anahuac, Travis tried to start a fire brake by writing directly to Ugartechea, pleading that his intentions at Anahuac had been pure and that he was no revolutionary. "I am extremely anxious to bring all our difficulties to a happy and peaceable termination," he pleaded, and then offered to help Ugartechea find a settlement, protesting even that he did not care what kind of government Mexico should impose so long as it protected the rights of person and property.[18] He was being disingenuous, of course, trying to forestall direct action against himself, and he failed, for even then the arrest order was on its way. In Matamoros Cós send out the directive on August 1, ordering that "the ungrateful and bad citizen W. B. Travis who headed the revolutionary party" must be apprehended, adding impatiently that "he ought to have been punished long since."[19] Travis had just finished his account of Anahuac—a self-serving document in which he protested that he acted as he did with the approval of local political authorities, and that "most men in this part of the country" applauded what he had done—when he learned of the order for his own arrest and that of others. He fled at once in company with Williamson and spent several days in hiding.

Behind him something startling happened. What Travis's intemperate actions could not do, the order for his arrest did. Peace Party men may not have liked Travis, but he was a Texian all the same. They had seen Austin imprisoned for a year and determined that no more of their countrymen would be political prisoners in a Mexican dungeon. That and the news that Santa Anna was going to send more *soldados* to Texas compelled them to do as Nacogdoches had done after Bowie read the captured dispatches. Rapidly, dramatically, they began to switch parties. San Felipe flatly refused to act on the arrest order and spent the next month defying orders from Cós and Ugartechea. "This military order," said Moseley Baker, one of those ordered arrested along with Travis, "may justly be regarded as the final success of the war party."[20]

As far away as New Orleans, these shifts in Texas politics were felt, and conclusions were being made. "It is impossible for Texas to remain long under the dominion of Mexico," said the New Orleans *Bee* in July. "The character of the Texonians, who are generally emigrants from the United States, is too essentially different from that of the Mexicans for them to remain long attached to the uncongenial laws and customs of Texas."[21] Austin reached New Orleans just days after that sentiment hit the press, and now he shared that same conclusion. Embittered by his imprisonment, disillusioned by what he now believed was the impossibility of there ever being a stable government in Mexico fit to govern Mexicans, let alone Americans, he was ready for the War Party. Texas must be "Americanized," he told a cousin. That was its only hope. Noting that even a gentle breeze could shake a peach off its branch, he asked "can it be supposed that the violent political convulsions of Mexico will not shake off Texas so soon as it is ripe enough to fall." He wanted a massive immigration from the United States, and quickly, to ripen the "peach." That done, Texas would not have to revolt under arms, for Mexico would see the inevitability of the province shifting nationalities. "The fact is, we must, and ought to become a part of the United States," said the empresario. Looking back on Santa Anna's promise to visit Texas soon, Austin now saw that the dictator may well have been playing with him, not mentioning that he might bring an army along for the visit. "We must rely on ourselves, and prepare for the worst," Austin advised. More to the point, he wanted all those new immigrants to bring their rifles with them when they came.[22] Perhaps not coincidentally, while still in New Orleans Austin bought three books on conquest, revolution, and the fall of empires.[23]

In several communities reaction to the arrest orders led to demands for another meeting to discuss their immediate future. This time, however, they did not speak of a convention. In July, in response to the uproar over Anahuac, the Peace Party people of Mina, at the northwestern tip of the Austin colony, suggested a convocation of delegates from all of Texas to assess their condition. Avoiding the use of the word convention got them around the prohibition against such bodies. It would be merely a meeting to talk, not to frame constitutions or memorials, and thus would not threaten the legal authority of the ayuntamientos. The Mina meeting never took place, but now on August 15 the men of Columbia, not far from Brazoria, issued a call for what they termed a "consultation." Supporters of the consultation movement remained purposely vague about what they expected. Some said it was merely consultative, to exchange views and then recommend measures to the ayuntamientos. Others maintained that it was, in effect, more than a convention, with power to make legislation and to decide the future of Texas within or without the shattered Mexican federation. Meanwhile, communities resurrected their committees of safety and correspondence, and suddenly Texas seemed alive with a spirit of resistance.[24]

In such an atmosphere, Travis no longer feared authorities acting on his arrest order, and he returned to San Felipe and revealed just how trimming his protestations to Ugartechea had been by immediately launching into renewed radical invective. "Huzza for Liberty, and the rights of man!" he exulted. "Texas is herself again." The Peace Party were all but disintegrated, "routed horse and foot," as he put it. "The Tories are dying a violent death." Their last gasp would come on September 12 when San Felipe held a meeting to decide what to do about delegates for the consultation. "I feel the triumph we have gained, and I glory in it," said Travis, but at the same time he warned that Texians must move swiftly, especially if Mexican *soldados* began to pour in from the south. "Let the towns be once garrisoned and we are slaves." The *ayuntamientos* must collect all the arms and ammunition they could find, and if Texians stood like men they would prevail. "If we are encroached upon, let us resist until our bodies & our property lie in one common ruin, ere we submit to tyranny." Valor must prevail. "And now let *Tories, submission men,* and Spanish invaders look out," he told Smith, promising that "we shall give them hell if they come here."[25]

It was an opportune time for Stephen Austin finally to return to Texas. On September 1 his ship approached Velasco at the mouth of the Brazos when the condition of things in Texas came vividly home to him. His vessel encountered a Mexican schooner trading fire with an American merchantman trying to evade the customs, and then a Texian-owned steamboat came out to assist the American ship. Thus, hostile gunfire heralded Austin's return to his home. There was no war yet, but it could not be far off. Inevitably, it must start as soon as Mexican reinforcements reached Texas, if not before. In his first public address to Texians in almost two years, the father of the turbulent colony acknowledged his disappointment that the peace and tranquility he had hoped to find on his return proved illusory. The fault lay entirely with Mexico and Santa Anna, he told them, for now the dictator gave them the stark choice of centralism. Texians would decide for themselves if they could accept that when they met in their consultation. "Texas needs peace and a local government," he declared. Could they remain peaceful when the Mexicans threatened their sacred rights of liberty and property?[26]

With Austin's arrival and his conversion to a consultation and resistance, some thought the War and Peace parties finally merged. "Now we meet on middle grounds," said his cousin Henry Austin. Frank Johnson and other War Dogs welcomed Austin to the cause, and when Austin arrived in San Felipe on the very day of the public meeting to decide on the consultation issue, the conference selected him its chairman. He threw his support to a consultation, and told men now that he advocated "no more doubts—no submission," and that "*I hope to see Texas forever free from Mexican domination of any kind.*"[27] Even as they conferred word came that Cós was arriving in Béxar with troops to reimpose Mexican authority. Their goal could only be to break up the settlements and subjugate the people, said Austin. A few days after the meeting he sent out a call to every *ayuntamiento* in the colony to send delegates to the consultation and vest them with full power to act "for the good of the country." Furthermore, they should raise their militia and enlist all the men possible, sending a full report of strength and numbers of men and arms to San Felipe.

Advised that Cós in Béxar was making a peremptory demand for the turnover of Travis and a list of other incendiaries, Austin saw no escape from the inevitable. "Conciliatory measures with Gen. Cos and the Military at Bexar, are hopeless," he warned. "War is our only resource. There is no other remedy but to defend our rights, ourselves, & our country, but by force of arms." To do that "we must unite."[28] Deeply torn by the condition of affairs, he wrote dejectedly but determinedly to a friend in Columbia. "War then is inevitable—It is impossible to avoid it," he said. "Now my friend tell me what we can do except to fight."[29]

Was war inevitable, even at this late date? Hypothetical history is pointless, and ultimately misleading, for with every suggested change from the known equation, all the other variables expand and the conclusions multiply exponentially. For years the Texians complained of poor government in Mexico City. Would better administration there have satisfied them? They wanted more regional and local autonomy. Would a state of Coahuila y Texas that functioned largely without interference from Santa Anna have satisfied them? Would even an independent Texas as a state in the so-called federation have answered their concerns and made them leave their rifles by their hearths? Would they have stayed peaceful—if complaining—if the Mexican military authority had not started threatening citizens like Travis? Judging from the past, the answer to all such questions would be "no," and the responsibility for that lay in the nature of the Texians themselves. For several years now, when Mexico acquiesced to their remonstrances about their rights, it produced only momentary calm. They came here with a cultural history of pushing for more and more and then taking it, and especially when dealing with indigenous peoples of color or alien nationality. By 1835 Texians had simply come to regard themselves as too different from Mexicans to coexist as a polity. Their interests, aspirations, society, religion, domestic institutions, and more were all too much at odds with those of Mexico, a conflict exacerbated by Mexico's seemingly congenital inability to govern even itself and its own people, let alone a distant province populated by men and women of another race and culture. If the dissonance did not come to a separation now, it would have in the near future just the same, and all the lenience and forbearance, all the gentle governance and sympathetic rule that Santa Anna might have shown had he chosen, would not have made a whit of difference to the outcome. The moment Spain opened itself to Moses Austin's dream of an Anglo colony west of the Sabine, there was going to be a rebellion someday. Now that day had come.

SOME MEN HESITANT about the wisdom of the militant stance, let alone any move toward independence, nonetheless felt great confidence in their prospects in any war. Lorenzo de Zavala, onetime leading federalist and office holder under Santa Anna, was now in exile in Texas and committed himself to its destiny. He knew Santa Anna better than any here, and he told Austin with confidence that the dictator was vulnerable. "Santa Anna can count on the support only of the priests and a few undependable rich men," he counseled on September 17. The army would not be enough to sustain him in the face of a general uprising in Mexico, and that could happen at any time. "The present attitude of Texas is his certain death," said Zavala. If he tried to invade, then "the rivers, forests, deserts, rifles, the scant sympathy the invading troops will find in the area, the ignorance of the language and above all American steadfastness will bring Santa Anna and his satellites to a quick end." In short, Zavala predicted, "Santa Anna fears Texas more than all the rest of the country because he instinctively fears that it will cause his overthrow."[30] Zavala's message was that there was really no reason to be alarmed or to fear Santa Anna at this time. He sought to calm excited feelings and counseled caution and restraint. However, such views, coming from a man once in Santa Anna's confidence, could also be understood as cause to bolster the determination of Austin and Texians to resist.

Within days the volunteers started to come forward, not as militia, but as regularly enlisted companies in service of Texas and not just their local *ayuntamiento*. A San Felipe company organized even as Austin sent out his call to Texians at large. In the face of the sudden escalation of the threat, Austin saw growing unanimity. "All are united and all are for War," he reported to the local committee of safety in San Felipe. At the same time he told them that in the coming hostilities he wanted no military command, but that he expected to fight as a common volunteer.[31] That was hardly likely, however. "All eyes are turned towards you," Travis told Austin on September 22. "Texas can be wielded by you & *you alone;* and her destiny is now completely in your hands." The people were ready for war, he said, and ready for the Father of Texas to lead them.[32] Within days others echoed more explicitly Travis's sentiments. Texians expected Austin to lead them against Cós when the time came, knowing that they needed his moral and symbolic cachet to bring unity and compel subordination.[33]

Austin coolly made a list of the challenges immediately before him. He and the consultation must frame some sort of government, even if only a provisional one in the emergency, leaving a more formal organization to less critical times. Before the consultation met on October 15 at San Felipe, he needed advisers now, and so he asked each *ayuntamiento* to send a man to form a Permanent Council. He must gather information rapidly from all over Texas in order to know what was happening and where, as well as how far and how fast to lead his people in response. Push too little and the Mexicans could gain the upper hand; push too hard and he still risked losing the wavering and uncertain elements.[34]

He need not have worried. By the third week of September, reports arrived of Mexican artillery landing at Copano Bay, one hundred twenty miles southwest of San Felipe, awaiting only the arrival of five hundred *soldados* under Cós to march on Austin's capital. In response, militia formed under the command of James W. Fannin Jr. intending to post themselves at the principal crossing of the Colorado River to retard or stop any such advance.[35] Austin sent a call to Warren D. C. Hall, ever-present in a Texas crisis, to raise a body of volunteers to come and help protect the consultation from attack so that its work might not be disrupted, and issued a similar plea to Nacogdoches.[36] The Columbia committee of safety actually suggested that every delegate going to the consultation ought to go "armed and equipped for battle," as they might have to defend themselves.[37] In several communities men met to pledge not only their lives and their rifles to the cause, but also parts of their fortunes to finance urgently needed munitions. Nacogdoches held a public meeting on September 21 at which men committed themselves for $4,001 and actually handed over $2,801 on the spot. Houston was there, paying $200 into the fund in the first overt act identifying himself with the war faction.[38]

Houston also helped muster militia, though ostensibly his purpose was protection of Nacogdoches from a supposed Indian threat from the north. Interestingly enough, and perhaps as further evidence that Houston still acted in some concert with expansionist dreamers in Washington, the Nacogdoches vigilance committee on which he sat sent a memorial to President Andrew Jackson hinting that the Mexicans might be about to lure Creek Indians from the north into a forced incursion into Texas. That would violate an international treaty between the United States and Mexico, and Houston and the rest of the committee implored the president to be ready to send troops to prevent such a violation.[39] The threat itself was an illusion. The goal almost certainly was to get United States troops located on the Texas border where, in the event of outright war between Texians and Mexico, it would be all but impossible to keep the Yankee regulars from becoming involved. In light of later events, it is also just possible that Houston wanted American soldiers there in case Texian forces were pushed to the Sabine in the days ahead.

The ultimate spark to set off the Texas Revolution came on September 25 in the form of a Mexican challenge sent by Ugartechea from Béxar to Gonzales. He had learned, or someone recalled, that four years earlier the Béxar garrison sent a small cannon to Gonzales for its defense in case of Indian attack. In the current situation, the Mexicans now demanded its immediate return. Some leaders in Gonzales believed this was only a pretext. Expecting that the Texians would not meekly turn over the cannon, Ugartechea or Cós could use a refusal as an excuse to attack the town and disperse its militia. The citizens held a town meeting the next day to determine their response, and while three men favored handing over the gun and avoiding a confrontation, the *alcalde*, backed by the majority, decided not to comply.[40] *Alcalde* Andrew Ponton tried to buy delay in his response. Most of the *ayuntamiento* were out of town, he protested. He believed that the cannon had been given to the town, not on loan but in perpetuity, for its protection. "The dangers which existed at the time we received this cannon still exist, and for the same purpose it is still needed here," he argued, though of course the

danger apprehended was from a far different source than in 1831. He
pleaded for time to learn more of the legality of the cannon's ownership,
and especially time to consult the political chief. Though he did
promise that he would hand over the gun once satisfied "after a mature
deliberation" that he ought to do so, he was clearly stalling.⁴¹ The day
before he sent his response to Ugartechea, he had already sent out a plea
to Mina, Gonzales's closest source of support, to send men to aid in
defense. He fully expected Ugartechea to send a force against them as
soon as the Mexicans received his answer. Situated as Gonzales was just
fifty miles east of San Antonio, and thus only two or three days' march
from the Mexican headquarters, it seemed very vulnerable.⁴²

The situation escalated rapidly by the hour. On September 27 the
alcalde of Béxar, Ángel Navarro, sent Gonzales a plea to hand over the
cannon before Ugartechea used force. The same day Ugartechea himself
sent another, peremptory, demand for surrender of the piece, and then
issued orders to Francisco de Castañeda to march on Gonzales with *soldados* and take the gun by whatever means necessary.⁴³ Two days later
Austin issued a proclamation about the growing emergency at Gonzales.
The refusal to surrender the cannon was but a defense of rights and
property, he argued, and the people of Gonzales acted purely in their
own defense. He predicted that Texians everywhere would fly to their
aid in an instant if they were assailed, and some companies of volunteers were already en route. Nevertheless, he reminded Texians at large
that they were all still on the defensive, and they ought to avoid making
any unprovoked attacks upon Mexican soldiers themselves unless to
defend themselves. If there was to be war, they must not be the aggressors, especially if anyone hoped for aid from the United States. Americans might rush to the aid of fellow Anglos attacked by a foreign enemy,
but if the Texians themselves started the shooting, they might be dismissed as mere hotheads undeserving of support.⁴⁴ Yet on the same day
that he sounded restrained in his public address, Austin wrote to Hall
that there was no longer an alternative to war.⁴⁵

Austin may have advised caution against precipitate action because
he had heard of a plan to stymie any Mexican movements in advance.
Cós himself landed at Copano on September 20 and was then reported
as being in Goliad on his way to Béxar with five hundred infantry. Philip
Dimmitt of Lavaca, a pugnacious volunteer leader, conceived a plan to
attack the Mexican column on its march and capture Cós, believing that

it would throw Santa Anna off his stride by taking his most trusted general and buy vital time for Texas to prepare for defense. It would also energize the remaining liberals in Mexico and be a morale blow to the centralists.[46] The possible benefits from such a coup—assuming it could be achieved—hardly offset the liabilities of a failure, and Austin refused to countenance the risk. Action would come soon enough, and the Mexicans could be expected to fire the first shots if the Texians only held their fire a little longer.

The same day of Austin's proclamation for caution, volunteers at Captain John W. Moore's farm on the Colorado received a messenger from Gonzales telling them that as many as three hundred Mexican *soldados* were expected to reach their community by nightfall. Men were mustering from the neighborhood as quickly as they could, but more were desperately needed. Families were packing their belongings on wagons and preparing to evacuate to avoid the anticipated outrages of looting. "What men we can muster will attack them tomorrow morning by way of annoyance," promised a member of the vigilance committee, and the Texians "will give the enemy a specimen of their skill in rifle shooting." But help must be immediately sent to them, he added, for "the frontiers are attacked."[47]

And so they were. Ugartechea sent Castañeda with one hundred mounted dragoons out of Béxar on September 27, and two days later the Mexican column reached the San Marcos River crossing just below Gonzales. That same evening Castañeda sent a demand for the release of the cannon. At the moment just eighteen armed men defended the town, among them George W. Davis, Almaron Dickinson, John Sowell, and Joseph D. Clements, who acted in the place of the absent *alcalde* Ponton. Clements returned the Mexican demand politely, saying he had not the power to act in the matter, but that Ponton would be back shortly. Meanwhile, the San Marcos ran too high for the dragoons to make a crossing safely, and the Texians prudently moored the ferry and all other boats on their side of the stream. It was agreed that the Mexican commander should wait until the next day to press his demand. The bluff of the "Old Eighteen," as they came to be called, bought valuable time. That evening Captain Robert M. Coleman arrived with thirty men from Mina, and then Captain Moore came in with another fifty, with additional arrivals expected momentarily.

The next morning Castañeda renewed his demand for the cannon, but also offered to negotiate the matter amicably if possible, since Ugartechea had advised him not to begin hostilities unnecessarily. Clements again protested that they needed to discuss the matter with Ugartechea himself, but failing that responded that "the only answer I can therefore give you is that I cannot now [and] will not deliver to you the cannon." The *ayuntamiento* stood behind him in that. "We are weak and few in numbers but will nevertheless contend for what we believe to be just." If Castañeda wanted the cannon, he must take it by force. Before long Texas lore credited Clements with coining the first defiant aphorism of the conflict, reshaping his reply to Castañeda into the simple words, "come and take it." Castañeda immediately reported this response to Ugartechea, adding that he felt quite certain the Texians were stalling for time while forces gathered to defend the cannon.[48] The next morning the Mexican commander received word that Texian numbers had swelled to about one hundred forty and that he was now outnumbered. He could never force his way across the San Marcos at the ford guarded by that many Texians, and so he tried to find an unguarded spot upstream.

Meanwhile, as yet unaware of the Mexicans' departure from the other side of the river, the Texians encountered for the first time in the face of the enemy the problems inherent in the independent, democratic, and strong-willed character of these volunteers. "We have as yet no head," Coleman observed. "Something will be done so soon as there is a commander in chief," he added, protesting that as it was "we are all captains and have our views." Coleman himself favored an immediate attack, but others thought differently.[49] The solution, in the best American volunteer fashion, was for the men themselves to elect their commander, an inevitable democratic expedient that, unfortunately, only guaranteed elevating a popular leader, but not necessarily a competent one. That night the policy of warfare by election began with the selection of Moore as colonel from a field that included Captains Coleman, Albert Martin, Edward Burleson, and Joseph W. E. Wallace. Even before then, however, Moore, Coleman, and Martin issued a joint appeal for reinforcements to aid them in repelling an attack. But they went beyond that, revealing that they anticipated being able to push aside or defeat Castañeda, for their goal was to augment their forces and march on Béxar itself to clear Texas entirely of Mexicans.[50]

Perhaps the little cannon added to their belligerence. On his arrival

Moore learned—if he did not know before—that the celebrated cannon, a modest gun tube of bronze or brass, reinforced at the breech to allow it to fire a six-pound iron ball, had been buried for safekeeping by locals on Castañeda's approach. Coleman immediately ordered it disinterred from George Davis's peach orchard, then took it to John Sowell's blacksmith shop where it was fixed securely on an axle and two wagon wheels. Sowell also forged several cannon balls, and then Coleman's adjutant, Captain James C. Neill, an actual veteran of the War of 1812, took over the gun and hastily assembled the first artillery company of the new insurgency, with Gonzales resident Almaron Dickinson directly in charge of the gun crew. Neill took them and the cannon to a nearby field and tried a practice round or two to make certain the piece worked.[51] It did, though with eighteen pieces of artillery at Béxar, some of them three times the size of the Gonzales cannon, the Texian "artillery" was not going to be much of a match.

On October 1, detecting the Mexican move upstream and fearing its intent, Moore moved his entire command, now swelled to perhaps one hundred sixty or more, across the ferry to follow Castañeda and, if possible, seize the initiative by a surprise attack. The Texians continued even after nightfall, covering about seven miles before they simply stumbled into Mexican outposts well past midnight. In a brief exchange of fire no one was hit, and then both sides settled down to await daylight, but dawn arrived shrouded in fog. The Texians tried to harass the Mexicans, who had taken cover on a wooded rise some distance away, but the poor visibility made effective fire impossible, and when Castañeda tried to dislodge them by sending some of his dragoons in a charge, the Texians themselves fell back to tree cover that effectively broke up the mounted attack.[52]

As they waited for the fog to lift, the commanders on each side agreed on a parley and met in the open between their lines. The discussion started rather amicably, Castañeda protesting that he did not come to fight but only to ask for the cannon. He was a federalist himself, he said, but Moore told him he was wearing the wrong uniform for that now, and if he really opposed the centralists then he and his command should join the Texians. That ended the discussion, and when Moore got back to his lines the Texians brought their little cannon forward and prepared to open fire, though for all the earlier practice with cast balls, they now loaded it with scrap iron, bits of chain, a broken iron kettle, and the like.[53] Earlier, while Neill and his men fretted over training with their little field piece, others determined that they needed one more hallmark of an army, their own flag. It seems to have been a spontaneous act, though certainly informed—if only subconsciously—by cultural recollections of the "Don't Tread on Me" and similar banners of their Revolutionary forebears. Responding much more to the immediate occasion before them than to any more general statement of purpose or ideals for disgruntled Texians at large, the Gonzales men found an apt expression. They asked local women to make a flag of white cotton to fly over the contested gun, and on it someone painted a silhouette of the cannon in its center, surrounded with defiant words loosely based on Clements's response to Castañeda's September 30 demand. As the little cannon burped out its first hostile fire toward the Mexicans on their hill, the ersatz banner proclaimed in hand lettering, COME AND TAKE IT! It would be the first rallying cry of the incipient revolution, though not its last.[54]

What followed was not much of a battle. After the first blast from their cannon, Moore led his men in a ragged charge on the Mexican position, but before they reached the foe's line, Castañeda mounted his men and ordered them to retreat to Béxar. He had orders to take the cannon, not to fight a battle. Even though his men were mounted, the Texians outnumbered him by sixty or more, not to mention the dreaded artillery, which did not even have time to get off a second shot. The Texians suffered no casualties at all, while the Mexicans lost perhaps two men killed, probably to the initial volley of American rifle and the shotgun blast from the cannon. It was an almost bloodless beginning to what would become a sanguinary little war.[55]

The news of the incident at Gonzales spread rapidly, and soon the inconsequential skirmish in which one side did not try to fight became a "battle," and better yet a Texian victory. The first word reached San Felipe on October 5 in an exaggerated report that had forty or more killed on each side. Few could still waver in the cause now. Even for those still undecided on the political questions before them, the fact that shots had been fired on Texian soil papered over such differences with a more immediate threat. "There are no peace-men, no parties here now," Austin declared that day. "All are war-men."[56] Noah Smithwick, who rushed to join at the news, recalled of those first volunteers that "some were for independence, some were for the Constitution of 1824;

and some were for anything, just so long [as] it was a row."[57] Volunteers flocked to Gonzales to be ready for the next move, whatever that should be. Back in San Felipe, men chafed in frustration that they had not been able to get there in time to be in the action. Only an attack of influenza kept Travis from being with the Gonzales volunteers. "Our frontier is attacked," he wrote a friend on October 3 when the news arrived, "& who says now that we shall not fight." It was time for differences to be put aside in the emergency. "Let us go at it heart & hand," he declared. "Stand up like men & we have nothing to fear."[58]

They could not know it, but that same day in faraway Mexico City Santa Anna finally issued the decree that dissolved all state legislatures and effectively killed state autonomy. Henceforward all officials in the states were answerable to him and the congress that he and his centralist allies completely dominated.[59] To that metaphoric imposition of slavery the Texians added the rumor that Cós brought with him eight hundred pairs of iron hobbles to shackle Texians who stood up for their rights. William Wharton published a broadside in Brazoria calling on every able man to turn out. "Five hundred men can do more now than 5000 six months hence," he argued. They could march on Béxar while Mexican numbers were still comparatively small, starve out a garrison that reports said was overtaxing local resources and already on short rations, and send Cós home wearing his own chains. Others in Brazoria actually advertised a $5,000 reward for Cós dead or alive.[60] At the same time, Wharton reminded Texians that the Mexican federalists in Zacatecas and the *tejanos* in their midst, though all men of Spanish or mixed birth and heritage, had volunteered in their communities and were "fighting our battles, more from sympathy, and from a detestation of oppression than from any pecuniary interest they have in the country." Texians needed to sustain and encourage "these generous and heroic individuals" in their "magnanimous efforts to render us a service."[61] It was going to be everyone's war, and not just the Anglos'. A century of separate revolutionary traditions and republican aspirations, fed by generations of revolutionary activity in Texas itself, seemingly gave them at last a common cause, if they could remain united.

Austin's own reaction to Gonzales was predictable now. "War is declared," he told the vigilance committee in San Felipe. "Public opinion has proclaimed it against military despotism." Now they must advance on Béxar and drive Cós and his garrison out. If they moved quickly they could accomplish that, and then "we should have peace," for the continuing uprising in Zacatecas and unrest elsewhere meant that Santa Anna simply had "too much to do at home" to send another army against Texas.[62] But immediately Texas needed men and guns. By October 4 the force at Gonzales had grown to three hundred or more, and he expected it would continue to rise beyond five hundred. Calling it the "Army of the People," he begged for muskets and rifles, and for money to buy weapons in Louisiana. "A few wagon-loads of muskets and fixed ammunition would be of the utmost service at this time," he told the committee, and while they were at it they should send an appeal east of the Sabine for volunteers to come and help the cause of republicanism and liberty.[63]

Even though no one was truly in charge of the growing resistance, Austin seemed to assume it by habit, and almost all deferred to his judgment. "We wish to do for the best in all cases and is only at a loss to know what is best," protested an ungrammatical leader in Columbia. [64] Three days after Gonzales, Austin felt cheered to see the volunteer turnout, and all seemed agreed that their policy must be to march on Béxar and drive Cós from Texas. That would virtually clear the province of Mexican soldiers. "No half way measures now—war in full," he told Burnet and other members of the Peace Party. "Now is the time—no more doubts—no submission." Privately he confided that he regarded the idea of separate statehood as evaporated, and that he looked now to eternal separation from Mexico. "It is yet too soon to say this publically—but that is the point we shall aim at—and it is the one I am aiming at." They must reach that point in logical and measured steps, however, "and not all at one jump," or they might leave the hesitant behind at a time when Texas needed everyone in line.[65] First they would drive Cós out of San Antonio and push him south of the Nueces. Then they would organize a government.[66]

For a brief moment it looked as if there still might be some accommodation to forestall further hostilities. Ugartechea sent a message to Gonzales two days after the skirmish telling the people that they were free to come and go unmolested and that he had no designs of making war upon them. Moreover, he told them that in a spirit of good faith Cós had stopped the march of three regiments of reinforcements at Saltillo, in expectation that "an amicable adjustment" of the current unrest could be found.[67] Ugartechea was less conciliatory with Austin, however, or else just frustrated enough to let his irritation show in address-ing an old friend. This same day he wrote Austin a scathing letter about "crimes and abominations," from the attack on Tenorio at Anahuac to the incident at Gonzales. Now he intended to march on Gonzales on the morrow with a force strong enough to impose his orders. Austin could prevent this by directing the surrender of the gun, for that was all Ugartechea wanted. If he failed to do so, however, then "I will act mili-tarily and the consequence will be a war declared by the Colonists."[68]

As soon as the men of Gonzales learned Ugartechea's intent, they begged Austin to come, and he did. Late on October 10 he reached their camps to find more than three hundred men gathered, and another one hundred just departed on a wasted march to meet a rumored threat sixty miles south at Victoria.[69] Unfortunately, Austin also found unrest among the men, thanks to the dark side of their democratic spirit. Many refused to serve longer unless they could be led by their own captains, and the captains themselves each approached Austin with his own par-ticular agendum. The little "army" having considerably outgrown Moore's initial command, he could not exercise authority over them all, and they had been making decisions in informal council. They knew that could not work for long, and had already scheduled an election for 4:00 P.M. on October 11 to choose a general to command them all. Austin's arrival broke the logjam over who should command, since all agreed that only he had the prestige to lead, and other would-be candi-dates simply bowed out. In each of the companies the captains polled their men at the appointed hour, and there being no opposition, Austin was unanimously chosen commander in chief.[70] As his first act, he named his staff, including appointing the old filibuster Hall adjutant for what he now called the "Army of Texas." That done, he announced to the men that in less than forty-eight hours they would be on the march to Béxar. It was time to take the "war" to the enemy.[71]

CHAPTER SEVEN

"Smoke Forced into a Bee Hive"

⚭

THERE WAS MUCH to do, and despite an illness that made Austin wish he had not been saddled with the command, he showed energy in attacking the challenge. Virtually all of the men in his new army came with their own weapons, clothing, horses, and in some cases even wagons. To cover them for their potential loss, he ordered appraisers to value each man's property employed for army purposes and issue vouchers for reimbursement at such time as Texas had a treasury.[1] Orders went to other companies known to be mustering to join the army along the route of march to Béxar, and at the same time Austin sent urgent word back to San Felipe to rush forward all volunteers arriving there. He expected that the one hundred men who had gone toward Victoria would rejoin him soon, but still he needed every man. He felt especially solicitous for news of volunteers from Nacogdoches.[2] The silence from that quarter worried him, for that was Houston's bailiwick, where he commanded the local militia. Houston's experience was needed, and Nacogdoches was known to have a substantial manpower reserve if they turned out.

Indeed, Houston's actions on hearing the news from Gonzales were curious, not the last time his course would appear peculiar. On October 5 he issued a call for volunteers, not in Nacogdoches and environs, but to Americans in the United States. Moreover, his announcement offered generous land bounties for men who came, regardless of the fact that Houston had no authority of any kind for such a promise. Whether he was playing fast and loose with the truth for the expedient of the moment—which had ever been a characteristic of "the Raven" as his

Cherokee friends called him—or if he expected that one day he would have the power to grant such lands himself cannot be surmised.[3] Whatever the case, however, Houston waited another three days before issuing a call for volunteers from Nacogdoches, a delay during a critical hour that he never explained.[4]

Austin could not wait on Houston, from whom he seems never to have gotten any information. Late on October 11 he issued orders for a general muster and inspection on the morrow so he could see and assess the tenor of his army. After that he wanted to put them on the road immediately. Knowing the nature of volunteers, he tried to instill in them and their officers some rudiments of discipline. They should not discharge their rifles indiscriminately in camp or on the march. Captains must furnish daily reports on the effective strength of their companies, and take care to have proper guard mounted on the march and in camp. To all he cautioned that the future success of their cause depended in large measure on their subordination now. "Patriotism and firmness will avail but little, without discipline and strict obedience to orders," he reminded them. "The first duty of a soldier is obedience."[5]

In a commendable effort at alacrity, especially from an inexperienced soldier who had never commanded more than a few men before, Austin made every effort to have his men cross the Guadalupe River on their way to Béxar immediately after their inspection on October 12. In fact, the crossing was under way by 11:00 A.M. when Austin got news of a second victory.[6] Hearing of the advance of Cós toward Béxar, twenty men in Matagorda gathered on October 6 and formed a company commanded by Captain George M. Collinsworth. They decided to march on Goliad, and by October 9 reached Victoria, their numbers swelled to forty-nine, with more joining every day.[7] They continued toward Goliad, less than thirty miles west, they too, like Wharton, hoping to capture Cós and either hold him for ransom, or capture with him a war chest rumored to contain up to $50,000. But there was no treasure, and Cós had left Goliad for Béxar four days earlier. All that remained behind him were about fifty men commanded by Lieutenant Colonel Francisco Sandoval.

Learning of the weakness of Mexican forces, Collinsworth immediately put his men on the march, and by sometime after nightfall they reached Manahuilla Creek, just a couple of miles from town. Just before midnight they came in sight of the Presidio La Bahía, having been joined en route by more men, including Ben Milam, the popular and rather

charismatic veteran of the Long expedition years before. Now the Texians numbered one hundred twenty or more. Collinsworth sent in a message demanding immediate surrender of the town. The response was
perhaps unexpected, for it came from the *alcalde* and he refused, even
though it was assumed that the civil authorities in Goliad had come
over to the Texian cause. Collinsworth did not waste time or wait for
daylight, but immediately sent volunteers armed with axes to break
down the doors of the presidio. They took Sandoval by surprise, and he
became their first prisoner. When the alarm went out, *soldados* began
firing into the dark at glimpses of Texian forms, but the skirmishing
lasted barely half an hour. At one point a Texian yelled to the defenders
to give up or the attackers would "massacre everyone of you," yet
another unfortunate Texian threat of no quarter to add to Bowie's and
Travis's. In the firing only one or two Texians took wounds, while the
Mexicans suffered three killed and another seven wounded. Finding
themselves badly outnumbered, twenty-one of the garrison surrendered,
but not before another twenty Mexicans managed to escape in the darkness.[8] Later after dawn Collinsworth proudly sent out word that "I am
now in possession of Fort Goliad."[9]

The little fort was a lot more important than the size of the captured
garrison suggested. It lay astride the only direct connection for supply
and communications between Béxar and Copano. Ports farther along the
coast at Matagorda or Galveston were too far away, and either behind
Texian lines, or too vulnerable to attack to be useful. The only other
port available was Corpus Christi at the mouth of the Nueces, and Cós
had left a garrison of almost one hundred men at Lipantitlán near San
Patricio, thirty miles upriver, to hold that line open. It would do him little good, for soon the Goliad victors would be on the march toward the
Nueces to cut off that route of supply, too. If they accomplished that,
then Santa Anna would be unable to send reinforcements or supplies to
Béxar by water, and instead would have to subject them to a grueling
march north across the mountains and deserts of northern Mexico.
Meanwhile, in the spoils of the Goliad capture the Texians found as
much as $10,000 worth of supplies that would be useful to them for
weeks to come, along with several hundred mainly useless muskets.
However, their "artillery" was virtually doubled by the addition of two
little four-pounder smoothbores. Before the end of the month that
would be augmented by some much more substantial guns. An iron six-

pounder belonging to a San Felipe blacksmith was sent off to be mounted on an oxcart to trundle to the volunteers, no one seemingly wondering why a smith—or anyone else, for that matter—would own his own cannon. Within days a twelve-pounder arrived, and soon thereafter a long eighteen-pounder, with another six-pounder on the way.[10]

The news of the Goliad capture enormously cheered Austin and his army, minor though the affair was militarily. The insurgents now had two successes in exchanges of arms with the Mexicans, and the momentum seemed with them. Word came from San Felipe that as many as forty men a day passed through on their way to join the Army of Texas, and the interim president of the council there, R. R. Royall, predicted that when news of their victories continued to spread "it will be like Smoke forced into a Bee Hive."[11] On October 11 Travis and the company he enlisted in finally reached the army just in time for the march to Béxar. Austin meanwhile continued to maintain the public posture that they were fighting for the 1824 Constitution and for the right of statehood in the federation, not for independence. He reminded his subordinates to emphasize this publicly, especially to Mexican soldiers, who seemed convinced that the Texians were bent on independence, an impression that Austin believed prevented many *soldados* and *tejanos* otherwise opposed to centralism from joining Texian forces.[12]

The army moved slowly, in part because there was only one road on which to march, and also no doubt due to the difficulty in maintaining discipline and getting the men to rise and take to the road as a unit. Austin issued more orders on taking care of their equipment and tried to enforce discipline by making public reprimands in front of their companies as the punishment for infractions. Serious offenders faced courtsmartial, he warned. Finding that he also had a number of men who simply attached themselves to the army on their own, without coming as a part of an organized company, he dealt with the potential disciplinary problem they could pose by ordering them to select a company and enroll.[13] On October 15 they actually had a brief and inconsequential skirmish with reconnoitering Mexican lancers whom the Texians easily pushed aside.

Austin also had to complete the organization of his force, trying to model it after a typical infantry regiment in the United States Army. At another election on the march the soldiers chose Moore as regimental colonel, Edward Burleson lieutenant colonel, and other lesser officers.[14]

Austin was also as yet uncertain what he would do when he reached San Antonio. Good reports suggested that the Mexicans numbered eight hundred at least—it was actually more like six hundred—including cavalry, lancers, and at least a dozen well-placed cannon with perhaps more not yet in position. "Against all these you present a band (brave perhaps to a fault) of untrained militia," William Jack told Austin, as if he needed reminding.[15] Already Austin was having trouble with Texians who did not want to obey orders. He had sent directions for most of the Goliad victors to remain there as a garrison at that vital spot, but those who stayed only did so reluctantly, and others simply refused to take such instructions, being bent on getting to the main army for the fight at Béxar.[16]

The army reached Cibolo Creek on October 16, now just twenty-five miles from Béxar, and Austin wisely decided to halt. He had already sent Milam ahead in command of a party of scouts to reconnoiter the best approach to San Antonio, learn what they could of Mexican defenses, and determine how much Cós knew of the army's approach.[17] Milam soon reported back that the signs of Mexican cavalry activity and their skirmish the day before suggested that the army had been spotted. That was enough to persuade Austin to await more reinforcements known to be on the way.[18] In the spirit of democracy that pervaded—and sometimes impeded—the army, he held a council of war of his officers and put future actions to a vote. They agreed it was best to wait for more men, and also approved Austin trying to open negotiations with Cós.

Interestingly, the council concluded that if given the chance, Austin should explain why Texians had taken up their arms, and also propose the terms on which they would lay them down again.[19] Nothing was said of asking for Mexican surrender, and the talk of Texians laying down their arms suggested that so far as the council was concerned, they might still be talking about guarantees of the 1824 Constitution and remaining within the federation as an independent state, which certainly ran counter to Austin's privately expressed views on independence. Cós could hardly recognize Texan independence. All he could do was stay or leave. Of course, it may have been a bluff, hoping to make a deal with Cós to evacuate to Mexico, which would automatically end the insurrection. Then they might hope that distractions elsewhere would simply prevent Santa Anna from sending any more troops and, by default, they would have either statehood or independence as they chose.

The next day Austin tried to open negotiations with Cós "to avoid the sad consequences of the Civil War which unfortunately threatens Texas." He did not say he would ask for the surrender of Béxar, but only suggested that "thus will be opened the way for the satisfactory adjustment of all the affairs of Texas."[20] Cós was having none of that. Pretending shock that Austin had taken the lead of the rebels, he declared that he had no authority to deal with insurgents until and unless they dispersed, released the prisoners they held, disarmed, and substituted peaceful petitions in place of acts of violence. He hoped to avoid a war, he said, but clearly the onus of responsibility lay with the colonists who were violating the laws and defying authority. He said Mexico would never "yield to the dictation of foreigners," showing that he no more regarded the Texians as true Mexican citizens than they did themselves. He flatly refused to negotiate, for to do so would constitute some recognition of the legitimacy of Austin's command. And then he warned that if the rebels did not cease—which he hardly expected—then the Mexican army would be compelled into "making of the Colonies a signal example."[21]

Meanwhile, inside the Béxar garrison, the Mexicans determined to hold their position. Martín Perfecto de Cós was just thirty-six, having risen from a mere cadet to a generalship when his near kinsman Santa Anna sent him to Texas in 1835 to impose control and new taxes. Even before Austin's army reached the Cibolo, Cós issued an address to his men. "The veil which has long concealed the perfidious designs of the colonists is at length withdrawn," he told them. "These ungrateful men have revolted against our government, and assumed the right to live as they like, without any subjection to the laws of the republic." Perhaps fearing the federalist sympathies of some even in his own command, he warned them not to believe protestations from the Texians about fidelity to the 1824 Constitution. They must be put down, Cós told his men. That he did not commence offensive operations even then was due to the need to wait for reinforcements and supplies, though he did not tell them that they were now cut off from either for quite some time. Rather, he complimented their discipline and valor, made no reference to the small but still embarrassing affairs at Gonzales and Goliad, and promised them the ultimate victory. They would "bring the rebels to repentance," he said. It would be hard, but "after fatigue comes repose, [and] we shall obtain it covered with glory."[22]

Having seen Cós's reply, on October 19 Austin held another council of war, giving some evidence of being unwilling to make major decisions without consensus. He had news that the Mexicans were barricading themselves in San Antonio. The more time the Texians gave them, the harder they would be to dislodge. Meanwhile, Bowie arrived with a few men from Nacogdoches, and Austin appointed him an aide on his staff with the honorary rank of colonel, though Bowie had no command of his own. Juan Seguín arrived soon thereafter at the head of 37 *tejanos*, and by October 21 the Army of Texas had grown to eleven companies with at least 453 men, and more coming in every day.[23] Yet sickness reduced the army's strength daily, too. For Austin now time was manpower, and the longer he remained inactive, the more it worked in the Mexicans' favor. It was time to advance and meet the enemy.

The magnitude of the task before them gave a jolt of reality to the little army. Cós had been reinforced to perhaps six hundred fifty now by small parties of *soldados* called in to his defense, with another one hundred on their way. Austin's numbers, too, continued to grow, to as many as eight hundred in the end, but the Mexicans were well emplaced behind defenses around the town, and even in its streets, as well as in the old mission San Antonio de Valero. In the early part of the century the mission had housed the Flying Company of San José y Santiago del Alamo de Parras, and from its tenure there locals commonly called the place "el Alamo." They had a dozen cannon, a British "Brown Bess" musket to almost every man, and ample ammunition. There would be no Gonzales- or Goliad-style pushover in taking Béxar.

There was no question of attacking Cós in his positions. Austin determined on the more prudent expedient of a siege to starve the garrison. First, however, he needed a base closer to San Antonio. He detailed ninety men commanded by Bowie, whose subordinate co-commander would be Captain James W. Fannin Jr., to find the spot he needed. Whatever their differences, Austin knew he could count on Bowie to be resourceful and daring, if perhaps impetuous. There were two missions, San Juan and San José, just south of San Antonio, that if taken might provide a good base for Austin's army to operate against both the town and its overland supply route to the Rio Grande. There were also reports that the Mexicans had stores of grain and other supplies at the missions that Austin himself desperately needed, for his army had no quartermaster stores other than what the volunteers brought with them from home.

Bowie's command reached the mission Espada on the afternoon of October 22 but found neither substantial food nor a good spot for the main army. However, he sent word back to Austin that he should bring the army forward and take a position north of San Antonio, while Bowie held Espada. That would have Cós cut off from support and leave him only one route of retreat to the southwest. In five days, he told Austin, he believed they could starve the garrison into surrender.[24] Austin saw the wisdom of the suggestion but put off moving the army for several days. He did, however, order Bowie and Fannin to move on to the missions San Juan and San José, which the Texians reached on October 23. Again they found almost nothing for the army to eat, and hunger was starting to be a problem. "You know the materials we have," Bowie wrote back to Austin as he retired to Espada. "They will fight—and fight desperately; but must *Eat.*"[25]

But the Mexicans seemed willing to fight, too. On the morning of October 24 Cós sent perhaps as many as one hundred mounted men out of his works and down the road toward Espada. It was probably nothing more than a reconnaissance to test Texian strength astride the vital road connecting him with Copano and other routes of retreat. A few shots were traded with no one hurt, and then the dragoons returned to the city. Bowie and Fannin sent urgent word to Austin that they needed more men to hold their vital position, at the same time urging Austin to push the main army closer to San Antonio so that they would be closer to each other for mutual support and close the door on Cós.[26] Austin's only reply was the promise of another fifty men, but he could not move the army, for suddenly he had a political crisis on his hands and a challenge to his leadership.

The day for the Consultation had come and passed, and of course Austin knew that a substantial number of men who had been elected delegates had stepped forward as volunteers. Should they now leave his army to attend the anticipated meeting, or ought they to remain with the army where even their small number was still important? For that matter, was it practical even to try to hold the Consultation in the sudden emergency? Austin convened a meeting of the army's officers and the elected delegates even before his election to command, and the result was a virtually unanimous resolution to be sent to the Consultation asking that all who could should rush to the army to join the delegates already there, who thereby determined to remain. If the time came when they could be spared, then they would go to the meeting. Mean-while, if enough men were left to form a quorum, then they were requested simply to meet from day to day and adjourn without taking any action until November 1. Clearly, some in the army's high com-mand thought that Béxar might be theirs by then and the delegates could be spared to go to the task of state building.[27] Apparently on his own authority, Austin himself announced on October 12 as his army was crossing the Guadalupe, that the Consultation was definitely post-poned until November 1.[28]

That date now approached, and if the delegates serving in the army were to reach the Consultation in time for its convening, they must leave momentarily. Immediately the army became a debating society. Some argued that the delegates ought to leave, since they had vital work to do. Others objected to any leaving while others stayed. Amid this dis-sension Sam Houston arrived on the scene. Having reached San Felipe to find that the absence of a quorum kept the delegates there from meet-ing, Houston rode on to find the army, his goal to persuade delegates to return with him. On his arrival he found a shocking ragtag of volunteers in every manner of dress and undress, armed with everything but relics from the days of the conquistadores, hard pressed for food, walking on moccasins, and wearing beaver hats and coonskin caps. To his compara-tively experienced eye, their discipline looked laughable, and if he did not say so aloud, he scarcely concealed his conviction that the ailing and hesitant Austin was not up to command. Indeed, it was soon evident that Houston believed himself to be the only man for the job.

On October 25, in yet another surrender to democracy, Austin assembled the army on the Cibolo, even calling Bowie and Fannin away from their outpost. He put to them the decision of whether or not the Consultation delegates should go or stay, and then allowed speakers to discuss opposing views. What became immediately apparent was another and even more immediate question: Should the army itself abandon the quest for Béxar and instead retire to some more secure loca-tion to build itself into a stronger, better disciplined and equipped com-mand? Branch Archer, an ardent proponent of independence, spoke first, advocating sending the delegates back to form a quorum and start the work of legislating in the Consultation. Houston followed, and many felt inclined to follow his charismatic leadership. He argued strongly in favor of withdrawal. They were too weak, too disorganized, too ill disciplined, and Cós was too strong. He advised their retreat to Gonzales for reshaping and reinforcing. He also urged that the Consultation must convene on time, and that the delegates with the army needed to be there. If the terms of his address seemed unwarrantedly defeatist, there was still some sense in Houston's position. Only a working civil government, even a provisional one, based on the mandate given to elected delegates, could speak with one voice and give direction to Texian affairs. Absent that, there was always the possibility that while many in the War Party stayed here with the army, some kind of rump government might be formed by the Peace Party faction in their rear. Such a junta could then repudiate what the army was doing, even outlaw Austin's leaders, and in the worst case make an accommodation with Santa Anna at the cost of independence, statehood, or even their remaining freedoms as Mexican citizens.

Houston was no coward, but he was by nature cautious and prudent in affairs of arms. He also surely realized that at the moment, and for several weeks to come, Cós posed no threat to Texians and would not so long as his communications with the Gulf remained severed. Santa Anna surely could not have serious reinforcements on hand before December at the earliest, and meanwhile those intervening weeks provided vital time to build the Army of Texas into a force guaranteed of victory when it marched again on Béxar. If they took the risk now and failed, the momentum of Gonzales and Goliad would be squandered. The effect of a failure on morale could seriously compromise civilian support, discourage foreign aid in money and men from the United States, and give a boost to Mexican spirits. Meanwhile, there would be no Texian government to stand up for the rebels. In short, they had too much to lose and not that much to gain from pressing their campaign any further now. It was a sensible approach.

Admittedly, however, Houston was also a man who rarely failed to take counsel of his own interests. Within a couple of days some found him exhibiting "the most discontented & envious of spirits mixed with the most unmeasured vanity."[29] He saw Austin as a weak leader both in politics and in the field. Vaunting ambition naturally suggested that Houston himself ought to command, and logic suggested that his military experience—though limited—made him a more sensible choice. If he still entertained notions of guiding Texas into the orbit of Washington and the United States, then he needed to be in a powerful position to make that happen, and command of the army could give him the necessary platform. If Austin wasted this little assembly on a pointless assault on Béxar now, then Houston's future might go up in the same plume of smoke as Texas's. A few even suspected that the Raven would risk the one to boost the other. "He is a vain, ambitious, envious, disappointed, discontented man, who desires the defeat of our army," complained one Texian, "that he may be appointed to the command of the next."[30]

The reaction to Houston's remarks was mixed, and some of it angry. He had reckoned without the enthusiasm of the men and the volunteers' natural impatience with delay. "He has endeavored to discourage our men by ridiculing a siege & alleging the impracticability of taking Bexar," complained one Texian in outrage when he heard Houston's remarks repeated two days later.[31] Having come forward for a specific purpose, they wanted to get it done and get home. To his argument in favor of withdrawal, some accused him of seeking deliberately to demoralize the men. Others said he was on the bottle again.[32] However, his argument about the necessity of the Consultation convening made sense to almost everyone.

William Jack followed Houston, in some measure probably echoing Houston's hesitance about attacking Béxar, though he supported sending the delegates to the Consultation. Then came a visibly weakened Austin.[33] Barely able to hold the saddle as he spoke, he told them that in his view the life of Texas depended upon their remaining here to clear Béxar of the foe just as much as it did upon the timely meeting of the Consultation. The choice was theirs whether to stay or withdraw, but he made it clear that he was going to remain in front of Béxar so long as there was a man to stand beside him.[34] He could see all of the problems with the army that Houston pointed out in his impolitic remarks, but he knew other things that Houston did not. Austin had brought some of these men to Texas more than a decade before. He knew them and had spent the ensuing years trying both to guide and contain their passions and independence. Houston was a much more experienced politician on the hustings and in legislative halls, and at least had brief experience in combat against the Creek Indians, but as a mere third lieutenant he never commanded more than a portion of a company. He had no experience at all leading volunteers like these in wartime.

There, for a change, Austin bested his record, for he had been leading these very men for years. He knew the strength of their enthusiasm, but also their volatility and mercurial nature. They had homes and families and farms they had abandoned to be here, and to which they wanted to return as soon as possible. The time it would take to regroup and train them was time in which their ardor could cool, and from the vantage of his greater experience and knowledge of these men, Austin knew that such a delay could be fatal. They had momentum now, and the Mexicans were dispirited and on the defensive. To surrender the advantage now might mean they could never gain it again. In other circumstances, Houston's program—setting aside its self-serving nature—would have been the prudent course. In this moment, however, Austin was right. As a result, and as the men seemed to realize, Sam Houston might have been the best available man to whip this mob into shape to meet Santa Anna's better trained and equipped forces. At this moment, however, the man to lead their army was Austin.[35]

The army sided overwhelmingly with all four speakers on the matter of sending the delegates—excepting Austin himself and his staff—to do their duty in the Consultation, and repudiated Houston's plea for withdrawal by voting to continue the march on Béxar.[36] Austin asked Houston to take charge of the party of delegates for the trip back to San Felipe. A few other delegates, Travis among them, volunteered to remain anyhow, but the rest, as many as twenty perhaps, left the next day. With them Austin sent a memorandum on his suggestions for the Consultation. He recommended that it reconfirm adherence to the 1824 Constitution, declare Texas a state within the federation as a result of the dissolution by the military of the properly elected legislature in Coahuila, organize a provisional government and appoint a governor and lieutenant governor, endorse the existing statutes of Coahuila y Texas, and pledge the credit of the new state to cover debts incurred in defending itself against the enemies of the 1824 Constitution. In a blow to Bowie and others designed to separate this resistance from the taint of their speculations, Austin also recommended declarations nullifying all of the corrupt land grants of the Monclova legislature. Finally, he called on the Consultation to devise a formal organization for the militia and appoint a commander in chief, and to begin the formation of a small corps of regular troops for permanent service.[37]

That done, Austin put the army on the road to the Salado Creek, sending Bowie and Fannin ahead to find the best spot from which to threaten Béxar.[38] The evening of October 27 Bowie and Fannin came to the mission Purísima Concepción on the San Antonio River, just two miles below Béxar, and they found what they wanted. It afforded an excellent campsite, and was close enough to the main road to interdict any wagon trains to succor Cós. Bowie sent *tejano* friends into San Antonio to scout the progress of the Mexican defenses, and they returned with word that at least nine cannon were in place and the *soldados* were fortifying the housetops. Bowie immediately sent word back for Austin to bring the main army up while he and Fannin spread out their men to hold the spot in the interim. It was certainly daring, for they knew that Mexican scouts had seen them, and in their position they were closer to San Antonio's several hundred Mexican soldiers than they were to Austin's army. Expecting the possibility of an attack before Austin arrived, Bowie and Fannin prepared to hold their ground. Sure enough, the next morning, beneath a dense, low-hanging fog, Texian pickets saw the legs of advancing horses. Cós sent both infantry and cavalry, the former to advance directly on the rebels, while the mounted lancers hoped to ride around them and cut them off from Austin.

What followed in the Battle of Concepción was the closest thing to a genuine battle yet in this infant revolution. At first Bowie just kept his men quietly in their positions beneath the river bank, waiting for the fog to lift, while the Mexicans sent a scattering of musketry their way without effect. When he could see clearly, Bowie saw just how dangerous a position he was in between enemy infantry and cavalry. Still he held his ground, and about eight o'clock the fighting began, the Mexicans sending volleys toward the Texians, and the defenders returning fire individually at will. After ten minutes the Mexicans brought up a small brass cannon to fire a scatter-load of canister to soften Bowie's line before an infantry charge, but as the yelling *soldados* surged forward, Texian fire brought down the cannoneers and turned back the charge. As new gunners rushed forward to try another round from the cannon, and as the infantry regrouped to charge again, the Texians turned them back at least twice more. Then Bowie ordered his men up from the riverbank to charge and take the cannon. They took it within seconds, found it loaded, and immediately turned it on the retreating Mexicans. Only then did the Mexican cavalry enter the fight, contenting themselves with firing from some distance a few ineffectual rounds from a small field piece of its own. That done, they withdrew and the battle was over, a third Texian victory, and now with a Mexican cannon as a battle trophy in the bargain. It came at a cost of one man killed and one wounded, while perhaps sixty of the foe fell dead or injured. Half an hour later the balance of the Texian army under a very apprehensive Austin reached the field.[39]

In fact, Austin at first tried to get his men to pursue the retreating foe right into San Antonio itself, but Bowie's men were too tired from the brief fight, and the rest of the army weary and disorganized from its march. Officers including Fannin and Bowie argued that the risk of attacking the fortified Mexicans in Béxar was too great, and against their remonstrances the commander finally yielded. It was probably the wisest course, yet it revealed again just how much command of this rabble of volunteers depended upon their sufferance, and how the spirit of democracy crippled any hope of dynamic and decisive leadership. Not until or unless the Consultation legislated a genuine army for Texas, under an appointed commander, and not until these local companies were formally enlisted under orders and obligations, and with pay, would the army commander have anything other than the moral force of personality to back his orders. Houston had been all too right about that. Even then, though, it remained an open question whether these men would ever cease being civilians on loan to the military and become real soldiers, assuming the revolt lasted long enough for that to happen.

Austin had hoped to capitalize on their momentum to carry Béxar. He feared a siege, not because he thought he could not succeed, but because he knew that every day of inactivity worked against army discipline, especially with November on the horizon and winter not far away. He could envision the army simply withering away as each man made his own choice as to the limits of his patriotism. One company actually left to go home during the march to Concepción and he could just as easily lose others. Sensing the fragile line remaining between discipline and disaster, he issued an immediate order even as the army rested from the march that any officer disobeying orders should be arrested immediately.[40]

He was soon relieved to learn that three hundred more volunteers were already on their way, and the news emboldened him to divide his army on October 30 by sending Bowie with between three hundred and four hundred men in a feint before San Antonio hoping to lure Cós into coming out of his defenses. The Mexicans did not take the bait, so the following day Austin led the other half of the army to a position north of the town, planning a simultaneous advance of the two wings that he soon had to cancel. Meanwhile, Bowie, apparently without authorization, sent his own surrender demand in to Cós, who returned it unread, explaining that he could not communicate with rebels.⁴¹ Austin sent his own surrender demand to Cós the next day, and received the same reply, though privately Cós sent word that his orders were to hold out to the last man.⁴² The following day, Austin held the now inevitable council of war among all of his officers except those with Fannin and Bowie. He put to them the question of whether or not they stood a chance of success by an immediate assault on Cós's defenses, and the vote against the idea was all but unanimous, only Milam voting in favor of storming the city. It was confirmation, if any were needed, that the only alternative now was siege. By another unanimous vote, they decided to take positions beyond range of enemy cannon, and there begin the investment of the town while awaiting the reinforcements and artillery of their own to make an assault practical.⁴³ On Austin's orders, Bowie held a similar council, with the same result. The only one who did not vote was Bowie himself. In the first sign of yet another crisis within the command structure of the army, he resigned.⁴⁴ Now more than ever, the army needed the political authority of the Consultation or a provisional government to keep the centrifugal forces within it from simply tearing it to bits.

Quite coincidentally, the Consultation actually achieved a quorum for the first time the very next day, but its shape and goals looked frustratingly ambiguous. The original plan for the meeting called for each municipality to elect five delegates. The committee of safety at Nacogdoches, however, proposed a plan to elect seven instead, and others followed suit. As the day grew closer, it became increasingly evident that it was important for everyone to be represented in San Felipe.⁴⁵ Travis, himself destined to be elected from San Felipe, offered a prescription for the kind of men needed. "I want to see that body composed of men talented, firm and uncompromising," he told Henry Smith.⁴⁶ It sounded more than anything like a call for the War Party, men like Travis himself and the Whartons. The citizens of Matagorda suggested their own template for a delegate: "'Is he honest' 'Is he capable' Is he identified with, and a friend to Texas."⁴⁷

But Austin had wanted Peace Party men there, too, for if all parties were not reflected in the decisions of the meeting, then it could only lead to discord. At Austin's request in September, Houston and Thomas

Rusk even sent an invitation to Shawnee and Cherokee leaders to the north inviting them to send their chiefs to attend "the Talk on the Brazos," though as observers not delegates.[48] Austin knew it would be difficult forming a coalition. Some of his old friends in the Peace Party did not hide their unhappiness that he sided with their reckless opponents, while he knew from long experience that many of the radicals in the War Party would be difficult to manage or control. Even united in a common cause, these factions came to the conference table—and perhaps the battlefield—with resentments and animosities of several years' standing, differences not soon to be resolved. "We know no party here, but are united in the General cause," a friend reported from Mina on September 23.[49] Alas, Austin knew that such sentiments were not universal, even in Mina.

Austin's roommate in San Felipe, Lorenzo de Zavala, felt uneasy about the Consultation for some time before it convened. Most of the delegates elected came with little or no experience as lawmakers, especially in what he called "the tactics of legislative assemblies." More perplexing, however, was the question of what they could and could not do. "What meaning has the word Consultation when applied to an assembly among a people where there are no public powers and where each citizen is a king like unto Adam?" he asked Austin back on September 17. "To whom is that council going to direct its decisions and who will put them into effect?" With the enemy at their doors, they needed a ruling authority with real power and a public mandate that many simply did not believe the Consultation would command. Instead, he feared that once the Consultation assembled and chose its officers, opposing parties would arise—coincident with the War and Peace parties—to vie for dominance. One would argue that they had full authority to pass legislation, and demand and quickly push for a declaration of independence, while the other more conservative faction would try to restrict the body's actions just to discussion and perhaps the framing of reports or resolutions, and adjourn, doing nothing about the current crisis.

"You can see that both parties are dangerous," Zavala declared, "and that the second is mortal." He believed that this was not the time to discuss absolute independence. Instead, the Consultation ought to adopt a declaration of provisional independence from Coahuila, create public offices for the immediate governance of Texas, and draft a declaration to justify such an action. Nevertheless, they ought as well to make it clear that Texas was a loyal state within the Mexican republic and only took this extraordinary step in defense of its rights. As soon as those rights were guaranteed, it would abandon the provisional government and rejoin the federation. It was very much the same program that Austin himself recommended to the Consultation when he sent the delegates back from his army a month later. Zavala did go a step further, though, and advocate that if Mexico remained in turmoil for a period of perhaps two years, then Texas should declare for complete independence.[50]

Some municipalities like San Augustine did not wait for the debate over authority to arise, and sent their delegates vested with "unlimited powers" to be governed entirely by circumstances. "This committee deem it impolitick to limit the capasity of their delegates," it concluded.

> Their interests being inseperably identified with their constituents, and in common with the balance of the citizens of the state, they knowing the wants, and agrievances of the people, having minds unbiased, with an eye single to good sound republican principles, will be willing to do what is right, and submit to nothing that is wrong, they [the committee] are willing to risk our all, to the mature and deliberate discussion and the final result of an unprejudiced decision of a majority of the members of said consultation in determining the course most advisable.[51]

Despite its grammatical eccentricity, it was about as good a definition of the idea of republican democracy as could be found in Texas, or anywhere else. It remained to be seen whether the Consultation could live up to it.

The Permanent Council met and tried to give some direction to affairs for a week prior to the scheduled opening of the Consultation, but with little force. Some municipalities sent no representatives to serve on it, while a number of its members—never more than twenty in number—brought no established voices or cachet from the years of confrontations leading to this moment. Worse, well aware of their powerlessness, the Council more often took orders from the army—as with the soldiers making Austin their general—than the other way around, for the army, such as it was, constituted the only real source of power at the moment. Austin himself used the Council to represent his own views in San Felipe, and acted in some measure as an unelected head of state in giving it directions that an uncertain and indecisive majority chose to accept. Indeed, the secretary of the Council actually told members that it was needed because Austin was absent, virtually confirming the group as little more than his alter ego.[52] In such a power and organizational vacuum, however, there was perhaps little else they could do. Throughout its brief service it repeatedly looked to Austin to tell it what to do, and the day before the Consultation was originally scheduled to meet, the Council's secretary acknowledged that with the convening of the meeting its own existence would cease, asking Austin to "provide for the continuance of a body of some kind at this place" with power sufficient to carry out the practical instructions of the Consultation.[53]

The Council was well aware of the problem of convening a quorum. "We are all united here and it requires more Pattriotism to keep men at home than to get them in service," complained the president of the Council on October 13. The next day, just twenty-four hours before the scheduled convening, not a single delegate was in San Felipe.[54] When the appointed time came, the convention simply did not have enough present even to try to convene. The next day, October 16, they did finally gather, with only thirty-two of an anticipated ninety-eight delegates present. Whole municipalities were unrepresented, and even from Austin's colony, in whose capital, San Felipe, the meeting was being held, only two representatives appeared. Zavala was there, and R. R. Royall, president of the Council, was already present. Henry Smith came from Columbia, and Houston had stopped by on his way to Austin's army. All they could do with no quorum present was to adjourn until the next day, and then, recognizing their organizational problem, they passed resolutions to adjourn until November 1 or such day as a quorum could be convened. The delegates present who wished to go to the army were free to do so in the interim, while those who did not go were asked to join the deliberations of the Permanent Council.

When November 1 came the Consultation again tried to meet, but with only twenty-five present. Houston was there, back from his rebuff in the army, and his arrival signaled that other delegates from the army would soon arrive. Again there was no quorum the next day, but on November 3 enough delegates appeared in the chamber to start conducting business, and divisions and conflicting ambitions quickly emerged. Austin had suggested Zavala as a suitable president of the meeting, since in the main he reflected Austin's own opinions on what needed to be done and the stance to adopt. But Houston almost immediately sought to dominate the proceeding, and given his political experience, the delegates naturally followed his lead. He moved the election of a president, and the result was not Zavala but Branch T. Archer, a man largely in the War Party camp. But when Archer looked over the men gathered in the room, he saw a great disparity of views. Perhaps a third of them shared his own mind. Another third came from the Peace Party, and the balance lay somewhere between. As a result, his first words were an appeal for unity and compromise. To remain partisan in this crisis was to commit suicide.

That done, he proposed that they proceed in the main to address the very questions that Austin said must be met, and from the order in which he spoke of them it is evident that he had either seen Austin's list or else had it right before him. They should draft a statement of the grievances that had brought them to resistance. Recognizing the power vacuum as evidenced in the inability of the Council to act decisively, he recommended that they establish a provisional government with both executive and legislative powers "to prevent Texas from falling into the labyrinth of anarchy." Of course, they must organize their military, begin to provide for its food and comfort systematically, establish military law for governance and discipline, and send agents to collect funds in Texas and abroad to finance the army and the government. They must also establish a land policy to make grants to the men from the United States who even then came to take part in their struggle. For fully a generation the United States had rewarded its own volunteers in its wars with land bounties for their service, and such was therefore suitable for Texas as well. And they had to do something about those fraudulent Monclova grants. Thus, even if Austin lost control of the presidency of the convention, he was thoroughly in charge of the incumbent's initial agendum.

If any doubt remained that the Anglos thoroughly controlled the Consultation—of the delegates who had gathered prior to this day not a single one was a *tejano* and only Zavala had Spanish blood—Archer concluded by reminding them that they were the descendants of the men of 1776 who wrested independence from Britain. They must comport themselves in a fashion to make the United States, "our mother country," proud of them. From the address one would have concluded that the *tejanos* were neither a part of the Consultation, nor even involved in their resistance.[55] It was an attitude not uncommon among the Anglo-centric War Party men, and did not bode that well for the unity that Archer eloquently solicited.

Houston continued to take the floor frequently, rising immediately after Archer to propose the thanks of the convention to Austin, Bowie, and Fannin for their success at Concepción. That done, Royall presented a lengthy report from the Permanent Council on its activities in order to bring the Consultation up to the moment on such military preparations as had been undertaken. Again Houston rose to propose thanks to the Council, and then yet again to suggest a resolution of thanks to a group of volunteers from Louisiana just recently arrived. None of these thanks resolutions were important business, but by standing so frequently Houston established himself as a leading presence being seen and heard.[56]

The real business of the Consultation began with drafting rules of order, and it adjourned overnight to give the committee time to finish their preparation. The next day the committee presented twenty rules that virtually echoed those commonly in use in legislatures throughout the United States and Europe. Emphasized was the requirement that debate be orderly and courteous. There were to be no *ad hominem* verbal assaults upon fellow delegates. More significant, however, was a prohibition of abstentions on votes. They needed decisions, and quickly, which made such a rule practical, but more subtly it also discouraged the wavering from taking refuge. They would have to be on record, meaning the moderates between the Peace and War factions must choose a side. Perhaps just as significant operationally, the president was to be prohibited from voting except to break ties, which meant that Archer's more militant voice was effectively stilled.[57]

Real debate only commenced on November 5, and two proposed courses of action emerged. One was for a declaration of causes to protest under their rights in the 1824 Constitution, as Austin had advised. Houston, still holding to the more moderate camp, introduced a resolution to that effect but withdrew it when the War Party's John A. Wharton, chairman of the committee to draft the statement, objected strenuously. The other course, introduced by James W. Robinson of Nacogdoches, called for an outright declaration of independence, but he could get no immediate debate on the subject. With more members arriving from the army almost hourly, the Consultation steadily grew to at least forty-eight with more on the way, and still not a *tejano* in the hall, and none likely since only Béxar elected any, and the siege there prevented a single delegate from coming.

As yet they evidenced little party alignment. On November 6 a motion by Houston to form a provisional government based on the 1824 Constitution carried 33 to 14. Archer then restated the question into a proposition for an outright declaration of independence, and it failed 15 to 33. Thus the lines were drawn, and it was evident that the firmest ground was in the center, largely where Austin wanted them to stand.[58]

They met from 9 o'clock in the morning until well into the evening, and on November 7 adopted their declaration of causes. It was a contradictory document, yet consistent in the implications of what it almost said. The declaration made plain their reasons for resistance, and just as in the 1775 declarations of their grandfathers, it emphasized that they resisted as loyal citizens of a mother country, not revolutionaries bent on secession and independence (though few could fail to anticipate—or fear—that such was the inevitable and logical outcome of this act). Santa Anna, they charged, forcefully overthrew the federal institutions of Mexico. They also charged that he dissolved "the social compact" between Texians and other states in the confederation, a perhaps disingenuous argument, since for years, in arguing for separation from Coahuila, Texian politicians maintained Texas's social distinction from Coahuila, and by extension from the rest of Spanish and ethnically Indian Mexico.

In response to these usurpations, therefore, Texians must exercise their "natural rights" and take arms in defense of the liberties guaranteed them in the 1824 Constitution. At the same time, however, in a step just short of declaring independence, they asserted that "Texas is no longer morally or civilly bound by the Compact of Union," and that Santa Anna and his present corrupt regime had no right to govern in Texas. In the current turmoil in Mexico, and given Santa Anna's repeated violations of the constitution he swore to uphold, they declared it their right to withdraw from the confederation and proclaim their own independent government should they so choose, though they stopped short of doing so now. Indeed, in a spirit of "generosity and sympathy common to a free people," they pledged their support to any other states in the confederation that resisted the despot, and promised that if or when Mexico returned to constitutional government and observance of the laws and conditions binding the confederation, then they would remain loyal to that government. Zacatecas, of course, had already been subdued, but it could rise again, and if other states heeded the call to rise, then Santa Anna could find himself too distracted on his home front to turn his attention to this weak outpost of resistance north of the Nueces. Should he come, they would not cease their resistance while he or his soldiers stood on their soil.

Scarcely noted or appreciated, however, were the three shortest yet perhaps most significant resolutions in the document. Texas assumed responsibility for the expense of the army it was now raising. They pledged the public faith of Texas to make payment on any goods purchased by its agents for whatever purposes. They promised all who volunteered for the army, regardless of whence they came, unspecified donations of land in reward. All three were the acts of an independent state, and could themselves be considered violations of the 1824 Constitution. The land donation was clearly a lure to men from the United States to come to their aid, thus anticipating a long period of resistance. Even more to the point, Texas possessed no land of its own to give as grants. Unsettled and untitled land there, as elsewhere, belonged to the central government. How could they give away what was not lawfully theirs unless implicitly they expected that shortly it would be?

The declaration revealed the independence faction clearly beaten, at least for the moment, though no doubt several, including Houston, went along with a more moderate approach—like Austin—out of expedience, biding their time until the proper moment to come out for absolute separation from Mexico. Houston himself moved that every member present sign the document. Mindful of their "fellow Mexican citizens" involved in the action of the convention, it voted to ask Zavala to translate the document and have five hundred copies printed in Spanish, though of the fifty-seven representatives who signed the broadside, not one came from *tejano* ranks. This was the Anglos' action, but like it or not, *tejanos* were irrevocably bound with them in whatever lay ahead.[59]

That done, they turned their attention to authorizing privateers to cruise the Gulf coast, sending purchasing agents to New Orleans and elsewhere to obtain arms and munitions, and approving $20 a month in pay for the volunteers then in service, backdating it to the date they left their homes in September and October, and including as well compensation for any personal property lost or damaged while in the ranks.[60] But then came time to discuss the plan for a provisional government reported by Henry Smith's committee.

It became immediately apparent that the committee lacked unanimity in its recommendations, and a minority report sought an airing on the floor. At issue was a statement that Texas was a "sovereign state" independent from Coahuila, and entitled to be governed by its own laws. Combining with that a preamble that echoed much of the wording in a similar section of the United States Constitution, some regarded this as essentially a declaration of independence.[61] The minority wanted to make its objections known, but by the closest of votes, 20 to 21, the house declined to hear its report. The War Party men would try to keep their radicalism in check, while the Peace Party men largely moved toward the center to find mutually acceptable accommodations. But when it came to the plan for a government, the factions remained apart, repeatedly delaying its consideration with parliamentary procedure.[62] Finally the report from Smith's committee went to another committee for revision, and that revised version went to the floor. Objectionable suggestions of independence disappeared, and in their place the new committee inserted an explicit oath of office requiring officials to swear allegiance to the 1824 Constitution. For two days they debated the plan, making minor changes and adding such things as a repudiation of the fraudulent Monclova grants, until on November 13 they adopted their final version.[63]

They approved a mainly conservative document of twenty-one articles that reflected primarily American ideas of republican government. The Consultation should elect a governor and lieutenant governor, a common practice of legislatures in the United States, and besides there was no time or machinery in place to allow for a general election. The governor should have full executive power, as well as being commander in chief of the armed and naval forces, but the Consultation would also elect a "general council," the delegation from each municipality choosing one of its own to serve on the body. A sort of super-cabinet to advise and assist the governor, presided over by the lieutenant governor, the Council was to exercise no legislative duties except in emergencies and when no convention or Consultation sat. Virtually everything relating to the welfare and management of the army, the defense of the state, contracting for loans, imposing taxes and duties, even establishing post offices, came under the Council's purview. Once the Consultation adjourned, the governor and Council would function as the provisional government until another Consultation should convene, or until another permanent government was established. Unfortunately, in their haste they neglected to consider what might happen if governor and Council did not agree. Their system created two largely autonomous authorities, with no check or balance and no system of arbitrating or settling disputes between the two, and—fatally—no separation of powers.

Articles also covered the judiciary, emphasizing that all trials should be by jury, and promised land to existing citizens and to all who should come to Texas during the war. As for any Texians who left the state to get away from service in defense of Texas, their lands and property should be forfeit. To help finance the government, a sequestration provision appeared in the document, making all debts due to Coahuila for land in Texas payable to the government here instead. This done, the document also provided that the Consultation adjourn when it thought fit, subject to reconvening on March 1, 1836, at Washington-on-the-Brazos some forty miles upstream from San Felipe. The selection of Washington was in part practical, as it was deeper in the interior and therefore more secure against invasion. Yet the importance of the name itself was hardly lost on these Anglos.

In spite of the rejection of debate on independence on the floor, strong language couched in the document hinted of more than just loyalty to the 1824 Constitution. Even though all governmental officers must swear an oath to "support the republican principles of the constitution of Mexico of 1824," that oath did not specifically bind them to fealty to that constitution itself—only to its "principles." The document also referred to the people of Texas as "free and sovereign," which hardly comported with their being subjects of any other authority, though, at the time, the United States largely considered itself a plural rather than a single entity, and the idea of state "sovereignty" had meaning to a degree later forgotten.[64] When he learned of the wording, Austin himself felt pleased. "This declaration secures to Texas *everything*, and without any hazard," he told the new government a few weeks hence. It was a platform broad enough for the War Party to find room to stand, without alienating the Peace men. To declare openly for independence risked alienating federalists in Mexico who resisted Santa Anna, and every weapon raised against the dictator south of the Rio Grande was as good as one in Texas for their cause.[65]

That done, they immediately afterward adopted a report from the committee charged with organizing the military, and it, like the "constitution" they had just approved, created two systems without providing for adequate coordination between them. It mandated a modest "regular," or professional, army of 1,120 men to be governed by the same regulations in use in the United States Army, under a major general to be appointed by the Consultation, commissioned by the governor, and subject to instructions from him and the Council. That seemed to guarantee civilian control of the military, but left unclear just which civilians it would be who were in charge, risking tearing the general between multiple masters. At the same time, the legislation created a Texas militia comprised of all able-bodied men between the ages of sixteen and fifty, and required all such inhabitants to assemble in one month to form companies. The major general should also command these militia companies, though the men themselves would be allowed to elect their officers from lieutenants through brigadier generals. The document said nothing about conflicting authorities between regular and militia officers, or whether companies in one branch were liable to orders from officers in the other, or who should take immediate command if volunteer and regular officers of identical rank found themselves in the same spot. It thus ensured that the confusion and difficulty, not to mention conflicting loyalties, which Austin faced in controlling his own army would continue.[66]

Meanwhile, the Consultation chose officers for the new government. The names of Austin and Smith went in nomination for governor, and Smith won by 31 to 22. While it reflected a minor triumph for the radicals, Smith being an outspoken—indeed intemperate—War Party leader, it was not the rejection of Austin that it appeared. His votes probably reflected the same rather solid bloc of Peace Party men and moderates that cast virtually the same number of votes against the "independence" minority report from Smith's committee. The core ballot for Smith likewise undoubtedly came from much the same delegates who had favored the "independence" report. Most of the difference, just twelve votes, would have come from delegates since arrived from the army, men who had served under Austin and observed two things. First, he was ailing and scarcely able to control his command. That boded ill for his stamina to run a government. But like most of the men already in San Felipe, they also knew of the enormous respect that Austin enjoyed in the United States. He had always been Texas's best ambassador wherever he went. Now Texas needed men, money, and supplies, and quickly. The choice between making Austin an adequate governor or an excellent emissary was not a difficult one. Indeed, Austin himself may have preferred this and so advised his friends in San Felipe, as he had quite certainly told them just days before that he had no desire or stamina to continue as a general in the field. They would make him an ambassador instead.[67]

The Consultation also elected Robinson unopposed as lieutenant governor, showing both the spirit of compromise as well as a lack of practical vision. Smith was an ardent—indeed bigoted—radical; Robinson had at least one foot in the Peace camp. With the governorship and the Council essentially independent entities, each led by men of conflicting views, the potential for conflict was inevitable. Less controversial on the face of it was the election of Houston as major general to command "the armies of Texas," an ambiguous phrasing that left open questions of whether he commanded the volunteers or just the anticipated Regulars. The delegates also elected the Council, choosing a good balance of men from both camps, but that was destined to change as Robinson's direction and the addition of more members quickly shifted it to an antagonistic posture toward the governor.[68]

Once Smith, Robinson, and the members of the Council took their oaths of office, the Consultation attended to some minor last business, but not before it felt Houston's attempted influence one last time. Except for the obligatory resolutions of thanks to their officers for their conduct, the last resolution introduced called for Austin to abandon the siege of Béxar and fall back to Goliad and Gonzales, establish guards, and furlough the main body of the men to go home until March 1, 1836, unless summoned before then. The house refused even to consider it and adjourned on November 14, calling on all members who could to go to Austin's army as soon as possible to bear arms in defense of Texas.[69]

From the time that his address failed to convince the army to withdraw from Béxar, Houston apparently rankled over what he saw as both an affront to himself and a dangerous policy for Texas. Throughout his life he did not take defeat gracefully. The very night after the speeches before the volunteers, his first public rebuff in years, Houston made one of his occasional visits to the bottle. He may not have become so irrational as to threaten suicide, as one witness later claimed, but he did get drunk enough that Bowie had to restrain him.[70] Now here in San Felipe the evening after the adjournment, he fought another losing bout with liquor, this time with Bowie and others present in his room at Jonathan Peyton's boardinghouse. Arriving that very day, and being introduced to Bowie, Anson Jones found the notorious speculator "dead drunk." When he met Houston, Jones found him little better, looking, he thought, like "a broken-down sot and debauchee." The revelers went late into the night with a loud drunken party before Bowie left with dispatches for the army. Others in the house heard their talk, and while the spree may have begun to celebrate the close of the Consultation and Houston's commission as major general, the chief topic of conversation soon turned to derision of Austin for not withdrawing his little army east of the Colorado River, a complaint likely growing from the renewed rejection by the Consultation that morning, and perhaps promoted by Bowie, who had reasons of his own to resent Austin. Jones had been at Peyton's listening to the session, and he complained of Houston's conduct to John Wharton and apparently to several others. In return Wharton warned him that "some parties" might take offense at his remarks— probably implying Bowie—and suggested that his life might be at risk unless he closed his mouth. Jones, however, continued his vocal denunciations during the two or three days he stayed in town, and in the end came to no harm.[71]

Not surprisingly, given the confusion during its calling, and the postponement due to lack of attendance, the Consultation found its share of critics in San Felipe. "My impressions of the Consultation, taken as a whole, were unfavorable," Dr. Jones recalled, though he had arrived at the very end of its sitting. "There appeared to me a plenty of recklessness and selfishness, but little dignity or patriotism." No doubt he thought in part of the behavior of Houston, an elected delegate and not just a visitor like Bowie. Much as the Raven may have reformed some of his earlier ways, he was seen in his cups too often in San Felipe for his own reputation. Jones concluded on leaving that posterity would say little in favor of the Consultation, but he was not being entirely fair. The delegates had produced a hybrid parliamentary republican blueprint. Certainly its prescriptions contained contradictory lines of authority, even though the delegates had had weeks since their election to be thinking of such measures. Still it provided a republican framework and a government that could earn allegiance as Santa Anna's authoritarianism never could from

Texians. No doubt men like Smith and Houston and Robinson pursued their own agenda, but that is ever in the nature of assemblies, even those of nations in genesis.[72] The greatest flaw, perhaps, was a sin of omission. Were the Texians bent on complete independence, even if somehow Mexico City restored the 1824 Constitution? They pretended the answer was "no." In any event, Santa Anna would not give them a serious alternative to "yes."

Now much of the decision for independence rested with Houston. He had not given up yet on getting the army away from Béxar for reasons—his wounded pride aside—that made sound military sense to him, especially now that he was charged with organizing and building the military forces of Texas. Had he known the condition of that army even then as he and Bowie charged their glasses, he would have felt renewed urgency, for Bowie himself brought news of disintegration and discord of which he had himself been a part, and he did not know the worst of it. The army was at risk of falling apart.

CHAPTER EIGHT

Dark Schemes

᏶ᎷᎷᏛ

THERE WAS A DARK irony in the fact that at the very moment that Texians arose in the name of freedom and liberty, some of them were torturing and murdering men on the lower Brazos for allegedly sharing the same dreams. Historically, slaveowners always overreacted to the faintest rumor of a slave revolt and rapidly exaggerated the supposed plans of the blacks. Everyone remembered the bloodbath that followed the uprisings on San Domingue, followed by a brief insurrection in Virginia in 1800 and the aborted 1822 rising planned by Télémaque Vesey in Charleston. Much more immediate in their consciousness was the 1831 revolt in Southampton, Virginia, when Nat Turner and three score other slaves rose up and went on a killing spree that left sixty or more dead whites in their wake. Now from the plantations near Columbia and the lower part of Austin's colony came rumors that slaves were plotting to take advantage of the crisis to rise in their own revolt.

Mexican authorities had always been hostile toward slavery officially, though they were willing to allow the various subterfuges by which Texians rationalized their chattels, and their own system of *peonage* was not much better. However, in the face of hostilities, Texians suspected that the Mexicans would encourage slaves to rise and create a second front in their rear. Even before hostilities commenced, Williamson said in a public address that the Mexicans would attempt to force emancipation on them, and Milam warned friends that he expected the Mexicans would try "to get the slaves to revolt."[1] Santa Anna himself certainly suggested that such fears were warranted. Noting the large number of slaves brought to Texas "under cover of certain questionable contracts," he asked his war planners: "Shall we permit those wretches to moan in chains any longer in a country whose kind laws protect the liberty of man without distinction of cast or color?" Even Austin argued before long, as he sought United States help, that the Mexicans intended to wipe out all Anglos in Texas and turn it over to blacks and Indians.[2]

As always happened in rumors of slave revolts, the fears soon escalated into male blacks attacking female whites. Even before the outbreak at Gonzales, the leaders at Matagorda recommended preparing to react to threats from its slaves, especially should Mexicans make a landing in the vicinity.[3] Thus, as soon as the rumor of problems on the Brazos appeared, whites there reacted swiftly and violently, especially as they distorted the story into a slave conspiracy to take over the cotton plantations, divide them among themselves, and then enslave their former masters. The commander of the Goliad garrison released men to go aid the containment, and in the end more than one hundred blacks were arrested. What followed was the tragedy that always closed such scenes. Texians whipped many of the slaves to coerce from them admissions and identification of leaders, and then the ropes began the hanging.[4] There may never have been such a conspiracy in the first place, but it was enough to cause Texians alarm at a critical moment, and the tortures and executions may have reminded the more reflective that such treatment at Mexican hands might be their own lot in the none-too-distant future.

For much of the month after the Consultation delegates left the army, an unaccustomed inactivity settled in on the Texians outside Béxar as the lack of organization, experience, training, supply, and more, incident on its hasty formation and march finally caught up with it. Austin needed time now to put it in shape. While he did so, and while Mexican authorities in Mexico itself still organized themselves to respond to the outbreak, the scene of activity shifted briefly eastward. Captain Philip Dimmitt took command at Goliad in mid-October with a very small garrison of just fifty men, and he wanted to advance south to the Nueces River to take the small Mexican post at Fort Lipantitlán near San Patricio. It would protect his hold at Goliad, while also giving the Texians an advance position deeper in south Texas from which they could threaten Matamoros on the Gulf or any overland relief expedition to Béxar. Indeed, Dimmitt believed from reconnaissance that as many as five hundred enemy cavalry were gathering in the vicinity to advance on Goliad.[5]

By the end of October, Dimmitt felt somewhat secure in sending thirty-five mounted men to take Fort Lipantitlán. Coincidentally, most of the Mexican garrison there—in fact it was a mere one hundred men strong—left that same day to move against Goliad. Thus, when the Texians reached San Patricio on November 3, they discovered there was no enemy to fight and occupied the fort late that same day, forcing the surrender of its remaining twenty-seven defenders without firing a shot. Contenting themselves with taking what they could carry that was of any use, they burned or broke down the rest of the fort, and on November 4 left to return to Goliad just as the balance of the Mexican garrison returned.[6] The two small parties met at a ford on the Nueces, the outnumbered Texians taking defensive positions on the edge of a wood and handily repulsing a Mexican assault in a skirmish that lasted barely half an hour. A week later the Texians reached Goliad once again with yet another small but bracing victory to their credit. Its real importance lay not in the capture of a fourth small garrison and the defeat of the rest, but in cutting off yet another possible route of relief for Cós and his garrison at Béxar. That set the stage for a genuine siege that could bring substantial gains.

General Cós found himself in an increasingly difficult position in Béxar by this time. Virtually all Mexican outposts in Texas had been dispersed, his route of supply to the Gulf was cut off, and Santa Anna in Mexico itself might not yet even know of his predicament. Furthermore, he could see Austin's ragtag army at Concepción before him. Cós had no reason to fear those rebels individually. He knew that overall his men were better trained and better armed, and he had the advantage in defense of his artillery, though his gunpowder was so miserable that when Texians captured ammunition from Mexican *soldados*, they threw away the powder and kept only the bullets. He had enough supplies to last for some weeks, so the immediate danger of starvation did not loom. But he also knew that there were thirty thousand or more colonists in Texas, which meant that the army of Austin might conceivably swell to several times his own numbers. Cós could withstand more than one assault, surely, especially if he pulled his command into the final defense of the Alamo's thick adobe walls. But even these ragged Texians with their hodgepodge of arms might conceivably overwhelm him from sheer weight of numbers if enough of them rallied to Austin's standard. Most troubling of all, however, Cós had no alternative but to wait and see what Austin would do. He could evacuate, of course, but he would have to leave his artillery behind, leaving Texas entirely in the hands of the insurgents, and thereby make it much more difficult for Santa Anna to retake. Not incidentally, it would likely ruin Cós's career in the offing, even if he was one of the generalissimo's favorites.

Cós might have been less apprehensive had he known that Austin faced serious dilemmas of his own. His own supplies were scanty, and he had to rely on his personal credit and that of officers like Bowie to buy food for his men from local farmers. His army did not swell as Cós feared. Indeed, immediately after the little scrape at Concepción, his strength slipped under six hundred as a number of men briefly left for home when the weather turned cold and the army had neither blankets nor shelters. Fortunately, more volunteers soon arrived, and by November 7 his numbers were between seven hundred and eight hundred, but they would decline again during the balance of the siege. Fearful that the Mexicans might slip from his grasp, Austin divided his army, leaving Bowie and Fannin at Concepción to patrol the southern approaches to San Antonio, while Austin took the balance north of town.

One of the first veterans of the war reached Austin's army in November when Neill, Dickinson, and the Gonzales "Come and Take It" cannon arrived. For all his increasing ill health and the pressure of a position for which he realized he was not qualified, army commander Austin could still muster a sense of the absurd now and then. Here he was with an understrength, ill-equipped, and already balky army of volunteers, trying to take by siege a force of experienced, well-equipped Mexican regulars and conscripts fortified behind strong masonry walls, and his artillery for the operation was a few ineffectual guns like this modest six-pounder. Seeing its influence as all but futile, he simply told Neill that he could shoot it at the Alamo if he wanted to, apparently taking no further interest. The gun crew took him at his word, and soon random members of the army were taking potshots at the Alamo walls, as they did when another piece from Concepción arrived, placing bets on where their balls would strike, more interested in the money and goods changing hands than on the negligible damage done to the enemy bastion.[7]

Austin was no military man, but instinctively he understood that when volunteers faced regulars, time was always on the side of the professionals. Knowing that his army could evaporate at any time as men lost heart or enthusiasm, or if the approaching winter turned too cold, he hoped to find an opportunity for an attack and a quick victory. Moreover, the political factionalism that hampered authorities back in San Felipe also infected the army's high command. Bowie, already inclined to the Houston clique, had resigned on November 2 when Austin consolidated his army, effectively ending Bowie's independent wing command. However, he remained with the army a few days, and rumors soon spread that he and Austin had had a falling-out. That mirrored more widespread problems. With the inactivity men became insubordinate, alcohol got into the camps, and desertion began to rise. Some men refused to answer the morning roll calls, and afterwards just wandered about as suited them, even walking close to Béxar itself to gawk.[8]

Seeing this, Austin's officers preferred to risk a siege, knowing that as unreliable as their men's commitment might be, their lack of training and discipline could make them even more unmanageable in an open-field engagement. Bowie's voice spoke loud in advocacy of a siege. Indeed, Moses Bryan believed that Bowie more than once wore down the resistance of the ailing commander, and was an "ambitious, self asserting" man who believed himself more capable of leading than Austin.[9] Evidence of that came on November 5 when Austin appointed him temporarily adjutant general in Hall's absence, and then the next day Austin announced that he would be leaving the army. He was tired, sick, and had seen enough of the dissolution. He was ready to abandon the siege, or at least hope of carrying it to a successful conclusion. Those who wanted to go with him to San Felipe could come along. He would leave Bowie nominally in command of the rest, with orders to hold an election to select a colonel to command them and then to resist as well as they could, and if Cós should evacuate, to press him closely to the Rio Grande.[10]

The election took place that same day, but among five candidates, Bowie came in last with only five votes. Edward Burleson, a thirty-seven-year-old veteran of the War of 1812 who had militia experience as an officer in Missouri and Tennessee and had led Texas militia against Indians, won overwhelmingly.[11] Then in a bizarre about-face, Austin announced that he would not leave after all, but would continue overall command of the army, while leaving Burleson in operational supervision. Austin's motives are cloudy. It may simply have been his health that led to indecision and vacillation. Or there may have been crafty policy in his action. By allowing the men to choose Burleson as their immediate commander, he rather placed himself above the carping of Bowie, William Wharton, Hall, and others, while at the same time his unexpected reversal so infuriated them that they all immediately and angrily resigned. Some noted an almost immediate improvement in morale in the camps thereafter as the dissidents left.[12]

For the next two weeks only minor skirmishes occurred as Cós sent out the occasional cavalry probe, or the Texians tried to get close enough to San Antonio to raid and snipe. Austin sent his own small mounted companies, one of them now commanded by Captain William Barret Travis, out into the countryside to intercept Mexican dispatches and an occasional herd of horses and any livestock that might be headed toward the beleaguered garrison. On November 18 when Bowie arrived with dispatches from Houston and others, Austin learned of the actions of the Consultation in San Felipe, including Houston's election as general in chief, and Austin's own selection to go to the United States as an emissary. Bowie also brought his own renewed ambitions. Learning from Houston during their party in San Felipe that the Raven was to take overall charge of Texian forces, but that he intended to remain in the interior organizing and raising more soldiers, Bowie returned hoping to win the Béxar army command for himself when Austin left. "Col. Jas. Bowie wanted to be in the Camps, yea and present when Genl. Austin resigned the command of the army," recalled Bowie's riding companion during the trip.[13]

But Austin did not leave immediately, for renewed disaffection erupted in the ranks. Men felt depressed and discouraged at the routine and inactivity, and as they learned the results of the Consultation, every shade of political opinion found something with which to object. Desertion reduced the force from more than six hundred men to just over four hundred. "This army has always been composed of discordant materials," Austin lamented. On November 21 he tried to order an assault on Béxar for the next morning in order to reinvigorate the men, but when dawn came half of the army simply refused to move. That convinced him at last that nothing more could be done with them. It was best for him to leave and go to his new assignment, and leave a small force there to watch while Houston built a proper army.[14] He ordered a new election for an army commander to be held two days later, but the results once again repudiated Bowie and saw Burleson securely in command when the *empresario* finally left for San Felipe. A week later Burleson reorganized the army into two divisions with Milam commanding the First, and Johnson commanding the Second, and some eleven small independent companies mostly engaged in scouting.

Still Bowie got another moment of glory when two days later word arrived that a Mexican mule train had been spotted five miles from Béxar. Some thought it came from the south intent on resupplying the garrison, though in fact Cós himself sent it out undetected. Burleson ordered Bowie to take a company of forty horsemen off to reconnoiter the train while he prepared to send an infantry detachment to intercept. Instead, perhaps impelled by rumors that the animals carried a treasure in silver, Bowie impetuously attacked the pack train in spite of being outnumbered almost four-to-one by the one hundred fifty *soldados* accompanying the mules. After the first rush stopped the train, Bowie dismounted his command and took cover to hold the Mexicans in place long enough for the infantry to arrive. The train guard tried to rush Bowie's position, but were forced back, just as Burleson came up to a position between Bowie and Béxar. Then Cós sent a relief party of dragoons out of town to aid the pack train, and Burleson was able to turn them back. Everyone but Cós's horsemen were dismounted, fighting from the cover of dry streambeds, meaning that no one really knew where anyone else was or in what strength, and the skirmish became a series of isolated and uncoordinated little battles until Bowie and Burleson united their commands and made a last push that drove the train guard out just as it was joined by its own reinforcement. The Mexicans pulled into the defenses of San Antonio, whose cannon soon opened fire and discouraged the Texians from further pursuit. They left many of the mules behind, but when the victors opened their packs expecting to find food or ammunition or, best of all silver, they discovered only fresh-cut grass destined to feed Cós's animals. Disgruntled by what one man called "this ludicrous affair" in fighting for nothing, the Texians derisively dubbed the little battle the "Grass Fight." Soon thereafter Bowie left the army, still destined to return one last time.[15]

When Austin held the election that put Burleson in command he also allowed the men to vote on whether or not to continue the siege of Béxar, and the majority assented. Despite the disappointment at finding only grass on those pack mules, still the fact that Cós risked sending out nearly a fifth of his garrison to gather fodder revealed that the animals in the Mexican garrison were close to starvation, and presumably the men would be, too. On December 2 Burleson announced that now at last was the time to attack, but his officers balked. In a council of war almost every one of them voted against an attack, and Burleson had no option but to announce a postponement. Once again in the face of apparent indecision, Texian morale plummeted. The men had been hungry for some time, San Felipe having as yet too little resource to send them adequate foodstuffs. The army was back up to about five hundred men, but they tired of inactivity and postponements. Some companies all but mutinied and refused to answer roll call. Worse, talk circulated of an expedition to Matamoros that promised not only easy action, but also plunder, and many of these men around Béxar wanted a share. So close to what might be a final victory, and with at last the first substantial battle of their revolution on the horizon, the Texians seemed almost ready to give up.[16]

It was the brink of disaster. Burleson called a general parade for the next day, and by the time he assembled the men the scale of the demoralization made itself painfully evident. Some companies refused to appear that day, and perhaps half of the army simply packed their belongings preparing to leave for home. "The spectacle becomes appalling," one man wrote in his diary. "All day we get more and more dejected."[17] Open drunkenness and a spirit of insubordination so prevailed that officers held almost no sway with their men. Burleson called another general parade of those remaining for December 4, and there announced to the men that he was calling off the siege and would lead them back to Goliad for the winter. After nothing but successes against the Mexicans every time they met since Gonzales, the seeming irresolution of the men and the fear that Cós knew of his plans and was too well emplaced to be budged combined to persuade him willingly to give up and retreat.

But at the last possible moment, with Burleson preparing to march the remnant of his army away from San Antonio, twin strokes of good fortune intervened. A Mexican deserter from Béxar arrived to report deplorable conditions and morale in the garrison and that the *soldados* might not have much fight left in them. Then the charismatic Milam, who had been away for a few days, arrived and saw with disgust that all their gains were about to be abandoned. He persuaded Frank Johnson to go with him to Burleson's tent and angrily walked there in full view of the men, who sensed that something was going to happen. As the Texians gathered around outside, Burleson sadly told Milam that he, too, wanted an assault, but his officers and men would not go along. They settled on an expedient that had some chance of success. If Milam, who was widely respected and admired in the army, could get enough volun- teers to go with him into an assault, then Burleson would try to keep the rest in place during the attack. If Milam failed, then Burleson could use the Texians to cover the withdrawal, and then they would all retreat to Goliad. If Milam made any gains at all, however, both commanders knew that it would inspire the rest of the men that there was action at last, and that fellow Texians needed their aid, and that they had a chance for another victory. However much it depended on the impon- derable of Milam's personal charisma, it was a mature and eminently sensible expedient.[18]

It worked. "Who will follow old Ben Milam into San Antonio?" he shouted when he left Burleson's tent. Close to five hundred volunteers remained in camp. Scores enthusiastically shouted "I will, I will," but still around two hundred remained silent.[19] The officer in charge of the New Orleans Grays, a volunteer unit arrived from Louisiana to take part in the uprising, managed to get his one hundred men to go along, bring- ing the assault force to about three hundred. It was not a lot to go up against a reported five hundred seventy *soldados* inside San Antonio, especially as they were well barricaded, but it was a start.[20] As he and other officers rallied the remaining volunteers, Milam persuaded Burleson to command them again and the die was cast. If it was the democratic impulse that had nearly led to complete dissolution and desertion of the army, it was that same impulse now that rallied around the prospect of action. True to form, the men were allowed to vote, and chose Milam himself to lead the attack.

Milam planned to seize some abandoned adobe and wattle *jacales* north of San Antonio and close to the town, and use those rude huts as a base for an attack into the streets. During the predawn hours of Decem- ber 5, Milam got the men into position, including their handful of small captured cannon, and at about 5:00 A.M. Colonel James C. Neill opened fire, sending a cannonball crashing into the wall of the Alamo. For the next hour or two a desultory artillery duel ensued, and under its cover Milam's advance crept forward to occupy houses within a block of the main plaza of the town. They swept onward, hugging the walls on either side of the streets as the two divisions moved deeper into the town. Mexicans finally spotted them when the Texians got within perhaps two hundred yards of the plaza, and immediately opened fire. Now the streets that gave them some protection began to work against the attackers, for Mexican field pieces positioned at the end of the *calles* fired down the streets with canister and the Texians had nowhere to hide. They broke into homes for cover, and all at once the engagement changed from a battle into a series of house-to-house skirmishes as the Texians continued their advance toward the plaza.[21]

After several hours of intermittent skirmishing and fighting, Milam's party was doing well, though meeting stiff resistance. They silenced some of the Mexican artillery in the street, and thus far suffered themselves only two killed and a few more wounded. But ammunition ran low, and there appeared to be plenty of resolve in the Mexican garrison to hold out long enough for Ugartechea to come reinforce them with, Milam and Burleson feared, as many as six hundred *soldados.* That would be more than enough to change the whole complexion of the siege, perhaps even lift it. Faced with this, while the gunfire still reverberated along the streets of San Antonio, Burleson sent a rider to San Felipe with an urgent call on Governor Smith for more men and materiel.[22]

Cós had seven field pieces in the plaza firing down the streets, with his heavier cannon mounted on the walls of the Alamo compound. Now he turned those big guns on the houses sheltering the Texians, which put the attackers between two fires. With axes and crowbars, Milam's men hewed their way through the walls from one house into another, while marksmen fired out the windows at the Mexican gunners at the end of the avenues. Texians on the roofs tried to snipe at the artillery-men, but Cós's own marksmen in the belfry of the church on the plaza neutralized them. Soon the Texian advance stalled as gunpowder ran short; they began to take casualties, and thirst reminded them that they had brought no water. All day the intermittent sniping continued, and that evening the Texians began digging in and barricading their end of some of the streets. Meanwhile, Burleson commanded the small reserve east of town, sending cavalry out repeatedly circling Béxar to make certain Cós did not attempt to break out and escape.

The next day, Milam and Johnson continued their slow advance, often encountering Mexicans in hand-to-hand combat over possession of a house. Texians got one of their cannon into the town and began to answer the Mexican artillery fire. That night they consolidated their gains with more earthworks, while the Mexicans threw up new defenses of their own.[23] When December 7 dawned, the sporadic fighting went on, the Texians steadily advancing against stubborn Mexican resistance, and now the attackers could use their cannon to blast fortified Mexicans out of houses. Finally, that afternoon Milam sensed that the time had come for an all-out attack that should carry the day. He consulted with the other officers to plan the assault, and had just walked into the courtyard of the old Veramendi house, where once Bowie lived as Veramendi's son-in-law, when a sharpshooter's bullet smashed through Milam's head, killing him instantly.

It was a critical moment. The men might have lost heart at the death of their inspirational leader if their officers did not act quickly. That evening they chose Johnson to succeed Milam, and then launched a successful morale-boosting night attack on Mexicans barricaded in houses close to the plaza. The next day, however, the Mexicans got their own brief spirit-lifting news with the arrival of—as feared—more than six hundred men and some artillery led by Colonel Domingo de Ugartechea. Somehow they evaded Burleson's patrols and got safely into town. Most of them were not soldiers, however, but prisoners in shackles, conscripted into service, and as soon as they were released from their irons it became clear that they would not fight, even under coercion. Instead, they threatened to attack the officers trying to organize them. Worse, Cós sent more than two hundred of his own men out the day before to find Ugartechea, but they simply deserted.

By the evening of December 8 only one remaining fortified house stood between the Texians and the plaza itself, and by midnight it, too, fell. That left the open plaza untenable for the Mexicans. Cós had lost too many of his good men to desertion and enemy fire. The newly arrived convicts were more of a threat than a help and would exhaust his dwindling foodstuffs even faster. His reduced command was not strong enough to hold all of his defensive lines, even if he withdrew them behind the Alamo's high walls. Once inside that compound, no other reinforcements could reach him and he could hardly hope to break out. There was no alternative left him but surrender. About dawn on December 9, while the skirmishing and the inexorable Texian advance continued, Cós sent out a white flag and commenced negotiations that went on until after midnight.

That very day San Felipe was reacting to news from Béxar. Burleson's rider reached the town late on December 8, bringing Governor Smith news of the critical state of the siege and the house-to-house conflict by Milam. The next morning Smith drafted a proclamation and delivered it to the printers Baker and Borden, whose press soon turned out a broadside exhorting his fellow citizens to act quickly. Milam's situation was critical, he said, with Mexican reinforcements daily expected to relieve Béxar. Characterizing the Texians' chances of success as "doubtful," the governor in seeming despair concluded that "all we have to hope from, is, that they are North American freemen, and will act worthy of themselves." Texians must rally immediately and go to Béxar ready to fight. "Never cease your exertions, while one stone can be found upon another, or a Mexican soldier [is] left to imprint with his footstep the soil of Texas." It was about as gloomy and uninspiring a call to arms as could be imagined, and it is just as well that by the time it came off the press, Béxar had fallen.[24]

In the end Cós surrendered, to be allowed to leave with one small cannon and limited arms to protect his men from Indian attack as they marched south. The remainder of their armaments, more than eight hundred muskets and twenty pieces of artillery, were to be left behind. The Mexicans had suffered as many as one hundred fifty casualties not counting the desertions, almost one third of Cós's command, against less than forty Texians, though the loss of Milam hurt sorely. The revolution had its first really significant victory, against not a single loss, and many believed that would be an end of it. The Mexicans, thus chastened, would not return, and Texas was free. Indeed, Burleson and most of the army soon simply went home, leaving a much-reduced command under Johnson to occupy San Antonio.

It was a tragic mistake, one that set up months of turmoil and dissolution, and put all the pieces in place for the collapse of the government and a disaster to Texian arms. Almost as soon as they assumed their offices, Governor Smith and the Council were at loggerheads. People found Smith "too illiterate, too little informed, and not of the right *calibre*" for the job he held. Opinions of Robinson at the head of the Council were little better.[25] For his part, the governor accused the Council of a want of patriotism. With them, he said, "it was all sordid self interest."[26] Their variant platforms on independence versus remaining in Mexico set up the discord, of course, and Smith's confrontational and impetuous personality guaranteed a stormy relationship.

Then there was the "sordid self interest." Texas politics never seemed able to free itself of the perennial clutch of land speculation. Of course, free or cheap land had been the mantra of the Anglo push west from the Appalachians to the Mississippi and beyond. These Texians were the sons of men who went west looking for land at as little as fifty cents an acre. Some had themselves already shifted from claims in Alabama to Mississippi and on to Texas. A few like Bowie nearly made great fortunes in Louisiana and Arkansas, not scrupling either at the way they obtained the land or in selling what was not their own. More, prominent Texian leaders such as Milam, Johnson, Samuel Williams, James Grant, and John Mason, and Bowie among them, tried again with great success to get massive land concessions from the pliant and purchasable Monclova legislature. Monclova sold the land to obtain money to help resist Santa Anna, but it was too little and too late.

When Monclova fell to Cós and he dispersed its legislature, the speculators took a hard blow. The fatal one came next, when the Consultation repudiated the Monclova grants. Not only were the speculators out the money they had paid, but they also lost any rightful title to sell the grant lands now declared to be public domain. Some of them responded with the idea of direct aid to foment and encourage federalist uprisings within Mexico. If they could succeed in overthrowing Santa Anna and installing the federalist Farías in his place, then the new regime would have the authority to legitimize the Monclova grants so long as Texas remained a state in the federation. The relatively conservative Council was much in tune with the idea, especially since some Council members themselves participated in the speculations. Ironically, even Smith favored the idea, believing that taking actual indisputable Mexican soil would somehow force the wavering into the inevitable shift from federalism under Mexico to independence under their own flag.[27]

The catalyst to turn idea into action was a forty-two-year-old Scot named James Grant. Born to a family heavily involved in the East India Company's trading ventures, he made a few voyages himself for the company before settling in Coahuila in 1823. By 1835 he was secretary of the Monclova legislature, a "shrewd schemer" to some, but a "scholar, gentleman and soldier" to others. Having escaped along with Bowie when the Monclova crowd were broken up, Grant was in Goliad early in November, and soon Governor Viesca joined him after his own escape. There they met with Dimmitt, who discussed with them the idea of leading an expedition against Matamoros, just up the Rio Grande from the Gulf and a port reputed to be doing $100,000 a month or more in shipping business. If they could take the port and themselves collect that revenue, they would be able to finance the grander scheme of spreading a successful revolt against Santa Anna through neighboring Tamaulipas and the reinstating of Farías and federalism. Not incidentally, such an uprising among Mexicans along the Rio Grande would likely mean that those loyal to the centralists would have to leave for their own safety. They were the wealthiest landowners, and thus their lands might be either forfeit or else sold at very attractive prices.[28] Several San Felipe mercantile interests also saw profit in the Matamoros idea, and some of them, too, sat on the Council.

The idea was not entirely foolhardy. The seizure of Matamoros could just as easily help finance the Texian uprising as one in Mexico, and its location on one of only two practical main roads from Mexico into Texas afforded an opportunity to reduce Santa Anna's routes of invasion by half. At the same time, plans were laid for an amphibious expedition of men raised in New Orleans and bound for Tampico under command of José Mexia, thus striking Mexico in two places at once. But there were political problems. In the November absence of any overall ruling authority in Texas, about all it needed to get up an expedition was finding men and money. There was no one from whom to gain permission. Austin favored the idea, but only if a Mexican federalist could be found to lead the enterprise. Otherwise there was the risk that if Texians commanded, then it would look like another land grab, and as well compromise the Texian insurrection by turning it from a movement in self-defense to one of conquest. Houston apparently showed some interest in the idea, not for its speculative motives, but because anything that distracted Santa Anna worked to the purpose of Texas, yet he took no active step on its behalf. Dimmitt was enthusiastic, suggesting Zavala to lead the expedition, thanks to his broad cachet among *tejanos* and Mexican federalists, but he had refused, at the same time warning that if either of the expeditions failed, then the other was doomed, the first but hardly the last prediction of disaster for the scheme.

Dimmitt actually got the project in motion when he took Fort Lipantitlán, for with it in his hands the road was clear to Matamoros. But then his enthusiasm for the plan waned. He felt uncomfortable seeing it fall into the hands of Grant and Viesca, with their mixed motives. He also learned that on November 14 the expedition to Tampico actually landed—ran aground and wrecked, actually—just one hundred fifty men strong, to find that the republicans in the local garrison had already revolted, to be put down by the arrival of centralist forces just before the Texian army "landed." As a result, Mexia's attack failed on November 15, and he was forced to escape on an American schooner, leaving thirty-one of his men behind. Three of them died of their wounds, and in a few weeks the rest went before first a court-martial, and than a firing squad. It was the first Texian setback, though few of the expedition had actually come from Texas. Dimmitt more than anyone else kept an ear tuned to sentiments in northern Mexico, and at the same time it became increasingly clear to him that federalist sympathy in Tamaulipas, while strong, was not strong enough. His own sentiments also shifted and in time he repudiated the federalists entirely and committed himself to Texian independence. That put him at odds with the federalist speculating supporters of the Matamoros plan, though he continued to support the idea of taking Matamoros for its military benefits.[29] It set him against Grant and Viesca.

Stymied in Goliad, Grant went to Béxar to try to interest the army then engaged in its desultory siege in his idea, while Viesca went to San Felipe to sell it to the governor and Council. Grant reached the army just as Burleson superceded Austin and as morale plummeted. As he saw it, the men were on the verge of leaving for want of a real commander. He appealed to Houston to come, then apparently suggested that he would himself make an able commander, but finally settled for acting as Johnson's executive officer in the operations that resulted in Cós's surrender. Burleson left soon afterward and that put Johnson in charge, himself heavily involved in the Monclova speculations. Most of the Texian volunteers also went home, many of the remainder at Béxar being men just arrived from the United States who had no local homes to go to, and who came in part to find land to make homes. They also filled their now idle time by plundering the livestock and grain of local *tejanos* regardless of their sympathies, giving evidence that to them all Mexicans were the same. They thus offered an audience ripe for the Matamoros hopes of Johnson and Grant. Both actively promoted their scheme to the men, promising land, booty, riches for the taking. "These glowing representations had the desired effect," recalled one of the men there. "The minds of these young men from the 'states' became inflamed with a desire for conquest, military glory, and loot."[30]

Meanwhile in San Felipe, Viesca's lobbying met receptive ears at first. On December 17, Governor Smith gave Houston instructions to take Matamoros, though he did not specifically order him to command the expedition himself.[31] Unfortunately, in a blatant example of the divided and uncoordinated nature of the government, the Council issued similar orders to Johnson. Houston, in turn, sent an order to Bowie that he should try to organize an expedition and lead it against Matamoros.[32] Without saying so explicitly, the implication was that Bowie was to try to raise the men from among the remaining companies at Béxar, which would put him directly in competition with Johnson. Suddenly governor and Council worked against each other with rival commanders to control rival expeditions and toward conflicting ends.

At Béxar, Johnson and Grant actively campaigned to enlist their soldiers in the Matamoros dream. Indeed, Johnson almost complained that his problem was not in finding volunteers to go, but in finding men willing to stay behind to provide an adequate garrison in San Antonio. "All—All wish to achieve new victories & to raise the glory of the Army of Texas," he declared. Johnson told Robinson that all would be well if he was "not interfered with by officers of the regular army," a bizarre virtual refutation of the legitimacy of the newly and constitutionally mandated military establishment. Indeed, he went further, giving evidence of just how little credence or fealty certain influential men paid to the acts of the Consultation. He could see through "the hostility which several persons in power have evinced to the Volunteer Army," he told friends the day before Christmas. Texas would have been ruined had it not been for the volunteers' adherence to their duty in spite of neglect. The hostility that he perceived to the volunteer army "created a multitude of evils too numerous to mention," he charged, thus excusing himself from the troublesome task of actually enumerating any. Only their patriotism held them together so that he and his officers brought order out of chaos and now had them disciplined and subordinate, a condition that only he seemed to perceive among those around Béxar.

Johnson completely bypassed Governor Smith and worked exclusively with the Council. At the same time, he either engineered or at least encouraged a flat refusal on the part of the captains of the several companies at Béxar to take orders from Regular Army officers. They wanted their own commander in chief—obviously Johnson—and would place themselves subject to Houston's orders only by their own invitation.[33] And meanwhile, rather unsubtly, he started castigating Dimmitt to Smith and the Council on a variety of trumped-up complaints, when Dimmitt cooled on the Matamoros adventure and displayed allegiance to Houston. At the same time, Johnson began running down Burleson as well.[34] The self-interest in his complaints was embarrassingly blatant.

Learning of the Council's backing of Johnson, Smith became incensed, especially when he and Houston and others heard rumors that Grant was calling for Houston to be replaced by Johnson, and meanwhile that Johnson and Grant really wanted to create a new polity called a Republic of North Mexico, independent both from Texas and Mexico itself, and were thus working exclusively to their own ends. As the whole affair became more and more complicated in ambitions, avarice, and politics, it was increasingly apparent just how dangerous the whole idea of a Matamoros expedition had become. In time this led to an ultimate rupture between Smith and the Council. The competition for its command between Smith and the Council in San Felipe, and between Houston and Johnson in the field, risked something close to civil war within a revolution. If Johnson actually led the expedition, he would command what at the moment would be a larger military force than Houston's, and if he succeeded then he was sure to eclipse the Raven in popularity and power. If Houston managed to take over the command, there was the risk of mutiny by the volunteers and a discrediting of the government in San Felipe. It did not help when the Council commissioned Fannin to act as a supply agent for the expedition on the same day that he accepted Smith's commission as a colonel and Houston's second in command in the Regular Army, thus virtually pitting Fannin in a test of loyalties against himself.

By early January, Smith had ordered Houston to take command of the enterprise, and Houston wanted to lead the expedition personally if it went at all. Meanwhile, Houston sent Bowie with orders to organize and take command, even though Bowie held no commission either in the Regular or volunteer forces. The Council now gave positive orders for Johnson to take command, yet also seemed to sanction Fannin assuming leadership. It only remained for Grant to try to take command, which he did on January 1, 1836, declaring himself acting commander in chief and putting his two-hundred-man army on the road for Goliad after he all but denuded Béxar of military stores and munitions, leaving the tiny hundred-man garrison commanded by Neill practically destitute.

By January 6 Johnson had temporarily withdrawn from the command, and the Council instead was considering Bowie as commander based on his orders from Houston. Then they suddenly appointed Fannin instead, and meanwhile Houston began giving orders to set the expedition in motion. If anyone needed evidence of the rapidly accelerating disintegration of the situation, it came on January 9 when a disgusted Smith, sensing that the affair had spun out of control, attempted to reassert his authority by canceling the expedition altogether, with Houston's assent now that he, too, had seen how dangerous it had become. But the Council refused to withdraw its authorization, whereupon Smith dissolved the Council after sending it an inflammatory critique accusing it of corruption. Unfazed, the Council continued to meet and itself impeached Smith on January 10, installed Robinson as acting governor, and then began moving against Smith's appointees with accusations of contempt and dismissal.[35] Soon thereafter it appointed several men to take the official archives away from the governor. Travis was one of those appointed, but he and most of the rest refused to carry out the order, and Smith stubbornly stayed in his office, now a powerless cipher.[36] Everyone was in charge, it seemed, and no one, and few could even keep up with all the shifts and changes. Then came word of Grant's acting on his own. "Some dark scheme has been set on foot to disgrace our noble cause," Bowie advised Houston.[37] The trouble was that Bowie's use of the word "scheme" should have been in the plural.

By the time Bowie reached Goliad, the Council had already passed a declaration that, as an officer in neither Regular nor volunteer forces, Bowie had no right to assume command in Goliad, and that Houston had had no authority to order him to do so. Unmindful of that, Bowie reached Goliad to find Grant joined by the mercurial Johnson, and both of them ignoring poor Fannin, whom the Council had most recently appointed to command. They also paid no heed to Houston's order for Bowie to assume control. Only when Houston himself arrived on January 14 did the morass begin to clear. Unable to stay out of the imbroglio, Houston had at least shown more judgment and maturity—as well as craft—than most of the others. Aware that he had enemies on the Council and among the volunteer officers, he stayed on his best behavior, halting the drinking sprees that had cost him respect in important quarters in recent weeks. He stayed constantly loyal to the governor, which under the articles drafted by the Consultation was his duty, and he also kept well aware of the several cabals against his own position. By mostly staying away from both San Felipe and the army, ironically, he may have saved his command.[38] The problem with these democrats, it seemed, was that they had created a system with overlapping powers, causing inevitable stalemate and making every elected official appear illegitimate. Only a popular outsider could rescue their loyalties, and Houston knew how to be an outsider when he wanted.

Now there was the danger that the army itself was beyond saving, or worse, that it might turn on itself. Grant had earlier reached Goliad to find Dimmitt refusing to acknowledge the legitimacy of his command or his expedition. Worse, Goliad followed a wave of independence feeling that finally got ahead of San Felipe's efforts at containment. In December, that same Anson Jones, who had been a Peace Party man reluctant to take rash steps, helped call a public meeting in Brazoria, and before it he placed resolutions calling for an outright declaration of independence from Mexico, suggesting a convention to meet in March 1836 to draft such a declaration and a constitution.[39] Almost immediately Dimmitt's garrison at Goliad did the same thing on December 22, as did coincidentally another public meeting at San Augustine.[40]

The proceedings of the Goliad meeting, however, had a distinct edge to them that reflected on the San Felipe government, and more particularly on Grant, Johnson, and this very army just arrived in its environs. It was framed not by the citizens, but by the men of the garrison. "They have seen their camp thronged, but too frequently, with those who were more anxious to be served by, than to serve their country," their declaration protested; "with men more desirous of being honored with command than capable of commanding." They had seen their energy and toil wasted by divided counsels, frittered away by indecision and ambition. "They have seen the busy aspirants for office running from the field to the council hall, and from this back to the camp, seeking emolument and not service, and swarming like hungry flies around the body politic." They had seen the captured command of Cós released, no doubt to rejoin Santa Anna and come against them again, because guarding the prisoners deterred men from the Matamoros dream. "A revulsion is at hand," they warned, and meanwhile Santa Anna and centralism were on the march, perhaps unstoppable. Why should they continue to stand in defense of the Constitution of 1824 when more than a decade of experience revealed that it posed no impediment to a dictator's aggrandizement? Their only recourse lay in complete independence. Furthermore, they thought they spoke only for the Texians, for at Béxar and here in Goliad, they believed that the *tejanos* had shown themselves infirm in the cause, too ready to continue under the tyrannical yoke of Mexico. "Let us carefully guard against deceiving ourselves," the soldiers said. "Men of Texas! Nothing short of independence can place us on solid ground."[41]

Its unfair slap at the *tejano* community aside, the Goliad declaration was perhaps the most sensible and mature assessment of the case before Texians to appear since the outbreak of hostilities. However, it caused a real problem for the Matamoros adventurers. Not only did it all but actually name Johnson, Grant, and the Council as self-interested scoundrels, which was embarrassing enough, but it and the other independence declarations risked compromising their expedition and their larger aims. If they really had visions of a Republic of North Mexico, any movement toward complete independence by Texas removed a substantial portion of territory to the south from their potential domain. On the other hand, if they still held to hopes of reinstituting the Monclova legislature and Viesca, thereby resecuring their massive land concessions and their personal fortunes, then independence would cost them everything. On Christmas Day, Johnson hastily advised Robinson and the Council that the volunteers felt unhappy over these declarations, and that "if we pretend to independence they will immediately quit us."[42]

Alas, the idea of an independent Texas risked seriously compromising the personal ambitions of some rather venal men, and in their own interests they were quite willing to compromise the cause they affected to serve. When Dimmitt raised a flag proclaiming independence, Grant ordered that it be taken down, protesting that Texas was still committed to the 1824 Constitution. Dimmitt refused, and in the standoff that followed, men feared that the opposing camps might fall to blows among themselves. "Col. Grant and we all expected to have a fight with his force," Captain William Cooke reported. "Both parties were kept in readiness for a fight."[43] Before that could happen, Dimmitt disgustedly resigned on January 10 and left just before Bowie and then Houston arrived. Between the two of them there was little they could do. Matamoros fever had spread throughout the command, and when Houston ordered Bowie to go to San Antonio to assess its defenses and take appropriate actions, Bowie could persuade only a handful of the volunteers to go with him. "I would myself have marched to Bexar," Houston told Smith on January 17, "but the Matamoras rage is up so high." Houston himself could accomplish little with the remainder, lamenting that "you have no idea of the difficulties I have encountered." More than once he addressed the men, trying to reawaken them to their duty to Texas, only to be rebuffed and as well to discover that Governor Smith had been grossly misrepresented to the men by Grant, Johnson, and others.[44] Unfortunately, since he had yet to see action in Texas's defense, while many of these men and their officers had, Houston did not enjoy a warm reception. Some thought he simply opposed Matamoros because he was not in charge of the expedition himself, a fair enough accusation in part, but Houston knew what they did not: that the potential gains from Matamoros did not offset the enormous risks, especially when he had to build an army to resist Santa Anna.

When Grant led the command on to Refugio, where he expected to meet reinforcements under Fannin, Houston simply went along for the ride, in some degree humiliated at his lack of influence with the men, and now more than ever convinced that volunteers were too unreliable to save Texas. Perhaps two hundred men arrived at Refugio on January 21, and there at last Houston's efforts baked half a loaf. At this same moment Johnson rejoined the command and displayed his orders from the Council placing him in charge of the army, a direct conflict with Smith's order to Houston, though Houston did not yet know of Smith's virtual deposition. It was also increasingly evident to Houston that two things utterly doomed the Matamoros movement. One was the blatant attempt to buy continued participation from the men with outright promises of plunder, and the other was the resultant expectation that if citizens were to be robbed of their property, then they would fight back, and twelve thousand people in Matamoros would be more than a match for two hundred Texians. On this basis he made an impassioned address to the army to convince them to give up the operation, and most of them finally did. Two of the companies with Grant agreed to enlist under the provisional government as volunteers for assignment elsewhere—though not as Regulars—and others agreed to remain at Refugio. About thirty had already left to go with Bowie to Béxar, and others returned to Goliad. Even then, none was willing to take orders from Houston, and Johnson's orders from the Council, combined with learning that Smith was essentially out of power, made Houston's own orders moot.

In disgust he simply left to ride back to San Felipe to report to Smith, a leader without a portfolio, in a capital with no government. But Houston's efforts weakened the resolve of many of the volunteers for the project, so that by the time the force finally left Refugio only two companies, about sixty-four men, were left. So many officers, political leaders, and men in the ranks felt disillusioned now with the confusion, crossed purposes, and selfishness of the movement that any chance of success was fatally compromised. When the Raven looked at his own situation, he saw cause for little but gloom. His army had all but abandoned him. His government was squabbling and impotent. Even his old comfort in the bottle was absent, as for some weeks now he kept himself "miserably cool and sober," as he told a friend.[45] He saw personal enemies all around him, both in the army and in San Felipe, and for his personal fortunes he resorted once more to simply absenting himself to let the situation settle on its own. Early in February, Houston would ride off to the Indian territory once more and let Texas fend for itself.

THEREAFTER THE MATAMOROS enterprise was doomed. Fannin landed at Copano with reinforcements early in February and moved to join the small band at Refugio, which then marched to San Patricio on the Nueces. By now all their hopes depended upon massive support from federalist Mexicans rallying to their standard, something that wiser heads like Houston and Dimmitt had known was not likely to happen. Meanwhile, overwhelming Mexican reinforcements reached Matamoros well ahead of them, and when Fannin learned of that, he pulled out of the expedition and withdrew to Goliad where he began what proved to be several weeks of catastrophic indecision, punctuated by requests that he be relieved of the responsibility of his command. Grant felt otherwise, however, and still believed that federalists would come to their aid with twice the numbers of *soldados* at Matamoros. While Johnson and thirty-four men foraged for animals and provisions in the country around San Patricio, Grant and another twenty-six moved on a few miles south to Agua Dulce Creek, unaware that several hundred *soldados* commanded by General José de Urrea were on their way. Urrea first struck San Patricio on February 27 and took Johnson by surprise. It was a totally one-sided affair and ended with all of Johnson's men killed or captured. Johnson himself became a prisoner but later escaped. Four days later Urrea caught Grant by surprise. With two hundred *soldados* facing less than a quarter of their numbers, the outcome was not in doubt. Only six men escaped being killed or captured in a mounted action that saw the Texians fleeing and the Mexicans riding them down. Grant himself rode some seven miles pursued by lancers before they surrounded him. He dismounted to meet the end, apparently defending himself well until felled in a flurry of lances, after which the officers repeatedly ran him through with their sabers.[46]

Grant never got within one hundred thirty miles of Matamoros, and all the planning, the intrigue, the political and military confusion and double-dealing ended in a bloody patch of grass south of the Nueces. More than that ended there, however. Matamoros had disintegrated the ill-conceived government created by the Consultation. It crippled for precious weeks the efforts of Houston and others to create an army of defense as opposed to Grant and Johnson's army of opportunity. It further confused the already uncertain goals of the revolt between Mexican federalism and outright independence. And in its outcome, it sent a shock through Texian ranks. The failure of Mexican federalists to come to the aid of the expedition revealed that in the coming fight with Santa Anna—and Urrea's arrival was a signal that Santa Anna would indeed be coming—Texians and sympathetic *tejanos* were going to be on their own. It is ironic that Grant and Johnson, having tried so hard to discourage talk of independence, should have gone to disaster just as a new convention finally wrestled with that very issue. Indeed, at almost the same moment that Grant and his men pointlessly lost their lives to pay for their ambition and folly, a group of Texian delegates two hundred miles northwest proclaimed at last for complete independence. The question now was whether or not the futile and destructive Matamoros dream had so seriously compromised the strength and resolve of Texians and *tejanos* alike that they might not be able to defend what they declared.

The "Father of Texas," Stephen F. Austin, walked a fine line for years attempting to keep relations peaceful between his restless colonists and their Mexican overlords. DETAIL OF A SILHOUETTE BY WILLIAM H. BROWN, CENTER FOR AMERICAN HISTORY, UNIVERSITY OF TEXAS AT AUSTIN

General Antonio López de Santa Anna, mercurial sometime liberal and sometime tyrant, faced the inevitable challenge to Mexican pride and union posed by Anglo-*tejano* Texas. CENTER FOR AMERICAN HISTORY, UNIVERSITY OF TEXAS AT AUSTIN

One of the last links to earlier attempts to wrest Texas from Hispanic rule, Jane Long was the widow of James Long, who led two abortive filibustering expeditions into the province and eventually lost his life. CENTER FOR AMERICAN HISTORY, UNIVERSITY OF TEXAS AT AUSTIN

FREEMEN OF TEXAS
To Arms!!! To Arms!!!!
"Now's the day, & now's the hour."

CAMP OF THE VOLUNTEERS,
Friday Night, 11 o'clock;
October 2, 1835.

Fellow Citizens:—

We have prevailed no our fellow citizen Wm. H. Wharton, Esq. to return and communicate to you the following express, and also to urge as many as can by possibility leave their homes to repair to Gonza les immediately, "armed and equipped for war even to the knife." On the receipt of this intelligence the Volun teers immediately resolved to march to Gonzales to aid their countrymen. We are just now starting which must apol ogize for the brevity of this communi cation. We refer you to Mr. Whar ton for an explanation of our wishes, opinions and intentions, and also for such political information as has come into our hands. If Texas will now act promptly; she will soon be redeemed from that worse than Egyptian bondage which now cramps her resources and retards her prosperity.

DAVID RANDON,
WM. J. BRYAND,
J. W. FANNIN, Jr.
F. T. WELLS,
GEO. SUTHERLAND
B. T. ARCHER,
W. D. C. HALL,
W. H. JACK,
WM. T. AUSTIN,
P. D. MCNEEL.

P. S. An action took place on yes terday at Gonzales, in which the Mexi can Commander and several soldiers were slain—no loss on the American side

and cut off their supplies. The inhab itants seldom raise enough for their own consumption, and 800 troops being thrown upon them, has brought the place to the door of starvation. Bread is out of the question with them, and they have no hopes of obtaining meat, except eating their horses or pil laging from the Colonists. The Vol unteers are determined never to return until St. Antonio has fallen, and every soldier of the Central Government has been killed or driven out of Texas. One great object of the Volunteers, is to intercept Cos between La Bahia & St. Antonio. After this if enough of our countrymen assemble, they will take St. Antonio by storm—if not they will surround the place—cut off their supplies and starve them into a surren der. Let all who can; turn out, and that immediately—Let no one say that business detains him; for what business can be so important as to crush the enemy at once, and thereby put an end forever, or at least for some time to come to this unholy attempt to bring us under the yoke of Military Despotism, or to expel us from the country. If St. Antonio is not taken, it will be a rallying point, where they will in a few months concentrate thou sands of troops. If it is taken they will have no foothold among us, and the power of the nation cannot re esta blish one. Fellow-citizens: there are ma ny fighting our battles, more from sym pathy, and from a detestation of oppres sion, than from any great pecuniary in terest they have in the country. These generous and heroic indivi-

In the immediate aftermath of the first clash at Gonzales, the "Free-men of Texas" were called to arms. CENTER FOR AMERICAN HISTORY, UNIVERSITY OF TEXAS AT AUSTIN

When colonists framed the Provisional Government of Texas they chose contentious, irascible Henry Smith as their governor only to see him embroiled in ineffectual feuding that made him all but powerless. CENTER FOR AMERICAN HISTORY, UNIVERSITY OF TEXAS AT AUSTIN

The Mission Concepción de Acuna is where James Bowie led one of the preliminary actions that presaged the siege of Béxar. CENTER FOR AMERICAN HISTORY, UNIVERSITY OF TEXAS AT AUSTIN

Texas's first military hero, Ben Milam, had a long history with the filibusters, then sparked new enthusiasm in those besieging Béxar in December 1835, leading the attack in which he lost his life. CENTER FOR AMERICAN HISTORY, UNIVERSITY OF TEXAS AT AUSTIN

More heroes would come, few more deservedly than James Bowie, frontier land speculator, legendary fighter, and martyr at the Alamo, a man who combined almost all of the motives of the Anglo Texians. CENTER FOR AMERICAN HISTORY, UNIVERSITY OF TEXAS AT AUSTIN

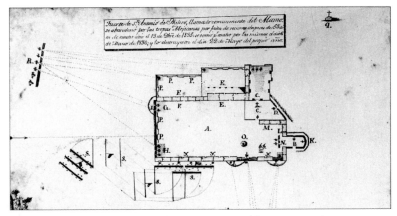

A plan of the layout of the Alamo compound by José Sanchez-Navarro, circa 1836. The famed church is at top right, noted as "C." CENTER FOR AMERICAN HISTORY, UNIVERSITY OF TEXAS AT AUSTIN

On March 6, 1836 the Alamo fell to an overwhelming force of attacking Mexican *soldados,* sending a jolt through Texas and beginning the most lasting of all Texas legends. CENTER FOR AMERICAN HISTORY, UNIVERSITY OF TEXAS AT AUSTIN

The facade of the church at the Alamo as it appeared in an early daguerreotype taken in 1849. Already some regarded it as a Texas shrine. CENTER FOR AMERICAN HISTORY, UNIVERSITY OF TEXAS AT AUSTIN

With the passing of Austin from the scene, the man who dominated affairs in the Revolution more than any other was General Sam Houston, one-time failure and inebriate, whose lasting impact as savior or self-serving schemer is still debated. CENTER FOR AMERICAN HISTORY, UNIVERSITY OF TEXAS AT AUSTIN

Hard on the heels of the disaster at the Alamo came the horrific murder of hundreds of surrendered Texians at Goliad, remembered in this naive painting, *The March to the Massacre.* Texians would remember Goliad as well as the Alamo in future encounters with the Mexican army. CENTER FOR AMERICAN HISTORY, UNIVERSITY OF TEXAS AT AUSTIN

While the Alamo garrison bought time, Houston and other founding fathers framed a declaration of independence and a constitution for Texas in this rude and drafty house at Washington-on-the-Brazos, hardly a likely looking candidate to be an "Independence Hall." CENTER FOR AMERICAN HISTORY, UNIVERSITY OF TEXAS AT AUSTIN

The new president of Texas under its new constitution was David G. Burnet, a recent arrival to Texas, who found himself almost as beleaguered as his predecessor, Henry Smith, yet who managed to keep the "government" functioning and more or less together even while fleeing from Santa Anna. CENTER FOR AMERICAN HISTORY, UNIVERSITY OF TEXAS AT AUSTIN

Uncertain that Houston would ever act to stop the advance of Santa Anna, Governor Burnet sent his secretary of war, Thomas Rusk, to accompany Houston and the army, to report back to the governor, and to assume command of the army, if need be.
HENDERSON YOAKUM, *HISTORY OF TEXAS*

A very stylized and romanticized painting depicting the *Surrender of Santa Anna* on April 22, 1836. Houston lies on a blanket at the foot of a tree, while the defeated Mexican general stands before him with hat in hand. CENTER FOR AMERICAN HISTORY, UNIVERSITY OF TEXAS AT AUSTIN

CHAPTER NINE

"Victory or Death"

༺∽༻

I N A DIFFERENT WORLD hundreds of miles to the south, Mexican
opinion on the revolt in Texas and its causes varied. Much of the population scarcely knew of it, and to many more it was only one of those
constant distant disturbances at the periphery of a restless nation. Ruling circles and the army elite held a distinct viewpoint, naturally, and
Captain José Enrique de la Peña expressed it rather succinctly. Eleven
years of living under the relaxed autonomy of the Constitution of 1824,
combined with inherent differences in beliefs and customs between
Mexicans and Anglos, brought about the uprising "or, better stated,
were the pretexts of which the colonists took advantage," he said. For
all the protestations of loyalty to federalism from Austin and others,
Peña believed like most Mexicans that the Texians' previous behavior
betrayed their "distorted aims." They repeatedly insulted the nation,
violated customs laws, attacked customs officers and military garrisons.
As Peña saw it, "they were the aggressors and we the attacked, they the
ingrates, we the benefactors." Federalism may have been destroyed by
the liberals who ostensibly espoused the cause in Mexico, but the Texians quickly capitalized on that by their appeals to continuing republican
uprisings in concert with their own. "They wished for us to destroy ourselves, the better to assure the success of their designs," he accused.
Thus, the Texians forced war upon Mexico, "for between war and dishonor there was no doubt as to the choice."[1] Regardless of whether it
was accurate in whole or part, or hardly at all, Peña's perception of the
case was what mattered to him, and to most Mexicans, and that perception justified—indeed demanded—that the army take action.

Indeed, it was an acceptable option. "War was the thing that could least frighten Mexicans, who seemed to have sworn not to live without it," quipped Peña.[2] Yet the nation came ill prepared to the contest. The nation's financial affairs were perpetually a mess. "The public treasury was badly depleted," he complained, and "all avenues of wealth had been blocked as a consequence of a civil war so barbarously prolonged," a situation made worse by the Texians' persistent evasion of tariff duties on the imports they smuggled into their colonies. Worse, as was inevitable in any authoritarian regime run by a strongman, Santa Anna needed a substantial army to enforce his authority, as in the repression of Zacatecas, and that cost money that must be wrung from the people by taxes. With wealth concentrated in the hands of a few, mostly the *creoles*, the burden of taxation fell heavily on them, making those opposed to centralization all the more unhappy. Moreover, Mexico's very size made problems for collection and distribution, with Mexico City largely cut off by considerable distances from far-flung provincial or state capitals like Saltillo.

As a result, officials in Mexico resorted to forced "loans" and taxes, and even that money did not always find its way to points of public necessity. Then too, the need to concentrate his military forces for the campaigns in the northern provinces meant that Santa Anna had to leave rather too few *soldados* to maintain order either against civil disturbances in the more settled states, or to give protection from Indian depredations in faraway places like Sonora and California. Peña had Santa Anna's Mexico specifically in mind when he complained of "the neglect, the apathy, or, even more, the criminal indifference with which all governments without exception have watched over the national interests." The two most important departments in the government were the Ministry of the Treasury, whose incumbent busily lined his own pockets while complaining that there was no money to pay soldiers or buy equipment, and the Ministry of War, run by a man of no real military experience. It appeared to Peña and other critics that Santa Anna was actually concentrating more of the nation's scarce wealth in support of the Texas campaign than was either justified or necessary, especially in taking more than six thousand *soldados* to meet a rabble whose army would never number more than nine hundred on any field.[3]

Santa Anna would hardly have agreed. From the moment of the outbreak at Gonzales in October, he began readying an expedition to

impose order and Mexican authority in Texas. Not to do so or to make
the attempt in a halfhearted manner simply carried too many risks. The
uprisings in Zacatecas and elsewhere already revealed the degree of
unrest in several pockets of the nation. He of all people knew from experience the danger that posed, for he had seen it so often in the past.
There were broader stakes than just Texas at risk, too. Coahuila was
deeply involved with the Texan unrest. Should the revolt spread there,
then the loss could be stunning, for Coahuila y Texas constituted the
largest state in Mexico, larger than all of Mexico south of it combined.
Even if Coahuila could be controlled, still an independent Texas would
always pose a threat to its stability. With Texas no longer a buffer
against further American spread westward across the Southwest, then
the territories of New Mexico and New California must inevitably
come under pressure in the future.

Santa Anna did not want and could not afford the trouble with the
United States that such pressure must inevitably create. Indeed, one
more reason for striking the Texian insurgents with quick and heavy
force was to put down their revolt before they could involve the Americans in their defense. The Texian idea of equality, mirroring the Founding
Fathers in 1776, posed a threat to social stability in Mexico itself, for such
ideas had shown that they could spread rapidly. Perhaps above all, the
collapse of federalism in Mexico had come because of the almost universal fear among the upper classes—federalist and centralist alike—of the
masses coming to power. It stands as one of the great ironies of the Texas
Revolution that slaveholding Anglos were more democratic than antislavery Mexicans. Indeed, the era's revolts, from 1776 to Mexico to
Texas, were led by oligarchies and vested interests seeking security for
the freedoms of their classes, suspicious if not hostile to unlimited popular sovereignty.[4] Thus, the revolt in Texas actually helped to drive some
fearful federalists in Mexico itself over to uneasy support for the new
regime because it promised more stability to their interests than the
alternative. Yet the revolts did spread the idea of democracy, and the
result would necessarily, decades later, be universal suffrage.

Santa Anna, as so often, was not in the capital but at home in Vera
Cruz on October 23, 1835, when he first learned of the outbreak at Gonzales three weeks earlier. Almost immediately he began planning his
response, ordering the Minister of War, José Tornel, to direct General
Joaquin Ramírez y Sesma to move from garrisoning Zacatecas to begin

organizing *soldados* at Saltillo. Santa Anna himself went to Mexico City in mid-November to put the government in shape to support the coming campaign. He put Major General Miguel Barragán in his office temporarily as chief executive immediately after Barragán named Santa Anna himself to command the newly designated Army of Operations to put down the rebellion. Sobering news awaited him. At the moment the sum of Mexican forces under arms was little more than thirty-five hundred, including the fifteen hundred already with Ramírez y Sesma. Santa Anna would have to resort to wide-scale conscription to fill his ranks, which he did. By December he assembled an army at San Luis Potosí more than six thousand strong. Many of his infantry were regulars, professionals of long service and experience, the backbone of any army. Others were reserves called out for the emergency, many of them untrained and inexperienced farmers, not a few of them draftees. There were also several regiments of cavalry, again divided between professionals and conscripts, and late that month Santa Anna put them on the long, hard march northward. Béxar had to be held. Not only was it strategically important, as it commanded a major overland route into the Texan interior, but it was also vital symbolically, both as the administrative center of Mexican Texas, and as a matter of wounded pride to be avenged for the attack on Cós. And as he had shown in Zacatecas, Santa Anna was inclined to make vengeance bloody.[5]

The greatest impact of the Texian revolt on the people of Mexico themselves came, ironically, from their own army as it marched north toward the Rio Grande. For a start there was the enforced conscription of men, what Peña called "the thoughtless violence with which forced recruiting was carried out." Santa Anna's orders to Ramírez y Sesma told him to "take advantage of the enthusiasm of the citizenry" by drafting men experienced with arms, but the "enthusiasm" existed mainly in his own fustian proclamation.[6] Wives and children saw their husbands and sons simply taken from them and thrust unwilling into the army, while at the same time officers and soldiers appropriated what they needed from the farmers and the *ranchos* as they passed. Even worse happened before they reached the Rio Grande. "The armies of all nations, no matter how disciplined, always carry licentiousness with them wherever they march," he observed in disgust, "and the greater their number, the greater the disorders committed." General Ramírez y Sesma, commanding the cavalry, apparently allowed his men to take pack mules, harness, horses, and whatever else they wanted from citizens along the road north. At the towns of Aldama, Candela, and Lampazos, he demanded that the citizens feed his men meat and tortillas. "We lived at times at the mercy of the generosity of townships and landowners," said Peña, "and at other, more frequent times, when these and the others are compelled to give us their stock, their flour, their corn, etc., in exchange for receipts they will never redeem from our most discredited treasury." Ruefully, Peña concluded that on the march to Texas "General Ramírez y Sesma, with his errors and abuses, really harmed us more than the enemy did."[7] Even then, the Texan expedition could do little more to upset what little equilibrium remained that Mexico's own pre-1835 experience had not already shattered.

Santa Anna's *soldados* were often resplendent in their finery. The majority of the men, the conscripts and militia, wore hand-me-downs from the regulars, mostly dark blue swallowtail coats with red facings and pants of canvas that once was white, but soon took on the shade of the march. The conscripts carried the British-made "Brown Bess" musket and bayonet, but little else as officers reserved the better equipment for the more elite units like the light infantry, or *cazadores*, who wore gray trousers beneath light-blue jackets trimmed in red, and leather shakos with green pom-poms. They carried a short flintlock Baker rifle with a bayonet that, like their leather accoutrements, was purchased from Britain, the principal supplier of arms to Mexico. Ramírez y Sesma's cavalry, upon whom so much of the Texas campaign depended, were the best dressed of all, with dark blue coatees in the French fashion, trimmed in red, and their leather accoutrements burnished white with pipe clay. The lancer wore blue riding pants with red stripes and leather seats and inside legs for long wear in the saddle. Above it all he had a black leather helmet with flowing black horsehair behind a pompom of green, white, and red. In battle he carried a carbine-length British Paget musket and a saber, but most dreaded of all was the lance, more than seven feet long, and tipped with a sharp iron arrow-shaped blade. It was these fearful weapons that accounted for almost all of the men who tried to escape the debacle at Agua Dulce Creek.

Through virtually all of the ensuing conflict Mexico remained a nation still culturally, politically, and economically reeling from a generation of internal uprising and warfare, though in the main its citizenry enjoyed at least the luxury of being largely removed from the direct impact or effects of the Texas revolution. Back on November 25 the Council had authorized Governor Smith to issue a total of up to nine commissions of letters of marque to men willing to employ their vessels as privateers against Mexican shipping. They even required that their privateers sail under the red, white, and green colors of Mexico, with "1824" on a white field to announce their allegiance to the constitution that Santa Anna was violating.[8] However, the ragged Texians posed no threat whatever to the nation's commercial relations any more than to its social structure, or really even to its political culture. Texian forces never set foot on Mexican soil south of the Rio Grande except as prisoners of war, ironically the only way any of them ever got to Matamoros, and thus no invader's heel trampled fields of maize or stepped over the hearths of citizens great or small. The culture of a nation and people deeply divided for centuries along lines of blood, land, wealth, and ethnicity remained virtually unchanged. Untouched, too, was a tradition of unrest and rebellion among the underclasses, a tradition that had been fostered during decades of repeated civil disturbances. Santa Anna, himself the leader of half-dozen revolts, a man who had switched sides from federalist to centralist, was not unaware that his regime was constantly the object of yet more projected coups, nor that his political opponents would take advantage of his absence in Texas to foment yet another plot.

Santa Anna rode into San Luis Potosí on December 5 in company with General Vicente Filisola. Two days later he gave Ramírez y Sesma orders to move on to Laredo on the Rio Grande, one hundred fifty miles south of San Antonio, and from there march toward Béxar, meanwhile sending word to Cós that help was on the way. Neither yet knew that Cós was on the verge of surrender. Ramírez y Sesma also received detailed orders on how he should attack the Texians. With almost Napoleonic thoroughness, Santa Anna tried in his orders to provide instructions on how to meet virtually any contingency that might present itself, whether Ramírez y Sesma met the Texians in the open field, whether he attacked or was himself attacked, how to use his artillery and cavalry, and more. Only if the foe was fortified in one of the missions outside San Antonio was Ramírez y Sesma to hold his forces in check until he knew as much as possible about enemy positions and strength. "Nothing will be undertaken without the definite information which assures a successful outcome which is a decisive defeat," Santa Anna told him.

It revealed the essentially methodical and cautious side of the man, as well as his anxiety to have one quick, overwhelming victory that could kill the insurgency in its infancy. He wisely understood that for a Mexican army that would be essentially an invader far from home on unfamiliar and largely hostile territory, with an attenuated supply line and an army composed substantially of unwilling conscripts, time and geography worked in favor of the rebels. He also advised Ramírez y Sesma of something else. Quite possibly he recalled those threats by Travis and Bowie in days past of giving no quarter to Mexicans who resisted them. Maybe he remembered, too, the treatment given to surrendered Mexican statesmen and soldiers after San Antonio fell to the Gutiérrez–Magee filibusters. No doubt much of the intemperate, and in some degree racially motivated, invective in Texas of the past few months had reached his ears, with its bombastic threats of death to those who tried to impose Mexican authority. Quite certainly his own harsh treatment of Zacatecas lay fresh in his memory. In the face of each new federalist threat to stability in Mexico City, he has responded with increasing severity, in the way of virtually all threatened regimes facing internal unrest. Inevitable logic suggested that this most dangerous peril yet deserved the most severe measures of repression. "The foreigners who wage war against the Mexican Nation have violated all laws and do not deserve any consideration," he told Ramírez y Sesma in closing, "and for that reason, no quarter will be given them," though he did not want such an announcement made to the *soldados* until the eve of battle. Texians had "audaciously declared a war of extermination to the Mexicans," he declared, "and should be treated in the same manner."[9]

Santa Anna also sent Filisola ahead to assume overall command of Mexican forces around Béxar until he could himself arrive with the main van of the army. Clearly, that Santa Anna himself wished to be present at the decisive battle, not having forgotten from his own experience how personal leadership at such moments could cement his hold on affairs at home. To ensure that, he must have the whole army in place to leave no doubt as to the outcome of the climactic battle. By December 18 he had his army all but complete and organized. Ramírez y Sesma's Vanguard Brigade of 1,541 infantry, cavalry, and artillery, with 8 field pieces, was already approaching the Rio Grande. Directly under Santa Anna at San Luis Potosí were two brigades totaling 3,379 infantry and a dozen cannon, and Urrea's small division of 601 infantry and cavalry and one small cannon. An additional cavalry brigade of 437 horse-men completed the army. That did not include the men still believed to be holding out under Cós. Unfortunately, it also did not include compe-tent physicians and surgeons to deal with the sick and wounded to come, nor more than one month's supplies. It was a worrying degree of ill preparation reflecting the hurried nature of the assembly of the army, the difficulties of its distance from Mexico City, and perhaps Santa Anna's own sometimes careless personality. He was by nature an instinctive, dynamic leader, quick, intuitive, sometimes inspiring. But as with most such men, logistical details often bored him, a potentially fatal difference between him and his model Napoleon. It had better be a short campaign.[10]

Just such details were on the minds of his adversaries, however. No sooner did Austin reach San Felipe than he prepared for his mission to the United States. As soon as Austin and his fellow commissioners reached New Orleans in January 1836, they began making good use of their time before heading for Washington, soliciting loans in the pre-specified amount of $320 to finance the war. They gave out certificates for more than four hundred by January 11, and more than one hundred on that day alone. The loans required an initial installment of $32, with no stipulation as to when and in what amounts the remainder was to be paid. Indeed, such further installments were to be at the option of the lender, making the $320 face value of the loan rather meaningless. In their position, however, the Texians felt a pressing need to raise what-ever cash they could as quickly as possible. The result of the next few months could well make any further installments on these loans super-fluous if the bid for independence failed. Thus, the loans raised no more than $25,000 by mid-January, but there was one carrot Austin's commis-sion could offer to induce further installments, that perennial lure of Texas: land. In lieu of being repaid, lenders were guaranteed, if they chose, to be able to take their reimbursement in land at fifty cents per acre. That was in itself enough to persuade lenders to keep making their installments, and to keep at least some hard cash coming in to the insurgents, money that Austin and later agents immediately spent in New Orleans on clothing, weapons, and munitions, some of it unfortu-nately misdirected to supplying the Matamoros fiasco.[11]

Meanwhile, the struggle to raise manpower proceeded in its halting and inefficient fashion. As soon as the Consultation authorized the new Regular Army, the colonels to command its regiments received instructions to set captains to work recruiting companies. From his headquarters at Matagorda late in December, Fannin, now lieutenant colonel of the as-yet-nonexistent First Artillery, directed his newly commissioned captains to fan out to any section of the country they chose to fill their sixty-four-man companies. "Enlist all you can," he implored. "Fill up your companies, and be ready for the field soon." Recruits must be brought to camp as quickly as possible and placed on "strict duty" to begin the work of making civilians into soldiers in the little window of time available before Santa Anna responded to Cós's fall.[12] Meanwhile, men still left their hearths in Gonzales, San Felipe, and elsewhere as more volunteers hastened forward, but now they were coming in twos and threes and by tens, rather than in the numbers that first turned out in October. Time, complacence, the Matamoros fiasco, and disruption and disillusionment in San Felipe had done their work. A sort of lethargy settled in. Nothing had happened in more than a month. No *soldados* had come to reassert Mexican authority. Perhaps it was already over.

All too soon in mid-January, Houston received an urgent appeal from Neill detailing the deteriorating condition of the garrison at San Antonio, and protesting that he had reports of Santa Anna's army moving toward the Rio Grande. Distracted by the Matamoros foolishness, Houston had sent Bowie and a small company to join Neill. He wanted the old Mexican fortifications in the town demolished so they would be of no use to the enemy in future. Moreover, he hoped to get permission from the governor to destroy the Alamo itself, believing that it could not be held by any garrison of Texian volunteers against determined Mexican regulars with artillery. But when Bowie arrived late on January 18 he found that Neill, despite his handicaps, had done much to improve the town's defenses. Between them, Bowie and Neill concluded that Béxar could in fact be held, and that it offered wonderful defensive possibilities, especially with the artillery now mounted on the walls of the Alamo. There were hundreds of captured Mexican muskets and some sixteen thousand rounds of ammunition, and soon Bowie was convinced that the place must be held even at the cost of a battle. Moreover, there were only two probable routes of invasion of Texas open to the Mexicans, either the Atascosita Road from Matamoros via Goliad, or the Laredo road that passed through Béxar. Hold Goliad and Béxar and

the Texians could forestall the enemy advance for some time, giving
Houston precious hours to raise that Regular Army or volunteers
enough to mount a serious resistance. Given enough men, Bowie and
Neill concluded, San Antonio could be held for quite a while. After all,
had not Cós done so for nearly a month?

During the next several days after his arrival, once more living in his
old home at the Veramendi house, Bowie helped Neill oversee more work
on the defenses and pleaded for reinforcements. The fact that the Matamoros expedition had robbed the community of almost all its draft animals meant that Bowie and Neill could not haul away the artillery
emplaced there even had they wished, and they could hardly just abandon them, for Béxar held the largest complement in Texas, twenty-one
guns in fact, exactly the same number as those coming with the Mexicans, though the Texians' guns were capable of throwing a considerably
greater weight of iron. "We will rather die in these ditches, than give it up
to the enemy," Bowie wrote to Governor Smith on February 2.[13] The garrison then was just one hundred twenty men, and already there were
reports that advance elements of Santa Anna's army, supposedly as many
as two thousand cavalry, had reached the Rio Grande, just one hundred
twenty-five miles distant. But then over the next three days the first Texian reinforcements arrived, small though they were. On February 3
Travis rode in by himself, now a lieutenant colonel in the Regular Army
and the vanguard of a company of cavalry he had raised that would come
in two days later. Then about February 6 after dark another half dozen
men appeared, informally led by the former congressman from Tennessee
and famous frontiersman and humorist, David Crockett.

ADVENTURING MEN bent on reaching Texas had for weeks been hur-
rying to join in the fight, some deciding to leave their bags and all but
what they could carry in saddle rolls behind in Natchitoches, Louisiana,
so as not to slow their journey. Their baggage could always be forwarded
later, though finding its owners in a constantly changing and chaotic
civil and military landscape presented no small challenge. Some never
again saw effects thus left along the way. For others, when the bags
finally reached Texas, the owners themselves were no more.[14] One
among that small but enthusiastic array of hastening volunteers was the
so-called gentleman from the cane, Crockett. He was America's first

genuine popular celebrity, a product in part of his own colorful character and shrewd capitalization on the current fad for "western men" from the frontier, and careful manipulation of his image by Whig politicians in the East who had used him as a tool in their campaign against President Andrew Jackson.

A South Carolinian who served in Congress with Crockett left a mixed reaction to this new star passing over the Texian firmament. "He was a dull, heavy, almost stupid man, in appearance," recalled William Grayson, "stout and clumsy in person with a blotchy fair complexion and light eyes, ungainly in address and manners." Grayson himself later recalled that he "never heard him utter a word that savoured of wit or sense." Indeed, Grayson rather thought that a simple look at Crockett's guileless face would disabuse anyone of the notion that the man was capable of wit or repartee. "He was the last man in the house that a stranger would have pitched upon as a wit and humourist," said the Carolinian, "yet by some freak of fortune he became the reputed author of innumerable queer sayings and stories, a man of infinite joke, an incarnation of frontier oddity." Upon acquaintance, in fact, Grayson found Crockett to be good-natured, kindhearted, and personally a favorite with many of his colleagues, however much the more seasoned politicians felt inclined to patronize, and in the end, use him for their own ends.[15]

Grayson largely misjudged Crockett. To be sure, he was a simple man, but one of complex instincts, an emblem of his times. His humor, in fact, had been the making of him, for within it he had the gift of encapsulating genuine wit with political satire, the resentments of poor whites toward the affluent and privileged who ran the country, and the stiff-necked and unpretentious pride of the newly risen common man. Nothing expressed it all better than his jibe that the only thing on earth he feared was receiving an honorary degree from Harvard College, reflecting as it did the disdain of the westerner for the effete east, of the unlettered for the educated, and the fact that Crockett's mortal political foe Andrew Jackson had been awarded just such a degree. Though he had some help, Crockett authored his own best-selling autobiography, a nationwide hit on its appearance in 1834. He wrote it in his own Tennessee vernacular, told his own story—with embellishments—and basked in the celebrity it brought him, a celebrity he instinctively knew how to manipulate to the fullest. Paradoxically, his greatest ambition was to be a gentleman, but he knew when to don the buckskins and act the role his public wanted. While in Washington attending Congress, he often met unexpected visitors to his lodging while wearing his politician's broadcloth suit, but he made certain to put on his fur hunting hat, drape himself recklessly across a chair, and lapse into colorful backwoods stories and exaggerated dialect. The pose lasted as long as the visit, but after guests left he became the Western gentleman again. "They came to see a b[e]ar," he explained to a friend, "and they've seen one—hope they like the performance."[16]

Most of America liked the performance, especially the Whigs. Themselves largely a party of Eastern affluent interests, they needed a man like Crockett on their side to lure the "common man" support away from Jackson. For a time it seemed it would work, and Crockett became more the tool of his sudden Whig friends than he would have liked to admit. But they lost interest in him in 1835 when he was defeated for reelection. Once they had swelled his ego with talk of the presidency in 1836, but out of office he was no good to them. A humiliated forty-nine-year-old Crockett told his constituents after his defeat that they could "go to hell" and he would go to Texas. As he passed through LaGrange, Tennessee, on his way west, he accepted an invitation to be feted at the local hotel, but made it clear that this was to be purely a social occasion. "I never expect to offer my name again to the public for any office," he insisted, protesting that he hoped merely to "spend the evening in a social manner leaving politicts out of the question." The people already knew his course in political life and the voters had chosen to reject him. "I have not chainged," he wrote them in the sort of orthography that once made him the darling of a nation.[17]

Still his motives now were mixed. Like so many others, he had run out his string east of the Mississippi. Rejected by his voters, virtually bankrupt personally, living in an estranged marriage, he needed to start over. A perennial seeker after cheap land, he saw that opportunity in Texas. When he left his home the revolution had not yet started, and he went with little if any idea of becoming involved in the ferment in the colony. However, by the time he reached Nacogdoches on January 5, it was apparent that at the very least a new state of Mexico was in the offing, if not a new and independent sovereignty in its own right, perhaps one later to become a part of the United States. The old politician in him could not miss the potential in that. Suddenly he told people now that in fact he came to fight in their revolt, and then it was suggested that if he wished, he could be elected to represent San Augustine in the forthcoming convention at Washington-on-the-Brazos. "I have but little doubt of being elected a member to form the Constitution of this province," he wrote home, but he declined the honor, perhaps with his eye on a bigger prize. If Texas won its independence, whether from Coahuila or Mexico itself, there would be greater offices, and likely they would go to the men who won glory in the army. Moreover, the voters themselves were going to be in the field now in the Regular and volunteer forces. The place for a politician with his eye on a governorship or perhaps something greater was in the army, and so he enlisted. "I had rather be in my present position than to be elected to a seat in Congress for Life," he wrote his daughter.[18]

Crockett enlisted for six months' service as a volunteer. He looked in other respects just like the great bulk of the men entering the ranks. Most of the volunteers entering the army of the revolutionary province of Texas had no uniforms at all. It would only be after a new provisional government was established at Washington-on-the-Brazos early in March that any official provision for uniforms was enacted, and that simply called for the acquisition of two thousand "gray" suits for its anticipated Regular forces, but almost certainly they were never delivered or even ordered, and thus none were seen on any soldiers. An earlier act by the Council at San Felipe in December 1835, creating a Regular regiment of cavalry to be commanded by Travis, specified at his suggestion cadet gray uniforms, cowhide boots, black cloth neck stocks or high collars, and fur caps. In January 1836 he placed an order for uniforms for his men and one for himself, yet since the Council's order did not specify any particular design other than the color gray, Travis apparently chose one on his own, no doubt settling for some standard pattern already manufactured in the United States for state militia. Yet by the time he reached San Antonio in February 1836, the new uniforms had not yet arrived and Travis was wearing only his civilian clothes, likely with nothing to mark him as a soldier except perhaps some ersatz insignia.

Indeed, civilian garb characterized the entire army, such as it was. Whatever they had on at home when they left to volunteer was what they continued to wear, and neither Houston nor the government could provide anything more for them before the revolution concluded. Some wore the buckskins usually associated with the typical frontiersman, while others dressed in anachronistic finery of everything from top hats to swallowtail coats. Most just wore homespun shirts and cotton or leather trousers, leather boots or brogans, and an incredible assortment of jackets and hats. The *tejano* volunteers wore the customary clothes of farmers and *vaqueros*, with only such adaptations as expedience or articles abandoned by fleeing Mexicans allowed.

There were just a few actual uniforms. A volunteer company raised in Louisiana and called the New Orleans Grays arrived in November 1835, dressed in obsolete gray United States Army clothing with short jackets. Then, too, a number of serving soldiers in United States Army posts on the western border of Louisiana deserted with the tacit approval of their commanders in order to fight with the revolutionaries, bringing with them their light-blue shell jackets and trousers. Ultimately, after only a few months of service, officers complained that all their men, regardless of how they came attired, were nearly naked as their clothing wore out.

Their equipment, too, was such as they could bring with them, carpetbags and blanket rolls, or rude homemade haversacks to hold their few possessions. Their guns were their own squirrel rifles and shotguns, a smattering of Kentucky rifles, here and there even something akin to a blunderbuss, but in the main those captured "Brown Bess" .75-caliber muskets taken from Cós and other Mexicans. At their belts they wore an assortment of Bowie knives, dirks, tomahawks, flintlock pistols, and even old swords and sabers from their fraternal lodges or their fathers' wars. They were truly an army of rags and patches.

Sadly, that frayed patchwork matched the chaotic disorganization created in the military by the Consultation. Soon the seemingly everpresent problem of democracy, confusion over command, appeared again. On February 12, Neill had to leave to attend his sick family. Bowie was nominally a colonel but in fact held no official commission other than election by volunteers who were no longer with him in any case. Travis was a lieutenant colonel with a commission in the newly formed Regular Army of Texas. He was also young, only twenty-six, and less experienced than the seasoned frontier fighter Bowie, but Bowie, not quite forty, was worn down, prone to bouts of drunkenness, and perhaps already showing signs of something like pneumonia or typhoid that would soon leave him incapacitated.

The best choice was to turn the command over to Travis, which Neill did. Moreover, it was the proper thing to do, since Neill was a Regular, and therefore a command entrusted to him by Houston, his lawful superior, ought to be handed over to another Regular. But the volunteer majority in the by-now one-hundred-fifty-man garrison objected. Echoing earlier declarations of volunteers and the expressed sentiments of men such as Johnson and Grant, they protested that they were not subject to the orders of the Regular Army unless they so chose. They immediately demanded an election for a new commander. Travis wisely acquiesced, allowing the volunteers to choose their own superior while he retained charge of the Regulars, and agreeing that the two men would then command jointly. The volunteers chose Bowie, naturally enough, thus commencing an uneasy relationship between the two. Bowie got drunk in celebration, caused trouble and embarrassment in town, and then apologized to Travis. Thereafter, whatever the two thought of each other, they worked together to strengthen their defenses and plead for reinforcements before the Mexicans arrived.[19]

It would not be long. By year's end Santa Anna had his forces on the move, and he himself left San Luis Potosí on January 2, 1836. Reacting to the news of the surrender and retreat of Cós, he had changed his line of advance. Now he ordered the main army north to Saltillo, and then due north toward the Rio Grande crossing at Paso de Francia. From there the Camino de la Pita led straight northeast one hundred forty miles to San Antonio. Urrea he put on the road east out of Saltillo toward Matamoros, eventually to deal with Grant and Johnson, after which he was to cross into Texas and move to rejoin Santa Anna. Ramírez y Sesma, already on the road, would march from Laredo to meet the army at Paso de Francia. Meanwhile, the disarmed Béxar garrison under Cós, just arrived in Laredo, turned, and went with the army back up to Paso de Francia to return to Texas to redeem itself. It was a difficult march for them all, some going long distances without finding any water along the way, and some of Ramírez y Sesma's men going without rations for two days at a time.[20]

Santa Anna steadily rethought and revised his planning as he got more information on Texian strengths and positions, and a fairly steady supply of intelligence—much of it of no use—filtered south to him from loyal Mexicans and *tejanos,* including from some in Béxar itself. It appears that some—perhaps all—of his commanders actually favored an approach via Goliad, which afforded them the advantage of a line of march closely paralleling the Gulf, allowing for more efficient and timely supply. Santa Anna, however, answered other imperatives. Béxar was symbolic of the rebellion, and had become a feather in its cap by the humiliation of Cós. It was politically and motivationally important to pluck that feather, a wise decision though it cost a hard march. Moreover, from what he knew at the time, Béxar appeared to be rather a soft target with so much of the garrison off at Goliad awaiting the march on Matamoros. Meanwhile, either at his behest or on its own initiative, the minister of war in Mexico City dispatched an emissary to Washington to try to counter any efforts by Austin's commission to involve the United States in the conflict.[21] He need not have worried. Austin would not reach Washington until March, and would achieve nothing, finally leaving in disgust and disappointment to go to New York.

By February 2 the advance elements of the army entered Monclova, and after the rest came up, Santa Anna sent them on six days later, only to encounter a heavy snowfall that made the march a nightmare for men who came unprepared for cold weather. Some became lost and confused and the whole operation bogged down in sixteen inches of white powder. Some men froze. Others deserted, and two days were essentially lost before the army reached the Rio Grande at last. At 4:30 on February 16 Santa Anna and the main van of his army began their crossing, with the cavalry under Ramírez y Sesma already ahead of them.[22] The next day they approached the Nueces, the southern boundary of Mexican Texas, and by the night of February 20 Santa Anna himself and his infantry advance elements camped on the Hondo River, just forty miles from Béxar. In two days, three at the most, they could come face to face with the Texians. That same evening as the Texian officers in San Antonio met in council to decide what to do next, the Mexican cavalry camped only a day's ride from the Medina River, itself scarcely ten miles from Béxar. Two nights later, while the garrison and townspeople in Béxar held a *fandango* celebrating George Washington's birthday, Ramírez y Sesma prepared to cross the Medina. The next morning a *tejano* came into town with the news that the Mexican cavalry had been spotted on the Leon Creek, just five miles south, and moving fast. At 3:00 P.M. that afternoon a lookout in the belfry of San Fernando church rang the bell as a signal. Mexican horsemen were in sight.

Knowing that their one hundred fifty or more were too few to hold the town against Ramírez y Sesma's cavalry by itself, let alone the thousands of infantry soon to appear, Travis and Bowie had already decided that in this event they would evacuate the town and retire within the walls of the Alamo, where they had already emplaced and fortified their twenty-one cannon and stored most of their supplies and ammunition. Bowie himself was now so sick that he had to be helped over to the mission, and Travis alone effectively exercised command thereafter. Lining the walls of the Alamo, the garrison watched as the Mexicans, with Santa Anna himself and his staff in the lead, rode quietly into San Antonio to occupy the town less than a mile away. When the Mexicans raised the red flag of no quarter over San Fernando and sent a demand for surrender, Travis ordered a round from his big eighteen-pounder cannon fired in response, and soon a few Mexican artillery pieces returned fire briefly. The siege of the Alamo had begun.

IT WAS TO BE the stuff of legend, a virtual replay of the ancient tale of a desperate few selling their lives to buy precious time for the many, a story enacted as far back as Thermopylae if not beyond. Yet nowhere in the American saga would so many important elements be in play at the same time to ensure the creation of such a truly epic legend, the cornerstone of Texian mythology and reality at one and the same time. Men who were already living semimythical heroes were here in the persons of Bowie and Crockett. Around them stood a small cadre of men seemingly willing to risk all in defense of ideals of liberty and democracy. Arrayed against them were the myrmidons of absolutism led by a cynical incarnation of brutality. It was good and evil, the future and the past, freedom and slavery, all locked in mortal combat, an epic in the making that was ripe for begetting the cornerstones of Texian identity, and pride. It may have been a small event in the course of history, but it would loom paramount in defining Texas and its people now and forever.

As if to punctuate the holy place it was destined to become to Texians, the battlefield itself had been a place of worship. The Alamo was a large rectangular compound around a central area more than an acre in size, its west wall facing San Antonio. Most of the walls, in fact, were simply rooms—now barracks—on whose roofs the Texians had emplaced their cannon. Set back from the southeast corner of the compound was the Alamo church, a partial ruin, with cannon emplaced on a platform where once the roof had been. The compound was a place that could be almost impregnable to all but heavy siege artillery if properly garrisoned, but it was simply too big, the length of its walls requiring many times Travis's numbers to be properly manned. Instead, Travis had only something over one hundred fifty, though in the days ahead scattered parties of reinforcements would get through the spreading Mexican encirclement to bring Texian strength up to somewhere around two hundred, perhaps more. It was simply far too few, though day after day Travis held to hope that more would be coming.

Many of the local *tejanos* joined the garrison, having themselves come to prefer independence to Santa Anna's rule. One of them was Juan Seguín. In April 1835 he had volunteered to lead a company of militia volunteers in a march to support the legislature meeting in Monclova as it faced a threat from Cós. Milam was in his company, and they actually skirmished briefly with Mexican soldiery before returning to Texas, disgusted with Mexican politics. "We pledged ourselves to use all our influence to rouse Texas against the tyrannical government of Santa Anna," he recalled later. Thereafter he kept in constant contact with agitators throughout the unhappy colonies and tried to bring about an actual uprising in Victoria or Brazoria, only to have Mexican military commanders stymie his efforts. But then came the outbreak at Gonzales on October 2. That same day, "well satisfied that the beginning of the revolution was close at hand," Seguín held meetings in the San Antonio area and set out to persuade *tejanos* to rally to the cause.[23]

The arrival of real hostilities forced the issue for the *tejano* community. Those on the fence could scarcely remain undecided much longer, while those still overtly loyal to the Constitution of 1824 and Mexico risked becoming outcasts in their own land. The overriding concern for *tejanos* in the gathering crisis had been self-government, the autonomy that would allow their province or state to be governed by those who knew best its interests and concerns. Despite mutual suspicions and resentments, they had been to date more than willing to cooperate with the Anglos when their ideological agenda intersected. Immediately after Collinsworth took Goliad on October 10, Seguín left with his company of volunteers to reinforce him, but then turned back to join Austin for the siege of Béxar. Lacking any Texian cavalry of his own, Austin desperately needed the *vaqueros* led by Seguín, and Austin soon appointed the *tejano* a captain in the new army. Seguín joined Bowie for the reconnaissance to the missions San Juan and San José, and then on to Concepción, where he took part in the fight with Cós's lancers. After that, thanks to his familiarity with the land, Seguín would spend much time with his mounted company riding through the countryside seeking food and forage for men and animals. Indeed, the *tejanos* did more of such duty than any other Texian soldiers, and they took on a burden of much of the reconnaissance work as well. But still Seguín was back with Burleson's army in time for the final assault and taking of San Antonio. Meanwhile, Seguín spent much of his time patrolling after isolated Mexican cavalry mounts, including one successful raid with Travis.[24]

The influence of prominent *tejanos* such as Seguín went far toward bringing their community together with the Texians in the crisis, and sensible commanders like Austin and Collinsworth took pains to ensure that *tejanos* knew that the insurgents did not regard them as the enemy. Collinsworth issued a proclamation in October promising to protect the lives and property of all citizens loyal to the 1824 Constitution without qualification, and the *tejanos* rewarded that protection by helping to provide food to volunteers whose own supply system was as yet nonexistent. After the surrender of Cós, when so many of the volunteers went off on the Matamoros fiasco or else simply went home, it was almost exclusively *tejano* horsemen like Seguín who kept an eye on the roads south of Béxar and the Rio Grande crossings, watching for any sign of a Mexican counterstroke. In San Antonio itself, historically the center of the *tejano* community, many of the *béxareños* gave aid to the garrison under Neill, and then Bowie and Travis. Neill was convinced that if attacked, the volunteers could count on support from eighty percent of the townsmen, and Bowie seconded that with testimony that the people had been of great assistance to the Texians. When the Council authorized the employment of *tejanos* to assist the garrison, it provided that they be paid fairly, and several officers made efforts to have the services and losses of *tejanos* who assisted the Texians recognized by the government.[25] "I think a distinction ought to be made between those who lost property while in our service," Travis wrote the very day that he got word of Mexicans on the Medina, "& those who were against us or were neutral."[26s]

Unfortunately, some believed that not enough of the *béxareños* had proved their loyalty. Indeed, there were unsubstantiated rumors that the bullet that killed Milam had come not from a *soldado*'s musket, but from a *tejano* gun.[27] After the siege, in fact, the majority of the *tejano* townsfolk remained at least outwardly neutral. Others felt the divisions over sentiment in particularly bitter ways. Some families actually split between loyalty to the revolution and to Mexico, Enrique Esparza siding with Santa Anna and his brother Gregorio going into the Alamo with a dozen other *béxareños*. The *tejano* clergy split, too, and there was no shortage of *tejanos* willing to send—or even carry—information south to Santa Anna's advancing columns.[28] If the Texians won and declared for outright independence, then the *tejanos* could be certain that they would be an inconvenient minority. If the Texians remained committed to the 1824 Constitution and prevailed, then *tejanos* would still be citizens of Mexico and would have its laws to protect them. Few were actually centralists in sympathy with Santa Anna, but forced to choose between some rights under a fellow Mexican dictator and the uncertainty of an Anglo ruling class in a new nation, the devil they knew seemed preferable.

Once Travis and Bowie withdrew into the Alamo, both felt chagrin at just how few of the local *tejano* men joined them, though there were certainly other *tejanos* from other communities among the Alamo garrison. "The citizens of this municipality are all our enemies," Travis complained before long, suggesting that all who had not come to fight with them should be outcast as "public enemies," after San Antonio was firmly in the hands of Mexican *soldados*.[29] Seeing the overwhelming force at Santa Anna's disposal, and the slimness of the Texian garrison, few could be blamed for choosing to wait to fight another day. Indeed, even some of the *béxareño* men who did come into the fort soon had second thoughts. Thanks to his marriage, Bowie probably had more intimate associations and sympathies with the *tejano* community than most Texians, and he had an instinct to stand up for an underdog, whether it be Protestant ministers trying to preach in a Catholic country or *tejanos* asked to make unthinkable decisions. He actually spoke with the *béxareño* men in the garrison, told them that Santa Anna had offered amnesty for any Mexican citizens who had taken up arms with the Texians, and advised them to leave while they could. Half a dozen did. Half a dozen remained, a division emblematic of the strained loyalties of *tejanos* as a whole.[30]

But Seguín's loyalty was clear to him. In January 1836 the new Provisional Government gave Seguín a commission as a captain of cavalry in its newly ordained Regular Army, making him the only *tejano* so recognized, and sent him orders to report to Travis in Béxar. While there he had reverted briefly to his position as *regidore* and oversaw the election of a delegate to the convention scheduled for March 1 at Washington-on-the-Brazos. He was still in San Antonio on February 23 when the Texians evacuated to the Alamo, and he and the others lined the walls of the mission compound to watch as the Mexican army rode into the town to begin the siege. Five days later Seguín joined the other officers in the Alamo in a meeting to assess their position. "Taking into consideration our perilous situation, a majority of the council resolved that I should leave the fort and proceed with a communication to Colonel James W. Fannin, requesting him to come to our assistance," Seguín recalled.[31] He left that same night for Fannin's garrison at Goliad, easily riding out through the as-yet incomplete Mexican encirclement. Learning the next day that Fannin was believed to be on his way, Seguín decided to await his arrival, but then he heard that Fannin had turned back and would not again attempt to relieve the Alamo. Immediately Seguín rode to Gonzales to meet with Houston and urge him to hurry to support Travis. Instead, Houston simply told Seguín to wait at Gonzales, and then on March 6 ordered him to return to the Alamo with a small train of provisions and new volunteers for the garrison.

The Alamo could have used those reinforcements. Within a day or two, and perhaps even hours, of the Mexican arrival on February 23, Bowie took a turn for the worse and disappeared into an improvised hospital from which he rarely emerged again, obviously desperately ill, and perhaps already dying. In the ensuing days it would be up to Travis to keep the defense going, to keep sending out riders with pleas for help, and to prepare for the inevitable enemy attack. Travis also seems to have instinctively understood that it was up to him to speak to the world for the garrison, and his dispatches soon took on the tone of a man addressing not just authorities in Washington, but posterity. "We will make such resistance as is due to our honor, and that of the country," he told Fannin that first day of the siege. He was "determined *never to retreat*." To another friend he wrote of his decision "to defend the Alamo to the last." Then on February 24 he sent out an address to "the People of Texas & all Americans in the world," making it clear that he knew the stage he occupied. Besieged, threatened with no quarter if he did not surrender, he called on patriots everywhere to rally to his aid.

"*I shall never surrender or retreat,*" he declared. "In the name of Liberty, of patriotism & every thing dear to the American character," he admonished men to speed to Béxar. Clearly, even if his newspaper in Alabama might have failed, Travis never lost his journalist's ear for the power of words, closing his plea with a declaration of "Victory or Death."[32]

Santa Anna, meanwhile, knew he had nothing to fear from the garrison and so took his time, waiting until the bulk of his army was in the vicinity, contenting himself instead with constructing batteries to shell the Alamo, and gradually extending his lines to encircle the compound and cut it off from succor just as the Texians had done to Cós. In the days ahead there were isolated skirmishes and frequent bombardment from the Mexican batteries, mostly reconnaisances sent forward to test the strength of Travis's command and defenses. Crockett seemed to circulate around the walls talking to the men, joking no doubt, showing them the "b[e]ar" and letting them see an example of frontier bravado that Travis thought animated their own spirits. One night he led a raid in on some *jacales* that gave shelter to enemy riflemen, and set them ablaze.[33] When not engaged in the skirmishing, Travis kept the men at work on their defenses. On March 3 there came encouragement when a rider got through with word of sixty men on their way from San Felipe and another three hundred expected, while Fannin, with some three hundred at Goliad, was finally supposed to be coming after all. If they all arrived in time, and if they could get through the Mexican cordon, Travis would have more than eight hundred, possibly enough to hold against any assault. But Travis did not believe that Fannin was really coming. Worse, he could see this afternoon the Mexican *soldados* building scaling ladders out in the open, betokening a heavy assault, and soon.

In a spirit of resignation, but not yet despondency, he sent out his last dispatches, one to the Convention at large and another to delegate Jesse Grimes. He detailed the almost miraculous fact that after ten days of intermittent shelling, he had yet to suffer any casualties. "The spirits of my men are still high although they have had much to depress them," he declared. Estimating that he faced somewhere between fifteen hundred and six thousand Mexicans, he pleaded for help but promised yet again to fight and die for Texas before he would surrender. His courage and that of his men would not fail them "in the last struggle," he said, revealing that the imminent possibility of death was certainly on his mind. Still he promised that "the victory will cost the enemy so dear, that it will be worse for him than defeat." He still did not doubt that this was the place to meet and stop Santa Anna, even if every day he could see the blood-red banner flying above the San Fernando tower in San Antonio, Santa Anna's reminder that he would take no prisoners. Above all, it was vital that the Convention decide on independence. Then every Texian would know what they were fighting for and rally to his aid. If the Convention failed to make such a declaration, he said, then and only then would he give up. The talk of independence made him even bolder, it seemed, for just after declaring his willingness to die, he boasted that if he had only five hundred more men, he could raise the siege and drive the Mexican army back below the Rio Grande.[34]

Yet it was with rather less bravado, and more reflection, that he added a brief private note to those the courier took out that day. Travis addressed it to the man then looking after his infant son Charles. "Take care of my little boy," implored the father. "If the country should be saved, I may make him a splendid fortune; but if the country should be lost and I should perish, he will have nothing but the proud recollection that he is the son of a man who died for his country."[35] These were the last words to come from Travis or the Alamo.

Within another day Santa Anna completed the ring around the Alamo, and no one was going to get in or out. From this point onward, it was almost certain that a strong assault would be successful. Travis had already succeeded in delaying Santa Anna for nearly two weeks, buying time for the convention being held at Washington-on-the-Brazos to wrangle interminably over a constitution and finally declare for complete independence on March 2, and also buying time, so he thought, for Houston to raise an army to defend Texas and to come to his aid. There was nothing more for the defenders to achieve by holding out, but until this time there seems to have been no thought of surrender, and indeed no expectation of humane terms if they did yield. Travis's March 3 letter would be the last words heard from the Alamo defenders. Their thoughts and feelings thereafter are forever shrouded in darkness. Almost forty years later a story appeared and went into Texas legend that told of Travis forming the defenders on the parade ground and drawing a line in the dirt with his sword, telling those willing to stay and die to cross it and stand with him. It may have happened, but more likely it was an invention, for the source of the story was decidedly unreliable.

Still, Travis's hired slave Joe claimed a few days later that on March 5, having given up altogether on the hope of reinforcement, Travis told the men that if no sign of help came that day, then on the morrow, March 6, they would either seek terms for capitulation or else try to escape or fight their way out.[36] One man did later tell a story of climbing over the wall that night and stealing through Mexican lines, and years later filed testimony that he had left the Alamo. All of these voices came after March 3, however. Once the gate closed on the courier Travis sent out that night, he, Bowie, Crockett, Dickinson, Esparza, and the rest ceased to speak, receding to scarcely more than shadows on the page until they came together one last time on their funeral pyres.

Santa Anna took no chances in planning his assault. Whatever his other failings as a commander, he was methodical. His officers preferred simply to continue the siege, confident that in another week or so, especially after heavy siege guns arrived, they could pulverize the Alamo into dust and force a surrender at no cost to themselves in life. Santa Anna wanted to take it by storm, however. Expecting that there would be more battles ahead, he needed to build the self-confidence of his army, especially among the inexperienced conscripts, some of them actually released convicts. He wanted to erase the shame of Cós's surrender with a glorious victory. To date, all of his outposts in Texas had been defeated by lesser numbers, even if the skirmishes themselves were minor. He needed real battlefield victory, and from the point of view of building morale and experience, Santa Anna made the right decision. Nor could he be unmindful of the continuing unrest behind him in Mexico proper. A crushing victory over insurgents here would send a loud message to the malcontents elsewhere to curb their republican zeal.

Nevertheless, Santa Anna made the right decision at the wrong place. Even if crumbling, still those Alamo walls posed a formidable defense, and must cost many lives even in an inevitable triumph. That being the case, he then made another correct decision, but again at the wrong time. He gave orders that his most seasoned and experienced regulars be the vanguard of the attack. It made sense, for they would perform better, with a better chance of success, while the conscripts and new men who followed could learn and take spirit from their example. But it also meant that the heaviest casualties would fall among his best troops, whom he would need for the campaign beyond Béxar.[37]

Santa Anna gave Cós a chance to redeem himself by commanding the first column of three hundred men, whom he would lead against the northwest corner of the Alamo compound with ladders for scaling and axes and crowbars for breaking into the barricaded adobe rooms. Colonel Francisco Duqué would take four hundred men similarly equipped against the north wall. Colonel Juan Morales should drive one hundred riflemen against the south wall and the fortified main entrance to the compound, while Colonel José María Romero and three hundred more struck from the northeast. That was only eleven hundred of Santa Anna's army. He intended to hold the balance in reserve under his personal command, ready to leap into any breach opened. Then sheer numbers would win the day. Meanwhile, Ramíres y Sesma's cavalry were to patrol in a circle around the Alamo at some distance to catch any rebels who went over the walls trying to escape.

Carrying their scaling ladders, the *soldados* approached in their columns in the pre-dawn hours of March 6. By 6:00 A.M. they had almost reached the walls undetected when enthusiastic soldiers ruined the surprise by shouting "Viva Santa Anna!" Dozing sentinels on the walls awoke and saw the attackers within perhaps fifty yards, close enough that at the first blast from Texian cannon on the walls half a company of *soldados* were cut down.[38] The alarm sounded quickly, and Texians ran to their posts. Travis, who had been asleep in his quarters, now ran to the north wall where his men already fired into the darkness at Cós's and Duqué's men preparing to raise their ladders. Joe heard him shouting for his men to "give them Hell," then saw him lean over the parapet to fire his shotgun into the throng, to be hit immediately in the forehead by a Mexican bullet. The Alamo's commander, perhaps the first defender killed, fell and died almost instantly, while Joe fled to cover and saw no more until it was all over.

In the next few minutes, with fighting almost all along the walls, the Texians soon realized they were too few to hold such a long line, and the Mexicans quickly probed for the weak spots. Defenders had no choice but to abandon one position in order to go to another more threatened, and soon most of them were on the north wall where the columns of Cós, Duqué, and Romero converged. Then Cós shifted around to the north end of the west wall and found that he could batter his way through closed windows and barricaded outer doors. Once through the single rooms inside, the *soldados* poured into the courtyard itself. At the same time Romero's men shifted back to the east wall and did the same. Seeing themselves about to be cut off as the enemy entered the courtyard behind them, the defenders on the north wall withdrew into the barricaded rooms of a two-story stone and adobe barracks on the east wall close to the church, rooms from which they knew there was no escape. Meanwhile, Santa Anna sent in four hundred reserves to help Cós finally push over the north wall, and at last the Mexicans held the courtyard.

The remaining Texians were confined either in those rooms in the long barracks or else in the church. At last Morales's men entered from the south, essentially ending the actual battle after barely half an hour. Before them now remained a bitter and brutal mopping-up operation as they went from room to room, using axes and crowbars or captured Texian cannon to bash in the doors before they rushed in to finish their work with bayonets. Some of them found Bowie alone in a sick room on the south wall, either dead already from his fever or else probably unconscious in a coma. They took him for a coward trying to hide under a blanket. Bayonets and a bullet through his head finished him, quite possibly without his ever knowing what happened.

Somewhere outside—no one would ever know where—fell Crockett. None who knew him or saw him go down lived to tell of his fate, while none of the Mexicans who killed him or saw him fall had any idea who he was. Some Texians later thought he fell in front of the church, others on the wall facing San Antonio, and still more believed he died on the parade ground. Several weeks later the first of a series of rumors appeared that he actually tried to surrender along with a few others who had exhausted their ammunition and could no longer fight. Their captors brought them before Santa Anna himself after the battle, only to be ordered to execute them on the spot. Perhaps so—perhaps not. Certainly men tried to give up. After all, when trapped in a room with nowhere to go, or cornered with empty rifles and muskets facing scores of *soldados*, there was no way for them to go on fighting, and no point. There could hardly be dishonor in giving up when the means of further resistance were exhausted and there was no point in the sacrifice, as Travis himself had suggested when he spoke of surrendering if the Convention did not go for independence.

In any case, all such men were put to death on the spot, begging for a definition of the line between death in battle and simple execution.[39]

Crockett, whose last known post was in the vicinity, may even have been with some defenders on the southeast corner who realized that further fighting was hopeless, and managed to go over the wall and run out into the chaparral. Two more groups unable to reach the church or the long barracks also went over the wall, perhaps as many as eighty men in all, more than a third of the garrison, but Ramírez y Sesma's lancers relentlessly ran them down. One desperate man managed to evade them long enough to take refuge in dense brush, into which the Mexicans simply fired and jabbed their lances until finally he was dead.[40] It is appropriate to Crockett's folk hero stature that his place of death could not be pinned down, as if symbolically he died everywhere, and nowhere. In future years rumors even appeared that he had not died at all, but like all true folk heroes lived on in new adventures.

In a few minutes more the *soldados* broke into the last of the barricaded rooms and into the church itself. Soon it was all over, those remaining few who attempted to surrender being shot or bayoneted where they stood. The next day Santa Anna ordered their bodies stacked with cord wood into three large pyres and set ablaze. While the remains of soon-to-be Texian heroes smoldered amid the black smoke of their pyres, the Mexicans collecting the several hundred muskets, rifles, pistols, and cannon of the defenders that littered the compound unwittingly took possession of another Texian icon. The iron artillery pieces Santa Anna retained either to augment his field artillery, or else to refortify Béxar once he left it behind. He regarded the softer brass and bronze pieces as essentially redundant and would not take them with him. It was hardly a priority just now, but at some time in the coming months he or a staff officer gave the order to melt them to prevent their being of any future use to rebels. Among those that disappeared in the crucible was Gonzales's "Come and Take It" gun, the spark that ignited the resistance five months before.[41]

Within just hours of the end of the fighting, Seguín and his small reinforcement approached San Antonio and listened for the signal gun that Travis had said he would fire periodically. "Arriving at the Cibolo and not hearing the signal which was to be discharged every fifteen minutes as long as the place held out, we retraced our steps to convey to the general-in-chief the sad tidings," he remembered. He also left two of his men behind to gather what information they could, and a few days later they rejoined him with confirmation of the fall of the Alamo.

Santa Anna had a complete victory. The Alamo and Béxar were his, and two hundred or more defenders had been killed, including two of the revolt's best-known leaders, Travis and Bowie. But as Travis had promised, it cost him dearly. One fourth of his sixteen hundred men in the attacking columns were casualties, more than two hundred of them dead or dying, and most of those from his best battalions.[42] Privately many of the generalissimo's officers felt appalled at the waste of life and disillusioned with their commander's leadership, an unfortunate situation with more campaigning ahead. When the Mexicans marched on a few days later, leaving a substantial garrison to hold Béxar, their high command was already deeply divided. Still, just the day after the fall of the Alamo, Santa Anna received a report from Urrea telling him of the ignominious end of Grant and the Matamoros debacle.[43] It hardly seemed that they should expect anything ahead of them but more victories and a successful defeat of the insurrection. He little suspected that he left behind him the birth of a legend, and a rallying cry and a spirit of revenge that would return to haunt him and help to keep the insurgency alive.

CHAPTER TEN

Atmosphere Devilish Dark

∘〰∘

NOT A SINGLE ONE of the Alamo defenders left behind definitive last words. In their final moments they were simply too
busy, too confused, or too afraid to think about speaking for posterity,
especially with no one likely to survive to pass it along.[1] Surely they
must have wondered at least one thing in common in their last hours:
"Where is Houston? Where is Fannin?" Where, indeed.

In the weeks that followed his abandonment of the Matamoros contention at the end of January, Houston behaved, as so often in his life, in a
manner to frustrate both those who knew him and those who did not.
The imbroglio over command of the Matamoros expedition between
himself, Grant, Johnson, and Fannin convinced Houston—rightly so—
that he had enemies in San Felipe, and that he could wind up as much a
fatality of the war between Smith and the Council as the governor himself. Worse, Texas itself appeared well on the way to the top of the casualty list. As soon as he reached Washington on January 30, 1836, he gave
the essentially impotent governor a scathing report on everything from
the poor condition of the volunteers he had seen to the weaknesses in
their government. Supplies were not forthcoming where they were supposed to be. Much-needed horses and draft animals failed to materialize.
Volunteers all but refused to take orders from any representative of the
discredited San Felipe crowd, and even some of the enlisted Regulars
flatly declined to march under his orders until properly clothed and paid.
The soldiers everywhere looked "truly destitute," he complained. Only
with great difficulty was Houston able to put together a garrison to guard
Goliad, a vital strong point on their best road to a Gulf port at Copano.

Then there was the mess in San Felipe. "I do consider the acts of the council calculated to protract the war for years to come," he declared. By backing the special interests of those behind the Matamoros enterprise, the Council had encouraged insubordination in the military, divided its high command, compromised the unity of purpose vital for an underdog in their situation, and diverted crucially important resources from the defense of Texas. On his return to Washington he had an opportunity, thanks to Smith, to read through all of the correspondence and public proclamations that told the sorry story of the disintegration in the Provisional Government. Now he found an order directed to him from the Council requiring that he disregard instructions from Governor Smith, even though their very organic law, imperfect as it was, made quite clear that the general in chief reported to the governor and not to the Council. It would be "an act of treason," Houston protested, and an attack on the basis of their government. Indeed, he went further. Treason had already been committed, but by those on the Council who sacrificed the security of Texas for what he believed to be motives of personal gain and political jealousy.

The Council had ordered Smith to require Houston to move his headquarters to Washington in December, and it was not hard to suppose that its motive had been to keep him out of the way and unaware of what was going on. "Their object must have been to conceal," he accused. Even though mysteriously no copies of the correspondence emanating from the Council relating to army matters made it to Houston, still he learned enough from what Smith showed him of their dispatches backing the Matamoros matter that he gleaned their purpose. "Every facility has been afforded to the meditated campaign against Matamoras," he complained, but "no aid has been rendered for raising a regular force for defence of the country, nor one cent advanced to an officer or soldier of the regular army." Worse, the Council repeatedly violated article after article of the organic law of the Provisional Government, compromising his own and Smith's authority, creating civilian men of power, like Grant, who stood completely outside any governmental control, unlawfully raising volunteer companies not subject to central command, and making Fannin insubordinate to his own oath as a Regular officer by commissioning him to do things counter to the instructions of Houston, his lawful commander. All in the interest of what Houston could only describe as "a piratical and predatory" expedition for plunder. He worried, too, for the impact of this behavior on the outside world from which Texians so much hoped and needed to receive support. "The evil is now done," he concluded. He only saw hope in the convention called for March 1, where a permanent government might be created and "where honest functionaries will regard and execute the known and established laws of the country, agreeably to their oaths." Absent that, "the country must be lost."

Houston even cited a statement by Fannin himself that he believed the ultimate objective of the Council was to remove Houston from his command. Thus, it was no wonder that the general saw conspiracies and plots in abundance. "Every effort of the council has been to mortify me individually, and, if possible to compel me to do some act which would enable them to pursue the same measures toward me, which they have illegally done toward your excellency," he told Smith. "They have loved darkness rather than light," he said delving for an apt aphorism, "because their deeds are evil." Houston made no effort to conceal his overarching concern for his own reputation in all this. He absented himself from all participation in the Matamoros episode in the end because, as he told Smith, "by remaining with the army, the council would have had the pleasure of ascribing to me the evils which their own conduct and acts will, in all probability, produce." Consequently, he now repudiated the Council and its actions, dismissing both as unlawful and not binding on him. Clearly concerned that he could be left the scapegoat for what ultimately happened to the Matamoros expedition, as well as for the general collapse of the infant military establishment, he refused to risk bearing responsibility for the mess, and decided to get himself as far away from it all as possible.[2]

Six days after giving Smith his report, Houston simply left Washington in company with John Forbes and rode north to Nacogdoches to meet with the Cherokee. He had already organized a treaty meeting with them before his ill-fated visit to Goliad. Now he simply washed his hands of the army and Texas political affairs, believing that any effort prior to March 1 and the new convention would be futile. Houston and Forbes concluded their treaty with Chief Bowl on February 23, and the next day cleared their accounts from their stay in Nacogdoches. As agents of a government that had no cash, they had to instruct Henry Raguet, the treasurer of the local vigilance committee, to make payments on account of the Provisional Government in merchandise taken from Raguet's own mercantile stock, just one more evidence of the crippling ineffectuality of the San Felipe Council.[3]

During those three weeks at Nacogdoches, Houston went all but silent to his correspondents. To a friend in Mississippi he wrote of confidence that the March 1 convention would declare for complete independence, but beyond that he essentially took himself out of the public arena, not to emerge again until the last day of the month when he returned to Washington and made a report on his Cherokee negotiations, significantly directed to Smith and not the Council.[4] It was perhaps wise for Houston to absent himself, for on February 12 Robinson, as acting governor, issued a proclamation accusing Smith of treason and of plotting to turn the Council over to "the military" for trial and punishment. Robinson did not name Houston in the document, but since Houston was in charge of the only portion of the military that was at all answering to the governor, the implication was clear enough. Indeed, the charges against Smith alleged correctly that he had been giving orders to Travis, Neill, and Houston, three men who constituted the bulk of Smith's support in the Regular Army, and who also happened to be known now as being on the record in favor of complete independence. Robinson and most of the Council still called only for secession from Coahuila.[5]

Houston's return to Washington on February 29 was hardly accidental, for the new convention was to convene the next day, and he was an elected delegate. Moreover, he expected to remedy much if he could as that body deliberated a new government and the ultimate course for Texas to pursue. He returned to find that the sentiment for independence advanced in his absence, thanks in large part to the appearance of the Mexican army marching on Béxar, and even now reports from Travis that he was besieged. Yet a strange lethargy prevailed both in Washington and in San Felipe, the deadly aftermath of the demoralization and indecision fomented by the disintegration of the government. Even as the Council voted to publish in the press Travis's stirring declarations of defiance and pleas for assistance, one man in Washington privately lamented that "the *vile rabble* here cannot be moved."[6] The paralysis spread throughout Texian forces, too. In Goliad, Colonel Fannin, despite having the wherewithal to aid Travis, simply stayed put. "I am in a devil of a bad humor," he wrote on February 28, "hoping for the best, being prepared for the worst."[7] But no one, it seemed, was actually prepared to do something.

There were several reasons, none of them likely to be satisfactory to the men about to die in the Alamo. The government itself was crippled and no longer commanded authority with the people, if it ever had. Houston was a general in chief without an army and with no backing in what barely functioned as a government. In any event, he did not favor trying to hold on to Béxar. Houston believed that the true strategic line of defense ought to run from Copano north through Goliad, then to the San Marcos River and along it through Gonzales to the edge of the hill country at San Marcos itself. Such a line covered the only three avenues available for an advancing army, the Atascosita Road through Goliad, the Béxar–San Felipe road that crossed the San Marcos at Gonzales, and the Camino Real that ran along the foothills from San Antonio to San Marcos and beyond. In Houston's thinking, Béxar was simply too advanced beyond that natural line of defense along the river, too exposed to being cut off and isolated.

Unfortunately, thanks to the damage done by the Matamoros frenzy, and to his own ignorance of the situation in February due to absenting himself to get out of harm's way, Houston simply did not know that if Béxar were abandoned nothing lay between it and San Felipe to stop six thousand Mexicans. The Alamo of itself may have been of no great military importance, but if Santa Anna had not halted his advance there for two weeks to deal with the garrison, March 1 could have seen his infantry on the Colorado just a day's march from San Felipe, and his cavalry much farther, in Washington or beyond, meaning that the existing government would be put to flight and the new convention might not be able to convene at all. In short, Houston's reading of the ground was entirely correct, but his reading of the strategic problem before him was all wrong.

It may have been a measure of the frustration of the situation he found on reaching Washington that Houston spent the evening before the convention getting drunk on eggnog, and thereafter slept much of the day. "It was a bad business," he later confessed of his behavior then. "I hated it."[8] In addition, if drink did not influence his judgment just then, Houston's experience with the Council, Fannin, and others left him so suspicious of conspiracies and so dismissive of incompetent amateurs that he looked skeptically at virtually all information coming from San Felipe. When he first saw Travis's entreaties for assistance, he doubted their veracity, if not their authorship. "A fraud had been prac-

ticed upon the people by the officers of the frontier, for party purposes,"
he allegedly said in a very definite echo of his diatribe to Smith, and further he declared that "there was not an enemy on our borders." It all
sounded so much like the claptrap that preceded the Matamoros fiasco.

He had met Travis, though they were not well acquainted, and even
if Travis had been loyal to Smith, still he had too many friends on the
Council to be trusted completely, and was besides too closely allied
with Austin. Moreover, as a soldier Travis was a rank amateur, and at
the same time had for years shown himself to have the pen of an incen-
diary and publicist, and thus could be expected to overreact and exaggerate his situation. Houston knew Fannin better, but as a result did not
trust him at all, having seen him acting as the tool of the Council. Fannin had shown himself anxious to take Houston's command, and Travis
might be just as ambitious, perhaps seeing holding on to Béxar as the
means to become a hero in Texas and ride that to power. Thus, Houston
dismissed both men's pleas for help at the Alamo. Four years later, one
Texian now in Washington recalled Houston declaring that the report of
the Alamo being threatened was "a damned lie, and that all those reports
from Travis & Fannin were lies, for there were no Mexican forces there
and he believed that it was only electioneering schemed [by] Travis &
Fannin to sustain their popularity."[9] Indeed, two years later Houston
told the brother of one of the Alamo defenders that he sent an order now
to Travis to evacuate the Alamo and retreat, something he could hardly
expect the garrison to do if he knew or believed that Travis faced the
Mexican army.[10]

When the convention gathered on March 1, Houston continued
expressing his skepticism, telling fellow delegates that Travis exaggerated his position and sought to aggrandize himself, even leading to speculation that Travis did not write the appeals, which after all came via
the Council in San Felipe and not directly to Washington. The unspoken
suggestion was that conspirators on the Council might have created
them hoping to lure Houston away from the convention, or perhaps
they were even authored by Mexicans or *tejano* traitors hoping to entice
more Texians into a trap.[11] That Houston took the situation in Béxar
with such apparent lack of appreciation may not speak well of his judgment and motives, but in the poisonous political atmosphere of which
he had all too much experience in the past two months, he could in
some measure be excused for excessive suspicion and caution. Besides,

if he took the reports at face value and left to try to assist in reinforcing Béxar, he would not be present in Washington when the anticipated new government chose its new general in chief. To preserve his own position, he had to be here where the political battles were to be fought, and trust that Travis could cope with the battles on his own front, whether real or chimerical.

The delegates came in out of a cold winter blast to convene their meeting, wearing their overcoats indoors in an unfinished hall rented from Noah Byers, and began their deliberations.[12] Forty-five of them represented twenty-one municipalities, though some had just one delegate present. Still they formed a quorum. Familiar faces filled the chairs: Martin Parmer, James Gaines, Zavala, and others. Béxar had three delegates there, two *tejanos* from the town and one delegate actually elected and sent by the garrison in the Alamo. Houston was there, too, though now representing Refugio rather than Nacogdoches as he had in the Consultation. They chose as president of the Convention Richard Ellis, a recent arrival in Texas not closely identified with either of the old parties, but shortly afterward, the Convention made its intention clear when it adopted a resolution to select a committee to draft a declaration of independence.[13] The vote on that resolution made the outcome virtually a foregone conclusion. Now it must be independence from Mexico or nothing.

Houston spent that evening working on a committee to draft rules of order, and the next day they went before the convention, differing little from parliamentary procedure elsewhere except in the excessive attention given to maintaining order and decorum in the hall, perhaps an anticipation of discord and contention. Indeed, the length and detail of the report suggest that it was in most respects prepared before the Convention met, and so, too, the report on the declaration of independence committee introduced immediately after approval of the rules. Again the members heard echoes of the 1776 declaration. It set forth all their grievances, including the arrest of Austin, denial of trial by jury, and new ones: the failure to provide public education and an explicit complaint about the religious obligations that, in fact, Mexico never really tried to enforce. Of course, these were minor compared to the fact that Santa Anna had launched "mercenary armies sent forth to force a new government upon them at the point of the bayonet." They had appealed to their fellow Mexicans to join with them in their resistance to oppression, but none came to their aid. "They are unfit to be free," the report said in condemnation of the rest of Mexico, "and incapable of self-government." Therefore, the right of self-preservation inherent to all humanity dictated that they remove themselves from any connection or fealty to such an oppressor, and thus they hereby declared Texas to be a sovereign and independent republic.

Houston himself guided the report through committee and on to the floor, and it was upon his motion that the Convention adopted it unanimously that afternoon.[14] The drafting committee had neither the time nor, apparently, the skills at command to produce a stirring document like Jefferson's of 1776. Instead this declaration was a wordy and somewhat querulous paraphrase of that earlier document. Euphoria over their act was almost immediately dampened by the receipt of a dispatch from Travis dated one week earlier. "I am besieged by a thousand or more of the Mexicans under Santa Anna," he wrote. Already his garrison had endured a day and night of bombardment, and Santa Anna had told him either to surrender (to be executed) or face no quarter.[15] Houston seemed stunned. For the first time in more than a month he attempted to stir some action. "War is raging on the frontiers," he proclaimed in a public letter written in the convention hall and soon distributed as a broadside. "Bexar is besieged." He exaggerated Travis's report of a thousand Mexicans to two thousand, and then called on citizens of Texas to rush to Travis's relief. "The enemy must be driven from our soil, or desolation will accompany their march upon us," he admonished. *Independence is declared; it must be maintained.*"[16] He signed himself as commander in chief of the army, yet it is clear that he felt he had no power to do more than make a stirring appeal, for three days passed before he attempted to issue a positive order. In retrospect it hardly mattered, for by this time neither Houston nor substantial reinforcements could have reached the Alamo before March 6. The garrison there was doomed before the Convention even knew it was in danger.

When he did start giving orders, however, Houston clearly felt he was in charge once more. That was because the convention renewed his appointment as general in chief. The motion to appoint a major general appeared on the floor March 3, to be tabled temporarily, even as the defenders in the Alamo stared out at that red flag flying over a church to announce their impending deaths. Meanwhile, the president appointed other committees to look into the condition of the army, its positions, officers, armaments, and supplies, and also to investigate mobilizing the country for defense. Interestingly enough, Houston appeared on neither committee, though he of all people should have been the most qualified to serve. Perhaps it was because he now joined the committee to draft a constitution for the new republic. In any case, he stayed unwontedly quiet in the parliamentary procedures of the next two days. On the morning of March 4, as Mexican *soldados* in San Antonio were preparing their scaling ladders, the Convention heard a resolution that in the crisis Texas needed one supreme commander to head an army with "subordination defined, established and strictly observed," not unlikely a sentiment induced by the Matamoros problem. Houston should be the man, to command all land forces, Regulars, volunteers, and local militia alike, and the resolution called for him to take command immediately. In the sudden sense of emergency, the Convention dispensed with its rule requiring resolutions to lay on the table for a day before debate, and that afternoon took it up at once. The delegates added amendments specifying that Houston should hold office only until they had a constitution and chose a president, who might then continue his appointment, and that otherwise he should answer to the Convention. The resolution passed, but only after some debate in which three delegates addressed the house in its favor and one spoke in opposition, an objection perhaps based in the natural contrariness of Robert Potter, the delegate in question and coincidentally the only delegate from Houston's former base in Nacogdoches, but also perhaps because Houston's drinking seems to have continued on a nightly basis, now involving others like Thomas J. Rusk, chairman of the committee to prepare a constitution.[17]

The Convention did not meet on Saturday, March 5, but Santa Anna did not take the day off, making his final plans for the assault of the next morning. Finally, on Sunday, as the battle smoke was still drifting over the scene of hundreds of dead Texians and Mexicans at the Alamo, the delegates convened again on Sunday immediately to consider Travis's March 3 dispatch just received, his out of the Alamo. The urgency and peril of his situation removed all doubt that might have remained from his earlier letter, as did his farewell declaration of "Victory or Death." A few minutes later Houston arose and asked permission to make a personal statement. Concerned as always with his reputation, and at the same time legitimately mindful of the need for approbation if he was to succeed in his new and unequivocal command, he took the first opportunity, safe from the reprisal of the Council, to make a public explanation of his conduct during the Matamoros affair, and of his relations with the discredited provisional government. That done, he thanked them for his appointment and announced that he would leave immediately to find what army there was left. His announced intention was to go to the relief of Béxar, even though he still expressed some doubts that the Mexicans actually held San Antonio.[18] At the moment he spoke, its garrison already lay dead in heaps on the walls and in the doorways and parade ground of the Alamo.[19]

And now tragedy followed tragedy for the revolutionaries. What excitement and optimism there was from the early quick victories, and then the declaration of independence on March 2, turned to shock and disbelief by March 11 when solid confirmation of the fall of the Alamo reached Houston and others. It was as if the British had burned Manhattan on July 5, 1776, with Washington and his army standing idly by. The funeral pyres in Béxar burned heroes and martyrs. The dead of the Alamo provided a rallying cry that inspired the rebels in the days ahead, but they also presented a problem for Houston himself, for his enemies might hold him culpable for not doing more to help them, as indeed some did, threatening to make Houston a living casualty of the battle. For the rest of his life he tried to explain or cover for his apparent failure to take the threat to Travis seriously. Just two days after he was forced to accept that the Alamo had fallen, he began to spin a new version of his involvement. He would say he had given emphatic orders for the Alamo to be destroyed and its guns removed, but Grant had taken all the draft animals necessary off toward Matamoros, and Bowie and later Travis refused to obey their orders. Before long he would be blaming Travis and Bowie specifically for "disobedience," while still acknowledging their heroism and sacrifice. In fact, he never gave any such an order, but merely a suggestion to Smith, yet in later days he would go on to try to blame the Council by inventing a fictitious order from it countermanding his own fictitious directive.[20]

And still, Houston moved with puzzling sloth. "Genl. Houston shew'd no disposition of being in a hurry to the Army," complained a man who met with him on the trip. One day after he left Washington he had covered barely ten miles, and two days later he had only moved another forty miles to the Colorado, all of it a distance a man in a hurry could have ridden in a single day. Moreover, he took back roads that added extra miles to his journey rather than the more direct Atascosita. Then Houston remained on the Colorado two nights and a day before moving on, and all told took five days to complete the two-day ride to Gonzales, which he reached about four o'clock on the afternoon of March 11.[21] Along the way he did not issue the first orders to start a concentration of remaining men at Gonzales until March 9, and only then did he send orders to Fannin, who commanded at Goliad almost all that remained of what could be called an army.[22]

That Houston showed no sense of urgency in getting to Gonzales is immaterial. There was no army there awaiting him anyhow. But to relieve Béxar he did have to get forces on the road to San Antonio, and quickly. The critical judgment against him is that he wasted three days on the road before starting to do so. Furthermore, given that Houston on horseback could move much faster than volunteers on foot, his delay in sending orders to Fannin only postponed the date that the two could meet to move on Béxar. Apparently Houston was never asked and never explained why he did not send orders immediately to Fannin and others from Washington. The three days he took to inform Fannin especially of his intentions are compelling evidence that Houston did not really believe the situation in San Antonio to be critical, supported by the fact that it was while he rested on the Colorado at the time he issued those first orders that he told a local man that he believed the reports from Travis and Fannin were politically motivated lies and that no Mexicans threatened either.

He spoke in another voice in his March 2 proclamation, to be sure. "Bexar is besieged by 2000 of the enemy," he had said. But if he genuinely believed that, then how can his remaining four more days in Washington—meanwhile making no attempt to influence concentrations of forces to relieve Travis—and wasting another three on the road before starting to react be explained satisfactorily? The only logical conclusion seems to be that he wrote the proclamation to try to arouse the people in anticipation of his renewed commission to lead them, while privately he remained unconvinced of the peril to the Alamo. It would be neither the first nor the last time that Houston said one thing for public consumption while protesting the opposite in private, nor is that necessarily to his discredit. People in power are often called on to wear two faces in the interest of some greater goal. Two weeks later in a private letter to Rusk, Houston unburdened himself. "You know I am not easily depressed," he said, "but, before my God, since we parted, I have found the darkest hours of my past life!"[23] He may have been referring to what he confronted since his arrival in Gonzales, but the reference to his previous life raises the specter of the deep depression, alcoholism, and withdrawal from the world that precipitated and followed his departure from Tennessee years before. Drink, indecision, fear for his reputation, could all account for his hesitation now on the road to Gonzales, and certainly he had already manifested all during the revolt to date. Moreover, the annals of history bulged with cases of men with little or no real experience at leadership who sought high command, only to freeze when they got it and realized the full weight of responsibility. Whatever the final explanation for Houston's sloth, unwittingly those three days of delay contributed to yet another tragic moment for Texas.[24]

Initially, Houston wanted Fannin to march at once north to the west bank of the Cibolo, where the general hoped to meet him with whatever force he would find at Gonzales and then race to the relief of the Alamo.[25] The irresolute Fannin had been begged before to send aid to the Alamo, and on February 26 he actually did leave with 320 men for San Antonio but got only two miles before the breakdown of some of his supply wagons collapsed his resolve and he turned back. Apparently in response to Houston's March 9 order, Fannin was ready to start out again for Béxar on March 12 when word of the Alamo's fall reached him. Thus, he did not move, and then came Houston's March 11 order to evacuate and pull back to the line of the Guadalupe near Victoria where he could protect Copano and have the river as a front line of defense.[26]

Once a rather decisive man, Fannin reacted to the Matamoros business with a fit of indecision, perhaps out of fear of responsibility in the face of a cripplingly divided government. By now he had retreated into a fog of irresolution, made worse by his sending a substantial portion of his command off to aid evacuating settlers. He did not want to abandon Goliad until his detachments returned, not knowing that they had been attacked and dispersed in several skirmishes in the vicinity of Refugio just north of Copano. One party of thirty or more were captured and executed by Urrea's command on March 15, and another body of one hundred twenty-five Texians lost a third of their number killed or captured the next day before they escaped. Then, as Fannin dithered, Urrea simply continued his rapid approach. By March 18 it was too late, with Urrea's advance riders already in sight of the Texian defenses.

The tragedy is that Fannin did not have to engage Urrea. Had Houston ordered him out earlier, without waiting until March 9, Fannin could have been well clear of Goliad and two days on his way to Béxar before learning that the mission was pointless. He might still have tried to turn back to Goliad, but more likely he would have hesitated in indecision to get instructions from Houston, who at this point would have ordered him on to Gonzales as he did subsequently. Houston's delay in sending orders makes him culpable for failure to take charge immediately in a critical situation. What happened subsequently to Fannin cannot be laid at Houston's feet, however.

Skirmishing with Urrea broke out that March 18, and Fannin intended to retreat as quickly as possible that night, but when fog set in after dark, he decided to wait until the next morning. He never got the chance. As he started after dawn on March 19, the pillars of smoke from the burning material he could not evacuate told the Mexicans what was happening and they rushed to encircle him. Unaware of his peril, Fannin moved slowly, further hampered by his wagons, and covered only six miles when he halted the column, having discovered that he had forgotten to pack any food for the men. Shortly after he resumed the march, he saw Mexican cavalry approaching on the road behind him and infantry soon thereafter. Instead of rushing on to the cover of woods, Fannin formed his command into a square out in the open. At once Mexican lines began to advance and attack. The Texians gave them volleys that stalled their approach, but soon it was evident that Fannin was surrounded and out in the open.

The fight continued on into the afternoon, stopping only with darkness. Fannin took some 60 casualties out of the 420 or more with him, while Mexican losses came close to 200 thanks to their having to attack in the open. That night the Texians dug rifle pits and threw up earthen breastworks, intending to fight on, but in the morning they found that now Urrea had even more men and also some artillery, making their position hopeless. After sending in a few rounds of canister to demonstrate his capability, Urrea humanely ceased fire and, as he expected, Fannin came out with a request for surrender terms. Urrea gave no guarantees, but Fannin believed he and his men would be paroled and sent to New Orleans, or else that is what he was told.[27] Of course, Santa Anna had given explicit orders that all rebels taken alive were to be executed as traitors and pirates. Urrea knew that but had no stomach for such business. As he marched the Texians back to Goliad, he sent a plea to his commander to relax his order and allow the men to be spared. In return Santa Anna sent Urrea a severe reprimand and an unequivocal order that all were to be put to death. Disgusted but resigned, on March 27 Urrea's officers had them marched out on the road to Matamoros, sparing them last minutes of horror by telling them they were on their way to gather cattle or wood, or even to ships to take them away. Then they were halted by the road and volleys and bayonets poured into them until 342 lay dead. Incredibly, 28 others managed to escape either by running or being mistaken for dead and left to rise and flee in the night before the rest were burned the next day.[28]

The revolt begun in a series of euphoric but inconsequential quick victories had suddenly taken a dramatic and disastrous turn. Just two days after the Goliad massacre, Henry Austin, one of Stephen's seemingly innumerable cousins, observed of recent disasters that "painfull as the event is in itself to me it came as the harbinger of Salvation to Texas—for I had long been convinced that some severe disaster alone could call the wretched set of men who have obtained the lead in public affairs to a sense of their duty to the people."[29] Indeed, despite Houston's expectations that it was worth his effort remaining in Washington to help create a more stable new government, it is evident that the same old party spirit and animosities prevailed, though now on a more *ad hominem* basis since they were all on record in favor of independence. Within hours after Houston's departure from Washington on March 6, Robinson, who still styled himself acting governor, wrote to Fannin that "we are too much divided for the benefit of our country." Instead, "party spirit lays hold with her infernal fangs," he said, perhaps at last beginning to recognize his own role in that demoralizing clash. "The spirit of party rages to an unprecedented height," he continued, then revealed that his real complaint was that the Council was still trying to rule but no one was paying any attention.[30]

In spite of his animosity toward Smith and Houston and other of the old War Party leaders, Robinson had at last acquired vision clear enough to see all the harm done, and the way to remedy. He addressed a letter to the Convention protesting the inclination of some like Houston to disregard his instructions as acting governor. Rather mendaciously he also tried retroactively to place himself on the right side of the issue by claiming that in the Consultation he had been for "*independence, and nothing but independence,"* whereas all of his public statements prior to this time put him firmly in the camp of those wanting only secession from Coahuila. But then he asked them now "so to organize, constitute and remodel the provisional Government, as to restore harmony, promote union, provide for the common defence and general welfare; and that the public interest may not be prejudiced or injured by the present unhappy state of dissention and disunion." He knew, he said, "the tenacity with which the human heart usually clings to power," but for himself now he protested that he neither sought nor wanted office. Rather, as soon as the Convention created new executive offices and filled them, he intended to leave his position and take to the field as a soldier. At last as good as his word, within a week Robinson would be a private soldier in Houston's little army.[31]

Certainly many in the Convention appreciated that the crisis took precedence over party. Robert Potter, the only man to oppose Houston's appointment as major general, immediately afterward proposed unsuccessfully that the meeting ought to adjourn so that its members could take their rifles and rush to the front. That was too extreme a measure, and so they remained, and in the days following framed and adopted an organization of their militia that enrolled virtually all able-bodied men between seventeen and fifty not already serving, established supply depots at Mina and elsewhere for the army, and began to consider the organization of the Regular Army.[32] They were creating at last the infrastructure that the old Consultation or provisional government ought to have had in place months before.

Then on March 9 they took up a draft of their constitution. It mirrored the United States Constitution in most respects, from the exact wording of its preamble to the organization of the several articles and sections. The new Republic of Texas should have a president, a senate, and a house of representatives, as well as a supreme court, and with minor alterations, their powers and duties duplicated those in operation in the United States. They did, however, embed in their organic law a few idiosyncratic ideas all their own, most notably a prohibition against ministers, priests, and other religious leaders holding any public office whatsoever. Even though they had suffered little if at all from the Mexican requirement of Catholicism, still it so rankled them that they determined to separate church and state as completely as possible. They also reiterated their concern for publicly funded elementary education by requiring Congress to establish such a system, placing Texas far ahead of the common education movement in the United States. At the same time, they recognized certain temporal exigencies that required some abridgment of personal rights. They allowed for military impressment of personal property needed for the war effort, and they omitted any prohibition of billeting of soldiers in private homes. They also continued the imposition of penalties on any citizens who left Texas to avoid giving aid or participation in the resistance effort.

That threat of forfeiture of property reflected another major concern of the framers, and that was property itself. They again repudiated all of the fraudulent Monclova land grants. They also cemented the stability of another form of property, slaves. Even then Southern leaders in Congress in Washington were responding to ambiguities in the United States Constitution on the status of slavery by proposing a "gag rule" to prevent any antislavery petitions or resolutions coming on to its floor. The Texians did not live in a vacuum. They knew what was happening to the east, and to prevent similar problems in their new polity they removed all uncertainty on the slavery issue from their constitution. They repealed all of the former expedients whereby slaves were contract or life indentures, and made it clear that slaves in Texas were slaves for life and that free blacks were not entitled to citizenship.[33] Some of the debate on these measures, especially the always touchy land issue, became lengthy and vigorous, but throughout it all the Convention got along harmoniously for the most part, and the old party lines gradually softened in the unity of independence.[34]

It helped that their sobering military situation virtually drove them together. On March 10 a report revealed that the known military forces of Texas amounted to just 60 enlisted men in the Regular Army overseen by 122 officers, most of whom were supposed to be raising their own companies, and 520 enlisted men in the volunteers. But one of those Regular officers was also an officer of volunteers, and of the Regular and volunteer enlisted men, at least 160 were in the Alamo. Volunteers and Regulars would never be combined under a single organization, though both would serve Houston in the days ahead. However, in a day or two when the fall of the Alamo was known in Washington, the totals reduced dramatically, to only about 420 enlisted men. The Goliad disaster that lay two weeks in the future eradicated all but a handful of those. Meanwhile, the government had on hand sufficient rations of bacon for less than three weeks, and flour, corn, and other foodstuffs in even lesser quantity.³⁵ Then late on March 15 they got Houston's official notification of the fall of the Alamo. The next day they authorized a formal appeal to the people of the United States, and sent it accompanied by Houston's fateful message of the fall of Travis and his men. However, they decided not to publish the news immediately in Texas itself, fearing the reaction to the disaster that in any case would soon be known to all. Immediately individual delegates began asking for permission to leave the Convention to go to the army in the emergency. In the suddenly urgent atmosphere of fear and uncertainty, the Convention even considered a resolution to send its own spies out in the field to forewarn them of any threat to their body.³⁶

The Convention, having adopted its new constitution, adjourned on March 17, but not before providing the day before for an interim government until officers could be properly elected. They mandated president, vice president, and cabinet officers for state, war, navy, treasury, and justice functions, and further provided that the Convention itself elect those officers by voice vote.³⁷ That same day, March 16, they elected David Burnet president, Zavala vice president, Samuel Carson secretary of state, Bailey Hardeman secretary of the treasury, Rusk secretary of war, Potter secretary of the navy, and David Thomas attorney general.³⁸ It was an interesting mix. Burnet was perhaps the oddest choice. For a start, though close to Travis, he had been firmly in the Peace faction until recent months, and was as well allied to the old speculators, having himself secured a substantial grant in the Kickapoo and Cherokee lands just west of Nacogdoches. Zavala, of course, was widely known and respected, close to Austin, and another centrist who came from Peace to War, secession to independence, not long since. Both elections may have been intended as signs of conciliation and unity between the old factions. Carson narrowly lost to Burnet, perhaps because he was a newcomer. Rusk and Potter had been pitted against each other for the war portfolio, but given Potter's hostility to Houston, it naturally seemed more prudent to give the job to Rusk, who had organized his own company the previous summer, stood with the rest in defiance at Gonzales, and for some time since had served as inspector general of the army. Potter instead got the navy office. Thomas was another newcomer to Texas, though a veteran of the volunteers and a lawyer, which may have been his chief qualification for the justice post, while Hardeman, another veteran, seemed chiefly qualified for the treasury position thanks to his success in his personal finances.

Until a congress could be elected and a judiciary appointed, these men would be the government. It was hardly an ideal situation, but at least the old divisions between governor and Council were past. There was now one civil authority in Texas, empowered with full political control, and overseeing one unified military establishment. When the Convention adjourned, Burnet and his cabinet immediately took over, and the day after the adjournment Burnet issued his first public address as president. Indeed, he was so concerned that he issued two proclamations on the same subject. He spoke hopefully of Houston and his growing army, but then turned to rumors of families starting to flee eastern Texas for Louisiana. It was a move that could spread panic, and every man who left the Republic was a soldier lost to its defense. "The best security for our families is to be found in a gallant bearing before the enemy," he argued. He called on all Texians to be calm and resolute, and urged them to organize themselves under the new militia law and hasten to Houston. "To the field then, my countrymen, to the standard of liberty," he exhorted. "The fall of the Alamo is the surest guarantee of our ultimate success," he told them. "The Spartan band who so nobly perished there, have bequeathed to us an example, which ought and will be imitated." But then in closing Burnet confessed that the new government itself was about to move, shifting seventy miles southwest to Harrisburg. "That removal is not the result of any apprehension that the enemy are near us," he tried to assure the people as he preempted the inevitable outcry. It was simply a move "for the common good," and in less than a week it was accomplished.[39] In fact, removal to Harrisburg placed the government much closer to Galveston Bay and communications with the United States via New Orleans, and also in the heart of a more populated region of the old Austin colony, sound enough reasons for a move. But the shift also removed them from an exposed spot well beyond the reach of Houston's protection at Gonzales, easily within reach of marauding Indians should the Mexicans incite them, and on a direct route of advance from Béxar. For all they knew, Santa Anna might well be on his way even then.

Thus, the government seemingly joined the very exodus it tried to discourage. Even before then, among the last acts of the Convention were provisions to provide aid to families suddenly forced to dislocate themselves in fear of Santa Anna's advance.[40] While some Texians found resolution for revenge in the fall of the Alamo and Goliad, other settlers perceived a danger they felt unready to face, and hundreds left their homes. Those close to the Rio Grande actually began their flight when Santa Anna first appeared. Houston found 374 men gathered at Gonzales when he arrived, and within two days that force rose nearly to 500, with another 100 known to be on the way, but when news of the Alamo spread through the camps, twenty or more of them simply deserted, no doubt to go to the protection of their families. Of a greater concern to the general, however, was that these men and others would now spread "dismay and consternation among the people." Two days later the news of the Mexican advance from Béxar persuaded Houston himself that he must pull back to the east side of the Guadalupe, but on March 14 he actually withdrew twenty-five miles farther east to the Lavaca.[41] Another day put the army in camp on the Navidad, a day's march from the Colorado, which was now his objective. Behind its swollen flow he could find relative security for a time as he summoned men, munitions, and supplies to him from scattered points.[42] Whether or not Houston took counsel of his own interests in remaining at Washington-on-the-Brazos until the declaration of independence, and regardless of his reasons for wasting several more days before trying to take decisive control of his military, he now genuinely had to buy time to build an army, and that meant staying out of Santa Anna's way. Yet his own very visible withdrawal contributed to the growing panic among the civilian population, who saw themselves left unprotected by their army. Houston actually encouraged their withdrawal, which dramatically escalated the exodus, and all along the way of his own retreat the general and his men found roads filled with refugees fleeing in panic. Wags afterwards called the frightened exodus the Runaway Scrape. Houston put Seguín in command of the rearguard of his little army, with special instructions to help keep these civilians out of the way of advancing enemy columns, a role Seguín continued to play for some weeks.[43]

It quickly became a panic, not helped by declarations such as that in Brazoria that the Mexicans were coming with the "avowed purpose of a general extermination of ourselves, our wives, our children and all who inhabit this country."[44] Weeks before Fannin had sent out silly and inflammatory warnings that the Mexican soldiery came intent upon raping the "*Fair daughters* of chaste *white women*," having supposedly tired of turning the women of their own country into prostitutes.[45] The appeal to the visceral old white fears about the sexual appetites of black men could easily be refocused on brown-skinned people as well, only adding to the panic, though in fact Texian women received uniformly gentle and even sympathetic treatment from the Mexican invaders. Despite Burnet's disingenuous protest that the abandonment of Washington-on-the-Brazos had nothing to do with Houston's withdrawal, the fact that it commenced immediately upon getting word of the army's retreat obviously suggested otherwise. Moreover, not only the government but the people of Washington abandoned the village. One by one other communities and isolated settlers between the Colorado and the Brazos took to the roads, often with little or no forethought or preparation, meaning the people took too little food, inadequate protection against cold weather, and often had no idea in mind of where they were going, knowing only their determination to get out of the way of Santa Anna. Many citizens did at least destroy what they could not take with them, to deny its use to the foe, but most simply fled.[46] On top of it all, they feared attack by the Indians to their north. "A constant stream of women and children and some men, with wagons, carts and pack mules, are rushing across the Brazos night and day," a visitor observed the very day that Houston reached the Colorado. "Thousands are moving off to the east."[47] Meanwhile, the panic spread as far south as Galveston, where a merchant guessed that five of every six civilians had fled "so panic struck that they are flying in every direction."[48]

The old fears about slaves reemerged, too, especially in the communities along the Brazos close to the Gulf. In Brazoria on March 17, even while exhorting men to flock to Houston's army, a citizens' meeting addressed the fear that Santa Anna intended "to unite in his ranks, and as instruments of his unholy and savage work, the negroes, whether slaves or free, thus lighting the torch of war, in the bosoms of our domestic circles."[49] Several slaves did run away, though few made common cause with the Mexicans. Rather, the runaways seemed generally to be at a loss as to what they should do next. Some just disappeared. Others wandered or returned to their masters' homes after the whites abandoned them. Two runaway slaves on the lower Lavaca inhabited their owners' house for some time, and actually caught a fugitive soldier from the Goliad massacre when he ventured into the house looking for something to eat. They threatened at first simply to kill him when he identified himself as a Texian, not because they knew or had any particular grudge against him personally, but more probably out of that eruption of pent-up frustration and anger that made slaves led by Nat Turner kill indiscriminately. Then they talked of handing him over to the Mexicans, to let them do the killing, but steadily their anger cooled, and in the end, recognizing a fellow fugitive from events beyond his control, they simply released him with food and directions on how to find Houston and the army.[50]

Behind them the fugitives in the Runaway Scrape left homes and barns that frequently gave shelter to Mexican patrols that often occupied whole settlements of log cabins for several days. At the same time some of the few men who escaped from the Goliad massacre made their way by stealth toward the Colorado or wherever they might find safety, and they, too, took advantage of abandoned homes. Mostly they moved singly, like J. C. Duval, who made a halting journey east to the Lavaca and beyond. He found a deserted Texian house recently vacated by Mexican *soldados*. All food was gone, but he found a comfortable bed, and managed to kill and cook an unlucky hog that wandered past.[51]

The Runaway Scrape continued for the balance of the uprising, shifting in scene as Houston's army gave up more and more territory. To provide some protection, Houston detailed one soldier to each family that applied for aid, even while trying to discourage flight by threatening to seize for the army all weapons in the hands of citizens who fled.[52] Many died of exposure, and many more at least temporarily lost the equilibrium necessary to survival. "People and things were all mixed, and in confusion," said a slave who stayed with his owner's family in the flight. "The children were crying, the women praying and the men cursing. I tell you it was a serious time." One mother who lost a son at the Alamo simply wandered in her distraction, following Houston's retreat to the Colorado, and thereafter she stopped and started, jumping from place to place. "I wish you could know how the people all did as they kept going about trying to get somewhere," she told a sister, "but no person knew where he was trying to get to." She used every exertion to keep her husband with the remaining family on the flight, and away from the army.[53] Yet there was also resolution and defiance. Another mother swore a vow as she abandoned her home that she would teach her sons "never to let up on the Mexicans until they got full revenge for all this trouble."[54] As usual, everyone seemed interested in placing blame. Houston laid the responsibility at the feet of the government in Washington, whose precipitate flight, he said, triggered the stampede. Leaders in the government pointed the finger at Houston for failing to stand his ground.[55]

Ordinary Texians and *tejanos* alike now felt the greatest impact of the war, but they never experienced the scorched earth that some feared. Since Texas as yet had none of the grander institutions of an established nation, there were none to be affected. Texas had villages like San Felipe but no cities to burn. More than enough *tejanos* remained loyal to—or fearful of—the central government that Santa Anna saw nothing to gain from destroying their municipalities at Béxar and Goliad. Indeed, the only communities razed were the small villages at San Felipe and Harrisburg, and no one knew then or later if they were burned by Mexican *soldados* or by Texians as they evacuated. Certainly whatever livestock, crops, or possessions remained behind during the Runaway Scrape quickly fell into the hands of Santa Anna's men. The direct effect of contact with Mexican soldiers, however, stayed close to their line of advance, which even though it followed the roads near which most Texian population had settled, still left thousands of more remotely located Texians virtually untouched.

Businesses everywhere along the Mexican route were at risk, even those operated by loyal *tejanos*, now just as likely to find themselves the victims of military impressment as those whom Ramírez y Sesma and others preyed upon during their march to the Rio Grande. Indeed, often as not it was the commands under Austin, Fannin, Houston, and the others who visited losses on farmers and business by impressing food and equipment they desperately needed, leaving behind chits and receipts that might mean little if the revolution succeeded, and nothing if it did not. Travis "purchased" a considerable quantity of goods and supplies for himself and his small command during his ride from San Felipe to Béxar, leaving behind a combination of expenditures paid for from his own pocket, and those for which he gave government receipts that vendors in future expended considerable time in trying to recoup, and then only in inflated Texian scrip.

Such education as there was found itself temporarily disrupted, either as teenaged boys went off to enlist when their schoolmasters went to the war or else as schools themselves closed on the enemy's approach. Their religious worship felt the same impact, at least insofar as that the very few established churches had to be abandoned. Accustomed, however, to conducting worship informally in homes and fields, the Texians still gathered to pray anywhere they chose. There were no "arts" to disrupt as yet, and as for culture, that of Texas was too new to be in any serious way distinguishable from what they had known where they came from. The war was too short to generate more than a few new patriotic songs, no painters came there to settle as yet, and even fraternal orders like Masonry had only just begun to gain a foothold a few months before the outbreak of hostilities. Texas had no literature, and of writers only a few passed west of the Sabine thus far, most of them publishing travel narratives in the east.

In the end, probably the biggest social impact of the revolution, other than the temporary civilian dislocation and the general economic loss to those unable to get themselves and their property out of the way of both of the armies, was the abrupt halt it put on the law. Texas already teemed with attorneys before 1836, mostly men like Travis who had come to start new careers knowing that wherever there was expansive cheap land, there must inevitably be lots of legal work dealing with titles. The efforts of the entrepreneurs like Bowie, who held often questionable titles to huge parcels they hoped to subdivide and sell, came to an abrupt halt, though that enterprising adventurer did not entirely abandon his speculating until history caught up with him at San Antonio. Indeed, land prices fell for a period as there was no money for buying, no new settlers to buy, and no guarantee of good title until the outcome of the war was known. And inevitably with the justices of the peace displaced or in the army, and the Mexican garrisons formerly responsible for peacekeeping now either captured or gone, civil order suffered, especially on the outer fringes of settlement, where lawless whites and opportunistic Indians raided settlers. When authorities caught the miscreants, often as not no police court could be convened to hand down an indictment, nor judges to try or juries to convict or acquit.

The war left communities largely on their own, each in its own way to meet the financial and manpower needs of the crisis, raising taxes to buy clothing and supplies for soldiers, soliciting voluntary contributions of everything there was to be had. Contribution more than anything else fueled the communities' ability to get by to the extent they did. Of course, every morsel that went to the armies was one that did not stay in the home, and families suffered as a result, especially the poorer ones with no slaves to augment their labor. With their men gone to the army, women and children faced getting in the spring planting of staple grains, while cotton, the main cash crop, had to be harvested by any hand available. In the absence of sufficient labor, much of the 1836 crop was lost, threatening an economic penalty to be paid that summer should any break in the Mexican naval blockade of Texian ports allow resumption of trade with the New Orleans market.

Perhaps worst of all, though, after the Alamo and Goliad and with the commencement of Houston's unexplained retreat, morale and enthusiasm dipped badly. After all, there had been no previous "nationhood" to generate aspirations of pride, and almost all of the colonists were natives from a host of other states and had not been Texians long enough to have developed a deep spirit of local patriotism. The Republic of Texas, less than a month old, was simply too new to have generated yet a genuine national identity out of the variety of often conflicting influences that led them to band together in resistance. Resentment of a distant and unseen adversary united them, but when that enemy became all too visible on their doorstep, it served instead to dissolve their resolution. The Texians needed success to generate the spiritual momentum to carry such a new and amorphous people through the fire. "Our atmosphere is devilish dark," one Texian wrote as the Runaway Scrape was about to begin. "If men stay at home, we are lost."[56]

CHAPTER ELEVEN

"Do You Feel Like Fighting?"

∽〰〰〰๑

T WO HUMILIATING DEFEATS at Béxar and Goliad, along with the losses in the Matamoros expedition and elsewhere, had cost the Texians more than six hundred killed in three weeks, with Houston and the rest in flight. From those bright days of December when the war seemed won, their fortunes had descended seemingly beyond repair. Yet what happened next exemplified a long-standing fact of democracies at war: When they are threatened on their homefront by a perceived alien threat, they rally. Almost everyone lost either a friend or a relation in the massacres, and that left in the living a resolve for revenge. Already volunteers came forward once more to Houston's banners, saying they should "Remember the Alamo" and "Remember Goliad," and so they would. Indeed, even before the Goliad massacre, Houston's army north of the Colorado grew to seven hundred or more.

While he tried to give them some rudimentary training, he got word on March 19 that Ramírez y Sesma's cavalry had been spotted only a few hours west of the river crossing at Burnham's Ferry. That left him little alternative but to pull back, burn the ferryboat, and move south along the east bank to Beason's Ferry, the next likely crossing, from which he at least offered a little more protection to the communities along the Brazos from San Felipe south. On his arrival at Beason's the situation before him dramatically brightened. The companies of volunteers that had been organized in Brazoria and elsewhere after the fall of the Alamo suddenly began to arrive. "Men are flocking to the camp," he said with relief on March 23. "In a few days my force will be highly respectable."[1] Indeed it would be, for the army soon grew to nearly fourteen hundred. Meanwhile, rains swelled the Colorado so much that when Ramírez y Sesma's cavalry appeared on the opposite bank on March 21, they could not cross. For almost a week the two opponents sat on opposite banks watching one another, Houston apparently confident that when the four hundred or more under Fannin joined him, he would be able to act. Then on March 23 came the news that Fannin had surrendered, his fate yet unknown but not hard to forecast. Realizing that the Goliad command would not be joining him now, Houston at first still told people that "on the Colorado I make my stand," but soon he decided to continue his retreat to buy more time. He knew that Urrea and other Mexican columns, especially the main one under Santa Anna, were on their way. It was not yet the time to fight. On March 26 he suddenly announced that the army would slowly march back toward the Brazos and San Felipe.[2]

The move bitterly disappointed the men. They knew they outnumbered the six hundred or so believed to be facing them under Ramírez y Sesma. If they could not attack and win with odds of more than two-to-one on their side, how could they hope to find a more favorable opportunity when Santa Anna's main force came on the scene? But Houston revealed that if at times he could not think or act clearly and decisively, at others he saw to the heart of the matter. His strength lay in being on the east bank where, if there was a battle, the Mexicans would be at a disadvantage being forced to cross the stream to attack him, all the while under the rifles and muskets of his own well-emplaced defenders. If he launched an attack, however, he forfeited that advantage and gave it to Ramírez y Sesma, a fool's option. Moreover, the Mexicans had artillery, while as yet Houston lacked field pieces.

If the general were not depressed enough over the news of Fannin—Houston could neither eat nor sleep for days—his mood only worsened when he issued the marching order and near-mutiny resulted. "There was a great dissatisfaction among the men of the army," a colonel told Postmaster General John R. Jones a few days earlier, the men frustrated at their lack of provisions and their insufficient numbers.[3] Two hundred or more simply left in disgust, either returning to homes to look after their families or just deserting. In the ranks a muttering began in secret and soon came out in the open suggesting that if Houston was afraid to fight, then they needed another commander who would. One of the captains, a veteran of Concepción and Béxar, did not scruple at labeling the general a coward, and others positively refused to move their companies. Resorts to the oratory that had served him so well in politics did not appear to move the men. That old problem of volunteers came back to visit once more. Their enthusiasm could be high at first, but they wanted a quick result, a fight while their blood was up. Failing that, their spirit waned fast, especially when they feared that their families might be at risk. It was the old problem faced by Austin at Béxar all over again, only this time their discontent took added impetus from the fact that in this new army under the new government, they could not simply vote their general out of power and choose another.[4]

Those who would take orders marched eastward on March 27, and by that evening they halted just outside San Felipe.[5] Yet after only one day in Austin's old capital, the general put the army on the march yet again on March 29, and no sooner did he leave than the panicked people remaining in San Felipe burned the village and joined the Runaway Scrape. The discontent in the ranks only continued and grew louder, some insisting that the army ought to march south to protect the lower Brazos settlements, others that they should move in some other direction. "Much discontent in the lines," Houston admitted. "Many wished me to go below, others above." Yet he kept his own counsel, as he would do much of the time hereafter. "I consulted no one—I held no Councils of war," he wrote to Rusk. When he put them on the road, it was northward to Groce's Landing on the east bank of the Brazos above Crump's Ferry.[6] Behind him he left as guards on the Brazos crossing two companies who refused to follow the army longer. Along the way he did relent enough to speak to the men once more, and in passing revealed that again he believed himself to be the object of men of fell purpose. "Evilly disposed persons" had told them he intended to march them as far as Nacogdoches, he said, thus abandoning virtually all of the settled portion of Texas. Instead, he said, he was taking them to Groce's, to a place where he believed he could put them in a defensive position in the dense woods lining the river bottom, a place so strong that they could defeat anything the enemy sent at them.[7] As so often, Houston said different things to different people. In fact, he did tell people he intended to withdraw to the Sabine. No sooner did he arrive at Groce's than he told one officer that "I will retreat to the Red-lands," meaning the territory near Nacogdoches.[8] A few years later, Houston even declared that his intent had actually been to "retreat and get as near to Andrew Jackson and the old flag as I could," meaning he did not at that moment intend to stop until he reached Louisiana.⁹ It was typical of Houston that he could be at the one moment candid and the next evasive or even mendacious.

A day's march brought the army to a camp on the west side of the Brazos protecting the ferry to its rear. From there he could fall back to the opposite side on short notice if he found he could not hold his line in the woods. By now the toll showed in Houston's correspondence. He sounded almost manic-depressive, full of boast and confidence in one paragraph, depressed in the next. "For Heaven's sake do allay the fever and chill which prevails in the country," he wrote to Rusk on March 31. Now he said he had planned all along to attack the enemy on the Colorado but was only prevented from doing so by the news of Fannin's disaster, and predicted that he would have prevailed, contrary to what he said at the time he refused to attack. It was a refrain he repeated again and again—a plan to fight, only to withdraw with the intention of fighting somewhere else. A general always had to be governed by contingency, of course, but there were those who feared that the contingencies guiding Houston's actions existed only in his imagination.

What was not imagination was the deterioration in his army. Almost half of his men had left him since he abandoned the Colorado line, and now he had only between seven hundred and eight hundred in camp beside the Brazos. Acutely conscious that men left out of disillusionment and in frustration at not knowing where or whether they ever would make a stand, he admitted that "I must let the camp know something," but then revealed that part of his hesitance in making any commitment was the fear of more dissatisfaction if contingency forced him to change his plans yet again. "I want everything promised to be realized by them," he told Rusk. Until he could be certain of that, he felt it better to frustrate them in darkness than to risk angering them even more by false light. "I hope I can keep them together," he added. "I will do the best I can."¹⁰ It was not easy, for a spirit of mutiny gradually grew in the ranks.

Houston and his army would stay in camp in that densely wooded swampy bottom for two weeks, mercifully unmolested by Santa Anna, who fatefully turned aside in search of other quarry after becoming convinced that the Texians would never stand and fight. The Mexican commander could afford to take his time. Indeed, he had shown little hurry about moving on after the taking of the Alamo. In part that was because of the heavy casualties his own attacking columns suffered at the hands of Travis's garrison. Moreover, Santa Anna wanted to wait for the arrival of more of his infantry and cavalry units still on the road to Béxar. Knowing how spread out his army had become on the grueling march north from Mexico, he very wisely concluded to let the men already in San Antonio who bore the brunt of the siege have a brief rest while he consolidated with them the rest of his absent units.

It was March 11, the very day that Houston reached Gonzales to start building his own army, when Santa Anna finally launched his columns eastward. His planning was sound. He sent one column to cooperate with Urrea in dealing with Fannin, and after they had taken care of the Goliad garrison, the two commands were to move along the coastal road clearing resistance as far as Brazoria. Meanwhile another seven hundred *soldados* were to march directly along the Camino Real through Mina and as far as Nacogdoches. Finally, the main body of the army, seven hundred men immediately under Ramírez y Sesma, was to take the road to San Felipe, to be followed shortly by six hundred more. The three columns moving roughly parallel to one another would be separated by between forty and fifty miles. They ought to be sufficient threat to prevent the Texians concentrating against any one even if they could muster the numbers to pose a real threat, while if they did, the columns were close enough to support one another if necessary, given two or three days' warning.[11]

Good news came within days of launching the campaign. On March 15, Ramírez y Sesma took Gonzales, only a couple of days behind the retreating Houston. Six days later, Fannin surrendered to Urrea, and two days after that, Victoria fell. Santa Anna himself may have concluded that the campaign was already a victory, with Béxar and Goliad fallen and Houston in flight, and on appearances well might he have done so. He reacted to the course of events by revising his plans. Now he decided to separate some of the men ordered to Ramírez y Sesma and send them toward Galveston, while ordering Ramírez y Sesma himself to turn southeast upon reaching San Felipe and move against Harrisburg, the new Texian capital. With Houston apparently in perpetual retreat, Santa Anna could afford to ignore him for a time and let him soak and wrinkle in the boggy Brazos bottomland at Groce's, while the Mexican army moved against the Texian government. Take them and the heart would go out of the staggering insurgency. Houston's army, without a govern-

ment, might not even need to be met. They could just as well disperse
to their homes or flee east of the Sabine.[12]

But there was a danger in that confidence, soon to be revealed in an
increasing complacence that appeared both in the commanding general
and in his most important immediate subordinate. "General Ramírez y
Sesma is a timid and irresolute commander," complained Peña, "dila-
tory in his judgment and apathetic in his movements." Even allowing
for Peña's prejudice against him, Ramírez y Sesma had been slow and
hesitating prior to this time. Now, instead of pushing across the
Guadalupe in pursuit of Houston, he waited for several days until his
division grew to thirteen hundred or more *soldados*, one hundred fifty
cavalry, and two field pieces. That was prudent in an unfamiliar country
against a foe whose forces, if any, were unknown. But in his uncertainty
he exaggerated Texian numbers to twelve hundred or more, encouraging
more delay.[13]

It did not help that Santa Anna himself stayed back in San Antonio.
He actually considered returning to Mexico City when he got news that
Barragán had died suddenly, and apparently believed that he could leave
the rest of the mopping-up of resistance to his subordinates. But then, at
least according to some, Santa Anna became concerned that Urrea was
accomplishing too much, which might make of him a potential rival.
Rather than risk Urrea taking home the credit for pacifying Texas, Santa
Anna decided instead to stay awhile longer to be in command at the kill.
On March 31 he left to join the center column in the field.[14]

None reckoned with the weather, for rains mired the roads and swelled
the creeks and rivers. Ramírez y Sesma, with his reinforcements, and now
joined by Santa Anna and also more men under Filisola, did not complete
crossing the Colorado until April 5. Three days later, three thousand
strong, they reached the Brazos opposite San Felipe, but the companies
left behind by Houston discouraged attempts to cross by boat. Santa
Anna left Ramírez y Sesma and eight hundred men to deal with San
Felipe's small guard, and himself took the van of the column south
thirty miles to Fort Bend, where he managed a crossing on April 12.
When word of that reached San Felipe, its guard pulled out at once and
Ramírez y Sesma began his own crossing of the Brazos. That put the
bulk of the Mexican army over the last defensible Texian river barrier
and well placed to cut off any line of supply for Houston via Galveston.
Indeed, Santa Anna now stood much closer to Harrisburg than Hous-

ton, and could effectively block any remaining line of retreat for the Texian army except the Coushatta Trace and La Bahía road to Nacogdoches. If Santa Anna's northern column moved quickly—which it had not, being stopped by high water on the Colorado at Mina—and if he had not subsequently redirected it toward San Felipe, which it finally reached on April 13, it might even cut off Nagogdoches and the Texians would have nowhere to go.

Santa Anna still conducted a well-planned, if somewhat leisurely, campaign, and in spite of obstacles from the weather. The initiative was all his, and he had been rethinking his plans. The absence of information about the whereabouts of his northern column worried him, but only a little. Now he wanted Filisola to march north with just five hundred men to attack Houston's camp at Groce's, while Ramírez y Sesma remained at San Felipe. Santa Anna himself at first intended to lead the men with him south toward Columbia and Brazoria, but on April 13 changed his mind. Perhaps caught up in the enthusiasm of the need for a bold and swift strike that could end it all there and then, he would move due east to take Harrisburg and capture the government if he could, and off he went at the head of just seven hundred men, ordering another five hundred under Cós to be sent to him by Filisola.[15]

When Santa Anna and his command approached Harrisburg on the evening of April 15, he found that he had missed his prey. The peripatetic government, such as it was, had left town abruptly and taken the road for Galveston, wisely ignoring Houston's earlier injunction that "you must not think of leaving Harrisburg" because the Mexican army was interested only in the Texian army.[16] In fact, the government had been functioning chiefly in name only since its creation and flight from San Felipe. With no treasury and as yet no elected congress, it could hardly do more, nor did it have the power to enforce its decrees. The loans being negotiated by Austin and his companions in Louisiana were not yet producing significant hard money, and some in the cabinet also worried about the pledging on such loans of large portions of the public land, the only real asset Texas possessed.[17] As soon as he reached Harrisburg, Burnet began trying to make something happen. Well aware of the power of print, he approached a man about establishing a press in the village, waving the lure of a monopoly on government printing.[18]

Burnet also sent an appeal to Henry Clay of Kentucky, then sitting in the United States Senate, begging him to make himself an advocate for

Texas in Washington. "Her government is almost a *fac simile* of your own," Burnet pleaded, and if Clay could bring about an early diplomatic recognition of Texan independence, it would greatly boost the cause, and might even "add a new and brilliant star to the constellation that illuminates the Northern Republic."[19] On April 1, Burnet actually ordered Secretary of State Carson to go to Washington to work with Austin and his commissioners to press for recognition.[20] Meanwhile, at home he issued a proclamation reinforcing their constitution's prohibition of the African slave trade, and ordering all military and naval officers to exercise vigilance in its enforcement, not out of hostility to slavery—though Burnet himself personally opposed the institution—but to appeal to Britain and others already on record with their own condemnation of the slave trade, essentially saying that Texas was ready to join their family of nations.[21] Sensible of the harm caused by delayed news, Burnet ordered a ship held at Galveston Bay early in April when he had only an intimation—proved untrue—"of a brilliant & decisive victory now about to be had by Houston." He wanted the ship held so that he could send off the announcement at once, only there was no victory.[22]

Diplomatic recognition would not be forthcoming in time to be of assistance to the Texian cause, and Texian efforts in the United States were further injured by the delay in getting accurate information. As late as the end of March, Austin in Washington did not yet know of the declaration of independence. Still he promised to raise money if he had to mortgage everything he owned, to the clothes on his back.[23] Though frustrated in their efforts to raise significant money in the United States, Austin, Archer, and Wharton did sufficiently popularize the Texian cause that private citizens and several communities contributed funds or actually sent men to Texas, and Cincinnati gave a pair of cannon to become known as the "Twin Sisters" that had already reached Houston. The bad news from home only added to Austin's anxiety. "My heart and soul are sick but my spirit is unbroken," he lamented in April.[24] Within a few weeks he gave up, however, convinced that his mission's trip to the United States had been pointless. No one was going to give Texas access to significant funds without knowing more than was known of affairs at home, and everyone, of course, wanted only to back a sure outcome. "Had I known as much of those kind of people last winter as I do now," Austin wrote on his way back to Texas, "I should not have spent any time upon them." His only goal now would be to help keep unity of purpose among Texians as they faced Santa Anna on their own.[25]

Meanwhile, Burnet tried to work with his cabinet in a collegial manner in order to maintain a smoothly running administration, and to the extent that was possible, he succeeded. He submitted major propositions to them for their counsel and looked toward consensus in formulating positions, as with the land-for-loans policy pursued by Austin's commission to raise money.[26] Burnet was especially concerned about the value of Texian credit overseas, since loans were all that they could look to for financing their cause. Then, too, he turned his attention to the relief of the refugees from the continuing Runaway Scrape. In April he ordered all fleeing families to stop where they were and that those who had not already found a temporary accommodation should go to Buffalo Bayou for a general encampment in a pleasantly located spot the government selected. The government would try to provide timber for them to erect huts and cabins, and to provide them with corn and beef. It was the first effort at public welfare, and though inefficiently organized and undersupplied, still it temporarily relieved the suffering of some. More to the point, however, it sought to halt the exodus that so demoralized other Texians.[27] Carson told him just how bad the fleeing had become. "Nothing can save the people from themselves," he warned a week earlier. "Their own conduct has brought this upon them." Should Houston retreat from the Brazos, they were lost. "Nothing can stop the people unless Houston is successful," he lamented.[28]

Most pressing of all, of course, was manpower. Burnet had already issued previous calls on all Texian men to step forward, even none-too-subtly appending to one call the provision of their new constitution that called for forfeiture of citizenship and the perennial talismanic land.[29] Burnet issued proclamation after proclamation throughout late March and early April, calling on men to come forward, even trying to shame them into enlisting by pointing out that men from the United States were coming in greater numbers to fight. The mediocre response revealed the ultimate weakness of a new government born in a storm and how little real authority it could yet exert over its people. Inevitably, in frustration at the near-futility of this, his most important mission, Burnet leaped to the inevitable extremity that crisis so often forced on republican insurrections otherwise founded on the rhetoric of personal liberty. In the emergency, he now proclaimed martial law for three months, dividing the Republic into military districts to be administered by appointed committees of vigilance to maintain order and organize militia. The committees were also to have full power to seize animals, weapons, and any other personal property deemed vital for the defense of Texas, and were as well to produce a census of all able-bodied males between the ages of eighteen and fifty-six, obviously with a view toward conscription. Any man failing to report within two weeks would be subject to arrest, and any who refused to enlist would be dealt with as deserters.[30]

It was a very harsh expedient, indeed just the sort of repudiation of personal liberty and property rights that so outraged Texians against Mexico. But it revealed the essential fact that, regardless of its shadow of a government, the Texas insurgency, like all political revolts against a greater power, lived in its army, and Burnet worried increasingly about Houston's intentions, and perhaps now his capability. On April 12, when he received word that Houston was retreating again and that Santa Anna was on the east side of the Brazos at last, the president privately expressed his dismay in a letter to Rusk, who was with the army. He hoped the government would not have to flee yet another capital. "We are a little disquieted at this point—but we will hold on," he promised; "a flying Cabinet is an odious term, which we by no means covet." But then in frustration he asked Rusk "what is the Army, the hope of Texas [doing]?"

> Is not this [enemy] to be arrested in their onward progress or is Texas to be overrun, her Seaports occupied and fortified, by a Contemptible Mexican force of 1300 men? Have we So far forgotten our wonted boasts of Superior prowess, as to turn our *backs* to an equal number of a foe that has given us every imaginable incentive to action. . . . Our friend the Commander in Chief has heavy responsibilities resting upon him. . . . the People of Texas are looking towards him with an ardent and anxious gaze. . . . The cry for Some [time] has been for a battle—A further retreat without a fight, would be infinitely disastrous. . . . Something must be done or we are lost as a nation.[31]

The next day definitive news of the Mexican approach forced the evacuation of Harrisburg. Burnet and Zavala left to look after their families, leaving only Hardeman and Thomas of the cabinet members still in the capital. David Thomas, now acting as secretary of war since Rusk had left to join the army, sent word to Houston that rumors had the *soldados* marching in all directions, toward Brazoria, toward Fort Bend, and elsewhere, but Thomas concluded quite correctly that Santa Anna's goal was to take Galveston and, as he put it, to "visit this place." Lose Galveston and Texas lost virtually all of its control of any useful coastline, he warned Houston on April 14. As for Harrisburg, it had not enough men at arms to form a picket guard, let alone a defense. When the Mexicans got too close, the few remaining officials would have to flee.

Yet his conviction that the capital was the target of the moment allowed Thomas to offer Houston some advice. "You need make no calculation of the enemy searching after you," he wrote the general. "If you fight them you must find them." It was an awkward way of saying something trenchant. Santa Anna indicated by his actions that he felt no concern about the Texian army and chose for the moment to ignore it, potentially a serious mistake if Houston took the initiative and capitalized on the opportunity. Thomas suggested that Houston might attack Santa Anna's advanced force, which he numbered at about fourteen hundred, almost exactly what Santa Anna would have when Cós joined him. Thomas hoped Houston could hit the Mexicans somewhere in the bottomland along the Brazos, but if that proved impractical, then he suggested an attack somewhere close to Galveston Bay to save war munitions there and the Texian vessels at anchor, as well as to keep open a line of supply.[32]

Thomas could advise Houston, but not order him, or he was not willing to try. As for President Burnet, he was as much in the dark as any and had already sent word to Rusk in Houston's camp to urge action. It had come to the moment, as inevitably it must, when so much depended on the army, and that meant on Houston. "If the army 'retreats' any farther," Burnet told a friend on April 14, he would have no choice but to send his family off for good, evidence of his fear that Galveston would be lost, and when that went, what was there to hold on to or to prevent the Mexicans from driving them back east of the Sabine?[33]

The frustration at Houston's seeming sloth and indecision mounted both in the army and in the government after he took the army into camp at Groce's on the Brazos. It lay behind Secretary of War Rusk's decision to go to the army in person, where he arrived on April 4. Houston reported the army in good shape, and at the same time forwarded reports that conditions within Mexican ranks were deteriorating as morale sank and hunger sapped their energy. Santa Anna "shall be closely looked to, and the first favorable moment seized with avidity to effect his total defeat," Houston wrote Thomas the day Rusk arrived. It should have been for Rusk to be sending reports back to Harrisburg, but the suspicious politician in Houston wanted his own version of affairs before the government in his own words. Despite his words, however, he did not move.[34] Within a few days men in the camps began to hold informal meetings in which they discussed deposing Houston if necessary in order to march on the enemy. They had elected their own generals before, and if Houston would not fight, they could elect someone to replace him regardless of the appointment from the Convention and the government, a body the men regarded with some derision for having itself adjourned to escape the Mexicans.[35]

Rusk did send his own dispatches. Three days after his arrival he reported the army in good condition, and grown in strength to almost fifteen hundred, and he too estimated the Mexicans under Ramírez y Sesma then on the Colorado as numbering only thirteen hundred, and in poor shape and worse spirits. "The propriety of making a move upon them is apparent," he told Burnet on April 6, "and that course will, I have no doubt, be adopted."[36] The very next day Houston aroused everyone's hopes with a general order declaring that "the moment for which we have waited with anxiety and interest, is fast approaching." He ordered preparations to be made to move on short notice, but then stopped short of calling an advance, and instead asked on the men to be calm, deliberate, and subordinate.[37] While he told others that "there is the most perfect harmony in camp," reports of discontent over inaction continued to come from his ranks.[38]

By April 11 he still had not moved. A day or two earlier, Houston received a letter from Burnet, whose own patience was exhausted. "The enemy are laughing you to scorn," the president complained. "You must fight them. You must retreat no further. The country expects you to fight."[39] Now one of Houston's own aides wrote an angry letter to Burnet criticizing the general's apparent sloth and asking for his removal. When he intercepted it, Houston erupted in anger. He had a "traitor" in his midst, he told Anson Jones over dinner.[40] "I am worn down in Body by fatigue," he complained to Burnet, saying he now slept only in the mornings after staying up most of the nights on watch. "Instead of being in a state of insanity I fear I am too irritable for my duties," he added in an imprecise sentence typical of his expression when excited. The reference to insanity may mean that he was battling depression again, and with it the indecision that so often afflicted him. It would hardly be surprising if he had found out that Rusk came to the army authorized by Burnet to relieve Houston of his position and to assume command of the army himself, which several urged him to do.[41] The fact that a few days earlier he specifically told a friend that "the army is in good *spirits*, and the General *sober*," may have had more to it than his crude play on words, if he was feeling the emotional disturbances that so often in the past drove him to the bottle.[42] Houston had now lost the confidence of the president and had in his midst a man who could at any time take away the command he had struggled so hard to retain.

In protesting the internal criticism of his command, Houston again promised the president that "I will cross the river soon and meet the enemy." Yet he did not move.[43] In fairness, his tardiness had some measure of prudent policy in it. He had to be certain that he would win if he ever did attack, for he could not afford to risk his army on drawn battles, let alone defeats, and there would be no second chances against a victorious Santa Anna. That meant that he had to be in some measure guided by Mexican movements. Unfortunately, as he waited and watched, looking for exactly the right opportunity—or dithering in indecision— he gave the initiative to Santa Anna and risked losing the opportunity already before him, for by now he had more than enough solid information from multiple sources to know that the enemy on the Brazos was at best only equal to his own strength, and likely inferior.

Finally on April 12, with reports that the Mexicans had definitely crossed the Brazos, he at last issued orders to cross the ferry behind Groce's as soon as possible.[44] That very day, however, Thomas sent him a frank letter informing him of Santa Anna's arrival and crossing at Fort Bend, and that now nothing stood between the Mexicans and Harrisburg and Galveston. "You have assured the Government that the enemy should never cross the Brassos [and] they have relied on your assurance," chided Thomas, "but they find your pledges not verified, and numbers of families exposed to the ravages of the enemy." For the first time during the insurgency, a member of the government spoke sternly to the general: "The country expects something from you, the Government looks to you for action, the time has now arrived to determine whether we are to give up the country and make the best of our way out of it or to meet the enemy and make at least one struggle for our boasted Independence. The Government does not intend to control your movements. But it is expected that you will take measures without delay to check the enemies movements."[45]

The general reacted with predictable defensiveness. "Taunts and suggestions have been gratuitously tendered to me," he complained, "and I have submitted to them without any disposition to retort either unkindness or imputation." He rehearsed the difficulties he faced since assuming command in March and inaccurately protested that his army two days earlier numbered only 523. Further, he mendaciously argued that his two-week halt on the Brazos had been against his wishes, but necessary to stop the panic among the civilian population. Even further from the truth, he protested that "there has not been even murmuring or insubordination" in his army. Any stories to the contrary were the malicious creations of his enemies. He could not perform impossibilities, he declared, and there at least he was right.[46] Houston reacted publicly by issuing that same day a proclamation to the people. "You have suffered panic to seize you, and idle rumor to guide you," he told them. Yes, the Mexicans had crossed the Brazos, but that only meant that "they are treading the soil on which they are to be conquered." Resorting to gross untruth, he explained that only sloth and apathy by some of his subordinates and their men had prevented him from meeting and beating Santa Anna before then.[47] But still, other than to cross to the east side of the Brazos, he did not move, though by April 16 Rusk, at least, was convinced that "a very few days will bring our armies into contact and I have no fear or doubts as to the result."[48]

By April 13 the army completed its crossing, but the general did not turn the column south toward where the enemy under Santa Anna was believed to be. That evening he dined with Jones, who complained of the desertions from the ranks and "a deep and growing dissatisfaction in the camp," and warned that if the policy of retreat continued longer, Houston would find himself all alone. Houston responded by complaining again of the traitors in his midst, impressing Jones as being undecided in his course and irresolute, hoping somehow to "get a bloodless victory" without fighting a battle.[49] Houston was so rattled now by the criticism within the army and from the government that apparently he shared his plans with no one, assuming he had any. Now he put the army on the road east along Cypress Creek, away from the known whereabouts of the Mexican forces. For all the pressure from some to attack, others like Secretary of State Carson wrote entreating him to retreat and only do battle if assured of absolute success. Indeed, Carson predicted that if the army withdrew to the Louisiana border, then volunteers from the United States would swell its ranks and then Houston could turn and strike Santa Anna decisively.[50]

As of April 15, some believed that this is precisely what the general intended to do, for on that day he called a conference and broached the idea of moving to Nacogdoches and beyond. The officers uniformly opposed it, but nevertheless the next day Rusk gave orders in anticipation of just such a movement, and some thought the general meant to go to the Sabine itself, meaning an abandonment of virtually all of Texas.[51] More than once while at Groce's he had told his officers that the only hope of saving Texas was for him to retreat to the Sabine, where he could cross to the safety of Louisiana and recruit his army to five thousand or more, then come back and drive the Mexicans out. This was neither cowardice nor defeatism, but it was not what Texian soldiers wanted to hear, and so Houston simply kept his plans from all but a few. Those officers in whom he did confide told him that they believed their men would refuse to march away from the enemy and toward Nacogdoches. Indeed, an impasse was avoided when Rusk suggested that instead of marching the army directly north on the road from Groce's toward Nacogdoches, he start the army west toward Harrisburg. That would get the men moving at least, and then Houston could be governed by exigencies.[52]

Then on April 16, unwilling to retreat any farther, the Texian army took the decision out of Houston's hands. Their line of march took them through Cypress City and a few miles beyond to the intersection with the road that connected Harrisburg to the south with Nacogdoches to the north. Those who knew the vicinity knew that the direction they took would determine whether they were to advance to fight or keep retreating indefinitely. The general still had not issued any orders in advance, either awaiting the very last moment to make a decision as he saw the temper of his command, or more likely still committed to continuing the retreat to the Sabine. The men suddenly took the decision away from him. At the crossroads some began shouting "to the right boys, to the right." A group of musicians marching at the front of the column took the right turn without awaiting orders, and the rest of the army followed, including Houston, who silently rode near the back files. Years later he claimed that this had been his intention all along, though if so it is strange that he would withhold from the men information that he of all people had to know would send a current of enthusiasm through the ranks, and stranger still that on a matter to become so controversial, not a single witness ever came forward to testify to receiving or witnessing a positive order from the army commander to march south.[53]

More to the point, he explicitly told at least some of the civilians with the column that he would be taking them and their livestock toward Nacogdoches and safety. When the column turned right, Pamela Mann, a farm wife who allowed the soldiers to use her oxen to pull the Twin Sisters, saw that her animals were not going north but south toward the enemy and concluded that Houston had deceived her as to the army's route of march. "With a heroism which might have been commendable had the oxen been taken by the enemy," wrote a soldier who watched her, she rode her horse to the head of the column and aimed a pistol at the leading officer, ordering him to stop or she would shoot. He did so, and then she rode to the cannon and again at gunpoint demanded that her oxen be removed. Despite the fact that she could have been stopped, officers allowed her to take her animals and go on her way to the north. Men with the army claimed that the officer she first confronted was Houston himself, and that Mrs. Mann accused him of lying to her about his intentions. If he had changed his mind since leaving Groce's, he certainly did not tell her.[54]

They came in sight of Harrisburg on April 19 to discover that Santa Anna had been there before them. The Mexicans took the capital four days earlier, less than twenty-four hours after the remainder of the government abandoned the village and moved toward Galveston. Santa Anna spent the next three days there, gathering information, including word that the Texian army had left its camp on the Brazos and was in motion. However, Santa Anna believed that Houston was going to continue his retreat to Nacogdoches, and continued to dismiss him as a threat. Instead, the general continued his fixation on capturing the government, and on April 18 burned Harrisburg and moved on toward New Washington on the northwestern point of Galveston Bay, only to miss catching Burnet and the others by just minutes as they embarked on a boat.[55]

Though he failed to snare Burnet and the others, Santa Anna justifiably felt increasing confidence that the campaign was all but over. He had driven the so-called government of the insurgents off the mainland and disrupted whatever administration it exercised. Houston's army was cut off from its civil leaders and was retreating toward the Trinity, maybe even toward Louisiana. Now Santa Anna had only to send his cavalry ahead to sever the rebels' line of march and then concentrate the rest of his own scattered army, and he could bring it all to a climactic end. And even if Houston escaped to Louisiana, that still left Texas firmly in Mexican hands. To try to stop Houston, on April 18 Santa Anna put the torch to New Washington and put his men on the march toward Lynch's Ferry, where information told him Houston would attempt to cross the San Jacinto River in his flight eastward. Only hours later the vanguard of Houston's army approached the still smoking remnants of its most recent capital.

On arrival in Harrisburg, Houston received a dispatch just captured from a Mexican courier with news that Santa Anna and a mere five hundred *soldados* were now at or near New Washington, isolated from the rest of their army and only about fifteen miles away. Now was the time to attack, and the next morning Houston put the army on the road. They had before them an incredible opportunity, due mostly to Santa Anna's complacence and failure to regard the Texian army as any longer a threat, as well as to the mere chance that Houston's line of retreat, followed by the change of direction dictated by the army itself, put it on the road behind Santa Anna. Houston issued yet another appeal to the men of Texas to turn out. "A few hours more will decide the fate of our army," he declared. "We view ourselves on the eve of battle. We are nerved for the contest, and must conquer or perish."

More important, Houston himself was now nerved by the news that he had a chance to strike an outnumbered Santa Anna himself, and suddenly his weeks of diffidence and hesitation gave way to confidence, though still he allowed Rusk to co-sign the proclamation, perhaps to give more confidence to those who had lost it in the general himself.[56] They must not be careless, however. "Great caution must be observed to conceal our movements from the enemy," he enjoined his men as they started their march.[57] Indeed, even as Houston made bold predictions of victory, his old uncertainty forced him to confide privately that "the odds are greatly against us," which on his latest information he knew not to be the case since he had seven hundred fifty effective men with him and believed Santa Anna to number as little as five hundred and no more than eight hundred. Still, "it is the only chance of saving Texas," he said. "We go to conquer."[58] Indeed, at last he made a speech to the army itself, exhorting them to "remember the Alamo! The Alamo! The Alamo!" In the ranks the men took up the chant, resolved to avenge the deaths of so many of their friends and fellow countrymen.[59]

The next day they continued a forced march for Lynch's Ferry on the San Jacinto, the same goal toward which Santa Anna now marched after burning New Washington. The first to reach it would hold the better ground, and Houston got there shortly before noon. His command had grown to about nine hundred once more by additions along the road, and he put his men in line along a grove of oaks backed by Buffalo Bayou near its confluence with the San Jacinto to await the enemy's arrival. "A scene singularly wild and picturesque presented itself," observed a man just arrived in a tiny company from Galveston. "Around some twenty or thirty camp-fires stood as many groups of men, English, Irish, Scotch, French, Germans, Italians, Poles, Yankees, Mexicans, &c., all unwashed, unshaven for months, their long hair, beard and mustaches, ragged and matted, their clothes in tatters, and plastered with mud; in a word, a more savage band could scarcely have been assembled." Houston ordered some beeves to be slaughtered for them to eat, and as they went at the work with their knives and their fires, their weapons lay scattered nearby. "Their guns of every size and shape, rifles without bayonets, no two perhaps of the same calibre, a few muskets, some with, some also without bayonets, were piled at hand, and each man was striving to warm a piece of meat for his morning meal."[60]

It was just then, about 2:00 P.M., that the Mexicans reached the field to find the rebels on the best defensive ground and leaving Santa Anna no option but to take the offensive, which with his contempt for Texian fighting ability did not trouble him overmuch. The Texians flew to their arms and prepared for a fight, forming their companies in the shelter of the woods to their rear. Santa Anna sent forward a portion of his small command of infantry to test Texian strength. They were hurled back by rounds from Houston's two cannon commanded by Neill, the Twin Sisters, small iron six-pounder smoothbores.[61] The only Mexican field piece with Santa Anna replied but soon withdrew. "I waited impatiently for the signal to close engagement, but it was not given," said one volunteer.[62] Many paused in like manner, then Houston's men revealed that their general still did not fully control them. In response to entreaties for a general attack, he protested that they were outnumbered and facing experienced and disciplined *soldados* who were expecting reinforcements any moment. An attack would be folly, and then he reiterated for the last time that their best policy was to retreat toward the Sabine.[63]

The men and officers would have none of it, and at last he allowed sixty of his cavalry led by Rusk to make a reconnaissance, but with orders not to precipitate anything more than skirmishing. Instead, the Texian cavalry got into a sharp fight and Rusk was almost captured, and then part of the infantry spontaneously attacked the Mexicans to support the cavalry and contemptuously ridiculed Houston's remonstrances for them to come back. He was in danger of losing his chance for a victory by losing control of his men. They repulsed the Mexicans in their front, however, allowing the Texians to retire to their own lines. Nightfall stopped the action with neither side holding an advantage. That evening Houston tallied his losses and felt relieved to have lost only two men wounded, Walter Lane, run through the shoulder with a lance and cut on the head by a saber, and Lieutenant Colonel Neill, wounded in the posterior.[64]

Still Houston felt angry at the insubordination. He had hoped by keeping his men concealed that Santa Anna would not be able to guess how many Texians faced him, but the engagement somewhat compromised the chances of surprise. Indeed, that evening the Mexican general realized his situation, concluding that the enemy in his front outnumbered him. Indeed, the unchecked enthusiasm of the Texians could have jeopardized their chances of victory, for however tired and hungry from their march they might be, Santa Anna's *soldados* were better trained and disciplined, and many were better armed. Houston expected that Santa Anna would launch an attack against him that night, though none was forthcoming.[65]

Now the battle raged in Houston's headquarters, where men and officers protested at his not sending the whole army forward during the day's scrap. Some openly condemned the general, saying they needed to attack now before Santa Anna was reinforced by Cós, known to be in the vicinity and on his way. Others passed among the campfires asking who would be willing to make an attack the next day regardless of what Houston said. The general himself kept to himself, revealing nothing of his intentions, if he had any. He may well have preferred to remain on the defensive and allow Santa Anna to attack him in defended positions. He certainly evidenced no anxiety about taking any initiative the next morning, for though he stayed up most of the night looking to his positions, he then slept well past dawn even after the army roused to reveille.

When the general did awaken on April 21, it was to the realization that his soldiers had been right. Shortly after 8:00 A.M. a Galveston volunteer saw a cloud of dust on the road from Harrisburg, and soon thereafter Cós arrived to reinforce Santa Anna to twelve hundred or more. Houston watched them march into Santa Anna's camps, and when the Texian who alerted him to Cós's coming expressed chagrin that delay had allowed the enemy to be reinforced, the general only responded that his men were tired and needed food and rest. Another twenty-four hours would see them in shape to fight, meaning Houston had no intention of acting this day.[66] He did send out a reconnaissance to glean a better picture of Mexican numbers, and while he awaited the result the frustration in camp grew. "Our men were becoming very much disheartened for fear we would not be permitted to attack them until they [were] reinforced so strong that we could not whip them," one Texian recalled.[67] By noon there was still no action, and in exasperation several officers finally demanded that Houston meet with them. In a heated discussion no immediate decision resulted. Some afterward claimed that the general expressed an intent to continue the retreat now that Santa Anna was reinforced. Others maintained that Houston had decided to attack. Whichever was the case, by three o'clock some kind of resolve emerged, though whether Houston made it freely or was forced to it remains a mystery. He sent a small party of men to burn a nearby bridge to isolate Santa Anna from yet more reinforcements believed to be on the road.

Finally, just after 3:00 P.M., Houston gave the order they all wanted, though Rusk seems to have given the same order independently. Seguín was there with a small company of *tejano* cavalry. He had continued his role in the Runaway Scrape until Houston sent him to watch Ramírez y Sesma's cavalry. Now Seguín was just about to eat a bite of lunch:

> General Rusk came to partake of dinner in my tent. When he had
> done eating he asked me if the Mexicans were not in the habit of

taking a siesta at that hour. I answered in the affirmative adding, moreover, that in such cases they kept their main and advanced guards under arms with lines of sentinels. General Rusk observed that he thought so too, however the moment seemed to him favorable to attack the enemy. He added: "Do you feel like fighting?" I answered that I was always ready and willing to fight, upon which the general rose, saying: "Well, let us go!"

Rusk did the same in several other company camps. The men formed into their companies, then both Rusk and Houston made speeches. Meanwhile, in the lines the men recalled Houston's recent exhortation, and they whispered to each other "Remember Crockett" and "Recollect Fannin," while others responded "Aye, and Bowie and the Alamo." Houston put Burleson's First Texan Volunteers in the center with the Twin Sisters. The Second Texan Volunteers commanded by Colonel Sidney Sherman took position on Burleson's left, and several other companies of infantry formed the artillery's right. Houston gave command of the sixty-one cavalrymen to Mirabeau Lamar in recognition of his daring behavior in the skirmish the day before and placed them on the far right.[68]

Houston sent them forward, hoping to cover several hundred yards to a rise that concealed them from Mexican view without giving away their movement. At the same time he got word that the bridge had been successfully destroyed, meaning that now the Texians themselves could not use it if forced to retreat. Irrevocably they were committed to what would almost certainly have to be the last battle of the revolt. It was a fortuitous moment. Santa Anna's men felt exhausted from their march of the previous day, not to mention being up much of the night erecting earthwork defenses. They spent most of this day so far on watch for an imminent attack, but by about 4:00 P.M. Santa Anna concluded, not unreasonably, that Houston was not going to make any move today, as indeed he had not intended to until forced by his officers. Consequently, the general gave orders that the men could relax their guard and get some much-needed rest. Santa Anna himself retired to a headquarters tent quickly erected behind his lines. Six years later Houston himself claimed that during his army's *siesta* the *generalissimo* entertained himself dallying with Emily West, a free black woman whom he may have appropriated a day or two earlier when the Mexican army burned the plantation of her employer Colonel James Morgan. Perhaps so, and perhaps not, but long afterward people and popular lore attributed the general's seemingly slow reaction to the outbreak of fighting to her distraction, whether intended or not.[69] What mattered most in the instant, however, is that the Mexican army was not ready for what was coming.

At 4:30 Texian cannon awakened them rudely with several rounds of grapeshot, scatter-loads. Then Lamar led his cavalry toward the left of Santa Anna's line in a charge designed to distract Mexican attention from the advancing infantry, while the infantry itself rushed forward, its musicians mischievously playing a popular song whose refrain asked "will you come to the bower I have shaded for you," though some thought it was actually "The Girl I Left Behind Me."[70] Houston himself moved with them on his horse, in spite of desultory Mexican musket and artillery fire that mostly went harmlessly overhead, and when he got within about forty yards of the Mexican line, he halted the men, calmly directed them to straighten their lines, and then ordered the first volley. "Then each man took cool and steady aim, and seven hundred rifles and muskets rent the welkin," recalled a witness. "It was our first and last volley."[71] Houston hoped to keep his men in line and send in more volleys, but the men were not about to be held back now that the long-awaited moment lay at hand. It did not help that Rusk, perhaps unwilling to risk one more hesitation from the general, took matters in his own hands, as he had earlier that day, and rode along the line yelling to the men, "If we stop, we are cut to pieces! Don't stop—go ahead— give them Hell!"[72]

Despite Houston's imprecations, his own lines immediately disintegrated as the men rushed forward and poured over the enemy breastworks and into the camps of the startled Mexicans, who had been in some degree paralyzed by that first volley. Santa Anna himself had been asleep and the fire awakened him abruptly. The first thing to meet his eyes when he emerged from his tent was his own men already in some state of disorder. "The mischief was already done," he confessed later. He tried to shift units to stop the disintegration, but it proved too late. One of his own best generals, Manuel Fernandez Castrillón, fell with a mortal wound, and then recent conscripts broke ranks and inadvertently prevented experienced regulars from using their arms. Then he and the others heard Texian voices yelling words perhaps not understood, but whose meaning was soon all too clear.[73]

"Remember the Alamo, Goliad, and Tampico!" they yelled. "In a second we were into them," recalled Lane, "with guns, pistols and bowie knives."[74] It was almost nothing like a battle, but rather a host of isolated personal fights that lasted just eighteen minutes. Seguín recalled that "the entire enemy line, panic struck, took to flight," and Lane gleefully likened the Mexicans' retreat to "running like turkeys."[75] The one Mexican field piece was soon captured while still loaded, and virtually all of Santa Anna's camp equipment, baggage, even flags, fell into the hands of ecstatic Texians.[76] Most of the Mexicans simply fled, while others who tried to make a stand were overwhelmed in a combat that became hand-to-hand. "We, having no bayonets, used the butt-ends of our muskets and rifles like the war-clubs of the Indians," recalled one volunteer, "many paying for it by having their shooting-irons break off at the breech."[77] All too quickly it became apparent that their rallying cries of "Remember the Alamo" and "Remember Goliad" were as much calls for vengeance, for now many Mexicans died in the same manner as the Texians in those massacres. Enraged Texians shot and bayonetted scores as they threw down their arms and tried to surrender, begging for mercy. Houston and other officers attempted to stop the slaughter, but to no avail. This was the soldiers' battle, and they had scores to settle. By the time they finished, six hundred fifty of Santa Anna's men lay dead, most of them paying with their lives for their commander's policy of no quarter elsewhere. Another seven hundred thirty were prisoners or would be within a few days when Houston sent his cavalry in pursuit, but by then the fury had subsided and the captured *soldados* had little more to fear in the way of reprisals. The Texians lost just nine killed or dying, and another thirty wounded, one of them Houston himself, with a shattered ankle.

Amid the cleaning up after the killing and looting was done, it became quickly apparent that Santa Anna himself had escaped. With all around him in chaos and the Texians close to taking him, he had accepted the offer of a servant's horse and galloped away toward Filisola's last known position, actually riding through the closing Texians. He got as far as the burned bridge, pursued by Texian horsemen, and when he saw he could not cross, he quickly hid himself in a thicket and escaped detection until nightfall. Then he waded the Buffalo Bayou and continued on foot, coming on an abandoned house in which he found clothing to disguise himself. The next morning he was walking out in the open when three Texian cavalrymen surprised him and he had no choice but to give himself up, though still not revealing his identity.

When the horsemen returned to Houston's camp with their prisoner, none of the Texians knew the man by sight. They were just putting him in a temporary "bull pen" made of ropes tied to pack saddles, when some of the *soldados* recognized their general. "Santa Anna, Presidenta Heneral!" they began shouting, which quickly alerted the Texians to the true identity of their prize.[78] "None of us knew it was Santa Anna or we'd [have] shot him right there," recalled one Texian who missed the battle but came into camp shortly afterward. Officers immediately had to quell the desire of many to wreak vengeance for the Alamo and Goliad.[79] At once they took him to Houston, then lying on a blanket beneath the shade of an oak tree, and in considerable pain from his wound. A Texian standing nearby talking with Lamar saw Santa Anna, spattered with mud and clearly nervous, squeeze Houston's hand to awaken him and then introduce himself. Houston motioned to a medicine chest nearby and asked him to be seated, saying with sarcasm that "such accommodation as we have is at your service." Once seated, the Mexican general asked for some of the opiate laudanum being used to treat Houston's pain in order to settle his own nerves.

Calmed, Santa Anna assumed a characteristic bravado. "You have conquered the Napoleon of the West," he said boastfully. "You have whipped me, I am your prisoner," he told the victor, "but Filisola is not whipped. He will not surrender as a prisoner of war. You must whip him first." Houston immediately charged him with the outrages at the Alamo and Goliad. Santa Anna pleaded that he actually had orders from his government to take no insurgent prisoners, trying to sidestep the fact that he was himself the real government in Mexico. But this was only initial sparring. The two soon got to the essential business before them. Neither was a fool. Whatever he might say later, Houston had to know that he did not defeat the Mexican army. Through his own luck, Santa Anna's complacence, and the Texian volunteers' impetuosity, he had simply defeated Santa Anna. He knew, and Santa Anna knew that Houston knew, that Mexico still had more than four thousand *soldados* in Texas, with substantial commands in hand on the road under Generals Filisola, Urrea, Antonio Gaona, and others. Mexico still had ample military force present to continue the war with much expectation of ultimate success, especially under better subordinates than the generalissimo himself, whereas Texian forces were widely scattered in small bands, and the only army under Houston was no match in numbers for Urrea and the rest.

Still, the Mexican commander well knew that hundreds of Texians out in Houston's camps wanted his blood to atone for the Alamo and Goliad. Alone and helpless, he had nothing to bargain with but his wits if he was to save his life. He could promise anything now, knowing that he could always come back for Texas another time if he chose. His boast about Filisola was a hollow declaration, for Santa Anna had a "but" to follow, believing that he could save his own life even at the cost of humiliation for his men and officers. "If I give him orders to leave the limits of Texas," Santa Anna said of Filisola, "he will do it." Houston took the bait, knowing that one lucky victory over Santa Anna's napping soldiers would not likely be repeated with Filisola and Urrea. Accepting the generalissimo's bargain, Houston had him send orders for Filisola and the rest of the Mexican forces to withdraw as far as San Antonio, where they would later be told what to do next. Then they agreed to an armistice until peace terms could be negotiated, though Santa Anna may not as yet have agreed to independence.

With no more to say to his prisoner, Houston ordered Santa Anna kept under guard in his own tent to protect his life from vengeful Texians, some of whom were already shouting that the Mexican commander should be turned over to them for swift justice.[80] Houston explained to the men that Santa Anna was worth far more to them alive than dead, for Santa Anna would almost certainly be amenable to anything to save his own life and could be compelled to use his influence to get the official government in Mexico City to acknowledge Texian independence. The dictator spent a very uncomfortable night on Houston's cot, fearful of sleep, and perhaps just as afraid of what the morrow might bring him. Before he went to bed he wrote a rather understated order to Filisola. Referring to the battle of San Jacinto by saying that he had "yesterday evening had an unfortunate encounter," the general adopted an even more hollow turn of phrase when he told Filisola that "I have resolved to remain as prisoner of war in the hands of the enemy." He ordered Filisola to march his own and Gaona's commands back to Béxar and there await further orders, while Urrea was to march to Victoria.[81] The next day Houston and Santa Anna signed a formal convention for an armistice.

San Jacinto had been one of the most one-sided victories in history, virtually an echo of Jackson's surprising and equally one-sided triumph at New Orleans in 1815. Yet one dramatic difference remained. Jackson got his victory after the war with the British had already been concluded, though he did not yet know the fact. Houston's victory, however, ended only one branch of Santa Anna's campaign. It remained to be seen if it could end a war as well.

CHAPTER TWELVE

"The Utmost Confusion and Rebellion"

෴

A NY VICTORY WAS a victory, even one over ineptly led and outnumbered foemen who were tired, hungry, and demoralized,
especially since almost every adjective applicable to Santa Anna's
defeated *soldados* also applied to Houston's army. Certainly the Texians
had the benefit of an ideological cause to fight for, and of the primal
instinct to fight to protect their own homes. Still, a week earlier morale
was such that they had been near disintegration, and perhaps only their
own spontaneous decision to fight before they evaporated gave Texas
the victory. Houston's great achievement lay not in his strategic planning, of which he gave evidence of doing rather little; or his leadership
in battle, of which he exerted even less; nor even on the march, where
his secretiveness left many fearing that he did not say what he intended
to do simply because he did not know himself. Rather, Houston's greatest personal contribution to the "victory" was that somehow he kept
these men together long enough that they could win a battle themselves. With his men and even officers constantly complaining about his
passivity and apparent want of a plan, still Houston provided a rallying
point for men willing to fight for Texas if or when the time came that he
would actually lead them.

Certainly he was not a great general on the evidence, but most Texians of the time perceived him as a great leader, and if not Houston, then
who else? When the Convention gave him the command, available
options were few, and none seem to have been considered. Austin was
too ill and lacked the confidence of the more militant. Burleson had
more experience in action but lacked the spark to inspire. Bowie could

inspire, but he was too tainted by his personal affairs, and all the others like Neill and Dimmitt and Fannin, even Travis, were simply names too small to win the kind of confidence needed for an army commander. It needed a big man, and Houston was a big man, even if for reasons having little to do with military competency. Still, Texians lived in an era and were themselves part of a culture that placed more trust in leaders of dominating personality than in men of great experience. In the end, then, maybe the Raven's real contribution to victory was his simply being himself. Fearing to risk doing wrong, he did little more that was right, but he was always there at the center of what happened around him, leaving no room for doubt that he was who he was, the physical embodiment of resistance.

Many a Texian volunteer, isolated out on the prairies, got the news from passersby, men like J. C. Duval who escaped the Goliad massacre and spent the next several weeks in hiding, dodging Mexican patrols, and trying to reach friendly lines. He learned of San Jacinto from one of Houston's scouts whom he met in a ruined settler's house. Given the word of the victory, Duval lit a fire in the remains of the fireplace, boiled coffee, and the scout shared with him a meager store of ham and potatoes, and massive biscuits. "Those biscuits! I shall never forget them!" Duval recalled. "None of your little thin flimsy affairs, such as are usually seen on fashionable tables, but good solid fat fellows, each as big as a saucer." He ate six of them, and no Texian relished a celebratory meal more.[1]

Their good fortune almost stunned the Texians. Indeed, even after the victory, while doctors treated Houston's own painful leg wound and his men and officers cheered themselves at their success, he briefly mistook an incoming party of several hundred prisoners under guard as a Mexican reinforcement about to launch an attack and exclaimed in despair that all was lost. Houston was as surprised as everyone else, and still in the embrace of disbelief. All across Texas people took the news when it came with something like the same incredulity. Those involved in the Runaway Scrape did not immediately start returning to their homes, and only after solid confirmation of the stories of San Jacinto became generally known did the fugitives come back, often to find their houses burned and their fields pillaged. No celebrations cheered the principal towns, because San Felipe and Harrisburg and Washington-on-the-Brazos no longer existed, and the fleeing government now made temporary quarters at Velasco. Mostly, Texians just felt an enormous burden of fear and anxiety removed from them, though perhaps not entirely. They knew not to trust Santa Anna overmuch, but at least enough to set to work rebuilding what they had lost and securing the government for their new Republic.

That still left four thousand Mexican soldiers in Texas and very much capable of continuing the war, even if Santa Anna's capture severed their head. To be sure, for days after San Jacinto, civilians and Texian soldiers like Duval encountered demoralized groups of Mexican cavalry traveling westward, clearly heading toward Béxar or beyond.[2] What Houston and his army did not yet know was that the condition of the other enemy columns in Texas was almost as bad as the one beaten on the San Jacinto. By the time Filisola's column reached the San Bernard River on its withdrawal, incessant rains turned the road into what the soldiers called "*mar de lodo*," seas of mud that slowed their progress and mired their wagons and cannon. "Artillery, cavalry, sick, baggage, mules, everything that accompanied the army, was a chaotic mass, buried in mud," Filisola complained on April 30. The soldiers simply could not walk when they sank to their knees in the mire. They discarded everything they could to lighten themselves, and still they bogged down. His soldiers could find no wood for their cook fires. They exhausted their own provisions, and both armies scoured the region clean of livestock and grain. The rain rusted their muskets and ruined their ammunition, and having come unprepared with adequate doctors or medicines, the men rapidly sickened with dysentery, and many died. "Had the enemy met us under these cruel circumstances, on the only road that was left," Filisola later protested, "no alternative remained but to die or surrender at discretion."[3] Complaining of the "inclemency of the season in a country totally unpopulated and barren, made still more unattractive by the rigor of the climate and the character of the land," Filisola felt he had no choice but to ignore Santa Anna's orders to retire when he finally got them, declaring instead that his duty to his soldiers forced him to take them home. In fact, the mud had beaten his men, leaving them demoralized and turning what had been an orderly strategic withdrawal into a retreat. Once he extracted them from the mire, he simply kept marching toward Mexico. Other than an isolated brush or two between small parties, there would be no more land engagements in the insurrection, and by late May, Filisola's consolidated army was across the Nueces and on the way to Matamoros.

Houston sent the Mexican prisoners of war from San Jacinto to Galveston Island, where they soon made quarters in round huts built from sod covered with roofs of reeds and rushes. The canton itself was not unpleasant, but after months on campaign without resupply, the poor men wore little more than rags, thus exposed to the changeable weather of the Gulf shore. Not surprisingly, their captors felt little sympathy with them, besides which the infant government could not afford the care and upkeep of its own soldiers much less the Mexican *soldados* it still held. Thus, an ingenious program came about of allowing Texian citizens to post a bond to take custody of one or more prisoners to employ on their farms, placing the burden of food and clothing on their temporary custodians until the government demanded their return.

For those remaining in the prison camp, there was little to do. In one hut the men passed their time by creating a small diorama depicting the Battle of San Jacinto, using bits of driftwood to represent the units involved. They intended to make it a gift to Houston.[4] Some found themselves the object of the curiosity of Texian guards who interviewed them for details on the Mexican side of the recent war, especially the fall of the Alamo. The place and manner of Bowie's and Travis's deaths were already generally well known from eyewitnesses, but of Crockett's there remained a mystery, and soon *soldados* told interviewers what they knew—or more likely imagined—of how he met his end. Prisoners in all circumstances and all wars soon learn to patronize their captors and tell them what they want to hear, and these Mexicans were no different. Feeling abandoned by their commander and resentful that he had led them to defeat, some began to blame him personally for all their ills. Sensing from the frequent specific questions about Crockett that he held a special place in the Texians' pantheon, some *soldados* may have resorted to an expedient to accomplish two goals at the same time. Soon stories came out of the Galveston camps that Crockett had been seen attempting to surrender, but that Santa Anna himself had ordered him to be shown no mercy. It satisfied Texian curiosity about one of their heroes, and conveniently made Santa Anna the villain.[5]

Santa Anna himself did what he had to do to get out of Texas alive. Houston sent notification of the victory to Burnet on the day after the battle, and so did Rusk, but the messages did not reach the president on Galveston Island until April 26.[6] That same day Rusk sent Burnet another message entreating him to come to the army's camp on Buffalo

Bayou. With the momentum of their victory, and with four thousand Mexican soldiers still in Texas, he believed that this was the time to press their advantage hard. "I have great fears of a different course being pursued," he confessed. "The rock on which Texas has heretofore split begins to rear its cragged head above the foaming spray, I mean unhallowed ambition." He did not specify the cause of his concern, but the fact that Rusk only mentioned Houston twice in his report of the battle, giving little indication that the general had provided real leadership however brave he was personally, suggests that Rusk feared a reemergence of the old policy of retreat and delay. Perhaps, too, Rusk and other cabinet members present in the army felt concerned at Houston overstepping his constitutional bounds in his discussions with Santa Anna. Then there was the fact that with peace apparently established, there would be a general election for a new president, and Rusk may well have spotted signs of higher ambitions in the commanding general.[7]

A few days later Rusk felt even more concern. Nearly two weeks after the victory, the army still camped on Buffalo Bayou. "We are gaining nothing," he complained to Burnet. "The golden moments of action drag heavily away when our Country is bleeding at every pore without the corresponding action upon our part." Voicing his own feelings as well as those of other cabinet members with the army—Hardeman and Vice President Zavala—Rusk threatened that "if things are to go on as they have done for the last few days we have no desire further to be connected with transactions that must result to the injury of the Country." Burnet must come, and with him the remainder of the cabinet, to impose some order in this irresolute atmosphere.[8]

Burnet reached the camps on May 1, and Rusk may actually have handed his own protest of that date directly to the president. Houston welcomed Burnet, perhaps not warmly, but with the ceremony due to a chief executive, and then informed him of the agreement reached with Santa Anna for Filisola's withdrawal to Béxar. The president was not entirely happy that such an agreement had been made without his consultation, but he forbore from complaint inasmuch as Rusk, an officer of the government, had been present and a party to the discussion. Besides, if Houston waited until Burnet could be involved in the talks, it would have delayed them for several days, time during which Filisola and the other Mexican columns might have continued their advance deeper into east Texas, making them that more of a threat and perhaps that much less amenable to obeying Santa Anna's order to retire. Houston, in short, had done the right thing militarily.[9]

However, the political implications of the armistice agreement with Santa Anna greatly irritated Burnet. He had no quarrel with Houston's guarantee of safety to the Mexican general, even though the clamor for Santa Anna's life only grew in the weeks ahead. The president did not even object at finding Santa Anna domiciled rather comfortably in a little house by the bayou, though under constant guard. But when Burnet met with Zavala, Hardeman, Rusk, the newly arrived Potter, and two new men, Peter Grayson who replaced the deceased Thomas, and James Collinsworth who replaced the absent Carson, he faced decisions of his own, and problems with the interference of Houston. Even before he called the first cabinet meeting, Burnet received from Rusk a list of suggestions scribbled in pencil that outlined what he felt they should seek in a lasting treaty with Santa Anna. What Burnet apparently did not know at first, however, is that Rusk's list came directly from Houston.[10]

By this time, Burnet felt such exasperation with Houston's conduct of the campaign in spite of the victory, and Houston felt so certain that Burnet had been turned into an enemy, that relations between the two became stiff to nonexistent. Still, the general tried to exert some influence on the peace terms by approaching the secretary of war. Recognition of the independence of the Republic of Texas must be a nonnegotiable fact, he said. He proposed that the southern boundary of the new nation be set at the Rio Grande and that Mexico pay reparations to Texas for all of the financial and property loss it suffered during the invasion, involving the United States as a guarantor that Mexico honor the terms. All hostilities should cease at once, civilians sympathetic to Texas who had been arrested, whether Texian or Mexican, ought to be released immediately, and all Mexican forces must immediately withdraw below the Rio Grande without further molesting the persons or property of Texian citizens. As soon as these terms were observed, Texas should release its Mexican prisoners, but Santa Anna himself ought to be held until the government in Mexico City ratified the terms.[11]

Burnet took the list given him by Rusk and used it as a template in subsequent discussions with the cabinet. Burnet met opposition on some points, Potter as usual being the most vocally discontented. Some objected to dealing with Santa Anna at all, basing their complaints on several things, one of them the fact that as the man who had overturned the 1824 Constitution, he was a usurper and therefore not lawfully head of state or anything other than himself a rebel. Moreover, another president now sat in Mexico City, and Santa Anna was merely a general, arguably with no power to make treaties. Nevertheless, in the end they decided that since Santa Anna was the only real power in Mexico, they must deal with him, as only he could likely enforce a treaty. Burnet drafted an agreement, therefore, and with only Potter dissenting, the cabinet approved it for presentation to Santa Anna.[12]

Houston had no choice but to recognize that with the campaign won, he filled no constitutional role in the peacemaking, perhaps explaining why his views went before the cabinet in Rusk's memoranda. He also felt it in his interest to distance himself as much as possible from the Burnet government, with a view toward his own future aspirations. His wound still troubled him greatly and showed no sign of healing as yet. Meanwhile, he had already issued an address to the people of eastern Texas calling on them to rally to his standard. Though the enemy was badly beaten and in retreat, he expected Filisola to concentrate at Béxar according to Santa Anna's instructions. Still, it was always possible that Filisola would decide to invade once again. "One bold push now will drive them entirely out of the country, and secure liberty, independence and peace to Texas," Houston declared.[13] But raising more troops and arms was the government's job, not his, and unless hostilities should resume, there seemed to him to be little for him to do.

Consequently, a few days after giving Rusk his recommendations for a treaty on May 3, Houston left the army to go to New Orleans to seek proper medical attention for his wounded foot. He issued one last address to the army, and it reflected more than his usual hyperbole. He complimented their patient and uncomplaining behavior during the hardships of the campaign, simply ignoring the fact of their frequent state of near-mutiny. He thanked them for obeying his orders promptly and maintaining unity in their ranks, glossing over their refusal to obey his commands more than once and their own internal divisions. He told them that they had defeated more than double their numbers and fought "in a manner unknown in the annals of modern warfare," which would have brought a smile from anyone familiar with Napoleon's campaigns of recent memory. Though Mexican *soldados* still occupied part of their country, he predicted that soon Texan soil would be free of their tread and independence secured. In a clear echo of the words that William

Shakespeare gave to King Henry V about "gentlemen in England now abed" who would be shamed in the presence of those who fought with him on St. Crispin's Day, Houston told his soldiers that in the years ahead for them "it will be fame enough to say, 'I was a member of the army of San Jacinto.'" There, at least, was no exaggeration.[14]

Houston's departure left a vacancy at a critical moment. On May 4 Burnet and the cabinet agreed to hand the army command to Rusk, who at first declined but finally accepted, while Lamar took an appointment as interim secretary of war in his place.[15] In the cabinet thereafter Lamar vehemently opposed any negotiations with Santa Anna. Still, with Hardeman, Grayson, Collinsworth, and Zavala in favor, and only Lamar and Potter opposed, Burnet had a clear majority and went ahead to present his draft treaty to Santa Anna. The Mexican general assented to all the terms, but then suggested that they actually conclude two versions of the treaty. One to be made public committed Santa Anna not to take arms again against Texas or to encourage his people to do so, pending the ratification of the treaty. It ended all hostilities on land and sea and required remaining Mexican troops to evacuate as quickly as possible to the south side of the Rio Grande, respecting private property on its march. All property previously seized by his army, specifically including slaves, should be restored to its owners. The armies were to take pains not to come into contact again with the other, and all Texian prisoners of war were to be released immediately, in exchange for a like number of Mexican prisoners being released from Galveston. The public agreement said nothing specific about when the rest of the *soldados* held at Galveston would be released, but the treaty promised them good treatment. Finally, Santa Anna himself was to be sent home to Vera Cruz "as soon as it shall be deemed proper."[16]

At the same time, Burnet and Santa Anna worked out a secret treaty, with the cabinet's assent. This one related specifically to undertakings agreed to by Santa Anna himself. In addition to committing him to facilitate all that was contained in the public treaty version, he further obligated himself to ensure that his own cabinet in Mexico City would favorably receive a Texian peace delegation with a view to settling outstanding differences and acknowledgment of the independence of Texas. He promised to conclude treaties of friendship and amity recognizing the Rio Grande as the lawful boundary between their two nations. Most vital of all, from his point of view, the public article providing for his return to Vera Cruz was expanded. Citing his return as "indispensable for the purpose of effecting his solemn engagements," the Republic was to provide not for his return when "deemed proper," but immediately.[17]

With the negotiations under way, Rusk felt compelled to shift the army to a better location, and the government itself suffered some disruption. They moved with their distinguished prisoner first to Galveston Island, but finding no suitable accommodation, they went on to Velasco near the mouth of the Brazos, where almost four years before, on June 26, 1832, the first blood was shed in the escalating difficulties between Texians and Mexico. There, fittingly enough, they concluded the treaties that brought peace, though not before Zavala and Potter left to attend their own affairs. Thus, only Collinsworth, Hardeman, Lamar, and Grayson remained of the cabinet, but still it was a safe three-to-one majority in favor of the treaties. On May 14 Burnet and Santa Anna signed both versions, as did the cabinet, Lamar abstaining.[18] The Texians knew they might invite opprobrium for dealing with the dictator, and especially for releasing him. The virulent reaction of Lamar told them so, and he would soon make his objections public. Santa Anna could not be trusted, some would say, as indeed many did. But Burnet believed that Santa Anna could be expected at least to look out for his own interests. If he did not get back to Mexico quickly, his rivals there might rise up, declare a new regime, repudiate any agreement made with Texas, and launch a new campaign to avenge Mexican honor. Moreover, once Santa Anna reached Mexico, should he violate the agreement, Burnet would make the private agreement public and Santa Anna would be shamed in the family of nations as well as at home. Shooting him gained Texas nothing but revenge. Holding him indefinitely a prisoner did nothing for independence. Releasing him under these conditions might just guarantee Texian independence.[19]

Burnet thought that he and the government achieved a coup with the treaties, but as soon as they published the public version, they discovered just how much they miscalculated the sentiment in the army and among the people. Part of the reaction stemmed from the general lack of confidence and trust in the government itself. Indeed, the new Texian government was hardly inspired. Many in the cabinet felt chagrined at Burnet's frequent indolence and the fact that sometimes he simply fell asleep during their meetings. Vice President Zavala thought the president a bureaucrat who lacked executive instincts or skills, contented rather with "composing notes and letters himself like an office clerk."[20] Rusk suspected Burnet's fitness for office though he supported the president's military policy toward the army, while Burnet began to wonder just what Carson had been about when he was urging Houston to retreat to the Sabine in direct opposition to the president's pleas for the army to stand and fight. Carson seemed too close to Houston, whom Burnet distrusted, and Navy Secretary Potter happily seconded any criticism of the general. It was not a very unified government even for peacetime, let alone the critical situation that it faced.

Moreover, the government had not been very effective in its efforts even before its disintegration at Harrisburg and partial reassembly on Galveston Island on April 19. For a start, it failed to publish the new constitution and get it widely distributed, meaning that most Texians simply did not know what the new laws of the land might be, or their obligations and responsibilities as citizens. After declaring martial law, the government tried in a desultory manner to raise troops through volunteering and the draft that the Constitution empowered it to enforce. It also sent agents to seize provisions and weapons from civilians under an impressment law to feed and arm the army. Meanwhile, Burnet issued a string of proclamations repeatedly calling for patriotic sacrifice, and at the same time waiving the threat of retaliation against those who fled or failed to do their part. Success was slim and sporadic. Hundreds of men came forward—mostly volunteers—to join the army, though how much that had to do with government appeals and how much with expedience is impossible to say, and hundreds also left the army when it suited them. As a result, the army inflated and deflated repeatedly during the campaign, and conscription officers found it all but impossible to do their job, thanks to the scattered and isolated nature of the settlements and farms.

Being so new and impecunious, and on the run almost from the outset, Burnet and his cabinet simply could not establish means of enforcement to compel acquiescence, and the president, at least, personally quailed from trying to punish people who fled in panic by confiscating their property or taking them into custody to face court-martial under martial law. It did not help that Houston all too publicly charged Burnet and others with inciting the Runaway Scrape with their own precipitate flight from Washington, the suggestion being that they were cowards. If nothing else stood between them, that alone alienated the president from the general, and to the extent that the divide between the civil leaders and their commander in the field became generally known, that, too, further weakened the moral force of the government.[21]

Then the soldiers and people learned that Burnet was going to release the butcher of the Alamo and Goliad. Within days the outcry commenced, and Burnet went immediately on the defensive for a wise decision that became a public relations nightmare. From all sides came protestations that Santa Anna's blood must pay for the deaths of Travis's and Fannin's commands. "A wild and intractable spirit of revenge is abroad among the people," Burnet observed a month after the treaty signing.[22] Some wanted the captive tried before a military tribunal. Others wanted him shot summarily, and still more insisted that at least he should be kept a prisoner until Mexico observed all of the stipulations of the treaty. Burnet protested that he would not condone what to him was murder. Besides, "Santa Anna dead is no more than Tom, Dick or Harry dead," he protested, "but living, he may avail Texas much." Still that mattered little to those with a taste for retribution.[23] Some communities met and adopted resolutions of protest demanding that the captive pay for his crimes, and a few took on a threatening tone suggesting that if the government did not act as it should, then the people would take the matter in their own hands.

Finally on June 1, when Burnet ordered Santa Anna taken aboard a ship for the voyage to Vera Cruz, a crowd gathered in Velasco and demanded the general's release to them or they would take him by force. "Yield to the public will," one citizen told Burnet two days later. "You had better resign your places you had best do any thing not dishonorable than to meet, and have this community to meet, the consequences that must, (depend upon it,) that must inevitably accrue."[24] The threat was implicit, yet Burnet held his ground, even when fresh volunteers arrived that same day and stood with the crowd. Lamar, himself opposed to releasing Santa Anna, supported the president to no avail, and on June 4 soldiers commanded by General Thomas J. Green ignored the secretary of war, took Santa Anna from his vessel, and incarcerated him under their own control, thereafter removing him to Columbia. Burnet at first feared that Texas would any day be branded with the stigma of assassination, but no one attempted to harm the prisoner.[25]

Nevertheless, harm was done, for Texians had violated their own treaties with the Mexican leader. Meanwhile, on May 20, even before receiving the details of the Velasco treaty, the interim President Antonio Montoya and the congress in Mexico City took their own action. They proclaimed renewed commitment to the war until Texas was conquered and pacified and Santa Anna released. Moreover, they specifically declared null any agreement entered into by Santa Anna while a prisoner, assuming he acted under duress. There was to be no peace with the insurgents.[26] Thus, both sides either violated or repudiated the treaties, leaving the matter of peace and independence in an indefinite limbo.

For all any knew, then, the war might well continue. Elijah Stapp, a signer of the declaration of independence at Washington-on-the-Brazos, advised Rusk in June that he thought the people seemed to be behind the government's conduct so far, especially after the victory at San Jacinto relieved some uneasiness about Houston. Still they expected the war was not entirely over, and civilians wanted the remnants of the Mexican army pushed across the Rio Grande without any arms or munitions that could be used against Texas again. Their own army was still weak. Remembering how Austin's army threatened to disintegrate the past fall, Stapp promised Rusk that "I am doing all I can to get men to Rally to the Standard and fight the Battles of Texas." They could breathe now, but they should not breathe too easy.[27] Even as Houston engaged in the climactic eighteen-minute fight on the San Jacinto, all around the rest of Texas it proved increasingly difficult to get men to volunteer, and desertion had always been a serious problem, as Houston saw from the shrinkage of his own army. Had San Jacinto been a defeat, or had Houston continued his withdrawal all the way to Louisiana, the idea of an independent Texas might never have been anything more than an idea.

Equipping the volunteers who stepped forward after victory remained haphazard at best. Of uniforms there were only dreams. The reality was whatever men wore when they left their homes. Contrary to popular misconception, not every man on the frontier owned a firearm, especially something capable of bringing down more than squirrel or rabbit. The British muskets captured from Cós at Bexar and those taken at San Jacinto scarcely met current needs sufficiently, and even in victory, as before, the army had to rely on appropriating private arms into public service at twelve dollars apiece.[28] Neither did the victory lessen the hardships that dogged soldiers and civilians alike during the short war. Stapp sent two sons to Austin's volunteer army the previous fall, and saw another one off now early in June, yet found himself, his wife, and their other five children all but shelterless and starving after returning home from the Runaway Scrape to find that Mexican soldiers had destroyed his farm and killed his livestock. "I am now here destitute," he pleaded, begging the army to allow him to draw food from public stores. He was not alone and, along with thousands of others, discovered that the coming of a shaky peace did not mean tranquility, not yet.[29]

For many Texians, there was old business to settle, loose ends to tie. Friends and relatives sought to learn the fates of men "gone to Texas" from whom they had not heard. "Will you pleas inform us if you received any time last Winter or Spring a Trunk or two and a chest for Robert Irvin Lewis a Soldier who went out to Texas and was killed at the Alamo," implored a friend in Natchitoches, Louisiana.[30] There was also opportunity upon which to capitalize. One Georgian who came to Texas in June urged friends back east to join him. "I think you would do well to visit Texas," John Bower wrote his younger brother in September 1836. "There is no cuntry in the world possesing as many advantages as Texas." It offered a healthy climate, fertile fields, and a new and seemingly unbounded opportunity for what so many had come seeking, fortune. "Any man that is [attenti]ve to business can make a fortune in five years," he declared. In spite of the stagnation and uncertainty caused by the war, he felt certain that once peace was securely established, the property he had acquired just in the past year would soon be worth a great deal, and this in spite of the fact that Santa Anna was still a prisoner and frequent rumors circulated that another Mexican army might be preparing to invade anew.[31]

Such optimism did not necessarily prevail among the *tejano* community, however. The equivocal state of things as of that summer left them in limbo, for they were men of Mexican blood, many of them allied to a cause whose independence remained unacknowledged. Thus, those loyal to Texas lived in the constant fear that a renewed Mexican effort to take Texas could jeopardize their lives and livelihoods, while those who sided with Mexico in the contest still did not know how they could expect to be treated by the Texians currently in the ascendancy. During the revolution even *tejanos* like Seguín, who fought bravely with the Texian forces, sometimes found themselves objects of distrust, even derision or worse. Their Catholic faith was openly challenged and their color brought them under increasing suspicion by their new white would-be rulers. Even Austin, who knew better than most the importance of *tejano* cooperation in the revolution, could not restrain an outburst in 1836 condemning Mexicans—and by extension the *tejanos* who shared the same blood—as a "mongrel Spanish-Indian and Negro race, against civilization and the Anglo-American race."[32] Even if Texians and *tejanos* made common cause against Santa Anna in the revolt, that did not make them brothers.

As a result, in the insurgency *tejanos* had been both friends and enemies, a problem encouraged by the fact that, of course, on the bare evidence of appearances, a white settler could not tell a *tejano* from a Mexican except by his dress, one reason that Houston urged Seguín to have his men wear little squares of white cardboard on their hats at San Jacinto to distinguish them from the foe. Indeed, Seguín's sad story provided a metaphor for the experience of many of his people during and after the revolution. The centers of *tejano* life had been Goliad, San Antonio, Nacogdoches, and Victoria, where they owned much of the land and livestock and operated much of the business community, as well as holding political offices. Yet within weeks of the end of hostilities in 1836 Anglos slowly began to freeze them out, challenging or revoking their land titles, denying their election to office, and even threatening their lives. Within a few years hundreds, including Seguín himself, simply left their homes to resettle in Mexico, where at least they could blend with the rest of the population. Those *tejanos* who fought with Houston might have believed they were fighting to create a new nation, but they could hardly anticipate that they were only helping create a country for another people, and that soon enough they would be outcasts in their own land.

In fact, Mexico and Mexicans, at least the leaders, had every desire to return to Texas and continue the war against the "gang of thieves" who dismembered their country.[33] The news of Santa Anna's capture resulted in a proclamation in Mexico City calling on citizens and soldiers to come forward to rescue their president and punish the rebels. The Mexican congress promised to press the war to a successful conclusion in spite of Santa Anna's instructions to Filisola, and the cabinet met in fevered sessions to address the crisis, though the people on the streets seemed much less inclined to risk more loss for a distant province. Nevertheless, the influence of the captured president remained considerable, and diplomats from the United States then in Mexico City expected that the mess would likely result in yet another internal revolution at terrible cost.[34]

Meanwhile, the army under Filisola actually received Santa Anna's order to withdraw on May 25 at Goliad, and immediately he put them in motion.[35] Urrea and others argued that they ignore Santa Anna's instructions and turn around to renew the attack, but Filisola remained adamant. Peña complained that "this countermarch is really cruel and harsh to me, for, in my opinion, after effecting a reunion with General Urrea, we should have marched to vindicate the honor of our arms, to avenge our companions, and to save those who might still be alive." Unfortunately, he found that the majority felt otherwise.[36] In time authorities relieved Filisola of his command and severely criticized him for abandoning Texas, replacing him with Urrea, who soon gathered that summer a new army at Matamoros numbering close to six thousand *soldados*. Continuing instability in Mexico itself forced Urrea to turn south rather than north, however, and he gave up the project of reconquering Texas.[37] No army would be marching north of the Rio Grande again any time soon. Still, neither would there be any recognition of Texian independence now or ever until the United States enforced it in another war to come. Ironically, a treaty with Santa Anna, repudiated both by the government of Mexico and the people of Texas, accomplished the all-important goal of getting Mexico's army out of the Republic.

In Santa Anna's absence, the Mexican congress began revising the 1824 Constitution in an effort to remake the nation, as well as to reduce the power of an executive become too strong. In the new system, the president would be the most subordinate official in the government, and the congress the most powerful. The former states became departments, forfeiting most of their autonomy to the central authority. The franchise was cut back to those who owned property. In an attempt to protect citizens against excesses—and perhaps with Santa Anna in mind—they created a fourth branch of government to act as a check on executive, legislative, and judicial branches. They even incorporated a bill of rights in what became known as the Constitution of 1836, a document that proved in the end no more capable of bringing stability to the poor distracted country than prior efforts. Meanwhile, the defeat, and his behavior after San Jacinto, cost Santa Anna much support in the centralist government, and signing the Velasco treaties all but disgraced him. By the time he returned home in 1837 he had been ousted as president and replaced by Anastasio Bustamente.[38] As so often before, Santa Anna simply retired to his home in Vera Cruz, patiently watching and waiting, knowing that his role in Mexico's destiny was not yet over.

Liberalism and republicanism were already all but dead in Mexico, with most of the established institutions—the church, the press, the political elites, and the middle classes—crying for strong central authority in the wake of the years of instability. What they got under the 1836 Constitution was more unrest, for though the centralists enjoyed a majority, they, too failed because they offered nothing better than the discredited federalism and simply could not manage or defeat the moderates and liberals still in their midst. Nothing addressed adequately the old issues of autonomy and the protection of the individual cultural, ethnic, and financial interests of differing regions that had so motivated the Texians themselves in their revolt. Bustamente lasted just four years before his overthrow finally abandoned efforts at constitutional rule and a military dictatorship took power, led by that mercurial genius of Mexican politics, Antonio López de Santa Anna.[39]

The prospect for orderly civil government appeared to be just as perilous north of the Rio Grande, unhappily. The Santa Anna affair crippled Burnet and his supporters for the balance of his incumbency. "The proceedings of D G Burnett and his Cabinet, has been throughout his whole administration so directly opposite to the necessities of his own Government and the expectations of the people here, that they have no confidence whatever in him," one man complained to Austin.[40] Austin himself, just arrived at Velasco from New Orleans on June 17, and though more restrained, still complained of Burnet's all but ignoring the Texian commissioners while they tried in Washington to gain American aid.[41] Zavala and a couple of other cabinet members argued in June that the government ought simply to resign and hand over the reins to the people, presumably to select new leaders. Burnet successfully forestalled such an extremity, arguing that the result would be anarchy, and they could all suffer the abuse if necessary rather than abdicate their responsibilities.[42]

Still, Zavala resigned on June 3, complaining that "the present Government of Texas has lost the moral confidence of the People."[43] Others left the cabinet before him—Rusk, Thomas, Carson—and most of them did not get along with each other. In all, the interim government's incumbency lasted just seven months, and yet thirteen men passed through the cabinet, not counting Zavala. "The cabinet is weak," complained a man who declined a position as secretary to the body a few days after Santa Anna's removal from the ship, "& altogether occupy a pitiful position both in the eyes of friends & enemies."[44] A disgusted Texian woman complained a few days later that the government were "the most imbecile body that ever sat in judgment on the fate of a nation."[45]

Burnet himself faced no choice but to confess that the Santa Anna episode all but emasculated the government, "shorn as it was, of all moral and physical power." Assailed by "the violent and dictatorial language of the army, the pragmatic and senseless denunciation of the newly arrived volunteers and the overheated anathemas of many citizens," he and the four cabinet members who remained in Velasco after mid-June could do little but maintain what he admitted was "a semblance of authority."[46] Bad as things were with the civil population, it got worse when Burnet found himself at war with the army. For a change, by July volunteers turned out in considerable numbers, indeed too many for the government to feed and clothe, leading Burnet on June 3 to try to put a stop to further volunteering.[47] The number of officers proliferated to the point that the Treasury had no idea of how many there were, their names, and whom it should be paying when it could. Newly arrived volunteers from the United States came with visions of land bounties, but no experience or history in the Texas struggle, and thus no loyalty to established leaders, while even among the veterans the Santa Anna business continued to rankle, and following the virtual abduction of Santa Anna, Burnet's own attitude toward the army soured.

Houston wisely stayed out of the imbroglio. He had returned from New Orleans, but came only as far as San Augustine a few miles west of the Sabine on the Nacogdoches road. His wound still refused to heal, and he delayed returning to assume command of the army once more.[48] Indeed, a foot wound could be quite painful and greatly impaired a general's mobility, but it is hard not to suspect that Houston also found it a useful expedient to absent himself from the political turmoil, just as he had when he went off to negotiate with the Cherokees after the Matamoros fiasco created the mess with Smith and the Council. A man with ambitions was wise to stay as distant as possible from these unseemly political wars, for with a regular election to replace the interim government only a few months away, anyone interested in seeking office risked being tainted by association.

Houston's continued absence made it necessary to find a more permanent commander for the army, and early in July, Burnet appointed Lamar major general and ordered him to supercede Rusk. Beneath the surface, however, Burnet and Rusk had fallen out. Privately Burnet suspected the war secretary of striving to build for himself a base of popularity in the army, as indeed he did after his performance at San Jacinto, while publicly the president maintained that he believed that Rusk did not want the army command permanently nor did he have the experience or skills necessary for leadership.[49] Rusk accepted his replacement manfully but then found the officers in the army greatly upset. "They Consider it as an unceremonious interfering of the Cabinet with the affairs of the Army," he shot back to Burnet. Then he attacked the cabinet for sloth, failure to feed and supply the army, even corruption, all of which was true.[50] To Houston, Rusk would be even more forthright. "The Cabinet, I fear, as a former Government had done, have been engaged in trying to destroy the Army," he said just days after the Lamar order came down, "and as a natural consequence the Army and People are exasperated agains[t] the conduct of the Cabinet."[51]

The reaction to Lamar's appointment took Burnet quite by surprise, for he expected it to be popular.[52] Lamar appeared to assume his command, only to find that at a meeting of some of the officers, mostly from Rusk's staff, and chaired by General Felix Huston, one of those men who had brought the troublesome new volunteers of whom Burnet complained, resolutions were adopted to defy the government and continue to take orders from Rusk.[53] At the same time at least one officer openly defied the president's authority to choose a new commander, and no doubt some believed it a move to politically injure Rusk and even Houston.[54] In that spirit of absolute democracy that so often crippled Texian affairs, Lamar asked to address the army itself, and he did, but then Rusk, General Thomas J. Green, and Huston spoke in rebuttal, and overwhelmingly the men voted to retain Rusk in command.[55] Nevertheless, Lamar began to issue orders as major general commanding. Then Green manifested a disinclination to accept Lamar's direction, and the insubordination of men whom Burnet characterized as "base and unprincipled" came out in the open.[56] It did not help that at this moment came confirmation of the reports of another Mexican army under Urrea poised for an invasion of Texas.

Matters escalated when Burnet tried to curb officers and men from plundering civilians under the excuse of military impressment, and when he nullified a number of commissions given to men who never actually took the field. It seemed clear that the president sought to curb the power of the officers, and when he did that it became at last apparent that the government had lost all authority with the army.[57] The officers struck back immediately. Fifteen of them, joined by three enlisted men and one civilian, met and framed charges and specifications against Burnet as the first step in what amounted to an attempt at a military coup. They accused him of usurpation on the ridiculous grounds that he assumed to be president and so styled himself "when there has been no law Establishing or enacting such office," implicitly resting their claim on the fact that the Convention at Washington elected Burnet and not the people. They charged him as well with treason for negotiating with Santa Anna, for providing food to Mexican prisoners of war, and for attempting to return Santa Anna to Mexico. Finally, they charged him with sedition in that he spoke publicly of Houston "in a contemptuous and ungentlemanly manner" for his policy of retreating, and also for attempting to discourage accepting further volunteers in May when it appeared that peace and independence were at hand and there would be no further threats of invasion. They also charged him with corruption in diverting public funds, interfering with officers in the conduct of their duties, and of "causing discontent & seditious conduct in the army . . . evincing a disposition to dissolve the same." Huston, Green, John Wharton, Benjamin Fort Smith, Neall, Burleson, Sherman, and several others signed as witnesses to the document.[58] Three days later they actually sent an order to an officer in Velasco to arrest Burnet and seize the government archives in his possession, but the officer chose not to obey, and the coup attempt quickly fizzled thereafter. "The good people of Texas have been insulted & outraged in the person of their Chief Magistrate," Burnet fumed. "A violent Revolution has been attempted, involving the overthrow of the Civil Authority, and evidently intended to create a Military Supremacy in the Government."[59]

The tensions approached the boiling point. That same day Lamar and Rusk narrowly averted fighting a duel after Lamar accused him of harboring a secret conspiracy to retain the command, but then Lamar withdrew the offending words that caused Rusk to demand satisfaction.[60] Instead, Rusk agreed to obey Lamar's orders, and the Regulars and several of the volunteer companies who recognized his authority moved to another camp, leaving the men under Green and Huston in place. Should those two generals continue to refuse to recognize Lamar's authority, then he threatened to charge them before a court martial. Worse, Green led a cabal that voted on bringing the captive Santa Anna to the army to face quick and unambiguous justice. Lamar hoped to intercept the prisoner beforehand and hand him over to the government. He also wanted the Mexican to pay for his crimes, but he wanted it done by civil law and "not by a rebellious mob of strangers who have been made such by an ambitious and weak General."[61]

Two days later, their difficulty adjusted, Rusk was on the verge of handing over the command to Lamar when Green and others found out about it and immediately protested. The officers were astonished, Green told Rusk. The volunteers had already spoken on whom they wanted as their commander in Houston's absence. "You not only destroy the Army but ruin yourself by transferring and disposing of the voice of 1500 Freemen just spoken on the subject," Green blustered. A day later Green simply refused to acknowledge orders from Lamar, and the army approached mutiny.[62] That very day Lamar reported to Burnet that "every thing is in the utmost confusion and rebellion." Rusk, at least, threw his whole support behind Lamar's authority, though the new commander suspected that it was only because Rusk saw his own cachet with the rebels on the wane. "The general Officers all seem determined to defy the civil authority of the land," warned Lamar. Only the election and convening of a congress, and that quickly, could forestall what he feared would be "dreadful disorganization and anarchy."[63] Even there it did not end, for as soon as Green's refusal to accept orders from Lamar became known, the army held another vote and once more repudiated Lamar in favor of Rusk as its commander. Faced with that, on July 18 Lamar simply resigned and went home.

Green preened in the victory over the government, crowing that in future "should any of their miserable creatures get impertinent, I will punish them with as little compunction of conscience as I would the thieving Wolf."[64] When Burnet tried again to appoint Lamar to army command early in August, the army met once more in a vote that rejected him, this time balloting nineteen hundred for the absent Houston and three hundred for Lamar. Now Rusk renewed his pleas for Houston to return to the army before it was too late, arguing that their mutual enemies "have used every effort against both you and me."[65]

The situation went so out of hand that seventy-seven men and officers urgently appealed to Houston on July 22 to come back to the army at once, and Rusk again made the same entreaty.[66] At the same time a few calm heads in the army began openly to question the idea of putting Santa Anna on trial, and Houston himself wrote to them to condemn the idea.[67] It was a propitious time for Burnet to issue a proclamation on July 23 calling for the anticipated general election of president, vice president, and congress six weeks hence.[68] With the threat of another Mexican invasion waning as Urrea moved his army south, there ought to be calm enough to organize and hold elections, and the president and cabinet felt anxious to be relieved of the opprobrium heaped daily upon them. Even the ever-complaining Rusk felt optimistic, confidently expecting that the balloting would produce at last "an efficient Government."[69] Included in the election was also a referendum on the proposition of applying for annexation to the United States, which had been much expected for some time. "There is a very strong party here in favor of union with the United States," Zavala observed back in May before his resignation, and he for one agreed. It was the only way many saw to obtain a stable government. Beyond that, and especially with the example of their current pitiful government before them, they worried about the ability of Texas "to march alone among the other independent nations."[70]

A FRENCHMAN WHO VISITED America only months before the Texas Revolution expressed frank wonder at the facility of New World people like these Texians for mixing rank self-interest with public spirit. "Sometimes he seems to be animated by the most selfish greed and sometimes by the most lively patriotism," observed Alexis de Tocqueville. "One must suppose these urges to be united and mingled in some part of their being." As the turmoil that so often disrupted or threatened to disrupt Texian fortunes demonstrated, there was good cause to wonder about their ability to achieve the right mixture of the two in order to govern themselves independently. Ironically, in its way the excess of democracy had made Texas almost as unmanageable as Mexico under its failed republican regimes, and threatened to do so again, yet somehow the Texians kept their commitment to the idea that in serving the will of the people as a whole they somehow also served the best interests of themselves individually. "For the sake of each other they think it their most important concern to secure a government which will allow them to get the good things they want and which will not stop their enjoying those they have in peace."[71] However difficult the process, Texians remained convinced that their prosperity and preservation remained rooted in the ballot box.

An election meant a resurgence of politics, of course, and the perpetually turbulent Green believed he saw Burnet and the cabinet inclining toward putting Austin forward for the presidency. He immediately notified Houston and Rusk, assuming that either or both of them might seek the office. The new government needed an energetic and aggressive leader to "fight them out of this war," he said, "or they will have a government of Negociation, to forever lay about and bootlick Santa Anna's royal feet." As for the aggressive policy he wanted, he raised an old specter that almost doomed Texas once, an attack on Matamoros.[72] In fact, on August 4 Austin did agree to be a candidate for the presidency. Soon thereafter, Henry Smith announced his candidacy, apparently so ignorant or deluded about the almost universal contempt for his previous administration that he actually thought he had a chance of success.

Almost at once the campaigning turned partisan and ugly. Opponents falsely charged Austin with involvement in the fraudulent Monclova speculations, and then went on to attack him for somehow being responsible for saving Santa Anna, a ridiculous charge that still Austin had constantly to refute. Houston saved the Mexican general, and wisely so, but in the current mood Austin could not say so much, and instead simply announced that he, too, thought Santa Anna deserved death. He was assaulted with charges that he had opposed independence, as indeed he had, at least publicly, until late 1835. What perhaps hurt him the most was the perception expressed by Green, that the ailing *empresario* was the candidate, and therefore would be the tool, of the discredited Burnet regime.[73] Burnet himself expressed confidence that Austin would be elected, and looked favorably on Lamar's interest in the vice presidency.[74]

The accusations about opposition to independence revealed the reemergence of the old party structure that largely went underground for the sake of unity during the revolt. The old Peace Party men who supported Austin prior to the revolt now seemed likely to stand with him again, while at least some of the War Party faction could be expected to back Smith if they could stomach him. As of August 15

Smith seemed to be running well ahead in the army itself, now camped on the Coleto. Indeed, Austin at one point started to go to the army to raise support, but gave up and turned back, probably due to increasing illness.[75] By the end of the month, with only the two candidates in the field, many in fact thought that neither could command sufficient support to establish a respectable government. Green, of all people, even approached the two with a proposition that whichever should win, he should appoint the other secretary of the treasury as an indication of coalition to unite the people.[76]

But then came news that made all previous speculations and combinations moot. On August 20 Houston announced his candidacy via the agency of a meeting at Columbia where six hundred men endorsed him, though he himself still remained in Nacogdoches, where he had continued his recuperation and his watching and waiting.[77] As of the end of July he expected to return to the army the last week of August.[78] He had said nothing yet publicly about any thoughts of his own as to the presidency, but he heard plenty from others. It was a necessity that "you should be made the first President of Texas," a friend with the army advised, warning Houston to beware even of Rusk.[79] On August 8, however, he issued his first criticism of the government, particularly for its handling of the Santa Anna affair and for trying to release him, rather a hypocritical stance since Houston himself had proposed an eventual release of the general. But now it was important for him to be on the right side of the army, and if that meant allowing the people to think Austin or Burnet really responsible for the Mexican general's survival, then it did not trouble the Raven's conscience overmuch.

Indeed, he now maintained that the constitution he helped frame at Washington was inadequate, that the Burnet regime had been unlawful, and the remedy was for the army to hold a convention and frame a new government. Tacitly Houston thus embraced the very military overthrow so recently thwarted by Burnet, and if the army were to create a new government, the recent vote of the soldiers left no doubt that Houston himself would be chosen president. It was not a call for creation of a military dictatorship like Santa Anna's, but rather for reframing a new government that would no doubt have executive, legislative, and legal branches. But then Mexico had a congress and a constitution and a high court, all backed and enforced by the military until recently under Santa Anna's control. Texas, like Mexico, lay close to anarchy and only strong government could save it from disintegration. The moment the military became involved in dictating the nature of government, liberal republicanism lay in danger, which Houston above all should have recognized.[80]

As for his own presidential ambitions, "General Sam" remained silent, even suggesting to Rusk that maybe he ought to seek the post, though perhaps it was a stratagem to sound Rusk's interests since the general had been warned about him. But Rusk denied any interest and rather said he thought Houston the fittest man.[81] Houston did begin reasserting himself more directly into army affairs at this time, however, and now was when he moved to Nacogdoches preparatory to returning to the army. On August 20 Rusk encouraged his speedy arrival, adding that "one proclamation from you here would now do us more service than all the Rickety Govts this side of——."[82] The declaration that Texas got that same day was Houston's candidacy for the presidency.

His correspondents urged his candidacy ever since the announcement of the election, but cagily he kept his own counsel. For one thing, he thought he perceived a conspiracy against himself among Burnet and some of the cabinet, believing they hoped to charge him with some dereliction of duty, even with desertion for leaving his command and going to New Orleans for treatment.[83] Indeed, rumors said that when Houston returned to his command, Burnet would give him no orders and try to retain Lamar in command somehow, though the army's reaction to Lamar put an end to any such scheme, if indeed it ever existed.[84] Meanwhile, Houston released his views on how best to unify Texas and safely see it through the crisis. He spoke against the crippling partisanship that dogged Texian politics for years, but other than his suggestion of an army convention to frame a new government and his trimming position on Santa Anna, he stayed carefully silent on other candidates and issues. That he waited until August 20 to get into the race reflected his lifelong canny political timing, a sense far superior to his military instincts. With less than a fortnight left before the election, opponents simply had no time to mount a campaign against him, nor for him to have to confront serious questions in the press. His victory at San Jacinto and his absence from the subsequent political turmoil were his chief assets, while his platform consisted of little more than his announcement that he yielded to calls for him to run because "the crisis requires it."[85] Eight years later he claimed that neither Austin nor Smith could have commanded the authority to get a new government up and running, and that only he commanded the prestige and the goodwill in all camps to bring about coalition and unity. It was a perfectly logical argument of much substance, though the Texian to whom he gave the explanation privately dismissed it as a "lame excuse."[86]

By September 2 Austin already predicted his own defeat. The army would go heavily for the general, and east Texas and the Red River area were also likely in the Houston camp. Smith's constituency was scattered, and Austin's old base of power even in his own colony stood fragmented.[87] The ailing *empresario* proved prescient, for on polling day Houston won overwhelmingly with 5,119 to 743 for Smith—who in any case withdrew to support Houston—and just 587 for Austin. The elections passed smoothly enough, choosing a new congress to take office. The ballot also contained a question on sentiment toward the idea of annexation to the United States, confirming the fact that many Texian leaders like Austin had always seen independence as a first step but the not the last. That referendum won approval, as did a continuation of the 1836 Constitution, thus at least eliminating Houston's idea of an army convention. A month later, on October 3, the Congress convened, though Burnet and the old cabinet remained in office and not due to be supplanted by Houston until early December. It was an intolerable situation, and after less than three weeks of polite but ineffectual coexistence, Burnet yielded to entreaties to resign early, which he did on October 22.

It was the end of the interim government and the last act of any provisional administration not directly elected by the voters of Texas. Even though Mexico had not and would not acknowledge the independence of Texas, the Revolution was over. Now it would be up to the hero of San Jacinto to see if he could arouse some new phoenix to fly from the ashes of Texan politics.

EPILOGUE

"Our Course Is Onward"

⚬⚬⚬⚬

INDEED THE REVOLT was over, though now Texians needed a revolution in their public affairs to counteract the tradition of division and self-interest that did so much to bring on the crisis, and to bedevil the insurgents throughout their time of greatest trial. Happily, Houston appeared equal to the task. His inaugural address appealed to all. "Our course is onward," he said in a hastily organized ceremony after Burnet's sudden resignation. "We are only in the outset of the campaign of liberty." He commenced at once to build an inclusive administration. Lamar won the vice presidency, and Houston named Smith to head the treasury department and Austin to be secretary of state. Within a few weeks Houston also disposed of that most divisive political liability, General Santa Anna. By an executive order he sent him not to Mexico, but to Washington, D.C., where he hoped that Santa Anna's making a renewed pledge to honor Texian independence to President Jackson's administration would help guarantee his compliance once he returned to Mexico. Austin magnanimously expressed a conviction that "I have *full confidence* that all will go right," even hoping that within six months Texas would become another star on Old Glory.[1] As he watched Houston in office in those first weeks, he found much to approve and little to fault, but he would not be around either to see Texas annexed, nor even to witness Texas's progress half a year hence. His illness only got worse, and on December 27 he lapsed into a coma, emerging in a delirium before he died to tell his friends that "the independence of Texas is recognized!"[2]

In terms of losses and destruction, the Texian Revolution paled in comparison with the most recent wars in Europe, and even here in America, though for the Texians at least, the percentage of their losses seemed dramatic. Probably no more than thirty-seven hundred men served as volunteers or Regulars during the entire period of the revolution, and most of them enlisted for no more than a single brief thirty- or sixty-day period. Yet just the tragedies at the Alamo and Goliad accounted for almost six hundred killed. Even though the battle deaths of Texians at the other engagements like San Jacinto and the siege of Béxar were minimal, still somewhere above seven hundred Texians died, making just deaths in the army almost 20 percent of total enlistments, with another hundred or more wounded. The inordinately high proportion of dead to injured is perhaps the most eloquent testimony of all to the unusual nature of the revolutionary actions, and to the continuing emotional and psychological impact of just those two disasters to Travis and Fannin.

Mexican losses approached more customary proportions of the experience of an army in the field, at least until San Jacinto. While he never had them all together at any one time, Santa Anna overall counted somewhere over six thousand *soldados* among his several columns. At none of the little skirmishes at Gonzales or Goliad or Concepción, or even in the siege of Béxar, did they absorb much loss. Indeed, in only two actions did Mexican arms suffer substantial injury. In the final assault on the Alamo, they lost two hundred killed and that many more wounded, many seriously, while at San Jacinto the Mexican dead amounted to six hundred fifty or more. In all, with those killed in the smaller actions and on patrols, Santa Anna's army may have lost as many as one thousand dead, and probably another five hundred wounded.

Thus, for both sides, casualty figures departed from the norm in nineteenth-century warfare, in which the wounded generally outnumbered the killed by two- or three-to-one or more. In this bitter little war, however, Santa Anna's vengeful policy toward "traitors" on the one hand, and an even more bitter determination for revenge on the other, ensured that after the Alamo few prisoners would be taken by either side, and the wounded were as likely to be murdered if caught. The concept of war crimes had not yet become a part of Western military ethics by the 1830s, though generally people at war knew excess from the legitimate and necessary cost of war. White Americans expected massacre from native adversaries. The killing of all combatants had often been a part of

Indian war ethics and was a frequent feature of the earlier contest between Indian and white for possession of the trans-Appalachian wilderness. But Europeans were expected to fight by a different standard, and the Texians at the time, and posterity since, concluded that Santa Anna stepped well over the line at the Alamo and Goliad. It is no wonder that so many Texians wanted Santa Anna put to death.

For years after 1836 many Texians dreamed of Santa Anna someday paying for his acts, though he never would. Instead, all too many of his *soldados* paid on the field at San Jacinto. There were far too many heartrending stories of vengeful Texians murdering helpless men trying to surrender, or wounded pleading for their lives, when they ought rightfully to have been made prisoners. Ironically, of the men with Santa Anna at San Jacinto, very few had even been present at the Alamo, and none were at Goliad. Perhaps most unfortunate of all, the actions at the Alamo and Goliad reinforced the perennial underlying racial distrust of dark-skinned peoples by the white Texians. It characterized their relations with *tejanos* during the war, and poisoned them in future. The seeming barbarities practiced by Santa Anna only confirmed long-held prejudices that made future relations between whites and *tejanos* and whites and Mexicans all the more difficult. The Alamo would be remembered, and for generations innocent Hispanics paid for the cruel lesson taught there by Santa Anna.

Both sides learned other lessons in this little war. For Mexico it simply reinforced what wise heads had known already for some time, and that was the near impossibility of ruling a province at so great a remove from the central authority, especially in an era of inadequate roads and otherwise poor communications. Unfortunately, the concomitant to that lesson, that a gentle hand was the wiser course in dealing with distant provinces, seems not to have gotten through. Zacatecas, Yucatán, Coahuila, and then Texas rose up in reaction to perceived repressive measures from the central government, even though they had tried in the main to be good citizens of the federation so long as left a reasonable degree of autonomy. But despite Santa Anna's troubles, he came back as dictator. The unhappy tradition of two generations of revolution and instability had not yet run its course, and turmoil and insecurity characterized Mexican politics for generations to come. The little affair in faraway Texas, while embarrassing, was hardly going to have any influence on something as fundamental to Mexican life and politics as that.

If the Texians learned some lessons from their narrow success, still they ignored others. For one, they resisted acknowledging the important role played by the *tejanos*, just as they also chose to ignore the substantial number of their white comrades who either sat out the Revolution entirely, or else for reasons of their own actively aided and supported the Mexicans. Rather, they soon began building their own myth of unanimity and exclusivity, of a revolution in which all of the people were united, and in which all of the revolutionaries were white Anglos. It was a myth that did much that was good in cementing Texians' image of themselves in the generations ahead, but also one that unfortunately supported and encouraged gradually making their *tejano* neighbors and onetime allies almost invisible. A decade after independence Texians narrowly missed denying *tejanos* the right to vote.

Nor did the Texians learn immediate lessons of the need for political unity, even though they saw their efforts to respond to the crisis repeatedly hampered by the political infighting between Houston, Austin, Henry Smith, Burnet, and others. Indeed, in the days and years ahead fellow Texians as much reviled as revered Houston. Public affairs in his new capital at Columbia, then later when the capital moved to a location named for Austin, remained chaotic throughout the ensuing nine-year life of the Republic. The flow of immigrants never ceased. "The country is filling up fast," observed a Louisiana man living on the Red River just three years after Texian independence. "The roads hereabouts are crowded with emigrants to Texas from Arkansas, Missouri, Kentucky, Alabama, Georgia & Mississippi."[3] When they reached their new homes out on the prairies, however, these new Texians and the old veterans of the revolt learned rather more from their revolutionary experience, though perhaps it is more accurate to say that the Revolution simply enhanced the lessons they learned all along about survival on this southwestern frontier. The wide expanses, the limited roads for communications, the hardness of some of the country, and the vagaries of the weather meant that to hold on to their new domain they needed hardened men well prepared for any contingency. Even with the Mexicans gone—for the moment—there were still the Indians on the Northern and Western fringes. Houston himself had been absent during the early stages of the Revolution concluding treaties with some of them in order to reduce the number of potential adversaries. Those peoples must be controlled or kept at a remove if the settlers of Texas were to be secure in their homes and plantations. On November 24, 1835, during the siege of Béxar, the authorities in San Felipe decreed the creation of the Texas Rangers, first as scouts for the army itself, but after independence they went on to become a growing force employed to control the Indians and, eventually, to break them down as a threat. When the war with Mexico erupted in 1846, the Rangers came into their own as a military force, a peacekeeping force, and a permanent fixture in Texan and Western lore.

The Texas campaign broke no new ground militarily. Texian authorities aspired to create a conventional military establishment very much on the model of the United States Army, even though their resources in manpower and materiel made it far more dream than reality. Meanwhile, they had little alternative but to conduct their campaigns entirely in reaction to Mexican movements after the fall of Béxar. Only at San Jacinto were they opportunistically able to seize the initiative and put the campaign on their terms for the final but crucial engagement. Their military lessons should have been of the crippling impracticability of the excessive democracy that permeated their ranks, but their actions after San Jacinto revealed that to be an admonition ignored. It was one thing for volunteers to elect their company officers, an old militia tradition in America, but for those same men to hold elections on the choice of their army commander, and on actual campaign operations, was simply foolish. Austin may have felt it necessary before Béxar in late 1835 in order not to alienate men by attempting to act by arbitrary authority, but in the summer of 1836 for the army repeatedly to reject an appointed commander, and for its officers to refuse to take orders from him, was simple anarchy. The attempt of the army to depose the president fell little short of an aborted coup. Thereafter, when Texas needed volunteers, as it would in two wars to come within the next quarter century, the volunteers still elected their company and even regimental officers, but the men in higher command usually received appointments on the basis of at least some experience and ability—or political connections—and decisions would be made in headquarters, not by the tent fire. As for the Mexican military, in the years ahead it would be just as riven with politics and revolts as the nation itself, a climate of instability in which development of military thinking was stultified amid the chaos of officers just trying to choose sides in internecine contests.

Of course, Texians and Mexicans met in hostilities again, though not in declared war between the two nations. In fact, the peace of the abortive Treaties of Velasco really inaugurated a period of overall calm interrupted by occasional but minor cross-border clashes, growing largely, among other things, out of the Texians' claim that their nation extended all the way to the Rio Grande, whereas Mexico acknowledged Texan claims just to the Nueces, and only grudgingly even to that line. In 1842, with Santa Anna again in charge in Mexico City, Mexican forces swooped across the Nueces and captured Lipantitlán and San Antonio. Eventually they withdrew, but Houston, now president of the republic, ordered a retaliatory expedition across the border commanded by Alexander Somervell. He led seven hundred men out of Béxar in November and captured Laredo the next month, and then took Guerrero. The expedition ran out of steam, and Somervell and part of the command returned to Texas. The rest decided to continue toward Mier, on the lower Rio Grande. On Christmas day they attacked the Mexican garrison and despite being outnumbered ten-to-one, continued the assault for two days before they were forced to surrender. Ordered at first to be executed, they were later sent off as prisoners, but when many escaped, only to be recaptured, Santa Anna reverted to his old harshness and ordered them shot. In the end, the men drew lots, and one in ten was executed. The rest either escaped again or remained prisoners for more than a year. In retaliation for the Mier episode, Jacob Snively led yet another incursion into Mexican territory early in 1843, penetrating through present-day Oklahoma and into Kansas, bent on preying on the Santa Fe Trail trade. In the end, he achieved nothing except a minor diplomatic incident when he ran into United States soldiers who claimed that the raid had crossed into territory claimed by the Union. It would be the last of the numerous Texian-Mexican clashes until 1846, when Mexican troops crossed the Rio Grande and engaged United States soldiers in the opening clash of what became known in the United States as the Mexican War, and in Mexico as the War of American Intervention.

It was in the United States that the greatest effects of the successful bid for Texian independence were to be felt, far afield from the prairies and plains over which the Republic flew the new flag it adopted at the end of 1836, a single gold star on a blue field, virtually the same flag raised by the brief Republic of West Florida a quarter century before. The moment Texas became independent, it went into play in the power struggle taking place in the United States between North and South over the issue of slavery and its expansion. The antislavery forces wanted Texas to remain independent. Even if it was a republic that embraced slavery, still that would have no impact on the balance of power between slave and free states in the Union. Southerners, of course, hoped eventually to see Texas come into the Union as another slave state, helping them to maintain the parity with the North in the Senate in Washington that seemed to be the only safeguard for the future preservation of slavery where it already existed. Indeed, many of the colonists originally went to Texas in order to pave the way for its one-day statehood, and back in the United States both pro-slave and antislave forces agitated and propagandized actively throughout the brief revolution.

Inevitably Texas one day became a part of the United States. No immediate neighbor populated so largely by Americans and governed so entirely on the American model could long remain outside the orbit of the Union, and certainly not in the era of Manifest Destiny. When the United States annexed it by treaty in 1845, the action only started anew the heated debate over slavery's future. In 1846 when the war with Mexico broke out, largely because Santa Anna held power again and was not about to recognize the independence he had accepted under duress ten years before, American victory resulted in the acquisition of the New Mexico Territory, along with California and most of future Utah and Nevada. The accession of so much territory only exaggerated the debate as Southerners demanded that all these territories be opened to possible slavery. Wrapped up as it was with the power struggle in Washington and fears for the existence of slavery where it already existed, and all of the associated questions of economic and social stability, that territorial contest finally put the Union on the road to Civil War.

The revolution in Texas did not make secession and internecine war inevitable. Had it failed, however, with no consequent annexation, and thus perhaps removed the immediate catalyst for war between the United States and Mexico in 1846, would those large-scale acquisitions in the Southwest and West that reawakened the territorial debate have come about anyhow? Almost surely the United States was going to expand to fill its continent sooner or later, though nothing is inevitable in history. Yet certainly the fact of an independent Texas put a new and potential trump card on the table in the already simmering sectional controversy in a nation that, otherwise, did scarcely more than watch while the Texas drama unfolded north of the Nueces. When the sectional simmer rose to a boil in 1861, Texians once more rose in revolt, though just as divided as they had been a quarter century earlier. The tradition of revolution that sent them to arms in 1835 to create a new republic had left within it one more final gasp of defiance to unwanted distant authority.

In the end that tradition of insurgency, with attendant causes, is what made it all happen in 1835 and 1836. Of course, men in Texas then answered a host of imperatives to take their rifles and muskets and stand against what they chose to perceive as tyranny. All interests are ultimately selfish, even what is called patriotism. No doubt a few really did hope to precipitate a revolt in order to gain the large land holdings promised by those fraudulent Monclova grants. No doubt, too, others agitated principally out of a desire to expand slavery, or because they resented being ruled ultimately by brown-skinned peoples whom they thought racially inferior. Some sought the quick profits of plunder from a regime they thought too disorganized and distant to defend itself, and no doubt some wanted a new and independent polity in order to achieve high station for themselves.

None of these influences brought about the Texian revolt, however. Rather they all operated on the fringes of the overwhelming causes. The term "manifest destiny" still lay a few years in the future when the "Come and Take It" gun first barked at Gonzales, yet the unstoppable dynamic behind that phenomenon was already well in train for a generation before. Americans began that century determined to head west in quest of land, opportunity, and a life less fettered by the restraints of Eastern society, including the growing power of government. They wanted to direct their own affairs in their own land, a wish coincidentally identical with that of the liberals in Mexico with whom the immigrants so long made a rocky common cause. Denying that autonomy was bad enough, but when councils in Mexico City repeatedly proved themselves incapable of providing efficient rule thanks to internal instability, revolutions, distance, and simple neglect or ineptitude, the situation in the colonies became intolerable. After a decade of experience taught them that Mexican rule meant seemingly capricious lurches from right to left and back again, when they saw the organic law either ignored or unable to maintain itself, and when their own voice in the councils that determined their affairs seemed so weak, Texians' ancestral instincts awakened.

Mexico seemed to have only the will to rule them, but not the skill or the internal stability to do so with security or efficiency. When the only future alternative in 1835 appeared quite logically to be more decades of upheaval and confusion, stunting economic policies, onerous interference in their public and even personal lives, and denial of rights whose concept of inalienability most of them brought from east of the Sabine, the choice became steadily more clear and unavoidable. They must rule themselves in their own land. Not only the practical realities before them impelled them to that course, but also the experience and tradition of a century of Anglo and Hispanic peoples alike in the New World. It was a hemisphere for revolution, and its destiny of revolt was not done yet.

During the first few months of secession and the formation of the new Confederate States of America, Southern men had no official national flag to follow. Quite coincidentally, in the interim they recalled a familiar design and flew it from their rooftops and campsites, a single white star on an azure field. Despite the adoption of later official patterns, many Confederates never lost their preference for what they called the "Bonnie Blue Flag." It was the Lone Star of the Republic of Texas all over again, now bursting its geographical bounds to become a generic symbol of resistance. Having emerged on the horizon beyond the Sabine a generation before, the Lone Star would rise once more.

ENDNOTES

CHAPTER ONE: "CAST IN A CONTENTIOUS CROWD"

1. Hiram Taylor to Mary Taylor, June 12, 1836, Hiram and Thomas Thomson Taylor Papers, Hill Memorial Library, Louisiana State University, Baton Rouge.
2. Robert Harvey, *Liberators: Latin America's Struggle for Independence 1810–1830* (Woodstock, NY, 2000), p. 2.
3. Ibid., pp. 2–6.
4. Ibid., p. 7.
5. Ibid., p. 1.
6. Philip Nolan to Barr and Davenport, n.d., Henry Raup Wagner Collection of Philip Nolan Papers, Yale Collection of Western Americana, Beinecke Rare Book and Manuscript Library, New Haven, CT.
7. Maurine T. Wilson, "Philip Nolan and His Activities in Texas" (master's thesis, University of Texas, Austin, TX, 1932), p. 86.
8. For more on Nolan, see Maurine T. Wilson and Jack Jackson, *Philip Nolan and Texas: Expeditions Into the Unknown Land, 1791–1801* (Waco, TX, 1987).
9. Jesús F. de la Teja, "Rebellion on the Frontier," in Gerald E. Poyo, ed., *Tejano Journey 1770–1850* (Austin, TX, 1996), p. 17.
10. Ibid., pp. 17–18.
11. The definition of *tejano* has been much mooted. See Adán Benavides Jr., "Tejano," Ron Tyler et al., eds., *The New Handbook of Texas* (Austin, TX, 1996), VI, pp. 238–39.
12. Thomas Maitland Marshall, *A History of the Western Boundary of the Louisiana Purchase, 1819–1841* (Berkeley, CA, 1914), pp. 2, 8, 10, 13.
13. Ibid., pp. 13, 18–19.
14. Ibid., pp. 38–40.
15. Ted Schwarz, *Forgotten Battlefield of the First Texas Revolution: The Battle of Medina, August 18, 1813* (Austin, TX, 1985), pp. 3–4.
16. Frank Lawrence Owsley Jr. and Gene A. Smith, *Filibusters and Expansionists: Jeffersonian Manifest Destiny, 1800–1821* (Tuscaloosa, AL, 1997), p. 62.
17. Walter F. McCaleb, *The Aaron Burr Conspiracy* (New York, 1903), pp. 105ff.
18. Matilda E. Moore, "The Bowie Brothers and Their Famous Knife," *Frontier Times*, XIX (February 1942), p. 201; William C. Davis, *Three Roads to the Alamo: The Lives and Fortunes of David Crockett, James Bowie, and William Barret Travis* (New York, 1998), pp. 44, 594 n.

19. Schwarz, *Forgotten Battlefield*, p. 28; Harris Gaylord Warren, *The Sword Was Their Passport. A History of American Filibustering in the Mexican Revolution* (Baton Rouge, LA, 1943), pp. 44–45.
20. Julia Kathryn Garrett, *Green Flag Over Texas* (New York, 1939), pp. 180–81.
21. Warren, *Sword*, pp. 64–69; Schwarz, *Forgotten Battlefield*, pp. 83ff; Garrett, *Green Flag*, pp. 224–28.

CHAPTER TWO: BAD CAUSES AND BAD MEN

1. Warren, *Sword*, pp. 79–80.
2. Owsley and Smith, *Filibusters*, pp. 166–69.
3. John Windship to William Plummer Jr., March 20, 1814, in Everett S. Brown, ed., "Letters from Louisiana, 1813–1814," *Mississippi Valley Historical Review*, XI (March 1925), pp. 573–74.
4. Warren, *Sword*, pp. 92–95, 238 n.
5. Ibid., pp. 113–14.
6. Ibid., pp. 121–22.
7. Baltimore, *Nile's Weekly Register*, IX, September 16, 1815, p. 33.
8. *American State Papers, Foreign Relations* (Washington, 1834), IV, p. 1.
9. Louis Aury to Maignet, February 10, 1812, Louis Aury Papers, Center for American History, University of Texas, Austin (CAHUT).
10. Stanley Faye, Commodore Aury, I, pp. 45, 92, typescript in Center for American History, University of Texas, Austin (CAHUT).
11. Stanley Faye, "Commodore Aury," *Louisiana Historical Quarterly*, XXIV (July 1941), pp. 631–33.
12. Aury to Victoria Aury, January 14, 1817, Aury Papers, CAHUT.
13. Faye, "Aury," pp. 634–35.
14. Ibid., pp. 640–41; Aury to his father, January 25, 1817, Aury Papers, CAHUT.
15. Warren, *Sword*, pp. 164–66.
16. Ibid., p. 171; Margaret S. Henson, "Henry Perry," *Handbook of Texas*, V, p. 160.
17. Warren, *Sword*, pp. 173–75.
18. Faye, "Aury," pp. 645ff.
19. Harris Gaylord Warren and Betje Black Klier, "Charles François Antoine Lallemand," *Handbook of Texas*, IV, p. 36.
20. Warren, *Sword*, pp. 200–203.
21. Ibid., pp. 208–210.
22. Ibid., pp. 222–23; Kent Gardien and Betje Black Klier, "Champ D'Asile," *Handbook of Texas*, II, p. 36.
23. Warren, *Sword*, pp. 228–30.
24. Marshall, *Western Boundary*, pp. 61–63.
25. Natchez, *Mississippi State Gazette*, June 16, 1819.
26. W[illiam] B[ollaert], "Life of Jean Lafitte," *Littell's Living Age*, XXXII (March 1852), pp. 435, 441 n.
27. Natchez, *Mississippi State Gazette*, August 14, 1819.
28. Warren, *Sword*, p. 238 and n.
29. Natchez, *Mississippi Republican*, August 18, 1819.
30. Warren, *Sword*, p. 240.

31. Jean Laffite to James Long, July 7, 1819 (copy), Mirabeau B. Lamar Papers, Texas State Library and Archives, Austin (TSL).
32. Felipe Fatio to J. Ruiz de Apodoca, July 16, 1819, Charles Adams Gulick Jr., and Katherine Elliott, eds., *The Papers of Mirabeau Bounaparte Lamar* (Austin, TX, 1923), I, pp. 33–34.
33. John Henry Brown, *Long's Expedition* (Houston, TX, 1930), p. 1.
34. New Orleans, *Louisiana Gazette*, November 4, 1819.
35. James E. Winston, "New Orleans and the Texas Revolution," *Louisiana Historical Quarterly*, X (July 1927), p. 319.
36. New Orleans, *L'Ami des Lois*, June 9, 1819.
37. New Orleans, *Louisiana Gazette*, August 26, September 4, 22, October 4, 1819.
38. J. H. Bell to Stephen F. Austin, September 21, 1819, in Eugene C. Barker, ed., *The Austin Papers* (Washington, 1924), I, Part 1, p. 348.
39. Davis, *Three Roads*, p. 51, n597.
40. Laffite to Long, September 30, 1819, Gulick and Elliott, *Papers*, I, p. 34.
41. Pierre Laffite to Juan Manuel de Cagigal, December 11, 1819, in Lyle Saxon, *Lafitte the Pirate* (New York, 1930), p. 231.
42. "A Friend of Liberty to ?," December 29, 1819, from unidentified newspaper in James Long Vertical File, CAHUT.
43. Laffite to Cagigal, December 11, 1819, Saxon, *Lafitte*, pp. 231–32.
44. Lawrence Kearney to Daniel Patterson, March 7, 1820, Record Group 45, Office of Naval Records, Captains' Letters, I, #108, National Archives, Washington, D.C. For Jean Laffite's probable death, see Bogotá, *Gaceta de Colombia*, April 20, 1823.
45. "Early Life in the Southwest, No. IV, Captain John McHenry, Pioneer of Texas," *DeBow's Review*, XV (December 1853), p. 576.
46. Ibid., pp. 576–77. Brown, *Long's Expedition*, is based almost verbatim on the McHenry account contained herein.
47. Ibid., p. 578.
48. Warren, *Sword*, pp. 252–54; "Captain John McHenry," pp. 578–79.
49. Austin to J. H. Hawkins, May 1, 1822, Barker, *Papers*, I, Part 2, pp. 504–505.

CHAPTER THREE: "THE LABYRINTH OF TROUBLE AND VEXATION"

1. Gregg Cantrell, *Stephen F. Austin, Empresario of Texas* (New Haven, CT, 1999), pp. 74–75.
2. Ibid., p. 75.
3. Stephen F. Austin to William M. O'Hara, March 10, 1819, Barker, *Papers*, I, Part 1, p. 339.
4. Cantrell, *Austin*, p. 75, agrees that at this point the Austins did not regard their land speculations as in any way a conscious preparation for Texas.
5. Examination of Moses Austin, December 23, 1820, Barker, *Papers*, I, Part 1, pp. 370–71.
6. Application for Colonization Permit, December 26, 1820, Ibid., pp. 371–72.
7. Moses Austin to Baron de Bastrop, January 26, 1821, Ibid., p. 379.
8. Stephen Austin to his mother, January 20, 1821, Ibid., p. 373.

9. Moses Austin to James Austin, March 28, 1821, Ibid., p. 385.

10. Moses Austin to Stephen Austin, May 22, 1821, Ibid., p. 393.

11. Maria Austin to Stephen Austin, June 8, 1821, Ibid., pp. 394–95.

12. Joseph Hawkins to Maria Austin, June 27, 1821, Ibid., pp. 397–98; Stephen F. Austin to ____, July 1, 1821, p. 399.

13. Austin to Moses Austin, July 4, 1821, Ibid., p. 400.

14. Cantrell, *Austin*, pp. 92–98.

15. Austin to J. H. Bell, October 6, 1821, Barker, *Papers*, I, Part 1, p. 415.

16. Austin to Martinez, October 13, 1821, Ibid., pp. 419–20.

17. John Sibley to George Sibley, October 29, 1821, G. P. Whittington, ed., "Dr. John Sibley of Natchitoches, 1757–1837," *Louisiana Historical Quarterly*, X (October 1927), pp. 504–505.

18. Christopher Long, "Old Three Hundred," *Handbook of Texas*, IV, p. 1142.

19. Cantrell, *Austin*, pp. 107–108.

20. Timothy E. Anna, *Forging Mexico, 1821–1835* (Lincoln, NE, 1988), pp. 87–90.

21. Ibid., pp. 118–19.

22. Andrés Tijerina, "Under the Mexican Flag," *Tejano Journey*, pp. 37–39.

23. Arnoldo De León, *The Tejano Community, 1836–1900* (Albuquerque, NM, 1982), pp. 2–3.

24. Ibid., pp. 8–9.

25. Ibid., pp. 11–12.

26. Tijerina, "Under the Mexican Flag," pp. 39–41.

27. Austin to Edward Lovelace, November 22, 1822, Barker, *Papers*, I, Part 1, pp. 554–55.

28. Cantrell, *Austin*, pp. 142–46.

29. Ibid., pp. 151–53.

30. Anthony R. Clarke to Austin, February 3, 1824, Barker, *Papers*, I, Part 1, p. 739; P. T. Dimmitt to Austin, June 1824, pp. 832–33.

31. Barker, *Papers*, I, Part 1, p. 821.

32. Gaines to Austin, November 10, 1824, Ibid., p. 939.

33. Austin to Colonists, June 7, 1825, Ibid., Part 2, pp. 1124–25.

34. Austin to Benjamin Edwards, September 15, 1825, Ibid., pp. 1203–1205.

35. Austin to Williams and Thompson, December 14, 1826, Ibid., p. 1532.

36. Austin to B. J. Thompson, December 24, 1826, Ibid., pp. 1539–41.

37. Austin to Citizens of Victoria, January 1, 1827, Ibid., p. 1558.

38. Tijerina, "Under the Mexican Flag," p. 45.

39. Sibley to Austin, February 18, 1827, Barker, *Papers*, I, Part 2, p. 1604.

40. Austin to Samuel M. Williams, May 8, 1831, Eugene C. Barker, ed., *The Austin Papers* (Washington, 1928), II, p. 661.

41. Woodville, MS, *Republican*, September 23, 1826; New Orleans, *State Gazette*, October 2, 1826; Alexandria, LA, *Messenger*, July 28, 1826.

42. Benjamin Morris to Josiah Stoddard Johnston, November 24, 1827, Josiah Stoddard Johnston Papers, Historical Society of Pennsylvania, Philadelphia.

43. "Gone to Texas," or simply "GTT," is one of the perennial mainstays of Texas settlement lore. In fact, this author has yet to see a single instance of this in a contemporary document, but the prevalence of the story is such that even if it was a myth, people of the time widely believed it to be true.

44. Amos Parker, *A Trip to the West and Texas in 1834* (Concord, NH, 1836), pp. 185–86.
45. William Gray, *From Virginia to Texas, 1835: Diary of Col. Wm. F. Gray* (Houston, TX, 1909), p. 111.
46. Davis, *Three Roads*, p. 230.
47. Cantrell, *Austin*, pp. 192–94.
48. Harvey, *Liberators*, p. 462.
49. Cantrell, *Austin*, pp. 209–11.
50. Tijerina, "Under the Mexican Flag," p. 44.
51. Cantrell, *Austin*, pp. 220–21.
52. Anna, *Forging Mexico*, pp. 224–25.
53. Ibid., pp. 228–29; Cantrell, *Austin*, p. 219.
54. Alexis de Tocqueville, *Democracy in America* (New York, 1969), p. 409.
55. Cantrell, *Austin*, pp. 220–21.
56. Austin to Lucas Alamán, May 18, 1830, Barker, *Papers*, II, p. 384.

CHAPTER FOUR: "WHAT WILL BECOME OF TEXAS?"

1. Barker, *Papers*, II, p. 498.
2. Austin to James F. Perry, September 22, 1830, Ibid., p. 495.
3. Tijerina, "Under the Mexican Flag," p. 42.
4. Austin to Henry Austin, October 14, 1830, Barker, *Papers*, II, p. 511.
5. Austin to Militia, October 18, 1830, Ibid., pp. 515–16; Austin to *Ayuntamiento* of San Felipe, October 18, 1830, p. 516.
6. Austin to Mary Austin Holley, January 4, 1832, Ibid., p. 732.
7. Austin to Mary Austin Holley, December 29, 1831, Ibid., p. 730.
8. Austin to Bradburn, December 30, 1831, Ibid., p. 731.
9. S. Rhoads Fisher to Austin, February 1, 1832, Ibid., p. 745.
10. Austin to James F. Perry, February 10, 1832, Ibid., p. 748.
11. Austin to Williams, March 21, 1832, Ibid., pp. 758–59.
12. Benjamin Franklin Porter Reminiscences, Benjamin Franklin Porter Collection, Auburn University, Auburn, AL.
13. Davis, *Three Roads*, pp. 205–206.
14. Hiram M. Thompson File, Pension Claims, Texas State Library (TSL).
15. Ramón Músquiz to Antonio Elosua, June 19, 1832, Músquiz to José Maria Letona, June 18, 1832, Nacogdoches Archives, TSL.
16. Davis, *Three Roads*, pp. 265–67.
17. Francisco Medina to Elosua, June 22, 1832, Nacogdoches Archives, TSL.
18. Bradburn to Military Commander of Coahuila y Texas, June 1, 1832, Ibid.
19. Mier y Terán to Letona, May 21, 1832, General Land Office, Applications, Austin's Colony, Volume 53, 163, TSL.
20. Davis, *Three Roads*, pp. 270–71.
21. Ibid., p. 273.
22. Williams to Bartlett Sims, July 1, 1832, Gulick and Elliott, *Lamar Papers*, I, p. 131.
23. Archie McDonald, "Battle of Nacogdoches," *Handbook of Texas*, IV, p. 923; James Bowie to Austin, August 8, 1832, Barker, *Papers*, II, p. 833.

24. See Davis, *Three Roads*, for a thorough background on Bowie's life prior to 1832.
25. Bowie to Austin, August 8, 1832, Barker, *Papers*, II, p. 832.
26. Bailey to David Shelby, June 27, 1832, Nacogdoches Archives, TSL.
27. New Orleans, *Louisiana Advertiser*, July 26, 1832.
28. Ugartechea to Colonel Guerra, July 27, 1832, Expediente XI/481.3/801, Archivo Historico Militar Mexicano, Secretaria de la Defensa Nacional, Mexico City.
29. Austin to Thomas F. Leaming, July 23, 1831, Barker, *Papers*, II, p. 678.
30. Cantrell, *Austin*, p. 255.
31. Tijerina, *Under the Mexican Flag*, pp. 44–45.
32. Ralph W. Steen, "Convention of 1832," *Handbook of Texas*, II, pp. 296–97.
33. Austin to William H. Ashley, October 10, 1832, Barker, *Papers*, II, p. 873.
34. Austin to Músquiz, November 15, 1832, Ibid., p. 889; John A. Williams to Austin, December 18, 1832, p. 903.
35. Ibid., November 30, 1832, p. 896.
36. Austin to Samuel Williams, December 6, 1832, Ibid., pp. 897–99.
37. Walter Lord, *A Time to Stand* (New York, 1961), p. 63.
38. D. W. Anthony to Austin, December 26, 1832, Barker, *Papers*, II , p. 910.
39. John A. Williams to Austin, December 18, 1832, Ibid., p. 903.
40. Sam Houston to Andrew Jackson, February 13, 1833, Eugene C. Barker and Amelia W. Williams, eds., *The Writings of Sam Houston, 1813–1863* (Austin, TX, 1938–1943), I, pp. 274–76.
41. Notes of Speech of General Houston to Convention at San Felipe, April 1833, Washington Miller Papers, TSL.
42. Address of Central Committee to the Convention, Barker, *Papers*, II, pp. 934–40.
43. Austin to Nathaniel Cox, April 2, 1833, Ibid., p. 941.
44. S. S. McKay, "Constitution Proposed in 1833," *Handbook of Texas*, II, p. 291.
45. Resolutions Against African Slave Trade, April 4, 1833, Barker, *Papers*, II, pp. 941–42.
46. Austin to Henry Austin, April 19, 1833, Ibid., p. 953.
47. Benjamin Lundy, *The War in Texas* (Philadelphia, 1837), p. 20.
48. Austin to Henry Austin, April 19, 1833, Barker, *Papers*, II, p. 953.
49. Davis, *Three Roads*, pp. 354–55.
50. Austin to Williams, May 31, 1833, Barker, *Papers*, II, p. 984.
51. Austin to Williams, May 9, 1833, Ibid., p. 966.
52. Austin to Luke Lesassier, May 6, 1833, Ibid., p. 962.
53. Austin to Wily Martin, May 30, 1833, Ibid., pp. 977–78.

CHAPTER FIVE: "CONFUSION DOUBLY CONFOUNDED"

1. Christon I. Archer, "Fashioning a New Nation," Michael C. Meyer and William H. Beezley, eds., *The Oxford History of Mexico* (New York, 2000), pp. 316–21.
2. Ibid., p. 328.
3. There is no good biography of Santa Anna available in English translation. Probably the best biography to date is Rafael F. Munoz, *Santa Anna: El Dictador Resplandeciente* (Mexico City, 1984).

4. Anna, *Forging Mexico*, pp. 257–58.
5. Archer, "Fashioning a New Nation," p. 330.
6. Anna, *Forging Mexico*, pp. 258–59.
7. Austin to Perry, October 2, 1833, Barker, *Papers*, II, p. 1007.
8. Cantrell, *Austin*, p. 272.
9. Austin to *Ayuntamiento* of Béxar, October 2, 1833, Barker, *Papers*, II, pp. 1007–1008; Cantrell, *Austin*, pp. 269–71.
10. Austin to Perry, October 23, 1833, Barker, *Papers*, II, p. 1008.
11. Ibid., p. 1008, Austin to Williams, November 5, 1833, p. 1014.
12. Austin to Williams, November 5, 1833, Ibid., pp. 1014–1015, November 26, 1833, p. 1016.
13. Cantrell, *Austin*, p. 274.
14. Austin to Williams, January 12, 1834, Barker, *Papers*, II, p. 1024.
15. Cantrell, *Austin*, pp. 277–78.
16. Austin to Perry, August 25, 1834, Barker, *Papers*, II, p. 1075.
17. Austin to Peter and Joseph Powell, January 18, 1834, Ibid., pp. 1043–44.
18. Robert E. Davis, ed., *The Diary of William Barret Travis August 30, 1833–June 26, 1834* (Waco, TX, 1966), January 13, 1834, p. 106.
19. Williamson address to the *Ayuntamiento*, and Memorial to General Congress of Mexico, April 28, 1834, Béxar Archives, Center of American History, University of Texas, Austin (CAHUT).
20. Austin to Perry, August 25, 1834, Barker, *Papers*, II, p. 1075.
21. Lemus to Juan Seguín, August 31, 1834, Jesús de la Teja, ed., *A Revolution Remembered: The Memoirs and Selected Correspondence of Juan N. Seguín* (Austin, TX, 1991), p. 129.
22. Davis, *Three Roads*, p. 372.
23. Teja, *Seguín*, p. 75.
24. David J. Weber, *The Taos Trappers: The Fur Trade in the Far Southwest, 1540–1846* (Norman, OK, 1971), pp. 221–22.
25. Tijerina, "Under the Mexican Flag," pp. 42–43.
26. Travis to David G. Burnet, September 12, 1834, Signature House Auction Catalog, October 20, 2001, item 24, p. 9.
27. Austin to Perry, August 25, 1834, Barker, *Papers*, II, pp. 1076–77, 1084–85.
28. Cós to Seguín, October 22, 1834, Teja, *Seguín*, p. 133. Spanish orthography would suggest that the Cós's name ought to be written without the accent, but since he signed his name with the accent, it is used here.
29. Travis to Smith, October 11, 1834, John Henry Brown, *Life and Times of Henry Smith* (Dallas, TX, 1887), pp. 27–28.
30. Cantrell, *Austin*, p. 291.
31. Austin to Jones, May 30, 1834, Barker, *Papers*, II, p. 1059.
32. Travis to Smith, October 25, 1834, Thomas W. Streeter Collection of Texas Manuscripts, Beinecke Rare Book and Manuscript Library, Yale University, New Haven, CT.
33. Travis to Smith, November 1, 1834, Brown, *Smith*, pp. 50–51.
34. Frank W. Johnson, *History of Texas and Texans* (Chicago, 1914), I, pp. 181–82.
35. Travis to Burnet, February 6, 1835, Alexander Autographs Catalog, April 29, 2000, item 126, p. 39.
36. Jodella K. Dyreson, "War Party," *Handbook of Texas*, VI, pp. 826–27.

37. Jodella K. Dyreson, "Peace Party," Ibid., V, p. 104.
38. Travis to Smith, November 1, 1834, Brown, *Smith*, pp. 50–51.
39. Davis, *Three Roads*, pp. 376–77.
40. Travis to Smith, November 13, 1834, Brown, *Smith*, pp. 56–57.
41. Cantrell, *Austin*, pp. 294–96.
42. Travis to Burnet, February 6, 1835, Alexander Autographs Auction Catalog, April 29, 2000, item 126, p. 39.
43. Anna, *Forging Mexico*, pp, 259–61.
44. Spencer Jack, Notes Concerning Trip to Mexico in 1834, etc., Lamar Papers, TSL.
45. J. H. Money to *Ayuntamiento*, June 26, 1835, Nacogdoches Archives, TSL.
46. Austin to Williams, April 15, 1834, Eugene C. Barker, *The Austin Papers* (Austin, TX, 1927), III, p. 63.

CHAPTER SIX: "WE SHALL GIVE THEM HELL IF THEY COME HERE"

1. Brazoria, *Texas Republican*, July 27, 1835.
2. James Kerr to Thomas Chambers, July 5, 1835, Béxar Archives, Center for American History, University of Texas, Austin (CAHUT).
3. Robert Wilson to Travis, May 13, 1835, Benjamin C. Franklin Papers, CAHUT.
4. Travis to Burnet, May 21, 1835, *Philpott Texana Auction Collection Catalog* (Dallas, TX, 1995), item #216.
5. Travis to Smith, June 9, 1835, Gulick and Elliott, *Lamar Papers*, I, p. 204.
6. Agreement, June 22, 1835, Lamar Papers, TSL.
7. Travis to Smith, July 6, 1835, Brown, *Smith*, pp. 59–61; Travis to the Public, September 1, 1835, [William Harris] Account of the ejection of Tenorio, 1835, anonymous account of Anahuac, June–July 1835, Lamar Papers, TSL; Tenorio to Ugartechea, July 1835, Eugene C. Barker, ed., "William Barret Travis, The Hero of the Alamo," *Publications of the Southern History Association*, VI (September 1902), pp. 416–17.
8. Travis to Smith, July 6, 1835, Brown, *Smith*, pp. 60–61.
9. James H. C. Miller to John W. Smith, July 26, 1835, Domestic Correspondence, Record Group 307, TSL; Thomas Thompson proclamation, July 26, 1835, Brown, *Smith*, p. 63.
10. Miller to Smith, July 26, 1835, Domestic Correspondence, Record Group 307, TSL.
11. Dyreson, "War Party," *Handbook of Texas*, VI, p. 826; Anson Jones, *Memoranda and Official Correspondence Relating to the Republic of Texas, Its History and Annexation* (New York, 1859), p. 1012.
12. Travis to Bowie, July 30, 1835, Henderson Yoakum, *History of Texas from Its First Settlement in 1685 to Its Annexation to the United States in 1846* (New York, 1856), I, p. 343.
13. Jones, *Memoranda*, p. 1012.
14. Pedro Ellis Bean to Ugartechea, August 11, 1835, Nacogdoches Archives, TSL.
15. Brazoria, *Texas Republican*, June 27, 1835; John Forbes to James B. Miller, July 24, 1835, Domestic Correspondence, Record Group 307, TSL.

16. Travis to Bowie, July 30, 1835, Yoakum, *History*, I, p. 343.
17. Travis to Smith, July 6, 1835, Matagorda, *Bulletin*, October 11, 1837.
18. Travis to Ugartechea, July 31, 1835, Barker, *Papers*, III, p. 95.
19. Cós to Political Chief in Department of Brazos, August 1, 1835, Cós to Ugartechea, August 1, 1835, Béxar Archives, CAHUT.
20. Moseley Baker to Houston, October 1844, Stephen F. Austin Papers, CAHUT.
21. James E. Winston, "New Orleans and the Texas Revolution," *Louisiana Historical Quarterly*, X (July 1927), p. 323.
22. Austin to Mary Austin Holley, August 21, 1835, Barker, *Papers*, III, pp. 101–103.
23. Cantrell, *Austin*, p. 308.
24. Brown, *Smith*, pp. 71–72.
25. Travis to J. W. Moore, August 31, 1835, Houston, *Morning Star*, March 14, 1840; Travis to Smith, August 24, 1835, Brown, *Smith*, pp. 72–73; Travis to Burnet, August 31, 1835, John H. Jenkins, ed., *The Papers of the Texas Revolution, 1835–1836* (Austin, TX, 1973), I, p. 379 *(PTR)*; Travis to Smith, September 1, 1835, Lamar Papers, TSL.
26. Austin to the People of Texas, September 8, 1835, Barker, *Papers*, III, pp. 116–19.
27. Davis, *Three Roads*, p. 459.
28. Circular, September 18, 1835, *PTR*, I, p. 456.
29. Austin to P. W. Grayson, September 19, 1835, Ibid., I, pp. 464–65.
30. Zavala to Austin, September 17, 1835, Ibid., I, pp. 454–55.
31. Austin to Committee, September 21, 1835, Ibid., I, p. 471.
32. Travis to Austin, September 22, 1835, Barker, *Papers*, III, pp. 133–35.
33. Eli Mercer to Austin, September 23, 1835, *PTR*, I, p. 485.
34. Austin to Perry, September 30, 1835, Ibid., I, p. 505.
35. Fannin to David Mills, September 18, 1835, Ibid., I, p. 457.
36. Austin to Hall, September 19, 1835, Ibid., I, pp. 465–66; Austin to Committee, September 21, 1835, p. 470.
37. Columbia Committee of Safety Resolutions, September 22, 1835, Ibid., I, p. 478.
38. Thorn et al., Pledges, September 21, 1835, Ibid., I, p. 476.
39. Forbes et al. to Andrew Jackson, September 11, 1835, Ibid., I, pp. 436–37.
40. G. W. Davis to Committee, September 25, 1835, Ibid., I, p. 487, E. Bailey Statement, September 26, 1835, p. 492.
41. Ponton to Political Chief, September 26, 1835, Ibid., I, p. 493.
42. G. W. Davis to Committee, September 25, 1835, Ibid., I, p. 487; E. Bailey Statement, September 26, 1835, p. 492.
43. Navarro to *Alcalde*, September 27, 1835, Ugartechea to *Alcalde*, September 27, 1835, Ugartechea to Castañeda, September 27, 1835, Ibid., I, p. 495.
44. Austin to Public, September 29, 1835, Ibid., I, pp. 500–501.
45. Austin to Hall, September 29, 1835, Ibid., I, p. 501.
46. Dimmitt to Austin, September 29, 1835, Ibid., I, p. 502; Dimmitt to ?, September 29, 1835, pp. 502–503.
47. Thomas Saul to Committee of Safety, September 29, 1835, Ibid., I, pp. 503–504; Saul to Asa Hoxey, September 29, 1835, p. 504.
48. Joseph D. Clements to Francisco Castañeda, September 30, 1835, Ibid., I, pp. 506–507; Castañeda to Ugartechea, September 30, 1835, p. 506.

49. Coleman to James B. Miller, September 30, 1835, Ibid., I, p. 507.
50. Albert Martin et al. to the Public, September 30, 1835, Ibid., I, p. 509.
51. Johnson, *Texas and Texans*, I, p. 270.
52. William Fisher to Austin, October 3, 1835, *PTR*, II, p. 25.
53. C. Newell, *History of the Revolution in Texas* (New York, 1838), pp. 53–54.
54. Jane Bradfield, *Rx Take One Cannon* (Shiner, TX, 1981), p. 17.
55. David Macomb to ?, October 5, 1835, *PTR*, II, pp. 47–50; Stephen L. Hardin, *Texian Iliad: A Military History of the Texas Revolution* (Austin, TX, 1994), pp. 12–13. Hardin's outstanding book is the best account of the military side of the Revolution and has been relied on heavily when original sources have not been used in this study.
56. Austin to ?, October 5, 1835, *PTR*, II, p. 43.
57. Noah Smithwick, *The Evolution of a State; or, Recollections of Old Texas Days* (Austin, TX, 1983), p. 71.
58. Travis to J. Randal Jones, October 3, 1835, William Barret Travis Papers, CAHUT.
59. Proclamation, October 3, 1835, *PTR*, II, p. 25.
60. Volunteers to Public, October 5, 1836, Ibid., II, p. 56.
61. William Wharton to the Public, October 3, 1835, Ibid., II, pp. 30–31.
62. Austin to Committee, October 4, 1835, Ibid., II, pp. 31–32.
63. Ibid.
64. J. H. Bell to Austin, October 6, 1835, Ibid., II, p. 57.
65. Austin to Burnet, October 5, 1835, Ibid., II, p. 42.
66. Austin to ?, October 5, 1835, Ibid., II, p. 43.
67. Edward Gritten to *Alcalde* of Gonzales, October 4, 1835, Ibid., II, p. 38.
68. Ugartechea to Austin, October 4, 1835, Ibid., II, pp. 39–41.
69. Moore to Hall, October 6, 1835, Ibid., II, p. 60.
70. P. W. Grayson to Austin, October 11, 1835, Ibid., II, p. 94.
71. Austin, Order No. 1, October 11, 1835, Ibid., II, p. 92.

CHAPTER SEVEN: "SMOKE FORCED INTO A BEE HIVE"

1. Austin General Order No. 2, October 11, 1835, *PTR*, II, p. 93.
2. David McComb to Benjamin Smith, October 11, 1835, Ibid., II, p. 98; Austin to Committee of Vigilance, October 11, 1835, p. 91.
3. Houston to Isaac Parker, October 5, 1835, Ibid., II, pp. 46–47.
4. Houston Orders, October 8, 1835, Ibid., II, pp. 68–69.
5. Austin General Order No. 1, October 11, 1835, Ibid., II, pp. 92–93.
6. McComb to Smith, October 11, 1835, Ibid., II, p. 98; Austin to Committee, October 12, 1835, pp. 101–102.
7. Collinsworth et al. Agreement, October 9, 1835, Ibid., II, pp. 76–77.
8. Craig H. Roell, *Remember Goliad* (Austin, TX, 1994), pp. 38–39; Ira Ingram to Committee of Safety, October 11, 1835, *PTR*, II, pp. 95–96; Hardin, *Iliad*, p. 17.
9. Collinsworth to Margaret C. Linn, October 10, 1835, *PTR*, II, pp. 84–85.
10. James Kerr to ?, October 11, 1835, Ibid., II, p. 97; Benjamin Smith to Austin, October 13, 1835, p. 123; Thomas McKinney and John Williams to R. R. Royall, October 26, 1835, p. 223; George Huff to Council, October 28, 1835, pp. 248–49; Royall to Austin, October 29, 1835, pp. 265–66.
11. Royall to Collinsworth, October 11, 1835, Ibid., II, p. 99.

12. Austin to Benjamin Smith et al., October 12, 1835, Ibid., II, pp. 102–103; Austin to Committee, October 13, 1835, p. 108.
13. General Order, October 14, 1835, Ibid., II, pp. 123–24.
14. Austin General Orders, October 13, 1835, Ibid., II, p. 109.
15. Jack to Austin, October 13, 1835, Ibid., II, pp. 114–15.
16. Benjamin Smith to Austin, October 13, 1835, Ibid., II, p. 121.
17. Hall to Milam, October 14, 1835, Ibid., II, pp. 127–28.
18. Austin to Committee, October 16, 1835, Ibid., II, pp. 138–39.
19. Austin Council of War, October 18 [16], 1835, Ibid., II, p. 151.
20. Austin to Cós, October 17, 1835, Ibid., II, pp. 142–43.
21. Cós to Austin, October 18, 1835, Ibid., II, pp. 153–54.
22. Cós to Troops, October 13, 1835, Ibid., II, pp. 111–12.
23. Davis, *Three Roads*, p. 433.
24. Bowie and Fannin to Austin, October 22, 1835, Stephen F. Austin Papers, CAHUT.
25. Bowie and Fannin to Austin, October 23, 1835, Barker, *Papers*, III, pp. 146–47.
26. Bowie and Fannin to Austin, October 24, 1835, Ibid., pp. 206–207.
27. Austin to Consultation, October 10, 1835, *PTR*, II, pp. 81–82.
28. Austin to Benjamin Smith et al., October 12, 1835, Ibid., II, p. 103.
29. George Huff and Spencer Jack to Council, October 28, 1835, Ibid., II, p. 248.
30. Ibid.
31. Ibid.
32. Moseley Baker to Houston, 1844, Moseley Baker Papers, CAHUT; San Antonio, *Daily Express*, December 8, 1935.
33. Thomas Cutrer, "William Houston Jack," *Handbook of Texas*, III, p. 889.
34. Moses A. Bryan to Perry, October 26, 1835, *PTR*, II, p. 222.
35. James L. Haley, *Sam Houston* (Norman, OK, 2002), p. 114, suggests that the army at this time did not actually trust Austin, though he fails to offer any support for this statement, one that the vote of Austin's army shows to be erroneous. Haley also dismisses as an "outrageous lie" the Moseley Baker source describing the adverse reaction in the army to Houston's remarks, but ignores several other contemporaneous sources that support Baker's account in most respects.
36. Austin to Council, October 26, 1835, *PTR*, II, p. 220.
37. Austin to Council, October 25, 1835, Ibid., II, pp. 215–16.
38. Austin to Bowie, October 27, 1835, Ibid., II, p. 230.
39. Austin to Convention, October 28, 1835, Ibid., II, pp. 242–43; Report of Bowie and Fannin, October 30, 1835, Adjutant General's Office, Army Papers, Record Group 401, TSL.
40. Austin, Account of the Campaign of 1835, Austin Papers, CAHUT.
41. Bowie to Cós, October 31, 1835, *PTR*, II, p. 273; Cós to José Tornel, November 2, 1835, pp. 298–99.
42. Austin to Bowie and Fannin, November 1, 1835, Ibid., II, p. 287.
43. Austin Council of War, November 2, 1835, Ibid., II, pp. 296–97.
44. Fannin to Austin, November 2, 1835, Ibid., II, p. 301.
45. Columbia Meeting Committee of Safety Resolutions, September 22, 1835, Ibid., I, pp. 478–79.
46. Travis to Smith, September 18, 1835, Ibid., I, p. 460.

47. Matagorda Meeting, September 26, 1835, Ibid., I, pp. 489–90.
48. Rusk and Houston to Bowl, et al., September 24, 1835, Ibid., I, p. 486.
49. Eli Mercer to Austin, September 23, 1835, Ibid., I, p. 485.
50. Zavala to Austin, September 17, 1835, Ibid., I, pp. 453–54.
51. Philip A. Sublett et al. to Committee of Vigilance at San Felipe, September 22, 1835, Ibid., I, p. 480.
52. Paul D. Lack, *The Texas Revolutionary Experience: A Political and Social History 1835–1836* (College Station, TX, 1992), p. 42.
53. Royall to Austin, October 14, 1815, *PTR*, II, p. 130.
54. Royall to Committee, October 13, 1835, Ibid., II, p. 119; Royall to Austin, October 14, 1835, p. 130.
55. *Journals of the Consultation Held at San Felipe de Austin, October 16, 1835* (Houston, TX, 1838), *PTR*, IX, pp. 246–50.
56. Ibid., pp. 250–52.
57. Ibid., pp. 252–56.
58. Ibid., pp. 257–58.
59. Declaration of the People of Texas, November 7, 1835, *PTR*, II, pp. 346–47; IX, pp. 260–61; Spanish version in R. M. Smythe Catalog Sale #181, item 316.
60. *Journals of the Consultation*, *PTR*, IX, pp. 264–66.
61. Lack, *Revolutionary Experience*, pp. 49–50.
62. Ibid., pp. 47–48.
63. Ibid., p. 50; *Journals of the Consultation*, *PTR*, IX, pp. 266–68.
64. *Journals of the Consultation*, *PTR*, IX, pp. 276–81.
65. Austin to Provisional Government, December 14, 1835, Barker, *Papers*, III, pp. 282–83.
66. Ibid., pp. 281–82.
67. Austin to President of the Consultation, November 8, 1835, Ibid., III, p. 247.
68. *Journals of the Consultation*, *PTR*, IX, pp. 271–72.
69. Ibid., pp. 283–85.
70. Baker to Houston, 1844, Baker Papers, CAHUT. Haley, *Houston*, pp. 114, 440–41 n, contemptuously—and unpersuasively—rejects the Baker account of Houston's drinking, as he tends to reject most claims of such intemperance, by instead condemning the authors and their motives. Baker's 1844 account does contain some gross misstatements, but it also contains much that is verifiable, and this, combined with the number of other references to Houston's occasional bouts with alcohol in this period, lends it probable credence on this point.
71. Jones, *Memoranda*, pp. 12–13; George M. Patrick to Moses A. Bryan, August 8, 1878, Texas Veterans Association Papers, CAHUT. Haley, *Houston*, pp. 117, 441 n, dismisses the Jones account of Houston's behavior at San Felipe just as he does Baker's account of the drunken episode with the army, and on equally unconvincing bases. Condemning Jones for bigotry toward Houston, he cites Cantrell, *Austin*, pp. 325–26, as support for the contention that Jones is unreliable on this episode. But Cantrell says nothing whatever about the Jones account being unreliable in this regard, and rather addresses stories that Houston intentionally sought to undermine Austin's command or engineer a battlefield defeat in order to discredit Austin, accusations that appear nowhere in the Jones account.
72. Jones, *Memoranda*, pp. 12–13.

CHAPTER EIGHT: DARK SCHEMES

1. Address of R. M. Williamson, June 22, 1835, *PTR*, I, p. 199; Milam to Johnson, July 5, 1835, Barker, *Papers*, III, pp. 82–83.

2. Randolph B. Campbell, *An Empire for Slavery, The Peculiar Institution in Texas 1821–1865* (Baton Rouge, LA, 1989), p. 42.

3. Ibid., p. 41.

4. White to Austin, October 17, 1835, *PTR*, II, pp. 149–50.

5. B. J. White to Austin, October 17, 1835, Ibid., II, p. 149; Dimmitt to Austin, October 19, 1835, pp. 165–66; October 20, 1835, pp. 172–73; October 21, 1835, p. 177.

6. Dimmitt to Austin, October 30, 1835, Ibid., II, pp. 267–68.

7. Sion R. Bostwick, "Reminiscences of Sion R. Bostwick," *Quarterly of the Texas State Historical Association*, V (October 1901), p. 88; Herman Ehrenberg, *With Milam and Fannin: Adventures of a German Boy in Texas' Revolution* (Dallas, TX, 1935), pp. 49–50.

8. Ehrenberg, *With Milam and Fannin*, pp. 43–48.

9. Moses A. Bryan, Recollections of Stephen F. Austin, September 25, 1889, Moses A. Bryan Papers, Center for American History, University of Texas, Austin (CAHUT).

10. Rusk to Bowie, November 5, 1835, *PTR*, II, pp. 333–34, Robert B. Irvine to Houston, November 7, 1835, pp. 349–50.

11. Election return, November 24 [actually November 6], 1835, Ibid., II, p. 496.

12. Bryan to Perry, November 7, 1835, Ibid., III, p. 345.

13. George Patrick to Bryan, August 8, 1878, Texas Veterans Association Papers, CAHUT.

14. Austin to Perry, November 22, 1835, *PTR*, II, p. 487.

15. Thomas Rusk, An Account of the Grass Fight, n.d., Thomas Rusk Papers, Center for American History, University of Texas, Austin (CAHUT); Edward Burleson to Provisional Government, November 27, 1835, *PTR*, III, pp. 5–6; William Jack to Burleson, November 27, 1835, pp. 7–8.

16. James Patrick and William Pettus to Provisional Government, November 30, 1835, *PTR*, III, pp. 49–50; Hardin, *Iliad*, p. 67.

17. Rita Maverick Green, ed., *Samuel Maverick, Texan, 1803–1870* (San Antonio, TX, 1952), p. 44.

18. Johnson, *Texas and Texans*, I, p. 352.

19. Hardin, *Iliad*, p. 78.

20. Alwyn Barr, *Texans in Revolt: The Battle for San Antonio, 1835* (Austin, TX, 1990), p. 44.

21. This account of the fighting in San Antonio is based, unless otherwise cited, on Hardin, *Iliad*, pp. 79ff, and Barr, *Texans in Revolt*, pp. 46ff.

22. Circular, December 9, 1835, R. M. Smythe Catalog Sale #175, item 398.

23. Burleson and Milam to Provisional Government, December 6, 1835, *PTR*, III, pp. 98–99.

24. Circular, December 9, 1835, R. M. Smythe Catalog Sale # 175, item 398.

25. Gray, *Diary*, pp. 111–12.

26. Henry Smith, "Reminiscences of Henry Smith," *Quarterly of the Texas State Historical Association*, XIV (July 1910), p. 50.

27. Davis, *Three Roads*, p. 488.
28. Robinson to Rusk, December 19, 1835, Rusk Papers, CAHUT; Brown, *Smith*, pp. 214–15; Stuart Reid, "'Go in and die with the boys,' Colonel James Grant and the Texan Revolution," essay furnished by Stuart Reid, Tyne & Wear, United Kingdom.
29. Dimmitt to Smith, December 2, 1835, *PTR*, III, pp. 77–78.
30. Reid, "'Go in and die.'"
31. Smith to Houston, December 17, 1835, *PTR*, III, p. 239.
32. Houston to Bowie, December 17, 1835, Ibid., III, pp. 222–23.
33. Johnson to Robinson, December 25, 1835, Ibid., III, pp. 325–27; Johnson to Wyatt Hanks and J. D. Clements, December 23, 1835, pp. 306–307.
34. Johnson to Robinson, December 25, 1835, Ibid., III, pp. 325–26; Johnson to Smith, December 17, 1835, p. 227, December 18, 1835, p. 244.
35. Robinson to Council, January 14, 1836, Ibid., IV, pp. 17ff; Robinson to Rusk, January 15, 1836, pp. 34–35.
36. Davis, *Three Roads*, p. 510.
37. Bowie to Houston, January 10, 1836, in Caiphas Ham, Recollections, Center for American History, University of Texas, Austin (CAHUT).
38. Haley, *Houston*, pp. 119–20.
39. Jones, *Memoranda*, pp. 13–15.
40. Address of San Augustine, December 22, 1835, *PTR*, III, pp. 287ff.
41. Goliad Declaration, December 22, 1835, Ibid., III, pp. 265–68.
42. Johnson to Robinson, December 25, 1835, Ibid., III, p. 327.
43. Cooke Account, n.d., #2169, Lamar Papers, TSL.
44. Houston to Smith, January 17, 1835, *PTR*, IV, pp. 46–47.
45. Houston to Don Carlos Barrett, January 2, 1836, Williams and Barker, *Writings*, I, p. 330.
46. Reid, "'Go in and die.'"

CHAPTER NINE: "VICTORY OR DEATH"

1. José Enrique de la Peña, *With Santa Anna in Texas, A Personal Narrative of the Revolution*, ed. Carmen Perry (College Station, TX, 1975), pp. 3–5.
2. Ibid., p. 6.
3. Ibid., pp. 4–8.
4. Anna, *Forging Mexico*, pp. 261–62.
5. Richard G. Santos, *Santa Anna's Campaign Against Texas 1835–1836* (Waco, TX, 1968), pp. 1–2.
6. Santa Anna to Ramírez y Sesma, December 7, 1835, Santos, *Santa Anna's Campaign*, p. 9.
7. Peña, *With Santa Anna*, pp. 22–23.
8. Ordinance & Decree, November 25, 1835, R. M. Smythe Catalog Sale #175, item 397.
9. Santa Anna to Ramírez y Sesma, December 7, 1835, Santos, *Santa Anna's Campaign*, p. 11.
10. Ibid., pp. 14–17.
11. Texian loan Certificate 296, January 11, 1836, R. M. Smythe Catalog Sale #176, June 4, 1998, item 44; Texian loan certificate 407, January 11, 1836, R. M. Smythe Catalog Sale #186, Part 2, April 22, 1999, item 494.

12. J. W. Fannin to J. W. E. Wallace, December 28, 1835, R. M. Smythe Catalog Sale #175, item 389.

13. Bowie to Smith, February 2, 1836, Army Papers, Record Group 401, TSL.

14. D. H. Vail to Edward Teal, February 22, 1837, R. M. Smythe Catalog Sale #175, item 385.

15. Robert D. Bass, ed., "Autobiography of William J. Grayson," Ph.D. dissertation, University of South Carolina, 1933, p. 206.

16. Galveston, *Daily News*, January 27, 1895.

17. David Crockett to Paris A. Gorman et al., September 30, 1835, R. M. Smythe Catalog Sale #175, February 26, 1998, item 380.

18. David Crockett to Wiley and Margaret Flowers, January 9, 1836 (copy), Samuel Asbury Papers, CAHUT.

19. See Davis, *Three Roads*, chapters 19, 20, and 21, for an extended discussion of Travis and Bowie and their relations, as well as for a general account of the siege of the Alamo.

20. Peña, *With Santa Anna*, p. 15.

21. Ibid., pp. 17–18.

22. Santos, *Santa Anna's Campaign*, pp. 50–52.

23. Seguín, *Revolution Remembered*, pp. 75–77.

24. Ibid., pp. 78–79.

25. Stephen L. Hardin, "Efficient in the Cause," in Poyo, ed., *Tejano Journey*, p. 56–57.

26. William Barret Travis Affidavit, February 22, 1836, Antonio Cruz File, Audited Military Claims, Comptroller of Public Accounts, Texas State Library, Austin (TSL).

27. Lack, *Revolutionary Experience*, p. 167.

28. Ibid., pp. 167–69.

29. Travis to President of the Convention, March 3, 1836, *PTR*, IV, p. 504.

30. Timothy M. Matovina, *The Alamo Remembered: Tejano Accounts and Perspectives* (Austin, TX, 1995), pp. 81–82.

31. Seguín, *Revolution Remembered*, p. 79.

32. Travis and Bowie to Fannin, February 23, 1836, *PTR*, IV, p. 419; Travis to Andrew Ponton, February 23, 1836, p. 420; Travis to the Public, February 24, 1836, p. 423.

33. Travis to Houston, February 25, 1836, Ibid., IV, p. 434.

34. Travis to the Convention, March 3, 1836, Ibid., IV, pp. 502–504; Travis to Grymes [sic], March 3, 1836, pp. 504–505.

35. Travis to David Ayres, March 3, 1836, Ibid., IV, p. 501.

36. Peña, *With Santa Anna*, p. 44.

37. The account that follows of the battle is based primarily on Davis, *Three Roads*, chapter 21. To date, the best account is Lord, *Time to Stand*.

38. Peña, *With Santa Anna*, p. 47.

39. There are several variant stories of Crockett's supposed surrender and execution, of which that given in Peña, *With Santa Anna*, p. 53, is neither the earliest nor the most controversial, though the focus of debate on the subject has been chiefly directed at Peña. For an examination of the problems with all such accounts, their derivative nature from each other, and the problems of assessing validity—if any—see William C. Davis, "How Davy Probably Didn't Die," *Journal of the Alamo Battlefield Association*, II (fall 1997), pp. 11ff. For a

summary of the assault on Peña's veracity, see William Groneman, *Defense of a Legend* (Plano, TX, 1994).

40. Joaquin Ramírez y Sesma Report, March 11, 1836, Expediente XI/481.3/1149, Archivo Historico Mexicano Militar, Secretaria de la Defense Nacional, Mexico City.

41. *PTR*, VII, p. 98.

42. Mariano Arroyo Report, August 1, 1836, Expediente XI/481.3/1151, Archivo Historico Militar Mexicano, Secretaria de la Defense Nacional, Mexico City; Santa Anna Report, March 6, 1836, Antonio López de Santa Anna Collection, Center for American History, University of Texas, Austin (CAHUT).

43. Santos, *Santa Anna's Campaign*, p. 86.

CHAPTER TEN: ATMOSPHERE DEVILISH DARK

1. Eyewitnesses do attribute last *known* words to Travis and Dickinson, but they may or may not be accurately reported, and in any case are not necessarily the last things the men said before their deaths.

2. Houston to Smith, January 30, 1836, *PTR*, IV, pp. 187–96.

3. Houston to Henry Raguet, February 24, 1836, R. M. Smythe Catalog Sale #175, item 381.

4. Houston to John Quitman, February 12, 1836, *PTR*, IV, p. 306; Houston and John Forbes to Smith, February 29, 1836, pp. 461–62.

5. Proclamation, February 12, 1836, Ibid., IV, pp. 307–14; Alexander Thomson and J. D. Clements to Smith, February 12, 1836, pp. 314–17.

6. Gray, *Virginia to Texas*, p. 120.

7. Fannin to Joseph Mims, February 28, 1836, William W. Fontaine Collection, Center for American History, University of Texas, Austin (CAHUT).

8. Mary Austin Holley, Notes, Mary Austin Holley Papers, CAHUT.

9. W. W. Thompson Affidavit, December 1, 1840, Home Papers, Box 2-9/6, Texas State Library, Austin (TSL); Thomas Ricks Lindley, "Drawing Truthful Conclusions," *Journal of the Alamo Battlefield Association*, I (September 1995), pp. 31–33. Haley, *Houston*, p. 123, is contemptuously dismissive of the Thompson account but fails to provide any convincing reason to doubt its veracity.

10. Milledge L. Bonham, Memorandum, Milledge L. Bonham Papers, South Caroliniana Library, University of South Carolina, Columbia.

11. Davis, *Three Roads*, p. 548.

12. Pay voucher, February 27, 1836, John H. Jenkins, *The Texas Revolution and Republic* (Austin, TX, 1986), item 134.

13. *The General Convention at Washington, March 1–17 1836* (Houston, 1838), *PTR*, IX, pp. 289–91.

14. Ibid., pp. 293–304.

15. Travis to People of Texas, February 24, 1836, Ibid., IV, p. 423.

16. Houston to the Public, March 2, 1836, Ibid., IV, pp. 490–91.

17. *General Convention*, Ibid., IX, pp. 305, 309–10; Lack, *Revolutionary Experience*, p. 87.

18. Houston to Collinsworth, March 7, 1836, *PTR*, V, p. 18.

19. *General Convention*, Ibid., IX, pp. 311–13.

20. Houston to Collinsworth, March 15, 1836, Ibid., V, pp. 82–83; Houston to the Senate of Texas, April 30, 1838, Williams and Barker, *Writings*, IV, p. 52; Lindley, "Truthful Conclusions," pp. 19–21, 25. Haley, *Houston*, exercises considerable flexibility with sources in his quest to absolve Houston of responsibility for his own actions when he passes along as fact Houston's post-Alamo claim that he "sent Jim Bowie with orders to the commander there to remove the artillery from the Alamo, *blow the fortress up and retire to Gonzales* [italics added] " (p. 119). Haley's citation for this assertion does not actually deal with Bowie and the Alamo, but rather discusses the Matamoros episode. The only contemporary source is Houston to Smith, January 17, 1836, *PTR*, IV, pp. 46–47, and in it Houston states: "I have ordered the fortifications in the town of Bexar to be demolished, and, *if you should think well of it, I will remove all the cannon and other munitions of war to Gonzales and Copano, blow up the Alamo and abandon the place* [italics added]." Houston's actual words gainsay everything Haley claims. He ordered Bowie to destroy the fortifications "in Béxar," that is, in the town, which the Texians were already in fact doing. He did not order the artillery removed to Gonzales or the Alamo blown up, but only offered those as suggestions to Smith "if you should think well of it."

    Haley repeatedly takes recent Texas scholars to task for being "revisionists" and "modernizers" when they are critical of Houston, but there can hardly be anything "revisionist" about getting facts straight and treating sources with respect.

21. Thompson Affidavit, December 1, 1840, Home Papers, Box 2-9/6, TSL; Houston to Collinsworth, March 7, 1836, *PTR*, V, p. 17; Houston to Burleson, March 9, 1836; Houston to Neill, March 9, 1836, p. 36; Houston to Fannin, March 11, 1836, p. 51. Haley, *Houston*, p. 123, acknowledges that Houston was not in a hurry to get to Gonzales, making the case that he had no need for haste in the circumstances, but then tries unsuccessfully to discredit the only source he cites that claims that Houston did dally. The Thompson affidavit, he says, was a politically motivated falsehood by an anti-Houston Texian. The fact that the affidavit was never made public—presumably its purpose if politically motivated—and that Thompson himself soon after making the affidavit signed a glowing public tribute to Houston are more than sufficient to compromise Haley's argument. I am indebted to Stephen L. Hardin for a 2002 essay in which this and other points noted below are made, along with their documentary support.

22. Houston to Collinsworth, March 13, 1835, *PTR*, V, p. 69. Houston does not actually say what date he sent the missing order to Fannin, but only says that he sent the order "from the Colorado." Since Houston's only other orders sent during his trip to Gonzales were also dated on the Colorado and on March 9, it seems safe to assume that the one to Fannin was sent the same day.

23. Houston to Rusk, March 23, 1836, *PTR*, V, p. 168.

24. Haley, *Houston*, p. 123, absolves Houston from accusations of sloth in getting to Gonzales by observing that there was no army there anyhow and thus no need for him to be there quickly. That is true, but surely misses the point. When Houston reached Gonzales was indeed immaterial. The problem is that he did not start to address taking control of the principal body of soldiers in near proximity to the Mexican army for at least two or three days after receiv-

ing his command. Haley also says that the March 9 order to Fannin ordered him to fall back to Gonzales. It did not. As Houston himself says, it instructed Fannin to move to "the west side of the Cibolo, with a view to relieve Bexar." That Houston's March 11 order was the first instruction sent to Fannin to evacuate Goliad is confirmed by another letter Houston wrote Fannin that same day, and enclosing his evacuation order. After giving Fannin detailed information on the news of the fall of the Alamo and its garrison, and of the known movements of Mexican forces into the interior, Houston concluded by saying "you are therefore referred to the enclosed order" (Houston to Fannin, March 11, 1836, *PTR*, V, p. 54). In short, the order to evacuate was contingent upon and a result of the information Houston had just imparted to Fannin about the Alamo, information he did not have on March 9 or at any time prior to his March 11 arrival in Gonzales.

25. Houston to Collinsworth, March 13, 1836, *PTR*, V, p. 69.
26. Houston to Fannin, March 11, 1836, Ibid., V, pp. 51–52.
27. This account of the Fannin-Goliad episode is drawn from Hardin, *Iliad*, pp. 166–74, Craig Roell, *Remember Goliad*, pp. 60–73, and Clarence Wharton, *Remember Goliad!* (Houston, TX, 1938), pp. 31–47.
28. Santa Anna to Urrea, March 23, 1836, *PTR*, V, pp. 175–76.
29. Henry Austin to Mary Austin Holley, March 29, 1836, Holley Papers, CAHUT.
30. Robinson to Fannin, March 6, 1836, *PTR*, V, p. 10.
31. *General Convention*, Ibid., IX, pp. 320–21.
32. *General Convention*, Ibid., IX, pp. 313–19, 324.
33. Ibid., IX, pp. 322–39; Lack, *Revolutionary Experience*, pp. 89–93.
34. Lack, *Revolutionary Experience*, p. 87.
35. *General Convention*, *PTR*, IX, pp. 343–44.
36. Ibid., IX, pp. 366–67.
37. Ibid., IX, pp. 519–20.
38. Lack, the *Handbook of Texas*, and other sources are silent on the actual date of the election of officers, and the journal of the Convention does not state when it took place, either. The executive resolution authorizing the election was dated March 16, and from that and a motion that same day unsuccessfully seeking to exclude any sitting member of the body from being chosen for executive office, it is clear that the election did not occur prior to that date. A letter addressed to Burnet as president dated March 16, 1836, also establishes that the election could not have taken place any later. *PTR*, IX, p. 367, Lamar to Burnet, March 16, 1836, V, p. 91.
39. Burnet Proclamations, March 18, 1836, *PTR*, V, pp. 125–27.
40. *General Convention*, Ibid., IX, pp. 367–68.
41. Houston to Collinsworth, March 13, 1836, Ibid., V, pp. 69–70; Houston to Henry Raguet, March 13, 1836, pp. 71–72; Houston Army Orders, March 14, 1836, p. 77.
42. Houston to Collinsworth, March 15, 1836, Ibid., V, pp. 82–83.
43. Seguín, *Revolution Remembered*, p. 108.
44. Brazoria Meeting, March 17, 1836, *PTR*, V, pp. 97–98.
45. Fannin to Robinson, February 7, 1836, Ibid., IV, p. 280.
46. Newell, *History*, pp. 92–93.
47. Gray, *Virginia to Texas*, p. 134.

48. Lack, *Revolutionary Experience,* pp. 224–25.
49. Brazoria Meeting, March 17, 1836, *PTR,* V, p. 99.
50. J. C. Duval, *Early Times in Texas* (Austin, TX, 1892), p. 79.
51. Ibid., pp. 83–86.
52. Houston Army Orders, March 21, 1836, *PTR,* V, p. 154.
53. Mrs. George Sutherland to her sister, June 5, 1836, Ibid., VII, pp. 24–25.
54. Quoted in Hardin, *Iliad,* pp. 163–64.
55. Houston to Rusk, March 23, 1836, *PTR,* V, p. 169.
56. Menard to ?, March 7, 1836, Ibid., V, p. 19.

CHAPTER ELEVEN: "DO YOU FEEL LIKE FIGHTING?"

1. Houston to Rusk, March 23, 1836, *PTR,* V, pp. 169–70.
2. Houston to Royall, March 24, 1836, Ibid., V, p. 180; Houston Army order, March 26, 1836, p. 200.
3. John R. Jones to S. A. Carson, March 25, 1836, Ibid., V, p. 193.
4. Hardin, *Iliad,* p. 183; Haley, *Houston,* pp. 130–31.
5. Houston to William Christy, March 29, 1836, *PTR,* V, p. 233.
6. Houston to Rusk, March 29, 136, Ibid., V, p. 234.
7. Hardin, *Iliad,* p. 186.
8. Robert Coleman, *Huston Displayed; Or, Who Won the Battle of San Jacinto? By a Farmer in the Army* (Velasco, TX, 1837), p. 18.
9. Hardin, "Houston's Generalship."
10. Houston to Rusk, March 31, 1836, *PTR,* V, pp. 254–55.
11. Santos, *Santa Anna's Campaign,* pp. 86–87.
12. Ibid., p. 90.
13. Peña, *With Santa Anna,* pp. 65, 77, 80, 96.
14. Ibid., pp. 94, 96.
15. Santos, *Santa Anna's Campaign,* pp. 94–97.
16. Houston to Carson, April 3, 1836, *PTR,* V, p. 308.
17. Carson to Burnet, March 27, 1836, Ibid., V, pp. 207–208.
18. Burnet to F. Gray, March 25, 1836, Ibid., V, p. 186.
19. Burnet to Henry Clay, March 30, 1836, Ibid., V, pp. 238–39.
20. Burnet to Carson, April 1, 1836, Ibid., V, p. 275.
21. Burnet Proclamation, April 3, 1836, Ibid., V, pp. 306–307.
22. Burnet to Morgan, April 2, 1836, Ibid., V, p. 293.
23. Austin, Wharton, and Archer to Bryan, March 31, 1836, Ibid., V, p. 249.
24. Austin to Bryan, April 24, 1836, Barker, *Papers,* III, p. 340.
25. Cantrell, *Austin,* pp. 346–47.
26. Burnet to Robert Triplett and William Gray, April 1, 1836, *PTR,* V, pp. 277–78.
27. Burnet Proclamation, April 9, 1836, Ibid., V, p. 399.
28. Carson to Burnet, April 4, 1836, Ibid., V, p. 316.
29. Burnet Proclamation, March 29, 1836, Ibid., V, pp. 227–28.
30. Burnet Proclamation, March 25, 1836, Ibid., V, pp. 188–89.
31. Burnet to Rusk, April 12, 1836, Ibid., V, pp. 444–45.
32. Thomas to Houston, April 14, 1836, Ibid., V, pp. 474–75.
33. Burnet to James Morgan, April 14, 1836, Ibid., V, p. 467.
34. Houston to Thomas, April 4, 1836, Ibid., V, p. 344.

35. Henry S. Foote, *Texas and the Texans* (Philadelphia, 1841), II, pp. 291–92.
36. Rusk to Burnet, April 6, 1836, *PTR*, V, p. 349.
37. Army Orders, April 7, 1836, Ibid., V, p. 360.
38. Houston to Raguet, April 7, 1836, Ibid., V, p. 361.
39. Burnet to Houston, April 7, 1836, Hardin, *Iliad*, p. 189. Hardin says this letter came via Rusk, but since Rusk arrived in Houston's camp on April 4, three days before the date of the letter, it had to have been sent by another means.
40. Jones, *Memoranda*, p. 16.
41. Houston to Burnet, April 11, 1836, *PTR*, V, p.434; Hardin, *Iliad*, p. 189.
42. Houston to ?, April 6, 1836, *PTR*, V, p. 345.
43. Houston to Burnet, April 11, 1836, Ibid., V, pp. 434–35.
44. Houston Orders, April 12, 1836, Ibid., V, p. 449.
45. Thomas to Houston, April 12, 1836, Ibid., V, p. 451.
46. Houston to Thomas, April 13, 1836, Ibid., V, pp. 456–57.
47. Houston to Citizens, April 13, 1836, Ibid., V, p. 453.
48. Rusk to Major Digges, April 16, 1836, Ibid., V, p. 492.
49. Jones, *Memoranda*, p. 16.
50. Carson to Houston, April 14, 1836, *PTR*, V, p. 470.
51. Hardin, *Iliad*, p. 192. Rusk to Digges, April 16, 1836, *PTR*, V, p. 492, certainly implies that Rusk expected the army to move through Nacogdoches and on east of the Trinity, and he would not likely have been giving orders without Houston's authority.
52. Foote, *Texas*, II, pp. 291–92.
53. Haley, *Houston*, p. 139ff, asserts that "Houston calmly ordered 'Columns right'," but the "eyewitness" evidence he presents to support the claim that Houston and not his men precipitated the turn toward Harrisburg dates from some years after the fact and turns out on examination not to be by eyewitnesses at the head of the column when it turned, and thus they were not able to speak knowledgeably of how the decision to turn was made or who made it. More to the point, even they do not speak of Houston himself giving any order, but of the order coming from their company officers. Meanwhile, there is ample, albeit equally after-the-fact, testimony to suggest that the army made the decision. The whole story is cloudy, since all accounts are based on latter-day recollections, all subject to error and false memory, but the tradition of an army decision as opposed to a Houston decision exists in greater quantity, and certainly receives implicit support from the total absence of any statement then or later from Houston's senior officers testifying to the commanding general having given them any instructions to turn south.
54. This account of the Pamela Mann incident comes from W. B. Dewees to Clara Cardello, May 15, 1836, *PTR*, VI, p. 286. It is the earliest known of five extant accounts of the affair and has apparently escaped previous notice. It agrees in virtually all particulars with the later accounts and was written less than a month after the fact by a man marching in the same company of volunteers that Mrs. Mann rode with at the time. Indeed, at the crossroads in question Houston detailed Dewees to accompany civilians, including Mrs. Mann, who took the road north while the army went south. The account does not state that it was Houston whom Mrs. Mann confronted, nor that he had lied to her about going north, but the account agrees so completely with other early and

later versions that include Houston as an object of her ire that it is evident that this story quickly gained currency throughout the Texian army in a matter of days, thus arguing that the other accounts that include Houston are independent and reflect the common belief in the army. Haley, *Houston*, pp. 140–41, attempts unconvincingly to dismiss the body of evidence in the several accounts of the incident as any sort of proof that Houston had told Mann he intended to head toward Nacogdoches. However, adding the Dewees account to all the other contemporary and later accounts of him stating such an intention simply amasses too much weight in its favor.

55. Santa Anna to Vicente Filisola, April 15, 1836, *PTR*, V, pp. 485–86; Hardin, *Iliad*, p. 191.

56. Houston and Rusk to the Public, April 19, 1836, *PTR*, V, pp. 504–505.

57. Houston to Karnes, April 19, 1836, Ibid., V, p. 503.

58. Houston to Raguet, April 19, 1836, Ibid., V, p. 504.

59. Hardin, *Iliad*, pp. 199–200.

60. Charleston, *Mercury*, August 28, 1844.

61. Thomas Ricks Lindley to the author, May 10, 1998.

62. Charleston, *Mercury*, August 28, 1844.

63. Foote, *Texas*, II, p. 296.

64. Houston to Burnet, April 20, 1836, *PTR*, V, p. 513; Hardin, *Iliad*, pp. 203–205; Walter P. Lane, *The Adventures and Recollections of General Walter P. Lane, A San Jacinto Veteran, Containing Sketches of the Texan, Mexican and Late Wars* (reprint: Austin, TX, 1970), pp. 12–13.

65. Houston to Burnet, April 20, 1836, *PTR*, V, p. 513.

66. Charleston, *Mercury*, August 28, 1844.

67. Thomas Ricks Lindley, ed., "Soldiers of the Texian Revolution," *Alamo Journal*, 129 (June 2003), p. 10.

68. Seguín, *Revolution Remembered*, p. 83; Charleston, *Mercury*, August 28, 1844.

69. James E. Crisp, "Did the 'Yellow Rose of Texas' really exist or is this just another story from Texas lore?" April 20, 1998, The War Room Web site at http://home.flash.net/-alamo3/warroom/warroom12.htm.

70. Charleston, *Mercury*, August 28, 1844; Lane, *Adventures and Recollections*, p. 14.

71. Charleston, *Mercury*, August 28, 1844.

72. Hardin, *Iliad*, p. 211.

73. Charleston, *Mercury*, August 28, 1844.

74. Lane, *Adventures and Recollections*, p. 14.

75. Seguín, *Revolution Remembered*, p. 83; Lane, *Adventures and Recollections*, p. 14.

76. Charleston, *Mercury*, August 28, 1844.

77. Ibid.

78. Lane, *Adventures and Recollections*, p. 15.

79. Galveston, *Daily News*, March 6, 1893.

80. Charleston, *Mercury*, August 28, 1844. This anonymous account agrees quite substantially with an account given by Houston himself in 1837 and published in Newell, *Revolution*, pp. 196–97.

81. Santa Anna to Filisola, April 22, 1836, *PTR*, VI, p. 15.

CHAPTER TWELVE: "THE UTMOST
CONFUSION AND REBELLION"

1. Duval, *Early Times*, p. 134.
2. Ibid., p. 131.
3. Charleston, *Mercury*, August 28, 1844.
4. Andrew Forest Muir, ed., *Texas in 1837, an Anonymous, Contemporary Narrative* (Austin, TX, 1958), p. 7.
5. See Davis, *Three Roads*, p. 737 n, and Davis, "How Davy Probably Didn't Die," pp. 11–37 passim.
6. Houston to Burnet, April 22, 1836, *PTR*, VI, p. 9; Rusk to Burnet, April 22, 1836, pp. 10–13.
7. Rusk to Burnet, April 26, 1836, Ibid., VI, p. 93.
8. Rusk to Burnet, May 1, 1836, Ibid., VI, pp. 144–45.
9. Burnet to the Public, September 6, 1836, Ibid., VIII, pp. 399–403.
10. Burnet to the Public, September 13, 1836, Ibid., VIII, pp. 460–61.
11. Houston to Rusk, May 3, 1836, Ibid., VI, p. 155.
12. Burnet to the Public, September 13, 1836, Ibid., VIII, p. 462.
13. Houston Order, April 26, 1836, Ibid., VI, p. 87.
14. Houston Address, May 5, 1836, Ibid., VI, p. 175.
15. Rusk to Burnet, May 4, 1836, Ibid., VI, pp. 170–71.
16. Treaty of Velasco, May 14, 1836, Ibid., VI, pp. 273–74.
17. Treaty of Velasco, Secret, May 14, 1836, Ibid., VI, pp. 275–76.
18. Burnet to the Public, September 13, 1836, Ibid., VI, p. 463.
19. Ibid., pp. 465–66.
20. Lack, *Revolutionary Experience*, p. 106.
21. Ibid., pp. 98–104.
22. Burnet to Grayson and Collinsworth, June 20, 1836, *PTR*, VII, pp. 2–7.
23. Burnet to A. Briscoe, May 21, 1836, Ibid., VI, p. 348.
24. Memucan Hunt to Burnet, June 3, 1836, Ibid., VI, p. 512.
25. Burnet to Grayson and Collinsworth, June 20, 1836, Ibid., VII, p. 207; Thomas J. Green to Houston, July 18, 1836, p. 481.
26. Tornel Proclamation, May 20, 1836, Ibid., VI, pp. 343–44.
27. Stapp to Rusk, June 1836, Smythe Catalog Sale #181, November 10, 1998, item 333.
28. Invoice, April 29, 1836, Ibid., item 331.
29. Elijah Stapp to Thomas Rusk, June 1836, Ibid., item 333.
30. D. H. Vail & Co. to Edward Teal, February 22, 1837, R. M. Smythe Sale Catalog #175, item 385.
31. John White Bower to Isaac Eben Bower, September 30, 1836, Bower Family Papers in possession of Adelaide Bower Wolfe, courtesy of Virginia S. McNeil, Hemet, CA.
32. Austin to L. F. Linn, May 4, 1836, Barker, *Papers*, III, p. 344.
33. Hardin, *Iliad*, p. 249.
34. Powhatan Ellis to John Forsythe, May 19, 1836, *PTR*, VI, pp. 332–33.
35. Filisola to Santa Anna, May 25, 1836, Ibid., VI, p. 371.
36. Peña, *With Santa Anna*, p. 124.
37. Newell, *History*, pp. 117–18.

38. Meyer and Beezley, *Oxford History of Mexico*, pp. 354–55.
39. Anna, *Forging Mexico*, pp. 261–63.
40. S. B. Dickinson to Austin, July 8, 1836, *PTR*, VII, p. 395.
41. Austin to Collinsworth and Grayson, July 9, 1836, Ibid., VII, p. 401; Austin Memorandum, July 10, 1836, pp. 411–12.
42. Burnet to the People, September 27, 1836, Ibid., IX, p. 14.
43. Zavala to Burnet, June 3, 1836, Ibid., VI, p. 515.
44. F. A. Sawyer to James Morgan, June 6, 1836, Ibid., VII, p. 46.
45. Lack, *Revolutionary Experience*, p. 106.
46. Burnet to the Public, September 27, 1836, *PTR*, IX, p. 15.
47. Burnet to R. Triplett, June 3, 1836, Ibid., VI, p. 507.
48. Houston to Raguet, July 4, 1836, Ibid., VII, pp. 362–63.
49. Burnet to Lamar, July 8, 1836, Ibid., VII, p. 391.
50. Rusk to Lamar, July 4, 1836, Ibid., VII, pp. 363–64.
51. Rusk to Houston, July 6, 1836, Ibid., VII, p. 371.
52. Burnet to Collinsworth and Grayson, July 8, 1836, Ibid., VII, p. 388.
53. Royall to Lamar, July 13, 1836, Ibid., VII, p. 443.
54. Burnet to Lamar, July 8, 1836, Ibid., VII, p. 391.
55. Lamar to Burnet, July 17, 1836, Ibid., VII, p. 471.
56. Burnet to Lamar, July 8, 1836, Ibid., VII, p. 392.
57. Burnet Proclamation, July 12, 1836, Ibid., VII, p. 427; Burnet Proclamation, July 14, 1836, pp. 445–46.
58. Charges Against Burnet, July 14, 1836, Ibid., VII, pp. 446–48.
59. Rusk to Burnet, July 31, 1836, Ibid., VIII, pp. 75–76; Burnet to Rusk, August 5, 1836, pp. 127–28.
60. Lamar to Rusk, July 14, 1836, Ibid., VII, p. 450.
61. Lamar to Burnet, July 17, 1836, Ibid., VII, pp. 471–72.
62. Thomas J. Green to Rusk, July 16, 1836, Ibid., VII, pp. 464–65; July 17, 1836, p. 470.
63. Lamar to Burnet, July 17, 1836, Ibid., VII, p. 472.
64. Green to Houston, July 18, 1836, Ibid., VII, pp. 480–81.
65. William Parker to ?, August 4, 1836, Ibid., VIII, p. 123; Rusk to Houston, August 4, 1836, p. 124.
66. William S. Fisher et al. to Houston, July 22, 1836, Ibid., VIII, p. 7; Rusk to Houston, July 25, 1836, p. 31.
67. A. C. Allen to Fellow Citizens, July 23, 1836, Ibid., VIII, pp. 10–11; Houston to Rusk, July 26, 1836, pp. 35–36.
68. Burnet Proclamation, July 23, 1836, Ibid., VIII, pp. 15–17.
69. Rusk to Henry Clay, August 3, 1836, Ibid., VIII, p. 112.
70. Zavala to José Antonio Mexía, May 26, 1836, Ibid., VI, p. 384.
71. Tocqueville, *Democracy in America*, p. 541.
72. Green to Houston, August 1, 1836, *PTR*, VIII, p. 93; Green to Rusk, August 1, 1836, pp. 93–94.
73. Cantrell, *Austin*, pp. 351–53.
74. Burnet to Lamar, August 8, 1836, *PTR*, VIII, p. 156.
75. Rusk to Houston, August 15, 1836, Ibid., VIII, p. 241.
76. Green to Austin and Smith, August 29, 1836, Ibid., VIII, pp. 344–45.
77. Newell, *History*, p. 120.

78. Parker to ?, August 4, 1836, *PTR*, VIII, p. 124.
79. R. Scurry to Houston, August 4, 1836, Ibid., VIII, p. 125.
80. Houston to Rusk, August 8, 1836, Ibid., VIII, pp. 159–60.
81. Rusk to Houston, August 9, 1836, Ibid., VIII, p. 182.
82. Rusk to Houston, August 20, 1836, Ibid., VIII, p. 279.
83. Haley, *Houston*, p. 160. Haley is silent on Houston in the election, as if he never declared a candidacy and his subsequent election was a spontaneous expression. Nothing could be further from the fact.
84. Ibid., p. 163.
85. Lack, *Revolutionary Experience*, pp. 258–59; Cantrell, *Austin*, p. 353.
86. Cantrell, *Austin*, p. 355.
87. Austin to Perry, September 2, 1836, *PTR*, VIII, p. 370.

EPILOGUE: "OUR COURSE IS ONWARD"

1. Austin to Perry, October 25, 1836, Barker, *Papers*, III, p. 439.
2. Cantrell, *Austin*, p. 364.
3. Samuel Clark to John S. Russworm, December 15, 1839, John S. Russworm Papers, Tennessee State Library and Archives, Nashville.

BIBLIOGRAPHY

Manuscripts

Adjutant General's Office, Army Papers, Record Group 401, Texas State Library, Austin (TSL).

Samuel Asbury Papers, Center for American History, University of Texas, Austin (CAHUT).

Louis Aury Papers, Center for American History, University of Texas, Austin (CAHUT).

Stephen F. Austin Papers, Center for American History, University of Texas, Austin (CAHUT).

Moseley Baker Papers, Center for American History, University of Texas, Austin (CAHUT).

Béxar Archives, Center for American History, University of Texas, Austin (CAHUT).

Milledge L. Bonham Papers, South Caroliniana Library, University of South Carolina, Columbia.

Bower Family Papers in possession of Adelaide Bower Wolfe, courtesy of Virginia S. McNeil, Hemet, CA.

Moses A. Bryan Papers, Center for American History, University of Texas, Austin (CAHUT).

Captains' Letters, I, Record Group 45, Office of Naval Records, National Archives, Washington, D.C.

Antonio Cruz File, Audited Military Claims, Comptroller of Public Accounts, Texas State Library, Austin (TSL).

Domestic Correspondence, Record Group 307, Texas State Library, Austin (TSL).

Expediente XI/481.3/801, Archivo Historico Militar Mexicano, Secretaria de la Defensa Nacional, Mexico City.

Expediente XI/481.3/1149, Archivo Historico Militar Mexicano, Secretaria de la Defensa Nacional, Mexico City.

Expediente XI/481.3/1151, Archivo Historico Militar Mexicano, Secretaria de la Defensa Nacional, Mexico City.

Stanley Faye, Commodore Aury, Center for American History, University of Texas, Austin (CAHUT).

William W. Fontaine Collection, Center for American History, University of Texas, Austin (CAHUT).

Benjamin C. Franklin Papers, Center for American History, University of Texas, Austin (CAHUT).

General Land Office, Applications, Austin's Colony, Texas State Library, Austin (TSL).

Caiphas Ham, Recollections, Center for American History, University of Texas, Austin (CAHUT).

Mary Austin Holley Papers, Center for American History, University of Texas, Austin (CAHUT).

Home Papers, Box 2-9/6, Texas State Library, Austin (TSL).

Josiah Stoddard Johnston Papers, Historical Society of Pennsylvania, Philadelphia.

Mirabeau B. Lamar Papers, Texas State Library, Austin (TSL).

James Long Vertical File, Center for American History, University of Texas, Austin (CAHUT).

Nacogdoches Archives, Texas State Library, Austin (TSL).

Washington Miller Papers, Texas State Library, Austin (TSL).

Benjamin Franklin Porter Reminiscences, Benjamin Franklin Porter Collection, Auburn University, Auburn, AL.

Thomas Rusk Papers, Center for American History, University of Texas, Austin (CAHUT).

John S. Russworm Papers, Tennessee State Library and Archives, Nashville.

Antonio López de Santa Anna Collection, Center for American History, University of Texas, Austin (CAHUT).

Texas Veterans Association Papers, Center for American History, University of Texas, Austin, (CAHUT).

Thomas W. Streeter Collection of Texas Manuscripts, Beinecke Rare Book and Manuscript Library, Yale University, New Haven, CT.

Hiram M. Thompson File, Pension Claims, Texas State Library, Austin (TSL).

Hiram and Thomas Thomson Taylor Papers, Hill Memorial Library, Louisiana State University, Baton Rouge.

William Barret Travis Papers, Center for American History, University of Texas, Austin.

Henry Raup Wagner Collection of Philip Nolan Papers, Yale Collection of Western Americana, Beinecke Rare Book and Manuscript Library, New Haven, CT.

Newspapers

Alexandria, LA, *Messenger*, 1826.

Baltimore, MD, *Nile's Weekly Register*, 1815.

Bogotà, *Gaceta de Colombia*, 1823.

Brazoria, *Texas Republican*, 1835.

Charleston, SC, *Mercury*, 1844.

Galveston, TX, *Daily News*, 1893, 1895.

Houston, *Morning Star*, 1840.

Matagorda, *Bulletin*, 1837.

Natchez, *Mississippi Republican*, 1819.

Natchez, *Mississippi State Gazette*, 1819.

New Orleans, *L'Ami des Lois*, 1819.
New Orleans, *Louisiana Advertiser*, 1832.
New Orleans, *Louisiana Gazette*, 1819.
New Orleans, *State Gazette*, 1826.
San Antonio, TX, *Daily Express*, 1935.
Woodville, MS, *Republican*, 1826.

Auction Catalogs

Alexander Autographs Catalog, April 29, 2000.
Philpott Texana Auction Collection Catalog, Dallas, 1995.
Signature House Auction Catalog, October 20, 2001.
R. M. Smythe Catalog Sale #175, February 26, 1998.
R. M. Smythe Catalog Sale #176, June 4, 1998.
R. M. Smythe Catalog Sale #181, November 10, 1998.
R. M. Smythe Catalog Sale #186, April 22, 1999.

Theses and Dissertations

Bass, Robert D., ed. "Autobiography of William J. Grayson." Ph.D. dissertation, University of South Carolina, 1933.
Crisp, James E. "Did the 'Yellow Rose of Texas' really exist or is this just another story from Texas lore?" April 20, 1998, The War Room Web site at http://home.flash.net/-alamo3/warroom/warroom12.htm.
Hardin, Stephen L. "Houston's Generalship: The Method, the Myth, and the Meaning." Paper presented at the Battle of San Jacinto Symposium, Houston, TX, April 19, 2002.
Reid, Stuart. "'Go in and die with the boys,' Colonel James Grant and the Texan Revolution," essay furnished by Stuart Reid, Tyne & Wear, United Kingdom.
Wilson, Maurine T. "Philip Nolan and His Activities in Texas," master's thesis, University of Texas, Austin, TX, 1932.

Books

American State Papers, Foreign Relations. Washington, D.C., 1834.
Anna, Timothy E. *Forging Mexico, 1821–1835.* Lincoln, NE, 1988.
Barker, Eugene C., ed. *The Austin Papers.* 2 vols. Washington, D.C., 1924, 1928.
———. *The Austin Papers, Volume 3.* Austin, TX, 1927.
Barr, Alwyn. *Texans in Revolt: The Battle for San Antonio, 1835.* Austin, TX, 1990.
Bradfield, Jane. *Rx Take One Cannon.* Shiner, TX, 1981.
Brown, John Henry. *Life and Times of Henry Smith.* Dallas, TX, 1887.
———. *Long's Expedition.* Houston, TX, 1930.
Campbell, Randolph B. *An Empire for Slavery, The Peculiar Institution in Texas 1821–1865.* Baton Rouge, LA, 1989.
Cantrell, Gregg. *Stephen F. Austin, Empresario of Texas.* New Haven, CT, 1999.
Coleman, Robert. *Huston Displayed; Or, Who Won the Battle of San Jacinto? By a Farmer in the Army.* Velasco, TX, 1837.

Davis, Robert E., ed. *The Diary of William Barret Travis August 30, 1833–June 26, 1834.* Waco, TX, 1966.

Davis, William C. *Three Roads to the Alamo: The Lives and Fortunes of David Crockett, James Bowie, and William Barret Travis.* New York, 1998.

de la Peña, José Enrique. *With Santa Anna in Texas, A Personal Narrative of the Revolution.* Edited by Carmen Perry. College Station, TX, 1975.

de la Teja, Jesús, ed. *A Revolution Remembered: The Memoirs and Selected Correspondence of Juan N. Seguín.* Austin, TX, 1991.

de León, Arnoldo. *The Tejano Community, 1836–1900.* Albuquerque, NM, 1982.

de Tocqueville, Alexis. *Democracy in America.* New York, 1969.

Duval, J. C. *Early Times in Texas.* Austin, TX, 1892.

Ehrenberg, Herman. *With Milam and Fannin: Adventures of a German Boy in Texas' Revolution.* Dallas, TX, 1935.

Foote, Henry S. *Texas and the Texans.* 2 vols. Philadelphia, 1841.

Garrett, Julia Kathryn. *Green Flag Over Texas.* New York, 1939.

Gray, William F. *From Virginia to Texas, 1835: Diary of Col. Wm. F. Gray, Giving Details of His Journey to Texas and Return in 1835–1836 and Second Journey to Texas in 1837.* Houston, TX, 1909.

Green, Rita Maverick, ed. *Samuel Maverick, Texan, 1803–1870.* San Antonio, TX, 1952.

Groneman, William. *Defense of a Legend.* Plano, TX, 1994.

Gulick, Charles Adams Jr., and Katherine Elliott, eds. *The Papers of Mirabeau Bounaparte Lamar.* 6 vols. Austin, TX, 1923.

Haley, James L. *Sam Houston.* Norman, OK, 2002.

Hardin, Stephen L. *Texian Iliad: A Military History of the Texas Revolution.* Austin, TX, 1994.

Harvey, Robert. *Liberators: Latin America's Struggle for Independence 1810–1830.* Woodstock, NY, 2000.

Jenkins, John H., ed. *The Papers of the Texas Revolution, 1835–1836.* 10 vols. Austin, TX, 1973.

———. *The Texas Revolution and Republic.* Austin, TX, 1986.

Johnson, Frank W. *History of Texas and Texans.* 5 vols. Chicago, 1914.

Jones, Anson. *Memoranda and Official Correspondence Relating to the Republic of Texas, Its History and Annexation.* New York, 1859.

Lack, Paul D. *The Texas Revolutionary Experience: A Political and Social History 1835–1836.* College Station, TX, 1992.

Lane, Walter P. *The Adventures and Recollections of General Walter P. Lane, A San Jacinto Veteran, Containing Sketches of the Texan, Mexican and Late Wars.* Reprint: Austin, TX, 1970.

Lord, Walter. *A Time to Stand.* New York, 1961.

Lundy, Benjamin. *The War in Texas.* Philadelphia, 1837.

Marshall, Thomas Maitland. *A History of the Western Boundary of the Louisiana Purchase, 1819–1841.* Berkeley, CA, 1914.

McCaleb, Walter F. *The Aaron Burr Conspiracy.* New York, 1903.

Matovina, Timothy M. *The Alamo Remembered: Tejano Accounts and Perspectives.* Austin, TX, 1995.

Meyer, Michael C., and William H. Beezley, eds. *The Oxford History of Mexico.* New York, 2000.

Muir, Andrew Forest, ed. *Texas in 1837, an Anonymous, Contemporary Narrative.* Austin, TX, 1958.

Munoz, Rafael F. *Santa Anna: El Dictador Resplandeciente.* Mexico City, 1984.

Newell, C. *History of the Revolution in Texas.* New York, 1838.

Owsley, Frank Lawrence Jr., and Gene A. Smith. *Filibusters and Expansionists: Jeffersonian Manifest Destiny, 1800–1821.* Tuscaloosa, AL, 1997.

Parker, Amos. *A Trip to the West and Texas in 1834.* Concord, NH, 1836.

Poyo, Gerald E., ed. *Tejano Journey 1770–1850.* Austin, TX, 1996.

Roell, Craig H. *Remember Goliad.* Austin, TX, 1994.

Santos, Richard G. *Santa Anna's Campaign Against Texas 1835–1836.* Waco, TX, 1968.

Saxon, Lyle. *Lafitte the Pirate.* New York, 1930.

Schwarz, Ted. *Forgotten Battlefield of the First Texas Revolution: The Battle of Medina, August 18, 1813.* Austin, TX, 1985.

Smithwick, Noah. *The Evolution of a State; or, Recollections of Old Texas Days.* Austin, TX, 1983.

Siegel, Stanley. *The Political History of the Texas Republic, 1836–1845.* Austin, TX, 1956.

Tyler, Ron, et al., eds. *The New Handbook of Texas.* 6 vols. Austin, TX, 1996.

Warren, Harris Gaylord. *The Sword Was Their Passport. A History of American Filibustering in the Mexican Revolution.* Baton Rouge, LA, 1943.

Weber, David J. *The Taos Trappers: The Fur Trade in the Far Southwest, 1540–1846.* Norman, OK, 1971.

Wharton, Clarence. *Remember Goliad!* Houston, TX, 1938.

Williams, Amelia W., and Eugene C. Barker, eds. *The Writings of Sam Houston, 1813–1863.* 8 vols. Austin,TX, 1938–1943.

Wilson, Maurine T., and Jack Jackson. *Philip Nolan and Texas: Expeditions Into the Unknown Land, 1791–1801.* Waco, TX, 1987.

Yoakum, Henderson. *History of Texas From Its First Settlement in 1685 to Its Annexation to the United States in 1846.* 2 vols. New York, 1856.

Articles

Barker, Eugene C., ed. "William Barret Travis, The Hero of the Alamo." *Publications of the Southern History Association,* VI, September 1902, pp. 417–21.

B[ollaert], W[illiam]. "Life of Jean Lafitte." *Littell's Living Age,* XXXII, March 1852, pp. 433–46.

Bostwick, Sion R. "Reminiscences of Sion R. Bostwick." *Quarterly of the Texas State Historical Association,* V, October 1901, pp. 85–96.

Brown, Everett S., ed. "Letters From Louisiana, 1813–1814." *Mississippi Valley Historical Review,* XI, March 1925, pp. 570–79.

Davis, William C. "How Davy Probably Didn't Die." *Journal of the Alamo Battlefield Association,* II, fall 1997, pp. 11–37.

"Early Life in the Southwest, No. IV, Captain John McHenry, Pioneer of Texas." *DeBow's Review,* XV, December 1853, pp. 572–84.

Faye, Stanley. "Commodore Aury." *Louisiana Historical Quarterly,* XXIV, July 1941, pp. 619–97.

Lindley, Thomas Ricks. "Drawing Truthful Conclusions." *Journal of the Alamo Battlefield Association,* I, September 1995, pp. 19–42.

————, ed., "Soldiers of the Texian Revolution." *Alamo Journal*, No. 129, June 2003, pp. 9–10.

Moore, Matilda E. "The Bowie Brothers and Their Famous Knife." *Frontier Times*, XIX, February 1942, pp. 199–205.

Smith, Henry. "Reminiscences of Henry Smith." *Quarterly of the Texas State Historical Association*, XIV, July 1910, pp. 24–73.

Whittington, G. P., ed. "Dr. John Sibley of Natchitoches, 1757–1837." *Louisiana Historical Quarterly*, X, October 1927, pp. 467–512.

Winston, James E. "New Orleans and the Texas Revolution." *Louisiana Historical Quarterly*, X, July 1927, pp. 317–54.

ACKNOWLEDGMENTS

A few friends have provided their usual unstinting cooperation and support in the preparation of this work, and they deserve acknowledgment, starting with Stephen L. Hardin of Victoria College, Victoria, Texas. The author of *Texian Iliad*, to date the finest study of the Texian war for independence, he has read the manuscript carefully and with his ever-incisive eye, providing the surest defense against the egregious misstatements that otherwise must surely have escaped both author and editors. His friendship and generosity are unsurpassed. Equally generous has been Thomas Ricks Lindley of Nixon, Texas, who always manages to turn up something everyone else has missed, and who shares unselfishly. T. Michael Parrish of Austin is a perennial benefactor of anyone working in Texas history, not only for his friendship and hospitality on research trips to Austin, but also for the periodic envelopes that arrive bearing copies of some arcane manuscript. Stuart Reid of Tyne & Wear, England, generously provided an outstanding essay on his ancestor James Grant and the disastrous Matamoros affair that almost killed Texian independence before it could be achieved. And finally, Bruce Nichols of the Free Press, as in the past, proved to be far more patient than he should have been with an author who lately seems to have gotten habitually haphazard with deadlines. The culprit promises that it will not happen again.

INDEX

ABOUT THE AUTHOR

WILLIAM C. DAVIS was for more than twenty years a magazine and book publishing executive and a prolific historian. He is the author or editor of more than forty books, most recently *Look Away!: A History of the Confederate States of America* and *An Honorable Defeat: The Last Days of the Confederate Government.* Davis has lectured widely in this country and abroad on the American Civil War and is currently Director of Programs at Virginia Tech's Center for Civil War Studies.